THE LION CONCISE
BIBLE
ENCYCLOPEDIA

Organizing Editor
Pat Alexander BA

Consulting Editors
John W. Drane MA, PhD
Lecturer in Religious Studies, Stirling University
David Field BA
Director of Studies, Oak Hill Theological College, London

Alan Millard MA, MPhil, FSA
Rankin Senior Lecturer in Hebrew and Ancient Semitic Languages, Liverpool University

Contributors
David Clines MA
Professor of Biblical Studies, Sheffield University

E. W. Crabb Dip Litt, Dip Th
Former Headmaster, Stanburn School, Stanmore, Middx.

Margaret Embry BA, BD
Lecturer at Trinity College, Bristol

David Gillet BA, MPhil
Director of Extension Studies, St John's College, Nottingham

Ralph Gower MEd, BD
Staff Inspector for Religious Education, County Hall, London

Colin Hemer MA, PhD
Research Fellow, Tyndale Library for Biblical Research

Kenneth Kitchen BA PhD
Reader in Egyptian and Coptic, School of Archaeology and Oriental Studies, Liverpool University

Alan Millard MA, MPhil, FSA
Rankin Senior Lecturer in Hebrew and Ancient Semitic Languages, Liverpool University

Margaret Moore BA, BD

The Rev. Stephen Parish Dip Th

John Paterson MA
Emeritus Professor of Geography, Leicester University

Canon R. W. F. Wootton MBE, MA
Leicester Diocesan Chaplain for Community Relations, Leicester

Illustrators
Mark Astle
Simon Bull
Pauline O'Boyle
Stanley Willcocks

The Lion Concise
Bible
Encyclopedia

LION·ISIS LARGE PRINT EDITIONS

Copyright © 1980 Lion Publishing

First published in Great Britain 1980
by Lion Publishing plc

Published in Large Print 1990 by Clio Press,
55 St. Thomas' Street, Oxford OX1 1JG,
by arrangement with Lion Publishing plc

CIP data for this title can be obtained on application
to the British Library.

Printed and bound by Hartnolls Ltd.,
Bodmin, Cornwall

Cover designed by CGS Studios, Cheltenham

INTRODUCTION

There are many today looking for a compact, helpful reference book to the Bible. This book has been designed to meet this need. It uses most of the text of *The Lion Encyclopedia of the Bible* which has enjoyed world-wide acceptance since its publication in 1978.

The larger Encyclopedia is in full colour and arranged by themes. For this Concise edition the text has been rearranged alphabetically. This has involved some shortening (notably of the Archaeology section), but most of the text still stands. The pictures and charts of the larger edition have been replaced by line drawings to give essential information or the feel of Bible times in a way which is more appropriate to this format.

The aim is to produce both an instant look-it-up book at an easily intelligible level for the beginner in Bible-reading and also a comprehensive, handy reference tool for those already more knowledgeable. So the level is not superficial; the content is carefully researched. But it aims to be simple and clear in style and presentation.

The articles reflect this practical aim. Some, on Bible times for instance, are longer than their importance warrants, compared with doctrinal subjects. But this information is not easily come by elsewhere. It cannot necessarily be found in the Bible itself, for instance. So the Encyclopedia majors on the historical, geographical and cultural setting of the Bible, to help the general reader understand the text of the Bible, and discover its riches in a new way. It is also designed to complement *The Lion Handbook to the Bible* (now also available in a Concise edition) which is a book-by-book explanation of the Bible text itself.

It is hoped that the sheer information presented here in such a practical way will, as in the case of the larger Encyclopedia, not only give pleasure and enjoyment but also help to make the meaning and message of the Bible clear.

AUTHORS OF MAJOR ARTICLES

Archaeology *Alan Millard*
Assyria; Assyrian and Babylonian religion *Alan Millard*
Babylonians *Alan Millard*
Bible translation *Canon R. W. F. Wootton*
Bible: modern English versions *Canon R. W. F. Wootton*
Building *Margaret Embry*
Canaanites; Canaanite religion *Alan Millard*
Clothes-making *Margaret Embry*
Daily life *Ralph Gower*
Dead Sea scrolls *Alan Millard*
Education *Margaret Embry*
Egyptians; Egyptian religion *Kenneth Kitchen*
Exile *Margaret Moore*
Exodus *Margaret Moore*
Family life *Ralph Gower*
Farming *Margaret Embry*
Feasts and festivals *David Clines*
Flood *Margaret Moore*
Food *Ralph Gower*
Geography of Israel *John Paterson*
Greeks; Greek and Roman religion *Colin Hemer*
Jesus' teaching *David Clines*
Law *David Clines*
Medicine *Margaret Embry*
Mining *Margaret Embry*
Pottery *Margaret Embry*
Prophets *David Clines*
Religion of Israel *David Clines*
Rome *Colin Hemer*
Temple *David Clines*
Towns *Ralph Gower*
Trade and commerce *Margaret Embry*
Travel and transport *Stephen Parish*
Villages *Ralph Gower*
War *Margaret Embry*
Writing *Alan Millard*

AARON

Elder brother of Moses and Miriam, born when the Israelites were slaves in Egypt. Moses was not good at speaking, so Aaron spoke for him to the Egyptian Pharaoh, pleading with him to obey God's command and let the people of Israel go. Pharaoh refused, and it was Aaron, with Moses, who warned him of the ten plagues God would send. Aaron gave Moses his loyal backing during the escape from Egypt. But at Mt Sinai Aaron gave way to the people's demands and made them a golden calf-idol to worship. Even so, God forgave him and made him the first high priest of Israel. Aaron was in charge of a special tent used for worship (the tabernacle). There he offered sacrifices to God for the sins of the people and prayed for them to be forgiven. But at times Aaron was jealous of Moses' position as the people's leader. He died before the Israelites entered Canaan and his son Eleazar became high priest after him.
Exodus 4:14; 5–12; 28:1; 32:1; Numbers 20:23–29

ABANA

Now called Barada, "cool". One of two rivers which flow through Damascus in Syria. When Elisha's servant told Naaman to bathe in the River Jordan and be healed, the Syrian general despised the muddy Jordan compared with the clear, fast-flowing

waters of Abana and Pharpar.
2 Kings 5:12

ABEDNEGO

The Babylonian name given to one of three Jewish exiles chosen for special service by King Nebuchadnezzer of Babylon. Shadrach, Meshach and Abednego, led by Daniel, courageously refused to eat the court food because, even in a foreign country, they were determined to obey the food-laws God had given the Jewish people. Later they refused to bow before an idol the king had set up. All three were thrown into a blazing furnace. But God protected them, and they came out unharmed. The king was most impressed. "No other God can do what this one does," he said.
Daniel 1–3

ABEL

Adam and Eve's second son; brother of Cain. Abel became a shepherd when he grew up, and offered a lamb to God as a sacrifice. This pleased God. But

A lion from the walls of Babylon's main street.

Cain was jealous because God did not accept his gift of fruit, and he killed his brother. The New Testament explains that it was because of Abel's faith that he, and not his brother, won God's approval.
Genesis 4:1–8; Hebrews 11:4

ABEL-BETH-MAACAH
A town in the north of Israel, near Lake Huleh, to which Joab pursued Sheba. Captured by Aramaeans of Damascus and recaptured more than once.
2 Samuel 20; 1 Kings 15:20; 2 Kings 15:29

ABIATHAR
The son of Ahimelech the priest in the days of King Saul. When David became king, Abiathar was made joint high priest with Zadok. But after David's death he conspired to put Adonijah on the throne, instead of Solomon, and was banished.
1 Samuel 22:20ff; 2 Samuel 8:17; 15:24ff; 1 Kings 1 and 2

ABIHU
See *Nadab*.

ABIJAH
The son of King Jeroboam I of Israel. He died as a child.
1 Kings 14

ABIJAH/ABIJAM
Son of King Rehoboam of Judah; he reigned for three years, about 913–911 BC.
1 Kings 15; 2 Chronicles 13

ABILENE
The region north-west of Damascus, governed by Lysanias.
Luke 3:1

ABIMELECH
1. Because he was afraid for his life, Abraham pretended that his wife, Sarah, was only his sister. Abimelech, king of Gerar, wanted to make her his wife, but God showed him the truth and prevented it.
Genesis 20; 26 (this story may be about another king of the same name who had a similar experience with Isaac)
2. A son of Gideon who killed his brothers to become king.
Judges 8:31ff; 9

ABISHAI
A nephew of King David, brother of Joab, and one of the king's generals.
1 Samuel 26:6–12; 2 Samuel 10:9–10; 16:9, 11–12; 18:2

ABNER
A first cousin of King Saul and commander of his army. When Saul was killed, Abner put Ishbosheth, Saul's son, on the throne. This led to war between the tribes who accepted Ishbosheth and the tribe of Judah, where David reigned. Abner became angry at the way Ishbosheth treated him and decided to support David as king of the whole of Israel. But he

was murdered by David's army commander, Joab, whose brother he had killed.
1 Samuel 14:50; 2 Samuel 3

ABRAHAM/ABRAM

Abram's name was changed to Abraham (father of nations) when God promised to make him the founder of the Hebrew nation. Abraham's original home was the rich and splendid city of Ur on the River Euphrates. He lived there for many years with his father Terah and his three brothers. He married Sarah, his half-sister. Terah and all his family moved from Ur to Harran, several hundred miles to the north-west. Terah died there, and God called Abraham to move on to Canaan.

Abraham obeyed. He lived as a nomad, moving from place to place with his flocks and herds. Wherever he camped, he built an altar and worshipped God. Famine drove him south to Egypt. But God told him to go back to Canaan. This was the land God promised to give the new nation. Abraham grew old, and still Sarah had no children. Following the custom of his time he had a son by Sarah's

Abraham and his family lived in tents, moving from place to place to find fresh pasture for their flocks.

servant-woman, Hagar. But this son, Ishmael, was not the child God had promised.

When Abraham and Sarah were both old, God gave them a son — Isaac. The new nation was to come through him. Isaac was still only a boy when God tested Abraham's faith as never before. He was told to take Isaac to a distant mountain and sacrifice him there. With a heavy heart Abraham obeyed, trusting God to keep his promise about his son. Isaac was bound on the altar. The knife was raised ready to strike. Then God's angel called out, "Do not harm the lad ... Now I know you will obey God whatever the cost." A ram, caught in a bush, was offered instead. Then God repeated all his promises to Abraham. "Your descendants will be as many as the stars in the sky. And all the nations of the earth will be blessed, because you obeyed me."

After Sarah's death, Abraham sent his trusted servant Eliezer to choose a wife for Isaac from his own family in Harran. Abraham is one of the really outstanding men of the Bible. His faith in God has made him an example for all time.
Genesis 11:31–32; 12:1ff; 17:1–8; 21:1–3; 22:1–14; Romans 4:1–3; Hebrews 11:8–19; James 2:21–23

ABSALOM
Favourite son of King David. He rebelled against his father and plotted to become king. David's men defeated Absalom's army in the forest of Ephraim. Absalom, escaping on a mule, was caught by his head in the branches of an oak. Joab, David's general, killed him — against the king's orders.
2 Samuel 15–19

Acacia tree.

ACACIA/SHITTIM
The wood from which the Covenant Box (ark) was made for the tabernacle. The acacia is one of the few trees to grow in the Sinai desert.
Exodus 25:10

ACCAD
Name of a region and a city in ancient Babylonia, founded by Nimrod. See *Babylonians*.
Genesis 10:10

ACHAIA
The Roman province of southern Greece governed from Corinth.
Acts 18:12, etc.

ACHAN
When the Israelites conquered Jericho, Achan disobeyed God's orders and took gold, silver and fine clothes for himself. Because of this the Israelites were defeated at their next battle.
Joshua 7–8

7

ACHISH
A king of Gath. Twice David fled to Achish from King Saul.
1 Samuel 21; 27–29

ACHOR
"Trouble Valley", near Jericho, where Achan was killed because he disobeyed God's command.
Joshua 7:24

ACTS
The Book of Acts continues the story begun in the Gospel of Luke, and is by the same author. It tells of the "acts" of (mainly) the apostles Peter and Paul. Because of its emphasis on God's power, it has often been called the "Acts of the Holy Spirit".

The book tells how the followers of Jesus spread the good news about him first in Jerusalem, then all through the local provinces of Judea and Samaria, and beyond "to the ends of the earth". It covers roughly thirty years, from the beginnings of the Christian church on the Day of Pentecost, to Paul's imprisonment at Rome.

Acts may have been written any time between AD 60 and 85. The author wanted to stress that the good news was for all people — not only for the Jews. He often takes care to show that Christianity is not a political threat to the Roman Empire.

The first seven chapters of Acts tell how the Christian movement began in Jerusalem itself, with the coming of the Holy Spirit in power on the Day of Pentecost. Filled with this new power the Christian group began to carry out Jesus' command to preach and teach. The church grew and spread. This section also records how Stephen, one of the first Christians, died for his faith.

Chapters 8–12 describe how, at first because of persecution, Christianity spread into Judea (the province around Jerusalem) and Samaria (where people belonging to a despised enemy nation were welcomed into the church). Saul's (or Paul's) dramatic conversion on the way to Damascus is followed by the account of how Peter learnt that the Christian message was for all nations, not only Jews.

The rest of the Book of Acts is taken up with the missionary work of Paul and his fellow-workers — his journeys in the Mediterranean world, his trials and his imprisonment in Rome (chapters 13–28). The message of the Christian faith is well summed up in several of the sermons recorded in Acts.

ADAM

1. The first man (the word "adam" means mankind), created by God to be like himself. Adam was put in charge of all the other animal life on earth. He was to live and work in the garden God had planted in Eden, and enjoy its fruits. Only the fruit of one tree was forbidden him — the "tree that gives knowledge of what is good and what is bad".

God never intended the man to live alone. He made Eve — the woman — to share his life. Tempted by the thought of being wise like God, Eve took the fruit, and she and Adam both ate it. Knowing they had done wrong, Adam and Eve tried to hide from God. Their friendship with him was spoilt. Because they disobeyed God, from that day to this the whole created world has felt the effects. And every life has ended in death.

Adam and Eve were driven out of Eden. They had children. But their family brought them pain as well as joy.
Genesis 1:26–27; 2–5:5

2. The place where the River Jordan was blocked, allowing the Israelites to cross into the Promised Land. In 1927 earth tremors caused the high clay banks to collapse at the same spot, and the Jordan was dammed for twenty-one hours.
Joshua 3:16

ADMAH

One of a group of five cities, of which Sodom and Gomorrah are best-known, now probably under the southern end of the Dead Sea. The kings of these cities formed an alliance and rebelled against four northern kings in Abraham's day. In the battle that followed, Abraham's nephew Lot was taken captive.
Genesis 10:19; 14:2

ADONIJAH

The fourth son of King David. When David was old, and the elder brothers were dead, Adonijah tried to seize the throne. But David had promised his wife Bathsheba that her son Solomon would succeed him. Adonijah's attempt failed. David forgave him but when Solomon was king he had Adonijah executed when he seemed once again to be trying to seize the throne.
1 Kings 1–2

ADRAMYTTIUM

A port near Troy (Troas) on the west coast of what is now Turkey. A ship from Adramyttium took Paul and his fellow prisoners on the first stage of their journey to Rome.
Acts 27:2

ADULLAM

David, on the run from King Saul and fearing King Achish of Gath, took refuge in a "cave" (probably a fort) near this town. His family and a group of 400 outlaws joined him in hiding. While he was there, three of David's bravest soldiers risked their lives to bring him water from the well at Bethlehem, which was held by the Philistines.
1 Samuel 22:1; 2 Samuel 23:13

AGABUS

A Christian prophet from Jerusalem who told the church at Antioch that a great famine was coming. Later he also warned Paul that he would be imprisoned if he went to Jerusalem.
Acts 11:27–30; 21:7–14

AGRIPPA

See *Herod*.

AHAB

Seventh king of Israel (about 874–853 BC). He reigned from the capital city of Samaria. Ahab went to war against Syria three times, and the third time he was killed. He was a successful ruler, but the Old Testament sees him as a wicked king who did more to anger God than all the kings of Israel before him. He married Jezebel, daughter of the king of Sidon, and began worshipping Baal (Melkart), the god of Jezebel's people. This involved him in a number of clashes with the prophet Elijah. On Mount Carmel Ahab watched Elijah stage a contest with the supporters of Baal, and win a great victory for God. When Ahab had Naboth killed so that he could take his vineyard, Elijah denounced him. Ahab died in battle at Ramoth-gilead. It was God's punishment for his sin.

1 Kings 16:29–34; 18; 21; 22

AHASUERUS

1. Hebrew form of the name of a Persian king known to us in its Greek version as Xerxes. Xerxes I (486–465 BC) divorced Vashti to marry Esther, a

A "relief" of Xerxes I (Ahasuerus) from the treasury at Persepolis, Iran.

Jewish girl, and make her his queen. Ahasuerus is also mentioned in the Book of Ezra. The people of the land complained to him when the returned Jewish exiles began to rebuild Jerusalem.
Esther; Ezra 4:6
2. Father of Darius the Mede.
Daniel 9:1

AHAVA

The name of a canal and a region in Babylonia where Ezra assembled the second party of returning Jewish exiles. Here they fasted and prayed for God's protection on their 900 mile/1,448 km journey to Jerusalem.
Ezra 8:15, 21, 31

AHAZ

King of Judah about 732–716 BC (co-regent from 735 or earlier). He introduced pagan worship and even sacrificed his own son. Ahaz was defeated when Israel and Syria launched a combined attack on Judah. Rejecting the prophet Isaiah's advice, he appealed to the Assyrian King Tiglath-pileser III for help but by doing so became his subject.
2 Kings 15:38ff.; 2 Chronicles 27:9ff.; Isaiah 7

AHAZIAH

1. The son of Ahab and Jezebel. He was king of Israel after Ahab but only for a short time (about 853–852 BC). He followed in his father's evil ways and worshipped Baal.
1 Kings 22:40ff.; 2 Kings 1; 2 Chronicles 20:35–37
2. A King of Judah, the son of Jehoram (841 BC).

He and his uncle, King Jehoram of Israel, with whom he had made an alliance, were murdered by Jehu.
2 Kings 8:24ff.; 2 Chronicles 22:1–9

AHIJAH

A prophet from Shiloh. Ahijah tore his dress into twelve pieces before King Jeroboam I to show how Solomon's kingdom would be divided. He told Jeroboam to take ten of these pieces, because God had chosen him to rule ten of the twelve tribes of Israel.
1 Kings 11:29ff.; 14

AHITHOPHEL

King David's trusted adviser who turned traitor and supported Absalom in his rebellion. When Absalom ignored his advice Ahithophel committed suicide.
2 Samuel 15:12–17:23

AI

The name means "the Ruin". After capturing Jericho, Joshua sent a small force against nearby Ai — and was beaten. The reason was because Achan had defied God's command by taking spoil from Jericho. Achan was punished, and Joshua attacked Ai again. He lured the men of Ai out by pretending to run away, and a hidden ambush force moved in and set fire to the stronghold.
Joshua 7 and 8

AIJALON

1. An Amorite town belonging by right to the tribe of Dan, but given to the Levites. Much later King

Rehoboam fortified the city and kept stores and arms there.
Joshua 19:42; 21:24; Judges 1:35; 2 Chronicles 11:10
2. A valley through which an important trade-route passed; near to the town of Aijalon. In this valley Joshua fought a great battle against the Amorites, and "the sun stood still".
Joshua 10

ALEXANDER
The name of several men (not all necessarily different) in the New Testament.
1. Son of Simon of Cyrene, the man who carried Jesus' cross.
Mark 15:21
2. A member of the high priest's family and one of the Jewish leaders in Jerusalem.
Acts 4:6
3. A Jew who tried to speak to the crowd during the silversmiths' riot at Ephesus (see *Demetrius*).
Acts 19:33
4. A Christian who lost his faith, at least for a time.
1 Timothy 1:20
5. A coppersmith who was bitterly opposed to Paul and the gospel. Paul warned Timothy against him.
2 Timothy 4:14

ALEXANDRIA
A great Egyptian seaport on the Nile Delta founded by Alexander the Great. The famous Pharos lighthouse tower stood at the harbour entrance. Alexandria was the capital of Egypt under the Ptolemies,

A Greek medallion showing the Pharos light-house at Alexandria. It was built of white marble and completed in about 280 BC. A beacon at the top burned day and night.

and remained a great centre of Hellenistic culture.

In Roman times grain-ships loaded up at Alexandria so that the people of Rome could have cheap bread. The city had a "museum" of arts and sciences and a famous library containing thousands of papyrus scrolls. There was a strong Jewish community, and it was here that the Old Testament was translated into Greek — the Septuagint version. Apollos, who became an important teacher in the early church, came from Alexandria.
Acts 6:9; 18:24; 27:6; 28:11

ALMOND
The almond was the first fruit-tree to blossom in Israel each year, sometimes as early as January. As well as being a favourite food, the nut also produced oil. The most famous Bible reference is Aaron's almond rod which flowered and produced fruit overnight.
Numbers 17:8

AMALEKITES
These people were related to Edom and Israel (like the Edomites they were descendants of Esau). They were a nomadic tribe and at the time of the exodus attacked Israel in the Sinai desert and further north. In the days of the Judges they often raided Israel. They were bitter enemies of Israel for many centuries.
Genesis 36:12, 16; Exodus 17:8–13; Numbers 14:43, 45; Judges 3:13; 6; 7:12; Deuteronomy 25:19; 1 Samuel 15; 30:1–20; 1 Chronicles 4:43

AMASA
King David's nephew, chosen by Absalom to lead his rebel army. After Absalom's defeat, David pardoned Amasa and made him commander of his own army in place of Joab. In revenge Joab murdered him.
2 Samuel 17:25; 20

AMAZIAH
1. The son of King Joash of Judah, who came to the throne when his father was assassinated. Amaziah (796–782 BC) was a good man, but victory over Edom went to his head. He challenged Israel and lost. He also brought back idols from Edom and refused to listen to God's prophet. The people plotted against him and eventually he was murdered at Lachish.
2 Kings 12:21–14:21; 2 Chronicles 24:27ff.
2. A priest at Bethel who opposed the prophet Amos. (See *Amos*.)
Amos 7:10ff.

AMMONITES

North of the Dead Sea, between the Arnon and Jabbok rivers, lived the Ammonites. They were related to the Israelites through Lot, and did not stand in their way on the march to the Promised Land. But they did attack later, during the days of the Judges and of Saul. King Nahash made peace with David. But his son insulted David's messengers and hired men from Aram to fight for him. David's generals captured his capital, modern Amman, and took control of the land. In the reigns of later kings, Ammonites often raided across the Jordan, and were again made subject when Judah was strong. After the exile, the Ammonite Tobiah interfered with Nehemiah's work.

The Ammonite kingdom was protected from raiders by a series of stone watch-towers. Excavation done in Ammon reveals ruined houses and tombs with pottery like that of the Israelites, stone statues, seals engraved with their owners' names, and a few brief inscriptions, which show that their language was similar to Hebrew. The main road east of the Jordan — the King's Highway — brought traders through the Ammonite kingdom on their way from Damascus to the Gulf of Aqaba. These were a source of wealth and a strong cultural and religious influence.

Genesis 19:38; Judges 3:13; 10; 11; 1 Samuel 11; 12:12; 14:47; 2 Samuel 10; 12:26–31; 2 Chronicles 20:1–30; 26:8; 27:5; Nehemiah 2:10, 19; 4:3, 7

AMNON

The eldest son of King David. He raped Tamar, his

half-sister, and in revenge Absalom had him killed.
2 Samuel 3:2; 13

AMON
King of Judah after Manasseh, his father (642–640 BC). Amon refused to obey God and worshipped idols instead. After only two years he was murdered by his palace servants.
2 Kings 21:18–26; 2 Chronicles 33:20–25

AMOS
One of the first of God's prophets to have his messages permanently written down. Amos lived in the eighth century BC. He kept sheep and tended fig-trees at Tekoa, a hill village in Judah. But God sent him north to Bethel in Israel, where King Jeroboam I had set up a golden calf-idol. Here he bravely gave God's message of justice and judgement against oppression and greed. The cheating traders could not make up for their dishonesty simply by offering sacrifices to God.

Amaziah, the priest at Bethel, who was in the pay of the king of Israel, told Amos to pack up and take his message back to Judah. But Amos continued to warn the people of Israel of judgement and exile if they did not repent.
Book of Amos

ANANIAS
1. Ananias and his wife, Sapphira, gave the apostles only part of the money they received from the sale of

land, though they pretended to give it all. Because of that lie, both died.
Acts 5:1–11

2. A Christian who lived in Damascus. Just after Saul (Paul) was converted, God told Ananias to go to the house where he was staying. Ananias restored Saul's sight when he had been blind for three days after seeing Jesus on the road to Damascus.
Acts 9:10–19

3. A high priest present when Paul was being questioned by the Jewish council (the Sanhedrin), and who ordered the guard to hit Paul. When Paul was tried by Felix, Ananias was the prosecutor.
Acts 23:2–3; 24:1

ANATHOTH

A town 3 miles/4km north of Jerusalem belonging to the Levites. The birthplace of Jeremiah.
Joshua 21:18; Jeremiah 1:1

ANDREW

One of the twelve apostles chosen by Jesus. Andrew and his brother Simon Peter were fishermen from Bethsaida on the Lake of Galilee. John the Baptist told Andrew that Jesus was the "Lamb of God". Andrew recognized him as the Messiah (Christ) and brought his brother Peter to hear Jesus teach. Later, when they were fishing, Jesus called both brothers to follow him. Andrew brought the boy with the loaves and fishes to Jesus when he fed 5,000 hungry people. When some Greeks who had come to worship at Jerusalem wanted to see Jesus, Andrew and Philip told him about them. Andrew was with the other apostles in Jerusalem after Jesus ascended to heaven. John 1:35–42; Matthew 4:18–19; 10:2; John 6:6–9; 12:22; Acts 1:13

ANGEL

The word means "a messenger". In the Bible it is used of the supernatural beings who surround the throne of God. Jesus tells us that they share in God's joy "over one sinner who repents".

Angels are also referred to as "sons of God" or "heavenly beings" and "heavenly powers", the "servants of God". Their work is to serve God. In heaven they worship God and on earth they act as God's messengers, bringing his word to men and women. They also help people. They took care of Jesus after his temptations and they care for his followers.

The Jews believed there was a complex hierarchy of angels, all of whom had their own names. The Bible has no clear reference to such a system. It names only two angels — Gabriel and Michael. It was Gabriel who brought news of the birth of Jesus.

The phrase "the angel of the Lord" is often used in the Old Testament as a way of describing how God sometimes came to people in human form to give them a special message. The "angel of the Lord" is also God's agent of judgement.

See also *Heaven*.

Luke 15:10; Job 1:6; 1 Kings 22:19; Psalm 103:20–21; Daniel 12:1; Luke 1:26–38; Matthew 1:20; 4:11; Hebrews 1:14; Genesis 16:7–14; 22:11–12; 31:11; Judges 6:11–21; 13:3–21, and many other places

ANNA

An old prophetess who was in the temple when Joseph and Mary brought Jesus there as a baby to dedicate him to God. Like Simeon, she recognized Jesus as the Messiah, and told others about him.
Luke 2:36–38

ANNAS

Former high priest, with his son-in-law Caiaphas, when Jesus was arrested. He questioned Jesus before sending him to Caiaphas.
Luke 3:2; John 18:13–24

ANTIOCH ("PISIDIAN")

A town in the heart of Asia Minor (present-day Turkey) visited by Paul and Barnabas on their first missionary journey. They preached first in the synagogue, but when non-Jews responded to Paul's message the Jews stirred up trouble and threw Paul and Barnabas out of the city. Two or three years later, Paul visited Antioch again, on his second missionary journey, to encourage the Christians in their new faith.
Acts 13:14–52

ANTIOCH IN SYRIA

Modern Antakya, on the Syrian border of Turkey. The most famous of sixteen cities with this name, founded by one of Alexander's generals in honour of his father. Antioch, on the River Orontes, had its own sea-port. Under the Romans it became the capital of the province of Syria and third largest city of the Empire, renowned for its culture. It had a large Jewish community. After the death of Stephen, persecuted Christians fled the 300 miles/483 km from Jerusalem to Antioch.

This was the start of one of the largest and most active of the early Christian churches. Many local people were converted, including a large number of Greeks, and it was here that they were first called "Christians".

Barnabas, who had been sent from Jerusalem to find out what was happening, set off to find Paul and ask him to help teach the new converts. They taught together in Antioch for over a year. Some time later the church at Antioch sent Paul and Barnabas out to teach in Cyprus and beyond. Antioch remained Paul's base, and for a long time the church there was second only to Jerusalem. The ancient city was levelled by an earthquake in AD 526.
Acts 11:19–26; 13:1; 15:35

ANTIPAS
See *Herod*.

ANTIPATRIS
A town rebuilt by King Herod and named in honour of his father, Antipater. When Paul's life was threatened he was taken under escort from Jerusalem to Caesarea on the coast. On the way they spent the night at Antipatris.
Acts 23:31

APOLLOS
A Jew from Alexandria who went to Ephesus and taught in the synagogue after Paul's visit there.

Aquila and Priscilla, friends of Paul, were able to teach him more about Jesus. Apollos then went to Corinth, where he spoke to the Jews with great power about Jesus as the Messiah.
Acts 18:24–28; 19:1; 1 Corinthians 16:12

APOSTLE

The word means "a person who is sent" — a messenger or representative. In the New Testament it is mainly used to refer to Jesus' twelve disciples, to Paul, and to other Christians who were involved in missionary outreach.

Jesus chose twelve apostles to be with him, to preach and to heal. After he rose from the dead Jesus told them to go and tell the whole world what they had learnt about him.

When the disciples were looking for an apostle to replace Judas Iscariot, Peter told them that they must choose someone who had been with Jesus from the very start of his ministry, and who had seen him after he rose from the dead.

Paul claimed that he was an apostle, because he believed that his experience on the Damascus road was not just a vision but a meeting with the living Jesus. He had been chosen by Jesus as his special messenger, particularly to bring his message to the non-Jewish world (the "Gentiles").
Luke 6:12–16; Acts 1:12–26; 14:1–4; 1 Corinthians 15:5, 7; Galatians 1:1; 2:7, 8

AQUILA

A Jewish Christian who was a friend of Paul. Aquila and his wife, Priscilla (or Prisca), were forced to

A Roman man and his wife.

leave Italy when the Emperor Claudius expelled the Jews from Rome (AD 48). Like Paul they were tentmakers and for a time Paul stayed and worked with them in Corinth. When Paul travelled to Ephesus, Aquila and Priscilla went with him (see *Apollos*). Later, Aquila and Priscilla moved back to Rome. In both places Christians met in their home.
Acts 18:1–3, 18–26; Romans 16:3; 1 Corinthians 16:19; 2 Timothy 4:19

AR
Capital of Moab, on the River Arnon. During their time in the desert after leaving Egypt the Israelites were told to leave this city in peace. God had given it to the Moabites, Lot's descendants.
Number 21:15; Deuteronomy 2:9; Isaiah 15:1

ARABAH
The rift valley of the River Jordan, stretching from Lake Galilee in the north to the Dead Sea in the

south and continuing on to the Gulf of Aqaba. The "Sea of Arabah" is the Dead Sea.

ARAM

A group name for various states in southern Syria, especially Damascus. See *Aramaeans*.

ARAMAEANS/ARAMAIC

At the time when Israel was moving into Canaan, a group of Semitic tribes settled into the land to the north. These were the Aramaeans (Syrians in the Authorized/King James' Version). We know some of their history from Hebrew and Assyrian records, and a few inscriptions written in Aramaic. There were several tribes, each centred on one city. They were scattered throughout Syria, across to Assyria, and down the River Euphrates into Babylonia where one branch became the nation of the Chaldaeans. Smaller kingdoms north of Galilee were soon absorbed by Israel and by the major Aramaean kingdom, Damascus.

In the reign of Solomon Damascus won independence from Israel, and a strong line of kings built up power there (see 1 Kings 11:23; 15:18). Until the Assyrians made Damascus a province in 732 BC its kings (including Ben-Hadad and Hazael who feature in the Bible stories) were often at war with Israel and Judah, trying to control the roads to Egypt and Arabia. From time to time they were able to dominate their fellow Aramaean rulers to the north, and in the sea-ports.

Because they were so widespread (this increased even more when Assyrian kings conquered and deported many of them to Assyria and Persia), their language — Aramaic — became the common language for diplomats and traders all over the Near East from about 750 BC. When King Sennacherib's Assyrian officials came to threaten Jerusalem, King Hezekiah's men begged them to speak in Aramaic. The decrees of the Persian kings were written in Aramaic. When the people living in the land had complaints against the Jews who returned with Zerubbabel, they wrote to the king in Aramaic. Part of the Book of Daniel is also in Aramaic.

After Alexander brought Greek to the Near East, Aramaic took second place for official purposes. But it remained the common language over a wide area and was spoken by the Jews in Israel in New Testament times. The New Testament contains several Aramaic phrases, for example : *talitha koum (cumi)*, *abba* (the everyday word for "father"), and *Eli, eli lema sabachthani* (Jesus' words from the cross).

Two Aramaeans dressed in caps and fringed robes, from an eighth-century BC relief discovered at Zinjirli, to the north of ancient Syria.

2 Kings 18:26; Ezra 7:12–26; 4:7–6:18; Daniel 2:4–7:28; Mark 5:41; 14:36; Matthew 27:46

ARARAT
The mountain country where Noah's ark came to rest when the flood waters drained away. The area, called Urartu in Assyrian inscriptions, is Armenia, on the borders of present-day Turkey and Russia. Mount Ararat itself is an extinct volcano nearly 17,000ft/5,214m high.
Genesis 8:4; Jeremiah 51:27

ARAUNAH/ORNAN
A man from Jerusalem who sold his threshing-floor to King David. Because of David's wrongdoing, Israel was suffering from a plague. David realized he was to blame for the trouble and obeyed God by building an altar on Araunah's threshing-floor. God saw that David was sorry for what he had done and the plague stopped. The temple was later built on this site.
2 Samuel 24:16–25; 1 Chronicles 21:18–30

ARCHAEOLOGY
The first notable steps in learning about the ancient world were taken in 1798 when Napoleon's invasion of Egypt included a survey of monuments there. During this invasion the Rosetta Stone was discovered. This is a stone block on which the same text was engraved in Greek and Egyptian writing. It helped people to decipher ancient Egyptian hieroglyphs for the first time (1824). Within a few years, a British diplomat in Baghdad, *Claudius James Rich*,

EXCAVATION OF A "TELL", THE MOUND OF AN ANCIENT TOWN.

City wall, partly washed away: later Middle Bronze Age

Egyptian scarab of about 1700 BC, and the forms of the pin and pottery (different from earlier ones) show the date of these floor levels

Part of a wall

Part of another structure, and typical black-surfaced juglet, lamp with wide rim, and Hebrew seal, date this level to time of the kings of Israel and Judah

Grave covered with stones: type of copper pin and pottery, and absence of walls date this to early Middle Bronze Age, about 1900 BC

Layer of wind-blown soil, built up while the tell was deserted — and in it a lamp of about 100 BC

Lamp from the time of Herod (37-4 BC) and red cooking-pot show when the uppermost floor was in use

Late Bronze Age floor, sealing pit

Objects on the floor and amongst burnt rubbish include a vase brought by trade from Mycenean Greece; a Late Bronze Age lamp (lip folds more sharply than earlier one); scarab of Pharaoh Tuthmosis III (after 1400 BC)

Building showing signs of burning — perhaps the work of invaders such as the Israelites or Philistines

Pit containing fifth-century AD lamp, the last trace of occupation on the mound

Pit dug early in the Late Bronze Age (about 1500 BC), perhaps to get bricks from an older wall; small jug from Cyprus tells us its age

approximate dates

50 BC

100 BC

900-600 BC

1400 BC
1500 BC

1550- 1200 BC

1800- 1700 BC

about 1950 BC

Excavation of a "tell", the mound of an ancient town.

had made the first accurate surveys of the sites of ancient Babylon and Nineveh. He also made the first representative collection of Assyrian and Babylonian seals and inscriptions.

Places in Israel were better known, because pilgrims had visited the "Holy Land" for centuries. In 1838 *Edward Robinson*, an American professor of Biblical Literature, undertook the first careful study of the country. From its geography and the way in which place-names survived, he was able to identify many of the towns named in the Bible. Most of his identifications remain satisfactory even today.

Egypt and Assyria In Egypt the task of clearing mounds of sand and tumbled stone from tombs and temples continued throughout the nineteenth century, and during this period a great many stone sculptures were taken out of the country.

Excavations began in Assyria when the French consul, *Paul-Emile Botta*, opened trenches in the mound of rubble that was ancient Nineveh. His work there was unrewarding, but nearby he discovered an Assyrian palace whose walls were lined with carved stone slabs (1842–43).

An English traveller, *Henry Layard*, was also interested, and in 1845 he found similar carvings in Nineveh, where Botta had failed to do so. Writing cut into the stonework and impressed on small tablets of clay was deciphered by 1850. This was the Babylonian cuneiform script. Documents written in this script have proved particularly valuable for biblical study.

The digging in Egypt, and in Assyria and Babylonia, was carried out by British, French and

Italian expeditions, quickly joined by teams from Germany and the United States. Most of the money raised for excavation came from museums, and some were intent only on acquiring spectacular exhibits for their sponsors. Others carefully noted many details and collected examples of the less exciting finds — pottery, knives, and so on. They measured buildings and drew plans on which they marked the positions of the objects they unearthed.

International expeditions still carry out this work, with permission from local departments of antiquities. Egyptian and Iraqi scholars also excavate independently. They pay special attention to preserving their national heritage. Even after a century and a half of exploration in those lands, it is clear that there is a great deal still to be found.

Palestine and Syria The early excavators were mostly concerned to find great monuments of imperial power to impress the western public, and so the cities of Palestine and Syria were by-passed. Apart from a few isolated trenches at Jericho and other sites (1866–69), the first digging was confined to Jerusalem. There *Charles Warren* traced the foundations of King Herod's temple wall and surveyed other ancient remains (1867–70). He cut through masses of fallen stones and rubbish (sinking shafts 211ft/65m deep and burrowing along the natural rock surface) to show how the shape of the city had changed over the centuries.

Into the twentieth century Near Eastern archaeology took a major step forward in 1890 when *Flinders Petrie* started to excavate at Tell el-Hesi, near Gaza in southern Israel. He realized

Sir William Flinders Petrie, whose work in Israel led to a break-through in methods of dating discoveries.

that, on any given site, the things he found at one height above sea-level were different from things found at another height.

This was most obviously true of the broken pottery. Taking care to separate the pieces according to their levels, he managed to work out a series of pottery styles that followed in order of time. He then gave dates to each style, by comparing them with Egyptian objects found in the same places. (The ages of the Egyptian objects were known from the discovery of similar pieces in Egypt, where inscriptions related them to the reigns of individual kings.)

Petrie's observations have become basic to all archaeological excavation. For several decades other archaeologists working in Palestine failed to realize their importance, and because of this many of their own conclusions have been proved wrong. But the basic idea of using pottery styles as a guide for dating other objects is now adopted by all archaeologists — though, of course, there have been some further important developments since.

As people's interest in the subject grew, museums and universities began to pay attention to sites in the land of Israel. Regrettably, the standard of excavation was often poor. Better techniques for observing and recording finds were developed by *G. A. Reisner* and *C. S. Fisher* during their excavation at Samaria in 1908–11. Following Petrie's example, the American, *W. F. Albright*, established the basic system of dating Palestinian pottery (at Tell Beit Mirsim from 1926 to 1936).

British archaeology had progressed by developing "stratigraphy", the close examination of the soil inside, and underneath ancient remains. *Kathleen Kenyon*, working at Samaria, was the first to apply this approach to an excavation in Palestine (1931–35). From 1952 she used it with conspicuous success at the difficult sites of Jericho and Jerusalem. So far this method of excavation is unsurpassed, although it makes far more demands on the excavator during the digging, and afterwards in interpreting his finds.

The work of excavation Mud is the commonest, and one of the earliest, building materials in the Near East. Walls made of mud-bricks dried in the sun will last for thirty years or so if they are plastered regularly to keep out the damp. Bricks baked in kilns were expensive in ancient times, so they were used only for important buildings.

Foundations were built of stone wherever it was available, and in very stony areas entire houses were stone-built. Roofs were normally made of wooden beams with matting and mud plaster laid over them.

These buildings easily collapsed through neglect, old age, fire, earthquake, or enemy attack. When they fell, people re-used the best pieces from the heap of debris, but most of it was left where it had fallen. In the course of time, new houses were built on top of the old ones. This meant that street levels became higher, and over the centuries the level of the whole town gradually rose. The results of this process can be seen all over the Near East in the ruin-mounds called *tells*.

Cities that once surrounded an inner fortress with heavily defended palaces and temples may leave an extensive area covered with low mounds, the fortress standing up as a great hill. Or the whole city may be a single mound. These tells can be 90–130ft/30–40m high, and 540yds/500m or more in length.

The most recent remains lie at the top of the mound. They may not be the ruins of the last buildings that stood there, because winter wind and rain quickly erode the dry mud-brickwork once the site is no longer occupied. At the lowest level, on the original soil, will be traces of the first town. There are many reasons why ancient towns were abandoned. The town may have grown up around a spring or well, at a ford of a river, or at a crossroads. If the spring dried up or the roads changed, the town may have died. Some political turn of events may have deprived a place of its influence and prosperity. Or the mound may have grown too high for people to live on top of it conveniently.

Cities like Jerusalem and Damascus, however, have never lost their importance, and they can be excavated only when buildings are demolished or areas are left undeveloped.

The dig The archaeologist digs into the mound from the top or at one side. As he cuts into it, so the remains of one period appear on top of another, much like the layers in a large cake sliced down the middle. Once he has disturbed the earth and the objects in it, they can never be replaced in exactly the same way. So his first job is to note where and in what layer of soil, each item is found.

A plan of the area will show horizontal positions of walls and other things. But the remains are rarely in absolutely even levels. A street may slope, or a wall may stand much higher at one point than another. Very often people of a later period will have dug a pit, for storing food or for rubbish, and that will go down from their own floor level deep into earlier ruins. Recording things by absolute levels (metres above sea level) would put rubbish from the bottom of the pit with bits and pieces from the earlier periods it had broken into. So the depth of any discovery has to be linked to the layer of earth in which it was found.

When the trench has cut into the earth the layers can be clearly seen in the vertical side of the excavation. Pottery lying on the floor of a room will belong to the last period that the room was lived in.

Archaeology

Pottery found underneath the floor will be older than the floor. The archaeologist has to note how the floor joins a wall, because a later wall may have cut through an earlier floor. If he does not notice, he could produce a wrong plan of the building, with the wall dated by objects on the floor.

Expert knowledge is necessary at every stage. Before any earth is removed, a surveyor has to measure the whole site and fix points from which measurements can be made. As work goes on he will plot the edges of the trenches and any other noteworthy features. A photographer is needed to record the stages of excavation, to picture important or fragile objects in position in the soil, and afterwards to photograph them and other pieces for publication.

Studying the finds Every object has a label fixed to it, or a mark written on it as soon as it is discovered, to show where it was dug up. Individual finds, such as pins, knives, jewellery, but not usually broken pottery, are listed and described. The pottery is sorted according to the place and level or layer of discovery. Someone who knows the whole range of discoveries can then choose sigificant pieces for detailed records.

Some pottery will need to be mended, and metal things will need treatment for rust or corrosion. Woodwork and other fragile objects will require special care to ensure that they do not decay any more. Samples of all sorts of natural remains can also give us information about the ancient environment, so shells, bones, and earth containing seeds, are all carefully collected.

Results Archaeology's main service is to illustrate the general context of the Bible and to show us what the biblical world was like. It may sometimes throw light on a particular verse; it may guide interpreters along some paths and bar others. It may appear to support historical statements in the Bible, or make it less difficult to accept them. But we must always remember two important facts. One is that much of our knowledge of the ancient world from archaeology is tentative and subject to change. Today's "assured results" may tomorrow be little more than a curiosity. Then we should also remember that ultimately it is pointless to speak of archaeology either "proving" or "disproving" the Bible. For the Bible's message is about God and his scope of archaeology to say anything about that.

ARCHELAUS
See *Herod*.

AREOPAGUS
"Mars hill", north-west of the acropolis in Athens, from which the Council of the Areopagus (which originally met there) took its name.
Acts 17

ARETAS
An Arabian king whose capital was Petra (in present-day Jordan). For a time Damascus was part of his territory. When Paul was in Damascus, Areta's governor planned to arrest him, but he escaped by being lowered over the walls in a basket.
2 Corinthians 11:32

ARGOB

Part of the kingdom of Og in Bashan, east of the Jordan. It was given to the half tribe of Manasseh, and was a fertile region with many strong towns.
Deuteronomy 3; 1 Kings 4

ARIMATHEA

The home of Joseph, a secret disciple of Jesus, in whose new rock-tomb the body of Jesus was placed after he was crucified.
Matthew 27:57; Mark 15:43

ARISTARCHUS

A Macedonian Christian, a friend and fellow-worker of Paul. He was with Paul when the Ephesian silversmiths started a riot. Aristarchus went with Paul to Jerusalem and later set off with him to Rome. When Paul was in prison in Rome he stayed with him.
Acts 19:29ff.; 20:4; 27:2; Colossians 4:10

ARMAGGEDON

See *Megiddo*.

ARNON

A river which flows into the Dead Sea from the east (now Wadi Mujib). It formed the border between the Amorites and Moabites. The invading Hebrews defeated the Amorites and their land was settled by the tribe of Reuben. The River Arnon remained the southern border.
Numbers 21:13ff.; Isaiah 16:2

AROER

A town on the north bank of the River Arnon, east of Jordan. The southern limit of the Amorite kingdom and later of the tribe of Reuben. Under Moabite rule from the time of Jehu to Jeremiah's day. Also the name of a town in the Negev, south of Beersheba.
Deuteronomy 2:36, etc.; 2 Kings 10:33

ARTAXERXES

Name of several kings of Persia. Ezra and Nehemiah probably returned to Jerusalem from exile during the reign of Artaxerxes I (464–423 BC).
Ezra 4:6–7

ASA

The son of Abijah and third king of Judah. He reigned for forty-one years (about 911–870 BC). When Asa became king he tried to wipe out pagan worship. He won a great victory when a huge Ethiopian army led by Zerar attacked Judah.
1 Kings 15:8ff.; 2 Chronicles 14:1ff.

ASAHEL

A nephew of King David. Asahel was one of David's bravest soldiers and commander of a large division of the army.
2 Samuel 2:18ff.; 23:24

ASAPH

A Levite who led the singing in King David's reign. His descendants served in the temple choir. Asaph wrote a number of psalms.

1 Chronicles 15:17ff.; 25:1ff.;
2 Chronicles 29:30; 35:15

Levite musicians playing harps and cymbals, drawn from a model.

ASCENSION

For forty days after Jesus rose from the dead he often visited his disciples. Then he returned to heaven. The disciples were with him on the Mount of Olives when Jesus gave them his final message. As they watched, they saw him "taken up to heaven . . . and a cloud hid him from their sight". This is what we call the "ascension".

Although the ascension was the end of Jesus' ministry on earth, it was not the end of his work. As the disciples watched Jesus being taken from them two heavenly messengers asked them, "Galileans, why are you standing there looking up at the sky? This Jesus, who was taken from you into heaven, will come back in the same way that you saw him go to heaven." The rest of the New Testament makes it clear that between Jesus' ascension and his return at the end of time he is with God, his Father, in the

glory of heaven. He reigns over the whole universe. He represents his followers before God and sends the Holy Spirit to help them.
Luke 24:50–53; Acts 1:6–11; Hebrews 1:3; 4:14–16; 7:24–26; John 16:5–15

ASHDOD
One of five Philistine strongholds in Old Testament times. When the Philistines captured the Covenant Box (ark) they took it to the temple of their god Dagon at Ashdod. Next morning they discovered the statue of Dagon flat on its face; the following day it was broken in pieces. Ashdod fell to King Uzziah of Judah in Isaiah's time. In New Testament times the city (called Azotus) was restored by King Herod.
1 Samuel 5; 2 Chronicles 26:6; Isaiah 20:1, etc.; Acts 8:40

ASHKELON
An ancient city on the coast of Israel, between Jaffa and Gaza. It became one of the main strongholds of the Philistines. Samson made a raid on Ashkelon, killing thirty men to pay what he owed in a bet. In the centuries that followed, Ashkelon was ruled in turn by Assyria, Babylonia and Tyre. In New Testament times Herod the Great was born at Ashkelon.
Judges 1:18; 14:19; 1 Samuel 6:17; Jeremiah 47:5–7, etc.

ASHTAROTH/ASHTEROTH-KARNAIM
A city east of the Jordan, named after the Canaanite mother-goddess. It was captured by Chedorlaomer in Abraham's time and later became a capital of

41

King Og of Bashan. One of the cities given to the Levites.
Genesis 14:5; Deuteronomy 1:4; 1 Chronicles 6:71

ASIA

The western part of Asia Minor (modern Turkey) including a number of important Greek city-states. Later the Roman province of Asia, including the whole west coast, whose most important city was Ephesus. Much of Paul's missionary work took place in this region.
Acts 2:9; 19:10; Revelation 1:4, 11

ASS (DONKEY) AND MULE

The most common of all pack animals, used for carrying heavy loads, and also for riding by rich and poor alike. The donkey is a descendant of the North African wild ass. The mule is cross-bred from a donkey (male) and a horse. Both ass and mule are sure-footed and can live in much rougher country than horses. The ass is the "hero" of the story of Balaam. Lost asses led Saul to a vital meeting with Samuel. And it was an ass which Jesus rode into Jerusalem on Palm Sunday, as a king coming in peace.
Numbers 22; 1 Samuel 9 and 10; Zechariah 9:9; Matthew 21:1–11

ASSOS

The sea-port on the west coast of modern Turkey from which Paul set out on his last journey to Jerusalem.
Acts 20:13

ASSYRIA

Assyria is the northern part of modern Iraq, along the Tigris river and eastwards to the foot of the Zagros mountains. The winter rains and the rivers that run into the Tigris provide enough water for farming. Barley and wheat grow on the plains. Grapes, olives, apricots, cherries and other fruit are grown on the hills. The countryside is covered with grass in winter and spring, unlike the land west of the Tigris. There, much of the land is desert, with craggy forested mountains to the east, which in winter are covered with snow. Assyria looked attractive to the wild tribesmen of the desert and mountains. The story of the land is one of constant war with these envious neighbours.

The Assyrians called their capital city, their country, and their national god by one name, Ashur. The city of Ashur is in the south of the country, on the west side of the Tigris. The second city, Nineveh, lies east of the river, opposite modern Mosul, 68 miles north of Ashur. Both cities were prosperous as early as 2500 BC and probably long before.

The Assyrian people First-hand records from Assyria begin soon after 2000 BC. The Assyrian king-list, an important record from a later date, shows that the Assyrians were in their land about 2300 BC. The texts prove that the Assyrians were a Semitic people. They used a language very closely related to Babylonian. They also show, as we would expect from the situation of the country, that the population was very mixed. Many non-Semitic people came in from the east and north. This seems to have happened peacefully, and, in later times, men who were not Assyrians by origin held important government posts.

Assyrians are commonly thought of as cruel imperialists. This picture, which comes partly from their wars with Israel reported in the Old Testament, has to be balanced against the situation of Assyria. Even when the frontiers seemed secure, threats existed, or could be imagined, from foreign rulers a little further away. These threats could only be dealt with by new campaigns. No doubt success encouraged further military adventures. But the Assyrians, like most people, prized peace and prosperity.

The Assyrian Empire   Between 1500 and 1100 BC Assyria became a leading state in the Near East, ruling as far west as the River Euphrates. Her kings wrote letters, as equals, to the kings of Egypt. Then Aramaean invaders from the desert almost completely overran the Assyrian homeland. This began a period of weakness that lasted until about 900 BC.

Then a line of vigorous kings began to regain their lost lands. They also tackled the problems of maintaining control over them. The warrior-kings Ashurnasirpal II (883–859 BC) and Shalmaneser III (858–824 BC) captured many cities and made their kings vassals. But as soon as the Assyrian army had gone home the subject kings rebelled. Tiglath-pileser III (745–727 BC) was the first to establish an effective system of provincial governors with firm control.

Exile   A common way of trying to break resistance was to take hostages. After a major rebellion large numbers of the population were deported to other parts of the empire and replaced with strangers from far away. (This happened in Israel when the Assyrians captured Samaria — 2 Kings 17:6, 24ff; see too 18:31, 32.) The famous emperors Sargon (721–705 BC), Sennacherib (705–681 BC), Esarhaddon (681–669 BC), and Ashurbanipal (669–627 BC) all followed this policy. Under the last two the empire grew too large, covering Egypt, Syria, the land of Israel, north Arabia, parts of Turkey and Persia. The frontiers could not all be defended, nor all rebels defeated. Babylon won independence in 625 BC, and, with help from the Medes, destroyed Nineveh in 612 BC.

Works of art Assyria's great empire brought enormous wealth. Some of it came as tax, some through trade. The kings were able to build great palaces and temples, each aiming to do better than ever before. From those excavated at Nineveh and at Nimrud (ancient Kalah, about 20 miles south) and at other places, we have recovered some fine works of art. Walls were lined with stone slabs carved in low relief to depict the king in religious,

King Ashurbanipal of Assyria hunting lions. One of a series of lion-hunt scenes which decorated his palace at Nineveh.

military, and sporting life. Furniture was decorated with ivory panels, carved or engraved, often plated with gold.

Many different influences — Egyptian, Syrian, Iranian — can be seen in the workmanship of these objects. But the basic culture of Assyria was drawn from the south, from Babylonia (see *Babylonians*). The most important of all Babylonian customs in Assyria was the cuneiform writing system on clay tablets. Thousands of these tablets have been found in the Assyrian ruins. Some deal with the administration of the empire. Some are diplomatic documents. Some are private legal deeds. Some are the records of the deeds of kings. Most outstanding of all is the library collected by King Ashurbanipal. This library held copies of every piece of literature and knowledge that had been handed down from the past. With its recovery, from 1849 onwards, modern study of Assyria and Babylonia began.

The Assyrians and the Bible story   The Assyrians come into the Bible story at the time of the last kings of Israel, when the prophets Amos and Hosea were at work in the north, and Isaiah was coming into prominence in Judah. They were the major world power, and the people of less powerful countries lived under constant threat of invasion.

"I will bring upon you . . . the king of Assyria", says Isaiah. The prophet's prediction to King Ahaz of Judah was terrifying. Ahaz was trying to win Assyrian help against his enemies, the kings of Damascus and Samaria (Israel). But God's messenger was telling him that this, the greatest power of the time, would soon overwhelm his own country. The Assyrian king was Tiglath-pileser III (745–727 BC). He did accept Ahaz and Judah as his vassal. Then he relieved the pressure by conquering Damascus and most of Israel and making them provinces of his empire.

It was Assyrian practice to make pacts with subject nations all around. If a subject stopped keeping the terms of the pact — if they failed to send an annual tax, or made friends with an enemy of Assyria — the Assyrians would try to change the situation by diplomacy. If that failed, they sent an army.

This happened to Judah. Ahaz kept the treaty, but his son Hezekiah — and King Merodach-Baladan of Babylon — joined a general rebellion when the Assyrian King Sargon died in 705 BC. Hezekiah took control of the Philistine cities which were subject to Assyria. After crushing the trouble in Babylon, Sennacherib, the new Assyrian king, naturally turned to deal with the rebel Hezekiah. His army overran Judah, as Isaiah predicted. Sennacherib's records claim: "forty-six of (Hezekiah's) strong towns ... I besieged and conquered. I brought out from them 200,150 people ... (Hezekiah) I shut up like a bird in a cage in Jerusalem his capital city ... the awful splendour of my lordship overwhelmed him ... he sent 30 talents of gold, 300 talents of silver ... to Nineveh." Jerusalem, however, remained uncaptured. In fact, the Assyrians never attacked Jerusalem again, although Manasseh, Hezekiah's son, joined an Egyptian-inspired revolt, and was kept captive for a while (about 671 BC).

Isaiah 7:17–25; 2 Kings 15:27–16:9; 18:7, 8; 19; 20:12ff.; 2 Chronicles 33:11–13

ASSYRIAN AND BABYLONIAN RELIGION

Like most peoples in the ancient world, the people of Babylon and Assyria honoured the great powers of the universe, and had favourite gods or goddesses of their own. They told stories about their gods, gave offerings to them in great temples and small shrines, asked for their help, and hoped for their good will. The gods were in control of everything, and their behaviour unpredictable.

Anu, king of heaven, was the chief of the gods. He was a remote figure. His son, Enlil, ruled over the earth's surface, and was treated as the king of the gods. Enki, or Ea, had charge of the fresh waters that gave life. Each had a wife and family. Ishtar was the wife of Anu, and far more prominent than he was in religious life. She was in charge of war and of love. Enki was given a son — Marduk — who became very important.

Marduk, also known simply as Bel, "lord", was the patron god of Babylon. His worship began to grow as Babylon's power increased during the period 2000–1000 BC. As time passed he was raised to be king of all the gods (see below). Marduk's son, Nabu, god of Borsippa near Babylon rose to high honour in turn.

There were other gods separate from these: Shamash, the sun, god of justice; Sin, the moon, worshipped especially at Ur of the Chaldees and at Harran; Adad, the god of rain and storm. Ideas such as fairness, truth, justice, and time, were also given the status of gods from soon after 2000 BC. In Assyria there was also the national god, Ashur, whose name was the same as the capital city and the land it ruled. Ashur's origin is unknown. As Assyria grew strong, her theologians identified him with Enlil, as king of the gods.

The Babylonian world was full of shadows. Evil spirits and demons lurked to catch anyone they could. They would slide under the door to attack a man in his sleep, or to snatch a child from its mother's lap, or bring diseases with the wind. Special priests recited prayers and spells over the sick or injured person, calling on the gods for help. Sometimes the affliction would be transferred by a ritual to a goat or some other substitute, which would then be killed or destroyed. People wore charms and amulets to ward off these evils. They also hung them in the doorways and buried them under the doorsteps. These last were sometimes model dogs inscribed with words such as "Don't wait, bite!"

Worship Each city had a main temple where the patron god of the city was worshipped. Here the people would gather for major festivals at the New Year and on the god's own special day. They lined the street when the god's statues were carried in procession, taken on tour from one shrine to another. Usually, it seems, ordinary citizens worshipped at small shrines set amongst the houses of a town. There they could ask the god or goddess for a son, pray for success in business, give him "thank-you presents", or make offerings to win attention, or persuade the deity to rid them of some misfortune. A priest would perform rites, speak the

The Assyrian king Tukulti-Ninurta I (about 1240 BC) depicted on an altar, standing and kneeling before the symbol of Nusku, the fire-god.

correct prayers, and accept the animal or goods offered in sacrifice.

Divination The gods had control of everything, according to Babylonian thought, but they did not reveal the future. People could not be certain about anything. So the Babylonians consulted omens. The livers and other parts of sacrificed animals were inspected for unusual symptoms, to see if the gods had "written a message" in them. They also used other unpredictable things — the flight of birds, or patterns of oil on water.

Astrologers worked out "omens" from the movements of the stars. The clear night skies made observation easy. And because each star was linked to a god or goddess, it was possible to make all sorts of deductions about the will of the gods. Some of these arts passed to the Greeks, and so to modern astrology. The zodiac is one legacy of the Babylonian astrologers. The 360-degree circle, and the 60-minute hour, were also first worked out by the Babylonian star-gazers.

Death and the afterlife All the dead were thought

to inhabit the underworld. There they lived in a land of dust, fed by offerings of food and drink made by their descendants. If no offerings were made, the ghosts of the dead would come back to haunt their families. So, too, would the ghosts of those who were not properly buried. Apparently the wicked had a worse time than the good, for some of the ancient kings served as judges in the underworld. Ideas of life after death were very vague, and offered the Babylonians no hope.

ATHALIAH
The only woman to rule over Judah (841–835 BC). She was a cruel, evil queen — like Jezebel, her mother — and put to death all the royal children except the baby Joash who was hidden by his aunt. When he was seven there was a coup, Joash was crowned king and Athaliah was killed.
2 Kings 11:1–16; 2 Chronicles 22:10–23:15

ATHENS
The capital of modern Greece which first became important in the sixth century BC. The city was at the height of its greatness in the fifth century BC when its most famous public buildings, including the Parthenon, were built. Athens was then a model democracy and centre of the arts, attracting play-wrights, historians, philosophers and scientists from all over Greece. In 86 BC the city was besieged and stripped by the Romans.

Although it lost its power and wealth as a centre of trade Athens still had a great name for learning in the mid-50s AD when Paul arrived on his second

Athens is dominated by the acropolis, surmounted by the Parthenon temple.

missionary journey, preaching about Jesus and the resurrection. The Athenians loved a discussion and called him to speak before their council. Paul used their altar, dedicated "To an Unknown God", as his starting-point. He spoke about the God who made the world and is near to each one of us.
Acts 17:15–34

ATONEMENT
The people who wrote the Bible were concerned with one problem above all others. How can men and women enjoy friendship with God? Because of sin they are separated from God, and their basic need is to be made "at one" with him. This is what the word "atonement" means.

However hard people try they can never make themselves acceptable to a holy God. We always fall short of God's standards.

In Old Testament times, sacrifices were offered in order to atone for sin. But this system could not be the final answer. A number of Old Testament writers saw that God himself would have to deal with the problem of sin. Isaiah wrote of the coming of God's servant to solve this problem: "All of us were like sheep that were lost, each of us going his own way. But the Lord made the punishment fall on him, the punishment all of us deserved."

The New Testament describes how God sent Jesus, his Son, to do just this. His death was the complete sacrifice for all men. When Jesus died on the cross he died in our place and suffered the death-penalty due for our sin. On the cross he became acutely aware of the agony of separation from God, and cried, "My God, my God, why did you abandon me?" Matthew goes on to tell us that the curtain hanging in the temple was torn from top to bottom. The fact that the curtain was torn in two announced in a dramatic way that we need no longer be cut off from God. Jesus had atoned for the sin of the world.

See also *Cross, Feasts and Festivals, Reconciliation, Redemption.*
Genesis 3; Leviticus 16; Isaiah 53; John 3:14–17; Mark 10:45; 15:34, 38; 2 Corinthians 5:14–21; Ephesians 2:14; Hebrews 7:26–9:28; 10:19–20

ATTALIA
Modern Antalya, a port on the south coast of Tur-

key, used by Paul on his first missionary journey.
Acts 14:25

AUGUSTUS CAESAR
The first Roman emperor, successor to Julius
Caesar. He ruled from 31 BC to AD 14. Augustus
ordered the census which brought Mary and Joseph
to Bethlehem.
Luke 2:1

A statue of the Emperor Augustus.

AZARIAH
Best-known of several Azariahs is the king of Judah,
also called "Uzziah" (791–740 BC). Azariah was a
good king, strong and powerful, who served God.
But he still allowed his subjects to worship idols, and
fame made him proud. He went into the temple to
offer incense, which only the priest was allowed to
do. His punishment was a severe skin disease which
forced him to live in isolation and make Jotham, his
son, acting king.
2 Kings 14:21ff.; 2 Chronicles 26

B

BAAL
See *Canaanite Religion*.

BAASHA
A man from the tribe of Issachar who seized the throne of Israel from Nadab, son of Jeroboam, and ruled from about 909 to 886 BC.
1 Kings 15:16ff.

BABEL
(Predecessor of ancient Babylon) After the flood, when people still spoke one language, they planned to build a city on the plain of Shinar (Sumer) in the land of the two rivers (Mesopotamia) — and a tower that would reach to heaven. God saw their pride and brought the work to a standstill by confusing their language, so that they could not understand one another.
Genesis 10:10; 11:1–9

BABYLON
A city on the River Euphrates, 50 miles/80 km south of modern Baghdad. Babylon was founded by Nimrod "the mighty hunter". It later became the capital of Babylonia and the Babylonian Empire. About 1750 BC, Hammurabi, one of the early kings of Babylon, wrote down on stone a great code of laws

which it is interesting to compare with the later laws of Moses.

After the defeat of Assyria in 612 BC Babylon became capital of a powerful empire extending from the Persian Gulf to the Mediterranean. In 597 and 586 BC King Nebuchadnezzar of Babylon conquered rebellious Jerusalem. On each occasion, many of the people of Judah were taken into exile to Babylon — among them the prophets Ezekiel and Daniel.

The city covered a huge area on both banks of the Euphrates. Both inner and outer city were protected by double brick walls 11–25ft/3–7m thick. Eight great gates led to the inner city, and there were fifty temples. The "hanging gardens" of Babylon was one of the wonders of the ancient world. These were terraces on different levels laid out with palms and many other trees and plants, providing colour and shade in a flat land.

In 539 BC the Persians, under Cyrus, took the city. Herodotus, the Greek historian, says they diverted the River Euphrates and marched along the dried-up river bed to enter the city. From that time on, Babylon declined. Nothing remains today but a series of widely scattered mounds, for the archaeologists to work on.
Genesis 10:10; 2 Kings 24:1; 25:7–13; Isaiah 14:1–23; Daniel 1–6

BABYLONIANS

The southern part of modern Iraq was the ancient kingdom of Babylonia. The city of Babylon first rose to power about 1850 BC for a few generations, then again under Nebuchadnezzar, 1200 years later, for an equally short time. It was the glory of Nebuchadnezzar's city that made Babylon famous in world history.

Civilization began in Babylonia long before Babylon became important. Cities grew up there soon after man learnt how to use the river waters to irrigate the land. Massive temples of mud brick have been excavated at Uruk (modern Warka, Old Testament Erech — Genesis 10:10). Their freestanding pillars are decorated with coloured mosaics.

Writing Here the oldest known writing was found, the beginning of the Babylonian cuneiform script, in which 800 or more simple pictures stand for common objects or ideas. The pictures quickly changed from representing objects to being used as syllables, for their sound values alone. (For example, drawings of a thin man and a king might mean "the king is thin" or "the thin man is king" as pictures; but they could be used as sounds to write the word "thinking".) Soon extra signs were included to show grammatical classes, subject, object and so on.

We cannot understand the very earliest clay tablets. But those of the next stage — about 3200 BC — are clearly written in a language we call Sumerian. They include lists of words by groups (stones, animals, professions), and the first meagre examples of literature, as well as accounts and deeds of sale. From the recognizable pictures, the signs quickly developed into groups of lines (these were easier to inscribe on clay), producing the wedge-shaped cuneiform script. The clay tablets survive well in the soil. They have given us more information about Babylonia than we have about almost any other ancient culture.

Sumerians and Akkadians The Sumerians may not have been the first people to live in Babylonia. But because they have left these documents, they are the first we can identify and name. Their origin is unknown, and we cannot relate their language to any other in the world. Side by side with them in the north lived Akkadian tribes. Their Semitic language was an early form of Babylonian, related to Arabic and Hebrew. The scholars of ancient Babylonia made translations from Sumerian into Akkadian, and these enable modern students to translate Sumerian.

Whoever the Sumerians were, their genius seems to have led to the invention of writing, perhaps of wheeled vehicles, and of city life in Babylonia. Stories copied out about 2000 BC recount the exploits of Sumerian heroes and gods. The most famous of these was Gilgamesh, king of Uruk soon after 3000 BC, who marched to the Lebanon mountains to fetch cedar wood, and perhaps into Turkey, too. His search for eternal life led him to the Babylonian Noah, who told the king how he was given immortality after surviving the flood. Gilgamesh was given two chances of gaining his goal. But he lost both, and returned home. He concluded that only through fame could a man's name live after him. Recent research has shown that some of these stories probably have a factual basis, even though they have mythical episodes.

About 2300 BC the Semites gained control of Babylonia under King Sargon. His capital was at Akkad, a place we have not yet discovered. His rule extended into north Syria, where he fought the king of Ebla. From this time on, the Sumerian language was less important than Akkadian. Sargon's family maintained his empire for about a century until attackers from the east broke their power. From about 2100 to 2000 BC a line of kings based at Ur had a kingdom which was almost as large.

Works of art Craftsmen in the third millennium (3000–2000) BC made fine jewellery in gold, silver, and semi-precious stones imported from the east and south. Smiths cast copper and bronze for weapons and statues. Stone carvers produced some of the finest pieces of Babylonian art — from great monuments to tiny cylinder seals (¾–2 ins/2–5cms high) which were rolled across clay to leave impressions of the pictures engraved on them. Outstanding examples of these skills were found in the Royal Tombs at Ur (dated at about 2400 BC). The local princes were buried in these tombs with their courtiers, dressed in their finery, and with chariots and wagons.

Inscriptions The small tablets which list rations and accounts seem least interesting of all the inscriptions. Yet they are of great value for the names they contain. By careful study we can separate Sumerian, Akkadian, and foreign names. From 2400 BC there are more names of the sort used later by Semites in the west (Canaanites, Hebrews). By 2000 BC large numbers of these "westerners" (Amorites) were pouring into Babylonia, and they took over the rule of the ancient cities.

Hammurabi The most outstanding of their kings was Hammurabi of Babylon, about 1792–1750 BC. He gained power for his city by war and by diplomacy. During his reign he revised the laws of the land and had them engraved on stone. These are "case laws" like those of Exodus 21 and 22. They begin: "If a man . . ." In Hammurabi's laws things are not forbidden on moral grounds, as they are in the Ten Commandments. Despite royal authority, these laws soon fell into disuse, but they were copied in schools for another thousand years.

Hammurabi's line (dynasty) collapsed when a Hittite army raided Babylon in 1595 BC. Kassite

The Ishtar gate, Babylon, and processional way leading to the temple of Marduk.

kings from the east took over, and, although they were not Semites, they quickly adopted Babylonian culture. The land was peaceful for 400 years, then a native dynasty arose.

Nebuchadnezzar and the empire Chaldaeans and Aramaeans from the west caused turmoil until the Chaldaean King Nabopolassar defeated the Assyrians (612 BC). His new empire contained most of the Assyrian provinces, although his son Nebuchadnezzar (605–562 BC) had to crush rebels in the west, including Judah. The wealth of the empire enabled these two kings to rebuild Babylon on an immense scale, with lavish decoration. The Book of Daniel describes how Nebuchadnezzar was struck down while boasting of his works (Daniel 4). His son was killed by a General Neriglissar (Nergal-Sharezer, Jeremiah 39:3), but Nabonidus in turn displaced Neriglissar's son. This king held strong religious convictions. He left Babylon in the care of his son Belshazzar, and lived for ten years in Arabia. After his return, the army of Cyrus the Persian took Babylon. The centre of world history moved away from the city for the last time.

Babylonian contributions to the world at large stem from the period about 3000–1600 BC, when the Babylonian writing system spread throughout the Near East. It took with it the knowledge of astronomy and mathematics (the divisions of the circle, the hour, and the day), which the Greeks borrowed. Other influences are harder to trace, but were undoubtedly strong.

See also *Assyrian and Babylonian religion*.

BALAAM

A prophet from Mesopotamia who was asked by Balak, king of Moab, to curse the Israelites at the time of their desert wanderings. They had just defeated the Amorites and Balak was afraid his country would suffer the same fate. At first Balaam refused to go and meet the king, but the second time he agreed. On the way, God's angel stopped Balaam's donkey and warned Balaam only to say what God told him. Instead of cursing the Israelites, Balaam blessed them three times. Later he tried to bring about the Israelites' downfall and gain the reward he had been promised by encouraging them to worship Baal. He was killed when the Israelites attacked the Midianites.
Numbers 22–24; 31

BALAK

A king of Moab who reigned at the time when the Israelites were waiting to conquer Canaan. (See *Balaam*.)
Numbers 22:2–24:5

BAPTISM

Jesus commanded his followers to be baptized to show they had become Christian converts. This practice had a Jewish background. In the time between the Old and New Testaments, people who became converts (proselytes) to the Jewish religion were baptized, or immersed in water, usually a nearby river, as a sign of cleansing. John the Baptist also baptized many people as a sign of their repentance and their inner cleansing by God.

But Christian baptism was not usually regarded as a "washing" from sin. Paul explains that when the person being baptized disappears beneath the water and then reappears, he or she has undergone a symbolic death, burial, and resurrection. Christians share in the death and resurrection of Jesus by the act of baptism: "By our baptism, we were buried with him and shared his death, in order that, just as Christ was raised from death . . . we might live a new life."

The fullest account of a baptism in the New Testament is in the story of Philip and the Ethiopian. Acts 8:37 shows one form of words that the early Christians would have used. The preacher says: "If you believe with all your heart you may be baptized." The person being baptized replies: "I believe that Jesus Christ is the Son of God." People were baptized sometimes "in the name of Jesus Christ", sometimes "in the name of the Father, Son, and Holy Spirit".
Matthew 28:19; Mark 1:4–11; Romans 6:3–4; Acts 8:26–39; 2:38; 19:5

BARABBAS
A robber and murderer accused of rebellion, in prison at the time of Jesus' arrest. The Roman governor, Pilate, knowing that Jesus was innocent of any crime and wishing to set him free, offered to release him. But the religious leaders stirred up the crowd to ask for Barabbas instead. So Barabbas was set free and Jesus was crucified.
Matthew 27:15–26

BARAK

An Israelite from Naphtali chosen by Deborah, the prophetess, to recruit a large army to fight Jabin, a Canaanite king at the time of the Judges. Barak's men won a great victory for Israel which ended twenty years of Canaanite rule.
Judges 4–5

BARNABAS

The nickname ("son of encouragement") of a Jewish Christian, born in Cyprus, who was a member of the church at Jerusalem. He was generous and warm-hearted, and he sold his land to give the money to poor Christians. When Paul came to Jerusalem after his conversion the Christians were still suspicious of him. But Barnabas welcomed him and introduced him to the apostles. The Jerusalem church sent Barnabas to Antioch to help the new Christians there, many of whom were not Jews. He went on to Tarsus to find Paul, and asked him to share in this work.

Barnabas and Paul set out together from Antioch on their first missionary journey and took John Mark, Barnabas' cousin, with them. On their return they reported to an important meeting of church leaders in Jerusalem. The two men later disagreed about asking Mark to come with them a second time. So Barnabas went back to Cyprus with Mark while Paul went on to Asia Minor (Turkey). Barnabas and Paul continued to be good friends and in his letters Paul speaks highly of Barnabas.
Acts 4:36; 9:27; 11:22ff.; 12:25ff.; 15; 1 Corinthians 9:6; Galatians 2

BARTHOLOMEW

One of the twelve apostles. He was with the other apostles after Jesus ascended into heaven, but we know nothing more of him. It is possible that he was the same person as Nathaniel, the man whom Philip brought to Jesus.
Matthew 10:3; Acts 1:13

BARUCH

A loyal friend of Jeremiah, the prophet, during the last days of Jerusalem, just before the Babylonians captured the city in 586 BC. Baruch wrote down the messages God gave Jeremiah. He stayed with Jeremiah after Jerusalem was destroyed, even when he was forced to go to Egypt. One of the books in the Apocrypha is named after him.
Jeremiah 36; 43:6

BASHAN

A fertile region east of Lake Galilee, famous for its cattle, sheep and strong oak trees. On their way from Egypt to Canaan the Israelites defeated King Og of Bashan, and his land was given to the tribe of Manasseh.
Deuteronomy 3; Psalm 22:12; Isaiah 2:13

BATHSHEBA

Wife first of Uriah the Hittite and then of King David. (See *David*.)

BEANS AND LENTILS

Broad beans can be cooked as a vegetable, or dried and ground into flour. The lentil grows in a small

Lentils (on the left) and beans.

flat pod, like a pea. It is red-coloured and is usually made into soups and stews (such as Jacob made for Esau), but can also be dried and ground into flour. 2 Samuel 17:28; Ezekiel 4:9; Genesis 25:34

BEAR

The Syrian brown bear was quite common in the hilly and wooded parts of Israel in Bible times. Bears will eat almost anything. They usually live on fruit, roots, eggs, bees' and ants' nests. But when they are hungry they may take a lamb from the flock. David, as a shepherd, had to protect his flock against them;

A Syrian bear.

and the Bible tells how bears attacked a mob who were jeering at the prophet Elisha. The Syrian brown bear still lives in the Middle East, but not in Israel.
1 Samuel 17:34–36; 2 Samuel 17:8; 2 Kings 2:24

BEATITUDES
See *Jesus' teaching*.

BEERSHEBA
The southernmost town to belong to the Israelites, on the edge of the Negev Desert, and on the trade route to Egypt. The well (*be'er*) which gave the town its name was dug by Abraham. Hagar came near to death in the desert of Beersheba. It was from this place that Abraham set out to offer up Isaac. Isaac himself was living here when Jacob left for Harran. Beersheba is also mentioned in connection with Elijah and Amos. The phrase "from Dan to Beersheba" became a common way to speak of the whole land, from north to south.
Genesis 21:14, 30–32; 26:23–33; 1 Kings 19:3; Amos 5:5

BELSHAZZAR
Ruler of Babylon, killed when Babylon was captured in 539 BC by the Medes and Persians. He had been acting king, ruling in the absence of his father Nabonidus. During a great banquet he was frightened by strange writing on the wall of his dining-hall. Daniel was called to translate the words. He warned Belshazzar that God had judged his kingdom and it had failed. Belshazzar would lose his life and

Babylon would be conquered. That very night the Persian army took the city by surprise.
Daniel 5

BELTESHAZZAR
This Babylonian name was given to Daniel. (See *Daniel*.)

BENAIAH
The best-known of several men of this name is the captain of King David's bodyguard who remained loyal when Adonijah tried to seize the throne. Benaiah played a leading part in proclaiming Solomon king, and became commander of his army.
2 Samuel 8:18; 1 Kings 1–2

BENHADAD
Name of three kings of Syria, probably meaning "son of Hadad" (the Syrian storm-god). Benhadad I (about 900–860 BC) helped Asa, king of Judah, against Israel. Benhadad II (about 860–843 BC) was an enemy of Ahab, king of Israel. Benhadad III (about 796–770 BC) went to war against Israel in the time of Elisha, the prophet. God freed the Israelites from the Syrians several times in answer to Elisha's prayers. He revealed to Elisha that Benhadad would die at the hands of his servant, Hazael.
1 Kings 20; 2 Kings 6–8

BENJAMIN
Youngest son of Jacob and Rachel. His mother died when he was born. With his brother Joseph he was the special favourite of his father. Their jealous half-

brothers sold Joseph into Egypt. Later, when the brothers were in Joseph's power in Egypt, he tested them to see if they would be equally cruel to Benjamin. But the brothers were changed men. They would not leave Benjamin behind in Egypt, even to save themselves. One of the twelve tribes of Israel was named after Benjamin.
Genesis 35:18–20; 43–45

BERNICE
The sister of Herod Agrippa II. (See *Herod Agrippa II.*)
Acts 25:13ff.

BEROEA
A town in northern Greece (Macedonia), 50 miles/ 80km from Thessalonica. Paul preached here on his second missionary journey. The Beroeans welcomed him because they studied the Scriptures. When Jews from Thessalonica stirred up the mob against him he had to leave. But Silas and Timothy stayed behind to teach the Beroeans more about the Christian faith.
Acts 17:10–15; 20:4

BETHANY
A village about 2 miles/3km from Jerusalem on the far side of the Mount of Olives, and on the road to Jericho. Mary, Martha and Lazarus lived here, and Jesus stayed with them when he visited Jerusalem. Jesus raised Lazarus from the grave at Bethany.
Matthew 26:6–13; Luke 10:38–42; 24:50;
John 11; 12:1–9.

BETHEL

A place 12 miles/19km north of Jerusalem where Jacob dreamed of a staircase from heaven to earth. God promised to protect him, and said he would give the land to Jacob's descendants. Jacob called the place "Bethel" (house of God). Centuries later, when the Israelites invaded Canaan, they captured Bethel and settled there.

When the kingdoms of Israel and Judah split up, King Jeroboam of Israel set up an altar and golden calf at Bethel, so that people could worship there instead of at Jerusalem. The prophets condemned this, and when the Israelites were taken into exile Bethel was settled by Assyrians. When the exiles returned, some of them lived in Bethel.

Genesis 28:10–22; Judges 1:22–26; 20:18; Kings 12:26–30; 2 Kings 2; 17–28; Nehemiah 11:31

BETHESDA/BETHZATHA

A large pool in Jerusalem. At the time of Jesus it was sheltered by five porches, and it is probably the five-porched pool that has been unearthed by archaeologists in the north-east of the city. The pool was fed by a spring which bubbled up from time to time. Many sick people gathered there, hoping to be healed if they were first into the water after this bubbling. It was here that Jesus healed a man who had been ill for thirty-eight years.

John 5:1–15

BETH-HORON (UPPER AND LOWER)

These two towns controlled the Valley of Aijalon and the ancient trade-route which passed through it.

Many armies took this route in Bible times. Here Joshua pursued the Amorite kings who had attacked the town of Gibeon. Philistines, Egyptians and Syrians also came here.
Joshua 16:3–5; 10:10; 1 Samuel 13:18

BETHLEHEM
The city of David, 5 miles/8km south-west of Jerusalem, in the Judean hills. Rachel, Jacob's wife, was buried nearby. Ruth and Naomi settled here. Bethlehem was David's birth-place, and the place where the prophet Samuel chose him as the future king, to succeed Saul. The prophet Micah foretold the birth of the Messiah at Bethlehem, although it was only a small town.

Centuries later the Roman census brought Mary and Joseph to Bethlehem. Shepherds and wise men came to kneel before their baby, Jesus — born in a stable in the "city of David". Not long after, jealous

The small town of Bethlehem straddles a ridge in the hills to the south of Jerusalem.

King Herod gave orders to kill all the boys in Bethlehem under two years old.
Genesis 35:19; Ruth; 1 Samuel 16; Micah 5:2; Matthew 2; Luke 2

BETHPHAGE
A village near Bethany, on or near the Mount of Olives, on the east side of Jerusalem. When Jesus came here on his last journey to Jerusalem, he sent two disciples to a nearby village to fetch the young colt on which he rode in triumph into the city.
Matthew 21:1; Mark 11:1; Luke 19:29

BETHSAIDA
A fishing town on the north shore of Lake Galilee, near the River Jordan. The home of Jesus' disciples, Philip, Andrew and Peter. Jesus restored the sight of a blind man at Bethsaida, and warned the people of God's judgement. Although they saw his miracles they would not change their ways.
John 1:44; Mark 8:22; Matthew 11:21

BETH-SHAN
A very ancient city in northern Palestine where the Valley of Jezreel slopes down to the west bank of the River Jordan. The Israelites failed to drive the Canaanites out of this district. After Saul and Jonathan were killed by the Philistines on Mt Gilboa, their bodies were fixed on the walls of Beth-shan, but later rescued and buried by men from Jabeshgilead. In New Testament times Beth-shan was known by the Greek name Scythopolis, and became one of the cities of the Decapolis, the only

one west of the Jordan (see *Decapolis*). The modern town of Beisan stands close to the mound of the old site.
Joshua 17:11, 16; Judges 1:27; 1 Samuel 31:10–13; 2 Samuel 21:12; 1 Kings 4:12

BETH-SHEMESH
A town about 12 miles/19km west of Jerusalem, given to the priests. It was near the borders of the Philistines. When the Covenant Box (ark) was returned by the Philistines, it came to Beth-shemesh. But some of the people here were punished for not treating it with respect. Later Jehoash, king of the northern kingdom of Israel, defeated and captured Amaziah, king of Judah, at Beth-shemesh.
Joshua 21:16; 1 Samuel 6:9–21; 1 Kings 4:9; 2 Kings 14:11–13

BETH-ZUR
A city of Judah, 4 miles/6km north of Hebron. Beth-zur was settled by the family of Caleb. Later it was one of fifteen cities fortified by King Rehoboam. Men from here helped to rebuild Jerusalem under Nehemiah's leadership. The place stood on one of the highest hill-tops in the land, and was the scene of one of the great Jewish victories in the Maccabean revolt (*1 Maccabees* 4:26–35).
Joshua 15:58; 1 Chronicles 2:45; 2 Chronicles 11:7; Nehemiah 3:16

BIBLE: INTERPRETATION
Some of the stories in the Gospels are so clear that

anyone can understand them. But is is not so easy to get the meaning of some other parts of the Bible. The Bible is an ancient book made up of many parts. It has many different writers, different audiences, different styles of writing and language. When we read a passage from the Bible it is useful to ask three questions:

What does the passage actually say?

What does the passage mean?

What does the passage mean today?

What does the passage actually say? To understand what the passage says we need to ask some further, more detailed questions. For example, it is important to ask: **when** and **where** the book, or passage, was written.

Was it before or after the birth of Christ?

Before the exodus or after?

When Israel was ruled by kings, or during the Roman occupation?

Where was it written?

In exile in Babylon?

In a prison cell in Rome?

At the royal court as an official record?

If we find out the answers to these questions we shall discover the setting of the passage in history. This helps us to understand what the writer intended.

A second useful question is: **why** was this passage written? If we can discover the purpose of the writer, we will begin to understand better some of the things he says. For example, some of Paul's letters were written to try to correct errors among groups of Christians. He points out their mistakes, and shows them a better way for the future. Similarly, it helps to know that the writer of the Book of Revelation wanted to encourage his readers who were suffering persecution for their faith.

It also helps to ask generally: **what** is this book about? The answer to this question will help us to read the book in the right way.

Is it the account of events in the life and death of Jesus?

Is it a list of the religious duties of the Hebrew people?

Is it a collection of religious poetry?

Sometimes it is important to ask what particular words mean. There are some special terms in the Bible — "atonement", for example, or "sin". It is important to understand their special meaning if we are to get the writer's message.

We need, especially, to ask: what *sort* of writing is this? In what form has it been written.

Is it history?

Is it poetry?

Is it a letter?

Then we can go on to ask the questions that apply to that kind of writing.

If we are reading a book of history, we can ask: what actually happened? What other important events were occurring at the same period? Why has the writer chosen these events to recount? And why does he recount them in the way he does?

But if it is a book of poetry, we should look at the writer's use of picture-language. What does he mean by his pictures? How was the poem or hymn used in worship?

It is worth looking in more detail at some of the forms of writing in the Bible.

History and biography The Old Testament has many books of history, such as Samuel and Kings, and we find New Testament history in the Gospels and Acts. If we are reading history, we need to enquire about the background to events.

What was going on in the wider world at the time?

What important affairs were taking place?

Then we need to look at the passage itself carefully.

What actually happens?

Who are the principle characters?

Where did this all occur?

Sometimes history books are written to prove or make a particular point. So it is important to ask what the writer was trying to show.

Law The main law-books of the Old Testament are Exodus, Leviticus, Deuteronomy and Numbers. These books contain long passages listing laws which cover many different aspects of life. It is useful to ask what part of life particular laws apply to.

Does the law deal with matters of behaviour and morals?

Are they state laws or social rules?

Are the laws about hygiene or family life?

Or are they religious laws — about worship, ritual and sacrifice?

Are they solemn ritual blessings and cursings related to Jewish religion?

When we read passages of the law, it is important to relate them to the particular periods in Israel's history to which they applied. When we come to the New Testament, we need to understand how far

Jesus' teaching overruled the law. Galatians and Hebrews, for example, show how the first Christians believed the scope of the law was altered.

Poetry Some Old Testament books are largely made up of poetry. Job, Psalms and the Song of Solomon are good examples. There are also passages of poetry in the prophets and shorter ones in the New Testament — for example Mary's song of praise, the Magnificat. We need to read these passages as poetry, not as prose.

Is the book written rather like a play, with characters? (The Book of Job can be looked at like this). Or is it the writer's personal feelings, which we can sometimes share? Examples of this include some of the psalms.

Or does the poetry have much picture-language? Some Old Testament poetry was written for official temple worship. A psalm, for example, may retell the great events in Israel's history. Sometimes it is important to know the history behind a particular poem — for example, David's lament over the death of his friend Jonathan. There are some special effects in Hebrew poetry. The one we see most often is the way the poet makes the same point in two slightly different ways in consecutive lines.

Wise sayings Some Old Testament books — particularly Proverbs and Ecclesiastes — are made up of "wise sayings". Some of these stand on their own: sometimes they are grouped into sayings with a common theme. Some of the sayings are common-sense comments on everyday living, often with a touch of humour. Others try to draw out general principles about human life. Some talk about life without God; others about the true source of happiness.

Prophecy   A large section of the Old Testament is made up of "books of prophecy". This does not necessarily mean that they foretell the future. The prophets who wrote the books were usually concerned to speak out against evils, or the disregard for God and his rules which they saw in society around them. But they also occasionally looked forward to what God had in store for the future.

When we read the prophets, we need to find out their background in history. There are other useful questions.

Is the writer using picture-language?

Is he writing a kind of poetry?

What do his word-pictures mean?

What was the prophet's purpose in speaking as he did?

Was the prophecy understood in a special way by the New Testament writers?

Parables   Many of Jesus' parables are written down in the Gospels. We also find parables, or picture-stories, in some of the Old Testament books of history and prophecy. We need first to find out what the main point of the parable was. Do the details of the parable have any special meaning — or are they there just to set the scene for the story? Many of Jesus' parables were told to help ordinary people understand what God's kingdom was like, and how he deals with men and women.

Letters   Many of the later books of the New Testament are letters from apostles or other Christians in various places. When we read these letters we must ask:

Who wrote this letter?

To whom?

What was his purpose in writing?

What is the main theme of the letter?

What did the passage mean to its first readers? If we have answered all the questions, and know what the passage actually says, it is not so difficult to find out what it meant to its original readers. We can try to find out what the main point of the passage is. What does it teach? If the passage was written to answer a specific need or situation, we can ask: Is there a general principle behind these events?

When we feel we know what the passage actually says, and what it meant for its original readers, we can confidently ask our final question.

What does the passage mean for us today? Is there a modern situation like that of the original reader? What would the writer have to say to such a situation? If not, is there a principle that still applies? What specific teaching is there in the passage? (It is often useful to compare it with other Bible passages dealing with similar subjects. Sometimes they may set it out more clearly — or add to the meaning of the passage we are reading.) Is there something we can learn?

About God?

About man?

About the world?

About the church?

About some other specific theme?

Can we find some example to follow? Is there a warning? Does it contain a promise that applies to us? Is there some action we should take in the light of this passage? Does it make us want to pray? Or to praise? Can we use the writer's words to express our own feelings about God? How does this passage, and its meaning, fit in with other passages we know with similar themes?

See also *Old Testament text*, *New Testament text*

BIBLE TRANSLATIONS

For many Christians in the first century "the Bible" was the Greek translation of the Old Testament (the *Septuagint*), which was begun in the third century BC. Soon after the New Testament was completed, translation work began. The first translation was probably into Latin. This was the official language of the Roman Empire, though Greek was the most widely spoken language among Christians, even in Italy. At first Greek was used in most churches.

From the second century on, there were many local translations of the Bible. But people felt that there should be a standard text that could be recognized and used by everyone. So in about AD 384 Pope Damasus instructed his secretary to revise the Latin New Testament. This man was Jerome. He is the first Bible translator whose name has come down to us (we know of earlier Jewish scholars who revised the Greek Old Testament). His Latin translation, the Vulgate (or Common Version), has been the standard Bible of the Roman Catholic Church ever since. Scores of other translations have been made from it including the first English ones.

Jerome was a good scholar and he did his work well. In order to translate the Old Testament he

For centuries the Bible manuscripts were copied by hand. This print from about AD 1340 shows a court secretary copying a manuscript in his library.

learnt Hebrew, living for many years in Bethlehem. Through his work, copied out by hand in many lands, God's word brought hope and new life to countless people.

In the second century, translators began work in Syriac, a dialect of the Aramaic language which Jesus himself spoke. Although old Syriac is no longer spoken, the fourth-century translation (known as the Peshitta) is still used in worship by Nestorian and Syrian Christians in Syria, Iran, India and other lands.

In Egypt the church at first used the Greek language. But as Christianity spread south, an Egyptian (or Coptic) version was needed. Translation began in the third century. The Coptic Bible is still used in worship.

After the Roman Emperor Constantine was converted (AD 312) Christianity spread rapidly, and new translations were soon needed. The Goths, who invaded the Empire in the River Danube basin, received almost the whole Bible in their own language from the missionary translator, Ulfilas. Much of the text survives in manuscripts, although the language has long been extinct.

St Mesrop worked out an alphabet for the Armenians, the first Christian nation in the world, and gave them their Bible in the fifth century. This is still the standard version of the ancient Armenian Church, both in the Armenian SSR (part of the USSR) and in the many lands where Armenians are scattered. The Ge'ez and Georgian Bibles, used to this day in the churches of Ethiopia and Georgia (USSR), probably also date from the fifth century.

Later there was a translation in Old Slavonic, the language spoken in Bulgaria, Serbia and southern Russia in the ninth century, when the Slavic tribes became Christians through the work of St Cyril. He invented the Cyrillic alphabet, and before long the whole Bible had been translated. This version is still the official version of the Russian Orthodox Church.

As well as these church translations, we know of at least one "missionary" version made *before* a church had been established. In about AD 640 a group of Nestorian missionaries, whose language was Syriac, translated the Gospels into Chinese for the Emperor Tai Tsung.

The Dark Ages In the centuries following the

break-up of the Roman Empire in the West, Christianity was spreading fast, especially in northern and eastern Europe. As the church grew, parts of the Bible were translated into many new languages.

The earliest real translation in England was Aldhelm's translation of the Psalms. Aldhelm was Bishop of Sherborne, in the south of England, AD 700. About the same time in the north of England the great historian, Bede, was concerned about priests who knew little or no Latin and so could not read the Bible. So he began to translate the Bible into Anglo-Saxon. He died in AD 735, working on his translation of John's Gospel on his death bed. Unfortunately, neither Bede's nor Aldhelm's work has survived. The English King Alfred (AD 871–901) was also a Bible translator, giving his people parts of Exodus, Psalms and Acts in their own language. Educated priests sometimes made their own versions, too. After the Norman conquest, various books of the Bible were translated into English, some in local dialects.

Other unofficial translations, mainly for church leaders and often in metre, were made in other languages. A translation of Matthew in Frankish (early German), made in AD 758, has survived. The earliest French texts date from the twelfth century; Italian from the fourteenth. The first Bible translations in Arabic probably appeared in the eighth century, though there were Christians in Arabia in the fourth century.

Forerunners of the Reformation In the latter part of the Middle Ages a number of new Bible versions appeared. These were designed to be read by ordinary Christians and the work was supported by people who were critical of the official church leadership. About 1170, a merchant of Lyons, Peter Waldo, found new purpose in life through reading the New Testament. He arranged for the Bible to be translated into Provençal (southern French). His followers formed the Waldensian Church, which was bitterly persecuted for centuries.

Nearly 200 years later, an Oxford theologian, John Wycliffe, was studying his Bible. He became convinced that it was so important that it must be available to everyone. As a result, by 1384 the Latin Vulgate Bible had been translated into English. Nicholas of Hereford, John Purvey and others were the actual translators of most of it. They followed the Latin closely, even in its very un-English order of words! By 1395 Purvey had revised the work in better and clearer English.

Some copies carried notes expressing the controversial views of the Lollards (as Wycliffe's followers were called). In 1408 a synod of the church met at Oxford and banned the writing, circulation or study of these English versions. But the appeal of the English Bible was too great. Many hundreds of copies were still circulating when the first printed books of the Bible appeared over 100 years later.

A similar movement took place in Bohemia (Czechoslovakia). Jan Hus, Rector of the University of Prague, was influenced by Wycliffe's teaching. He was burnt at the stake in 1415, but his followers began the work of Bible translation. The Czech New Testament, printed in 1475, was the result.

Printing and the Reformation   Around 1450, at

Mainz in Germany, Johann Gutenberg pioneered the process of printing from movable metal type. His work began a new era in the history of books, and with them, of the Bible. The first major work to emerge from the press was the Bible (1456) — in Latin. Ten years later it was printed in German at Strasburg, from the text of an unknown fourteenth-century translator. In 1471 the first Italian Bible was printed and this was soon followed by the French New Testament. The first Dutch Scriptures appeared in 1477. Next came the whole Bible in Catalan (for Spain, 1478).

All these versions were based on existing manuscripts and translated from the Latin. But with the revival of learning, texts in the original languages began to be studied. Jewish scholars had preserved the Hebrew Bible and in 1488 they printed it in Italy. The Greek New Testament was first published by the great Dutch scholar, Erasmus, in 1516. Although he was not himself a translator (except into Latin) Erasmus, unlike many others, was very much in favour of translating the Bible into ordinary speech. He wrote:

"I wish that the Scriptures might be translated into all languages, so that not only the Scots and the Irish, but also the Turk and the Saracen might read and understand them. I long that the farm-labourer might sing them as he follows the plough, the weaver hum them to the tune of his shuttle, the traveller beguile the weariness of his journey with their stories."

Meanwhile, in Germany, a young monk called Martin Luther was anxiously studying his Latin

Bible. As he read, he was especially struck by Paul's words in Romans 1:17 "The gospel reveals how God puts people right with himself. It is through faith from beginning to end." He describes the great release and freedom these words brought. "I felt completely reborn . . . My love for that sweetest word 'righteousness of God' was henceforth as great as my hatred for it had been hitherto. In this way this passage of Paul was truly the gate of Paradise."

Luther was a lecturer in the university at Wittenberg. He proclaimed this message, and made a close study of the Hebrew Old Testament and Erasmus' Greek New Testament. Then he undertook the task of making a new translation in German, in the clearest possible language. The New Testament appeared in 1522 and the task was completed in 1532. It has remained the best-known German Bible ever since.

The English Bible   About the same time, William Tyndale, who had been a scholar at Cambridge soon after Erasmus, and was influenced by his writings, began to translate the New Testament into English. The church authorities gave him no encouragement. So he went to Germany to finish his work. The first New Testament printed in English appeared at Worms in 1526. Copies soon reached England and were eagerly studied. The authorities denounced them and the Bishop of London bought large quantities and burnt them. Tyndale's reaction was to publish a better version! He revised it twice, and by 1566 it had been printed forty times. He went on to write other books and to translate part of the Old Testament. But the New Testament is his great legacy to the English-speaking world, for the Authorized/ King James' Version of 1611 follows it very closely.

In 1535 Myles Coverdale published the first whole Bible in English. It was printed abroad but soon found its way into England. In 1533 the clergy of the province of Canterbury had asked King Henry VIII for an official translation of the Bible. They wanted this "delivered to the people for their instruction". A dedication to the king was added to the Coverdale Bible. It seems that when the scholars assured him that it did not contain any heresies Henry authorized its circulation.

Coverdale did not work from the original Greek and Hebrew. He based his work on that of Tyndale, Luther and the Latin versions. His translation is still used today, in the version of the Psalms that is still printed in *The Book of Common Prayer*. Coverdale was the first to include chapter summaries, as in the Authorized/King James' Version, and to separate the Apocrypha from the Old Testament books. In the older versions the apocryphal books were set out in the same way as they are in the Greek *Septuagint*.

In 1537 came the first Bible actually printed in England. It had on it the name "Thomas Matthew", the pen name of John Rogers, a fellow-worker of Tyndale's. It is made up mostly of Tyndale's translation, including his Joshua to Chronicles, not previously published, and contains a good deal of extra material in the form of indexes and notes. It was the first Bible to be published "with the King's most gracious licence", a privilege granted to Coverdale's Bible in the same year.

In 1538 an order was issued with the king's

authority that the clergy must provide "a book of the whole Bible of the largest volume in English" to be set "in some convenient place within the church, whither your parishioners may most conveniently resort to the same and read it . . . It is the very living Word of God that every Christian person is bound to embrace, believe and follow if he look to be saved".

The book the king intended was the Great Bible, Coverdale's revision of Matthew's version. It appeared in 1539. Its second edition contained a preface by Archbishop Cranmer, encouraging everyone to read the Bible. It also contained a note: "this is the Bible appointed for the use of the churches." One of the two bishops who had examined it for the king was Tonstall, who as Bishop of London had burnt Tyndale's New Testament. All controversial notes had been dropped. Before Henry's death in 1547 Tyndale's and Coverdale's translations were forbidden and large numbers were destroyed. But the Great Bible remained in the churches throughout the reign of Edward VI and some even in the reign of the Roman Catholic Queen Mary (1553–58), although the church services were once more in Latin.

Meanwhile, in Geneva, scholarly English exiles were at work on a revision. This appeared in 1560, dedicated to Queen Elizabeth I. It contained the first translation of Ezra to Malachi directly from Hebrew. The Hebrew idiom was kept wherever possible, in the New as well as the Old Testament. The Apocrypha was included, with a note about its value. The Bible also contained some notes about its meaning. It became a very popular Bible. In Britain, as well as in Geneva, it was printed seventy times in Elizabeth's reign. In Scotland this was the Bible officially read in churches, and it continued to be used for some time after the Authorized/King James' Version had appeared. It is sometimes called the Breeches Bible, because in its translation of Genesis 3:7 it says that Adam and Eve made themselves "breeches".

Meanwhile the Great Bible was being revised. This was mainly the work of the bishops, with Archbishop Parker playing a leading part. So the new version which appeared in 1568 became known as the Bishops' Bible. The revisers aimed to improve the accuracy of the text, to change expressions offensive to public taste and to avoid controversial notes and interpretations. But the result was not so good as the Geneva Bible. Although it was used in churches, it proved to be less popular.

King James' (Authorized) Version   When he came to the throne in 1603 James I of England (VI of Scotland) agreed to a new revision. He himself took a share in organizing the work, which was entrusted to six teams of scholars. After they had done their work, two scholars from each team worked over the whole Bible before it went to press. The work was based on the Bishops' Bible, but using the original Hebrew and Greek. Names were given their familiar forms, and familiar ecclesiastical words (like "church" and "bishop") were to be kept. Notes in the margins explained Greek and Hebrew words and linked parallel passages. Words added to complete the sense were printed in a different type. New chapter summaries were included.

This version enjoyed enormous prestige for 350

years. The main reasons for this are probably the beauty and rhythm of its language. All early editions included the Apocrypha. This was not omitted from the Geneva Bible till 1640, and much later from the Authorized Version. Since the first edition the spelling has been greatly modernized, the chapter summaries reduced and marginal references expanded. In 1701 Archbishop Ussher's dates were added in the margin and continued to appear for 200 years.

The Douai version One year before the Authorized Version, the standard Roman Catholic version, the Douai Bible, was published. This was the work of Gregory Martin and others at the English College at Douai, in France. His New Testament appeared in 1582 when the college was at Rheims. He tried to translate the Vulgate word for word, sometimes making little sense in English. Some unusual words taken over from the Latin are explained in a glossary. Full notes explain the text and points of doctrine.

Many found the language of the Douai Bible hard to understand, and so Bishop Challoner issued two revisions of the Old Testament and five of the New up to 1772, much influenced by the Authorized Version. His last revision came to replace the original Douai as the official Roman Catholic version.

Pioneer missionary Bible translators When missionary work began again after the Middle Ages, the first translations were made by Roman Catholics. They generally began with the Ten Commandments, the Lord's Prayer and selected parts of the Gospels or Bible story books, as well as the catechism. But in 1613 Jesuit missionaries published the whole New

Testament in Japanese.

The first Protestant version was in Malay, and was made by employees of the Dutch East India Company.

The first whole Bible was John Eliot's 1663 version in "Massachusetts". This is a complex American Indian language, with some words 15–20 letters long.

Bible translation in India began in earnest with Danish Lutheran missionaries. Ziegenbalg's New Testament in Tamil appeared in 1711 and the Old Testament was added by Schultze in 1728. But a new era began when the first English missionary, William Carey, reached India in 1793. He spent forty years working at Serampore in Bengal with two colleagues and many Indian helpers. When he died, his press had produced translations of the whole Bible or New Testament in 37 different languages or dialects. These included Burmese and Chinese. He had also compiled grammars and dictionaries. It was an amazing achievement.

The Bible Societies In 1804 the British and Foreign Bible Society was founded "for Wales, for the kingdom, for the world". At first it issued existing Bible versions. But its members soon took an interest in new translations. They issued the Hindustani (Urdu) New Testament, translated by the pioneer missionary, Henry Martyn, in 1812 and the first modern African translation in 1816. This was in the Bullom language for Sierra Leone. Since then there have been translations into about 480 African languages. Christians were the first to write these languages down, using the Roman script. The first complete New Testament for Africa was in Amharic, for Ethiopia, in 1829. The first whole Bible in an African language was in Malagasy in 1835.

A similar process began in the Pacific (with Tahitian in 1818) and in Latin America (with Aymara, for Bolivia, in 1829).

By this time other societies had begun work. The Netherlands Bible Society, the American Bible Society and the National Bible Society of Scotland, all began the work of Bible translation. In India, Africa and the Arab lands Roman Catholic missionaries also worked on Bible translation.

The modern missionary movement grew all through the nineteenth century, and until 1939 translation went ahead at a great rate. Practically every missionary society had a part in it. The chief translators were generally missionaries, though nationals were also involved. Some played a major role. Nigerian-born Bishop Samuel Crowther, for example, worked on the Yoruba Bible (Nigeria, 1862) and Pandita Ramabai on the Bible in Marathi (1912). The Bible Societies helped set the work up. They gave money where it was needed. They had the translations printed and distributed and generally helped out with any problems. Only the Netherlands Society trained its own linguists and sent them out as translators.

Missionary Bible translation today There have been great changes in Bible translation since World War II.

The Wycliffe Bible Translators were founded in 1934 to bring people the Bible in their own language. Thousands of languages were still without it. This group has now expanded into the largest missionary society in the world. It has over 3,000 missionaries, who carry out a carefully organized programme in about 700 languages.

Each translator is first trained in linguistics. They usually have to give the language a written form for the first time. This is no easy task, especially when it contains sounds unknown in any European language. Then the translator has to write a grammar and a complete list of words used. He is usually helped by a national who has at least some knowledge of another language known to the missionary. Years may pass before he can begin even the simplest translations. Meanwhile the tribal people have to be taught to read. And then the translation must be tested all the time, to make sure that people can understand it.

A still larger programme, covering some of the major languages of the world (Hindi, Chinese, Arabic) has been carried on by the United Bible Societies. This organization unites sixty or so national societies all over the world. Both Roman Catholics and Protestants co-operate in this work. The second Vatican Council encouraged Roman Catholics to supply their people with the Bible in their own language.

Consultations are held to gain wide support for the new translation. Some people are bound to resent any changes in the Bible they have known from childhood, and their views must be taken into account. If a new translation is decided on, translators will be chosen and trained. They will make the first drafts, sharing them with each other and noting criticisms. Then their agreed draft will go to a team of experts on the Bible and the language, who will send their criticisms in writing. If the translators do not accept these, they will be discussed at a meeting of the experts. Church leaders will also receive drafts, so that when the work is finished they will support it and help churches to accept it. A Bible Society translations officer will keep in close touch with a number of projects like this. He will make regular visits, offering advice and suggestions and occasionally settling disputes.

Today thousands of people are working to make the Bible clear in terms which ordinary people can understand. There are still many hundreds of language groups, mostly small ones, with no existing translation that meets their need. And languages are always changing. United Bible Society scholars reckon that, to keep up with this change, some revision, if not a new translation, will be needed in every language every thirty years. Certainly there will be enough work to keep the Bible translators busy for many years to come, bringing God's message to everyone in his own language.

BIBLE: MODERN ENGLISH VERSIONS
The Revised Version In 1870 the Church of England passed a historic resolution, to prepare a revision of the Authorized Version, making only necessary changes. Teams of Old and New Testament scholars were appointed, and Church of Scotland and Free Church scholars were invited to join. They were to make "as few alterations as possible" in "the

language of the Authorized Version". No changes in the Greek and Hebrew text were to be adopted without a two-thirds majority. Two parallel groups were formed in the USA to co-operate with suggestions and criticisms.

The Revised Version New Testament, printed in 1881 and telegraphed to Chicago, aroused great interest. It was based on a far more ancient Greek text than the Authorized Version, relying chiefly on the fourth-century Vatican and Sinaitic codices (see *New Testament Text*). Many marginal notes referred to the sources of the original text. Quite a number of well-known words and verses in the Authorized Version were left out because there was no good manuscript authority for them. This led to strong opposition, though without good reason. The translation is often over-literal or pedantic. But the Old Testament translation (1885) was a great advance on the Authorized Version. Many meaningless passages were made clear through new knowledge of the Hebrew; poetic passages were set out as poetry; paragraphs were used; and a good reference system was introduced in 1898.

The Revised Standard Version The American scholars who had been associated with the English Revised Version produced the American Standard Version in 1901. In 1937 the council which held the copyright for this decided on a revision. The New Testament appeared in 1946 and the Old Testament in 1952. Its language is a compromise between the out-dated language made familiar by the King James' Version, and modern English. Most, but not all, of the out-of-date words have gone. Quotation marks are used for speech. In some places ancient translations have been followed where the Hebrew text seems clearly wrong. And in Isaiah some changes have been introduced in the light of the Dead Sea Scrolls.

In 1973 a new edition, known as *The Common Bible*, was issued. It was authorized by Roman Catholic authorities as well as the RSV committee.

The New English Bible In 1946 the Church of Scotland approached the main British churches and suggested an entirely new translation. The idea was welcomed and soon three teams of scholars were at work, with a further group to advise on questions of style. Dr C. H. Dodd was the general director. The New Testament appeared in 1961, the Old Testament in 1970. This is the first official inter-church translation in Britain and the first major version to depart from the Tyndale/Authorized Version tradition.

The New English Bible takes all the latest research into account. The Dead Sea Scrolls have thrown new light on the Old Testament text. Newly-discovered documents in languages related to Hebrew have revealed the meanings of some difficult words. It is intended to be in modern English without the old-fashioned "biblical" language of the Authorized Version. But there are still frequent echoes of it. Some of the words are long and difficult and it did not capture the idiom of modern English.

The Jerusalem Bible In 1966 Roman Catholic translators published the Jerusalem Bible. This was a new version made from the original languages. It was similar to the French *Bible de Jerusalem*, and included the introductions and notes from the French translation. This translation has been widely used by Protestants as well as Roman Catholics. Its language is more lively and modern than that of the Revised Standard Version.

The Good News Bible   (Today's English Version) The Good News Bible, produced by the American Bible Society (New Testament 1966, Old Testament 1976) has broken new ground. The aim is a reliable and accurate translation using words which make the meanings clear to everyone. This includes people who have no Christian background, people without much formal education, and people who use English as a second language. It is based on a careful study of linguistics and provides a pattern for translations in many other languages all over the world.

The basic aim is to provide in English the closest *natural* equivalent of the original language.

A second important aim concerns the level of language. Scholarly, poetical and technical religious terms are avoided. And so are all slang expressions. The result is a "common language", which should be clear and acceptable to all readers of English.

Other modern English translations by groups and individuals are as follows:

1902 **The Twentieth Century New Testament**
The thirty or so translators included ministers but not textual experts. Easy to read and understand.

1903 R. F. Weymouth, **The New Testament in Modern Speech**
Long sentences are divided, and section headings added. Uses dignified and sometimes old-fashioned language.

1913 and 1924 J. Moffatt, **A New Translation of the Bible**

A good translation, especially in the Old Testament. Rearranges and changes parts of the text, for reasons which Moffatt explains elsewhere.

1923 and 1927 E. J. Goodspeed, **The Complete Bible: an American translation**

A very readable version. The Old Testament was the work of four other scholars.

1941 and 1949 **The Basic English Bible**

A successful experiment using a vocabulary of only 1,000 words.

1941 **The Confraternity Version**

A Roman Catholic translation made in the USA. A revision of Challoner's New Testament. The Old Testament translation is based on the Hebrew.

1945 and 1949 Ronald Knox, **The Holy Bible**

A Roman Catholic translation based on the Latin Vulgate, by a master of English style.

1947–1957 J. B. Phillips, **The New Testament in Modern English**

A free and racy version which has been very popular.

1945 and 1959 **The Berkeley Version**

The New Testament by Dr G. Verkuyl; the Old Testament by a team of scholars in the USA. A conservative version.

1958 K. S. Wuest, **Expanded Translation of the New Testament**

Designed to help Bible students who do not know Greek.

1958 **The Amplified New Testament**

Produced in the USA. Includes alternative and additional words to bring out the meaning.

1971 K. Taylor, **The Living Bible**
A popular American paraphrase into everyday language, designed for family reading.
1971 **New American Standard Version**
The American Standard Version of 1901 with modernized English.
1973 and 1978 **The New International Version**
A translation by a team of Protestant evangelical scholars mainly from the USA. Clear, dignified and readable.

BILHAH

Rachel's servant, who became the mother of Dan and Naphtali.
Genesis 29:29; 30:3–7

BITHYNIA

A Roman province in the north-west of Asia Minor (Turkey). Paul was forbidden "by the Holy Spirit" to preach here. Yet Bithynia was not forgotten. Peter sent his first letter to Christian believers living in Bithynia, among other places. We know that this area soon became a strong centre of Christianity, for early in the second century the Roman governor Pliny wrote to the Emperor Trajan about the Christians there.
Acts 16:7; 1 Peter 1:1

BLOOD

The New Testament often describes the death of Jesus by the phrase "the blood of Christ (or Jesus)". The background to this unusual phrase is in the Old

Testament, where the word "blood" is used in a number of distinctive ways:
— When blood is shed a person's life is over: "The life is in the blood."
— Life is the gift of God, so no one must shed another's blood.
— The blood of animals was shed in sacrifice. It represents the animal's life poured out in death. Since life is the gift of God, this blood must not be used for food (this ruling applied to every animal killed, not only in sacrifice).

So when the New Testament uses the phrase "the blood of Christ" it refers to the violent death of Jesus on the cross. Indeed, some modern versions simply translate the phrase as "the death of Christ".

See also *Atonement, Cross, Redemption*.
Genesis 9:4–6; Deuteronomy 12:15–16, 20–28; Ephesians 1:7; 1 Peter 1:18–19; Hebrews 10:19–22

BOAZ
Hero of the Book of Ruth. Boaz was a rich and generous farmer in Bethlehem who married Ruth and became the great-grandfather of King David.
Ruth 2–4

BODY
In the Bible the word "body" is often used to stand for the whole person. So it can sometimes be translated as "self". For instance: "Offer your bodies (your selves) as a living sacrifice." The New Testament speaks of the "resurrection body", the new form we will have when God raises us from death. This means a full, continued life for the whole

person, not merely some disembodied existence as a spirit.

Paul uses the idea of the body — in which different parts have different functions — as a picture of the church. Christians are like the different parts which make up a body. Each has a different part to play in the church, working under the direction of Jesus.

The New Testament places great importance on the physical body. It is "the body" which is the temple of the Holy Spirit, and our "bodies" which are to be used for God's glory.

Romans 12:1; 1 Corinthians 15:35–49; Romans 12:4–5; 1 Corinthians 12:12–30; Ephesians 4:15–16; 1 Corinthians 6:15–20

BOZRAH

An ancient city in Edom, south-east of the Dead Sea, about 80 miles/128km south of modern Amman in Jordan. The prophets foretold that Bozrah would be utterly destroyed.

Genesis 36:33; 1 Chronicles 1:44; Isaiah 34:6; 63:1; Jeremiah 49:13, 22; Amos 1:12

BREAD

See *Food*.

BUILDING

Skill in building developed slowly in Israel. As slaves in Egypt the Israelites had made bricks for massive building projects. But when they entered the land of Canaan, they showed little interest in building. The spies reported "large and well fortified" cities in

Building

Canaan (Numbers 13:28). But the Israelites destroyed many of these, and the buildings that replaced them were not very impressive.

It was not until the time of David and Solomon that real skill was used, and this must be due mainly to the help and instruction of Phoenician masons and joiners sent by King Hiram of Tyre (see 1 Chronicles 14:1). Buildings put up later, after the alliance with Phoenicia had broken down, reverted to the cruder style. The more elaborate buildings of later times still, owe much to Persian, Greek and Roman influence.

The materials available for building were mud, stones and boulders, limestone and wood.

Bricks were widely used where stone was not plentiful. Mud and straw were mixed, shaped — by hand or in wooden moulds — into squares or rectangles, and then dried in the sun. Mud was also used as mortar, sticking loose stones together to make a rubble wall.

Builders' tools found in Egypt, dating back to about 2,000 BC: a wooden mallet, bronze chisels and plumb-bob.

The limestone of Palestine is soft and easily cut, but it was not much used for ordinary building work. Sites of old quarries have been found, showing the marks of picks, and unfinished blocks of stone. Hammers, saws, picks, and axes were used as tools. To detach a large block of stone, the rock was split with hammers along the natural faults and wooden wedges hammered in and then soaked. As the wood expanded, the rock cracked.

Stones were roughly finished in the quarry, but then sent to the building sites for final trimming. This accounts for the piles of stone chips excavators have found at the palace of Lachish and the later citadel in Jerusalem. But for Solomon's temple, as 1 Kings 6:7 records, the stone was prepared at the quarry, so that there was no sound of hammer, axe or iron tool in the holy place.

Forests were plentiful in Israel at that time, particularly in Galilee. For building purposes conifers were often used.

Building work meant mainly constructing houses and city walls, and digging wells, cisterns, water tunnels and grain silos. These were usually an individual or village community effort. (Compare the building of the walls of Jerusalem by united effort under Nehemiah — Nehemiah 3–6.) There was no question of skilled craftsmen doing all the work.

Houses were built on a stone foundation, but the walls were made of brick, plastered on both sides with mud. Sometimes long stones were used as reinforcements and wooden columns were put up on a stone foundation, as supports to extend the reach of the house. Rubble walls were then built between these columns, making small rooms which led off an open court. But normally the house had only one room. Wooden beams were laid across the top of the walls and the roof was made of matting, covered with a plaster of straw, mud and lime. There was usually only one storey, but the roof itself became an extra working-space. A staircase outside the house, or a ladder inside, led up to it. There was a railing round the edge of the roof to prevent accidents.

Town walls were made of rubble or boulder masonry, sometimes plastered and strengthened by towers. The boulders were only roughly shaped, but carefully fitted together. Houses were built along the inside of these walls, but beyond that there was little attempt at town planning. Houses were built wherever there was a space.

As time went on, many houses had a cistern underneath to store rain water. These were dug out of solid rock, but needed to be lined with slaked lime to stop the water leaking away. Pools for storing water were often cut out of rock and in several cities excavations have revealed tunnels cut to make water more accessible. One at Megiddo is from Israelite times.

Masons and carpenters also made things for everyday use — stone basins, water jars, loom weights, millstones; wooden yokes, ploughs, threshing-boards, carts and furniture.

Special projects Special building projects of Bible times include David's palace; Solomon's fortifications; the temple and buildings around it in Jerusalem; Ahab's palace at Samaria; Hezekiah's water tunnel in Jerusalem; the rebuilding of Jerusalem after the exile; then the many buildings of Herod the Great and his successors (the temple, Herod's palace, the fortress of Machaerus, the Herodium, Massada, and the harbour at Caesarea). Under Pontius Pilate, an aqueduct was constructed to bring water into Jerusalem.

The temple built by Solomon at Jerusalem must have been the most spectacular early project. Cedar-trees were supplied by Hiram, king of Tyre, who was one of Solomons's allies. Hiram also sent skilled craftsmen. And at this point, for the first time since the Israelites occupied the land, we find finely dressed and shaped stones — ashlar masonry. The corners are well jointed, and bonded; blocks are closely aligned without the use of mortar; and the technique of "headers" and "stretchers" is used (stones laid alternately widthwise and lengthwise for extra strength).

The walls of Solomon's temple had three courses of finished stones, surmounted by brick on a row of cedar beams. The wood helped to absorb shock in case of earthquakes. The roof and doors were timber; the floor, walls and ceiling were lined with boards of fir and cedar, decorated with carvings. (See 1 Kings 6.)

The fortifications of Solomon's cities at Hazor, Megiddo and Gezer had city walls of the casemate design (two walls with partitions across, the hollows filled with rubble, or left as store-rooms) and city gates with three guard-rooms either side. Under the paved floor of the gate there was a stone drain.

Hezekiah's tunnel was built to bring water from the Gihon spring into the city of Jerusalem. In 1880 an interesting inscription made by the workers was found. It describes two groups of quarry-men, 150ft/45m underground, about to meet in the middle after a long (1750ft/530m) and winding route from each end. They can hear one another's picks.

"On the day of the piercing through, the stone-cutters struck through each to meet his fellow, axe against axe. Then ran the water from the spring to the pool . . ."

Because of King Herod's building programme the building trade at the time of Jesus had an important position in Jerusalem. Herod is said to have prepared 1,000 wagons for transporting stones, some of which may have been quarried from the caves under the city itself. Stones 5–10 tons in weight were produced and were moved to the buildings, perhaps on rollers. Arches and vaults were constructed on the Roman pattern.

Jerusalem in Herod's day was also a typical city of the Roman Empire. Excavations of first-century Jerusalem have uncovered large houses built on a lavish scale. There is underfloor heating and piped water. A paved Roman road in a village nearby is flanked by stone holders for torches, to serve as street lights. The houses of the poor continued to be simple, but probably most had more than one storey.

CAESAR

The title of Roman emperors in New Testament times. Augustus reigned when Jesus was born. Tiberius reigned after him. Peter and Paul were probably martyred when Nero was Caesar. Jesus sometimes used the word to mean "the ruling power".
Mark 12:14–17; Luke 2:1; 3:1; Acts 25

CAESAREA

A Mediterranean port built by Herod the Great. He named the town after the Roman Emperor Augustus Caesar. Statues of the Emperor stood in a huge temple dedicated to him and to Rome. Traders on their way from Tyre to Egypt passed through Caesarea. So it was a centre of inland as well as sea-trade.

Caesarea was the home town of Philip the evangelist. It was also the home of Cornelius, the Roman centurion who sent for Peter, asking him to explain God's message. It was here that Peter learned that "the Good News of peace through Jesus Christ" was for non-Jews as well as Jews.

Paul several times used the port on his travels. The Roman governors lived at Caesarea, rather than at Jerusalem, so it was here that Paul was taken for trial before Felix after his arrest. He spent two

A section of the aqueduct built by Herod the Great to carry water to Caesarea.

further years in prison here. From Caesarea he sailed for Rome after his appeal to Caesar.
Acts 8:40; 21:8; 10; 11; 9:30; 18:22; 23:33–26:32

CAESAREA PHILIPPI

A town at the foot of Mt Hermon and close to the main source of the River Jordan. Herod the Great built a marble temple here to Augustus Caesar. And one of his sons, Philip, changed the town's name from Paneas to Caesarea. It was known as Philip's Caesarea to distinguish it from the port.

Jesus had taken his disciples to this part of the country when he asked them, "Who do you say I am?" The answer came from Peter: "You are the Messiah, the Son of the living God."
Matthew 16:13–16

CAIAPHAS

High Priest in Jerusalem AD 18–36. At the trial of

Jesus he and his father-in-law, Annas, found Jesus guilty of blasphemy and sent him to Pilate for sentence. Caiaphas was the high priest mentioned in Acts, who persecuted the first Christians.
Matthew 26:3, 57ff.; Luke 3:2; John 18:13ff.; Acts 5:17ff.

CAIN
Eldest son of Adam and Eve. He worked as a farmer. His brother Abel was a shepherd. Because God was pleased with Abel's offering of a lamb, but not with Cain's offering from his harvest, Cain was furious. In a fit of jealous anger he killed Abel, and as punishment lived the rest of his life as a nomad.
Genesis 4; 1 John 3:12

CALAH
A very ancient city of Mesopotamia on the River Tigris, later a leading city of the Assyrian Empire. Excavations at the site, now Nimrud in Iraq, have unearthed inscriptions and ivory-carvings which throw light on the times of the kings of Israel.
Genesis 10:11–12

CALEB
A spy sent by Moses to find out all he could about Canaan and the people who lived there. Of the twelve spies who reported on what they had seen, only Caleb and Joshua believed God would make it possible to conquer the land. Because of their confidence in God, Caleb and Joshua were allowed to settle in Canaan — all the other Israelites born in Egypt died in the desert.

Numbers 13–14; Joshua 14:6ff.

CALL

The God of the Bible is a God who calls people and speaks directly to them.

In the Old Testament the story of the nation of Israel begins with the call of Abraham, and shows how the Israelites were God's people, not because they had earned the right to be his children, but because God himself decided to "call" them.

It is the same in the New Testament. Jesus called people to follow him, to respond to his teaching about his new kingdom, and the early church did the same. Christians are "called" to salvation, to eternal life, to a life of endurance, to a life of peace, to go on being changed by the Holy Spirit.

In both Old and New Testaments the personal nature of God's call to his people is often emphasized. God calls men and women to specific tasks: Abraham, Moses, Samuel, David, Isaiah, Jeremiah, Ezekiel and many others. In the New Testament Paul was "called to be an apostle", and to travel abroad to preach the gospel.

See also *Election, Grace*.

Genesis 12:1; Hosea 11:1; Matthew 11:28–30; Mark 1:20; 2:14; Acts 2:39; 2 Thessalonians 2:13–14; 1 Timothy 6:12; 1 Peter 2:21; 1 Corinthians 7:15; 1 Thessalonians 4:7; Exodus 3; 1 Samuel 3; 16; Isaiah 6; Jeremiah 1:4–10; Ezekiel 1–3; Romans 1:1; Acts 9; 13:1

CAMEL

In the Old Testament, usually the one-humped Ara-

One-humped Arabian camels.

bian camel, invaluable to desert nomads. It can live on poor food and go for several days without drinking. In ordinary use it can carry a load of about 400 lbs/180 kgs, as well as its rider. Camels are mentioned in the stories of Abraham, Jacob and Job. The Israelites were not allowed to eat camel-meat.
Genesis 12:16; 30:43; Job 1:3

CANA
The village in Galilee where Jesus turned the water into wine at a wedding. During another visit to Cana, Jesus healed the son of an official from Capernaum. Nathanael, one of Jesus' twelve disciples, came from Cana.
John 2:1–12; 4:46–53

CANAAN
Son of Ham. Because of his disrespect, Noah, his grandfather, put a curse on Canaan and his descendants (the Canaanites).
Genesis 9:18–27

CANAANITE RELIGION
At Mount Sinai God had commanded Israel to have no other gods but him. The Israelites, when they

111

Baal was the Canaanite god of weather and fertility.

invaded Canaan, must therefore avoid all contact with Canaanite religion. But even before the Israelites invaded Canaan they had begun to worship Baal, the Canaanite god. When they settled in the Promised Land, Baal became a serious rival to Israel's own God. The Book of Judges describes the troubles this caused, and how men like Gideon opposed Baal-worship. Although little is said about it in the time of King David and King Solomon, later, when Ahab became king of the northern kingdom of Israel, Baal almost ousted the God of Israel. This was the work of Ahab's queen, Jezebel, who came from the Canaanite city of Sidon and brought many priests of Baal with her.
Exodus 20:3; 23:23, 24; 1 Kings 16:29 and the chapters that follow

Canaanite gods Canaanite gods and goddesses were the powers of nature personified. Baal, which means "lord", was the title of Hadad, the weather-god (his name probably has the sound of thunder). He controlled the rains, mist, and dew, and so held the key to the good harvests which were essential if the Canaanites were to survive.

Baal's wife was Astarte, also known as Anat, goddess of love and war. His father was El, the chief of the gods, but at the time of the Israelite conquest he had become a shadowy figure. El's wife was Asherah, mother goddess and goddess of the sea. Both Asherah and Astarte were often simply called "Mistress" (Baalat).

Other leading deities were Shamash, the sun; Reshef, lord of war and of the underworld; Dagon, the corn; and many lesser ones who made up the families and courts of each senior god. This general picture varied from place to place, as each town had its own patron or favourite deity, often called "Lord" or "Mistress" of such-and-such a place.

Stories of the gods   Stories of these gods and goddesses are known from Canaanite (Ugaritic) and foreign sources. They were brutal and blood-thirsty, delighting in battle with each other, and in uncontrolled sexual relationships. They interfered in human affairs simply to satisfy their whims, regardless of the suffering caused. At the same time, they could be kind and generous. They were no more than reflections of their worshippers, dressed up as gods.

Naturally these stories had their effect on the worship of the Canaanites. Religious festivities became a degraded celebration of the animal side of human nature. Even Greek and Roman writers were shocked by the things the Canaanites did in the name of religion. So it is hardly surprising that the Bible totally condemns their wickedness.

Deuteronomy 18:9; 1 Kings 14:22–24; Hosea 4:12–14

Temples and priests The important gods had richly endowed temples in the leading cities, with priests, choirs, and temple servants. On holy days the kings would go in procession to offer sacrifices. Some of these were burnt entirely; some were shared between the god and his worshippers. On occasions of great celebration the ordinary people probably joined the processions and watched the ceremonies from a distance. But the temple buildings were not large, and only the privileged could go into them.

It was a matter of pride for a king to make the temple as grand as he could, covering the statues of the gods and the walls of the shrine with precious metal, and supplying golden dishes for the god's food. As well as a statue of the god, or of an animal that was his emblem (Baal was represented by a bull, Asherah by a lion), there was also an altar for the sacrifices, an altar for incense, and perhaps a number of stone pillars inside the temple. The pillars were thought to be the homes of gods or spirits. There were also stone pillars, altars, and a wooden pole or tree trunk in simpler open-air shrines ("high places"), where the ordinary people could easily go to make a sacrifice, or to pray. The pillars sometimes stood for Baal, and the post for Asherah (see Deuteronomy 12:3).

When a sacrifice was offered, the priest often examined the entrails of the animal to forecast the fortune of the worshipper (see *Assyrian and Babylonian Religion*). Other ways of telling the future were by looking at the stars, by making contact with the dead, and by prophetic trances. The priests were also in demand to heal the sick by prayers and incantations.

Sacrifices   The sacrifices offered to the gods were normally animals and foodstuffs. The fact that Israel was commanded to avoid human sacrifice, and later information from Greek and Roman writings, shows that this was practised, but it is not clear how common it was. Probably it was a rite used in extreme circumstances, when only the greatest sacrifice was thought adequate to persuade the god to act favourably. The god Molech, who is named in connection with this sacrifice, seems to have been a god of the underworld.

The Canaanite and Hebrew languages share several words for sacrifices, priests and other religious matters. There are some other expressions that are similar, too. There was obviously a common stock of words; but the ideas indicated by them differed from place to place and from faith to faith.

Leviticus 18:21; Deuteronomy 12:31; 2 Kings 3:27

Israelite and Canaanite religion   The religion of the Canaanites was totally different from Israelite religion. No evidence for a series of rules of conduct like the Ten Commandments has been found among the Canaanites. There is no known mention of love for any god and there seems to have been little joy and happiness in Canaanite worship. On the other hand, our information is limited, and it should be noted that kings were expected to care for the poor, the widow and the orphan.

It was a strong temptation for the invading Israelites to respect the gods already in the land, and supposedly responsible for its fertility. As well as this, worship of the Canaanite gods was much less demanding than the strict Israelite laws and rituals. Many of God's people gave in to the temptation. The result was the gradual slide towards disaster recounted in the books of Kings. The God of Israel demanded total loyalty.

CANAANITES

About 1300 BC "Canaan" was an Egyptian province covering Lebanon, Syria and what later became the land of Israel. The name may have belonged at first to the coastal plain, then have been extended to include the people of the forested hills — the Amorites (see Numbers 13:29; 35:10; Joshua 5:1). Besides Canaanites and Amorites, there were other groups living in the land. Deuteronomy 7:1 lists five others. So the term "Canaanites" came to include a mixture of peoples.

Trade Those living on the coast were traders. In fact, trade was so much a part of Canaanite life that the word Canaanite came to mean "merchant" in Hebrew (it is used that way, for instance, in Proverbs 31:24). The major ports were Tyre, Sidon,

A Canaanite ruler celebrates a victory. This scene is carved on an ivory found at Megiddo, dating from between 1350 and 1150 BC.

Beirut and Byblos, in the tongue of Canaan that stretched northwards (the coast of modern Lebanon). From them cedarwood, jars of oil and wine and other goods were exported to Egypt, Crete, and Greece. In return came Egyptian luxuries and writing paper, Greek pottery, and metal ores. Beyond the boundary of Canaan, but sharing many Canaanite characteristics, was the great city of Ugarit (near modern Latakiya). This city too, was a wealthy commercial centre.

The position of Canaan as a bridge between Asia and Egypt, as well as her trading activities, laid the people open to cultural influences of all sorts. Palaces and temples might be built in Egyptian style for a resident governor or garrison in one city. Syrian styles might be followed in another. Scarabs and other Egyptian jewellery were fashionable — alongside Babylonian cylinder seals and Hittite goldwork from Turkey. These influences are seen most plainly in the way the Canaanites used both Egyptian ("hieroglyphic") and Babylonian ("cuneiform") writing.

The alphabet   Canaan's great legacy to the world is almost certainly the alphabet, invented here between 2000 and 1600 BC. Egyptian influence led to paper (papyrus) becoming the normal writing material. Because this has not survived the centuries in Canaan, examples of the infant alphabet are very rare. They are limited to more durable items — names scratched on cups, for instance.

Cities and rulers   Canaanite cities were surrounded by defensive walls of earth and stone to keep out raiders and wild animals. Inside, the houses were crowded together, as they are in the old cities of the Near East today. The ordinary people worked for themselves on small patches of land, or at various crafts, or were employed by the king, landowners, and merchants. Beyond the city lay scattered villages of farmers and herdsmen.

The rulers of the cities were constantly quarrelling and fighting with each other. And some were liable to attack by bands of brigands and outlaws who hid in the forests. The Amarna Letters, found in Egypt, describe this state of affairs in about 1360 BC. And the Bible books of Joshua and Judges show that it was much the same a century or two later. This made the conquest easier for the Israelites. A united Canaan would have been much more difficult (see the list of kings in Joshua 10 and 12).

Canaanites and Israelites The language of the Canaanites was closely related to Hebrew, perhaps even the same. The life of the Canaanite farmers was not very different from the life of the Israelites in Egypt before they became slaves. So the Israelites were able to settle easily into their Promised Land. It was tempting to fall in with other Canaanite ways, too. But the Canaanite religion was a far cry from the love of God and obedience to his clear, moral laws. So the Israelites were forbidden to mix and marry with these peoples.

CAPERNAUM

An important town on the north-west shore of Lake Galilee at the time of Jesus. It was Jesus' base while he was teaching in Galilee. Levi (Matthew) the tax-collector lived at Capernaum. So too did a Roman

army officer whose servant Jesus healed. There may have been an army post here. Many of Jesus' miracles took place at Capernaum, including the healing of Peter's mother-in-law. Jesus also taught in the local synagogue. But despite all this, the people of the town did not believe God's message, and Jesus had to warn them of coming judgement.
Mark 1:21–34; 2:1–17; Luke 7:1–10; 10:13–16, etc.

CAPPADOCIA
A Roman province in the east of Asia Minor (Turkey). There were Jews from Cappadocia among those who heard Peter in Jerusalem on the Day of Pentecost. Later the Christians in Cappadocia were among those to whom Peter sent his first letter.
Acts 2:9; 1 Peter 1:1

CARCHEMISH
An important Hittite city from early times, on the River Euphrates. The ruins now lie on the border between Turkey and Syria. When the Egyptian Pharaoh (king) Neco went to attack Carchemish, Josiah, the king of Judah, made a needless attempt to oppose him, and was defeated and killed in the plain of Megiddo. In 605 BC Neco himself was defeated at Carchemish by Nebuchadnezzar, king of Babylon.
2 Chronicles 35:20; Isaiah 10:9; Jeremiah 46:2

CARIA
A small state in south-west Turkey which emerged after the fall of the Hittite Empire. The Indo-European Carians remain virtually unknown. We

are not yet able to read their alphabet. They served as mercenary soldiers in Egypt, where their inscribed gravestones have been discovered, and in Judah.
2 Kings 11:4, 19

CARMEL
A mountain range which juts into the Mediterranean Sea close to the modern port of Haifa. The ancient city of Megiddo guarded one of the main passes through the hills some miles inland. It was on Mt Carmel (1,740ft/535m at the highest point) that Elijah, God's prophet, challenged the prophets of Baal to a contest. Elisha, who followed Elijah as prophet, also seems to have made a base there.
1 Kings 18:19–46; 2 Kings 2:25; 4:25

CATTLE
Long before Abraham came to Canaan, herds of cattle were kept to provide milk and meat, and leather from skins. The ox pulled the farmer's plough and his threshing-sledge, and was harnessed to wagons and carts. Cattle were killed in the tabernacle and temple sacrifices. A man's wealth was reckoned by the numbers of cattle and sheep he owned. Bashan, to the east of the Jordan, was famous for its cattle.
Genesis 1:24; 13:2; Leviticus 1:2

CEDAR
The beautiful, giant cedar of Lebanon, which once grew in great forests. Although the cedar is still the national symbol of Lebanon only a few of these trees remain, high in the mountains. In Solomon's day

The cedar of Lebanon.

King Hiram of Tyre exported vast quantities of cedar. The wood is a warm red colour, and long-lasting. It could be carved and decorated, and was used to panel Solomon's temple and palace.
1 Kings 6:15–7:12

CENCHREAE
The eastern port of Corinth in southern Greece, from which Paul sailed to Ephesus.
Acts 18:8; Romans 16:1

CEPHAS
See *Peter*.

CEREALS
Barley, wheat, millet and spelt were a major part of the normal diet in ancient Israel. Wheat made the best flour and bread; it was used to make the bread the priests offered to God. Barley, which ripens before wheat and is harvested in early summer, was

the food of the poorer peasants. When Egypt's barley crop was ruined by the plague of hailstorms, the wheat, which came up later, was saved. Spelt is a poor kind of wheat; and millet, which is rather like rye, makes the worst bread of all. It is mentioned in Ezekiel as food fit for a time of famine.
Exodus 9:31–32; Ezekiel 4:9

CHALDEA
South Babylonia; Abraham's family home. See *Aramaeans*.

CHEBAR
A canal running from the River Euphrates in Babylonia (S. Iraq). It was by the Chebar that the prophet Ezekiel, in exile with the Jews in Babylonia, saw some of his great visions of God.
Ezekiel 1; 3; 10; 43

CHEDORLAOMER
A king of Elam.
Genesis 14

CHERITH
A desert stream east of the Jordan. Here God provided food and water for Elijah during years of drought and famine, until the stream itself dried up.
1 Kings 17:3–7

CHILDREN
See *Family Life*.

CHINNERETH

The Old Testament name for Lake Galilee, from a place on its western shore. The name is used in descriptions of the boundaries of lands belonging to the tribes of Israel, and of nearby kingdoms. See *Galilee*.
Numbers 34:11; Deuteronomy 3:17; Joshua 11:2, etc; 1 Kings 15:20

CHORAZIN

A town where Jesus taught, near Capernaum, on a hill above Lake Galilee. Jesus was deeply troubled that these places which heard his teaching did not show any change of heart and life as a result. The site of Chorazin is now a deserted ruin.
Matthew 11:21; Luke 10:13

CHRONICLES

At first glimpse, the books of Chronicles seem to retell 2 Samuel and Kings in a duller way. The writer was in fact repeating the account for readers who knew the earlier books. He had two main reasons for writing his own history of the kings of Israel:

He wanted to show that, in spite of the disasters, God was keeping his promise to look after his people. The writer pointed to the nation's success under David and Solomon, and to the good reigns of kings Jehoshaphat, Hezekiah and Josiah.

He wanted to describe how the temple worship in Jerusalem began, to set out the duties of the priests and Levites, and to show that David was the true

123

founder of the temple (although Solomon had actually built it).

The author, the "Chronicler", was probably writing specially for the Israelites who had returned from exile to rebuild Jerusalem. They needed to understand their past. He underlined the fact that the nation's success depended on its loyalty to God.

1 Chronicles begins with a section of family trees, from Adam to King Saul (chapters 1–9). The remainder of the book is taken up with the reign of King David, and his preparations to build the temple (chapters 10–29).

2 Chronicles opens with the reign of King Solomon and the building of the temple (chapters 1–9). After recounting the revolt of the northern tribes under Jeroboam, chapters 11–36 deal with the history of the southern kings of Judah up to the destruction of Jerusalem in 587 BC.

CHURCH

The church is the community of those who believe in Jesus. In the New Testament the word always refers to people, never, as it often does today, to a building. In fact for several generations Christians had no purpose-built meeting-places.

Jesus promised Peter that he would establish the church, and it was Peter's sermon on the Day of Pentecost that led to the first 3,000 people being baptized and joining the Christian group. In the Old Testament God had chosen the Israelites to be his special people. The New Testament states that all those who believe in Jesus — whatever their race —

are now God's chosen people, his "church". They are being prepared for the day when he returns — the great "wedding-day" of Jesus and his people.

In the New Testament, the word for church refers both to a local group of Christians and to all Christians throughout the world. Paul teaches that Jesus Christ is head of the church, and that no Christian stands alone but is part of the whole: "Though we are many, we are one body in union with Christ, and we are all joined to each other as different parts of one body."

In New Testament times there was no organization of the local church comparable with what we know today. Some churches had leaders, sometimes called "elders" or "bishops" who taught and looked after the members. But many others had no "official" leaders, and special gifts, such as preaching or healing or caring for others, were exercised by different members. There must have been great variety in the gatherings of these churches, as different people took part.

Matthew 16:18; Acts 2; 13:1; 1 Corinthians 12:12–28; Romans 12:5; Colossians 1:18; Ephesians 4:11–16; 1 Corinthians 12:1–11; Acts 2:42–47; 4:23–25; 1 Corinthians 11:13–34; 1 Timothy 2–3; Titus 1:5–9; Revelation 19:5–9

CILICIA

A region in south Asia Minor (modern Turkey) which became a province of the Roman Empire in 103 BC. Tarsus, where Paul was born, was the chief town of Cilicia. Behind it, running north-east, lay

the wild Taurus mountains, cut through by an impressive pass known as the Cilician Gates.
Acts 21:39; 22:3; 23:34

CINNAMON
Oil distilled from the bark of the cinnamon tree, and used to flavour food and wine.
Song of Solomon 4:14; 8:2

Flowers of the cinnamon tree.

CIRCUMCISION
Circumcision is a minor operation to cut away the loose skin covering the end of the penis. It is widely practised by primitive peoples, and was carried out on every Israelite baby boy on the eighth day after his birth.

When God promised Abraham that he would be the founder of a great nation, the nation of Israel, he commanded that all his male descendants should be circumcised. This was to be the physical sign that they belonged to the people of God.

As time went on, the sign came to be more important than what it represented, and the prophets often had to remind the people that the outward sign on its own was not enough. It should be matched by love of other people and obedience to God.

The New Testament makes a similar point. "True circumcision", or memberhip of the people of God, is really a matter of what we believe and how we behave. Therefore non-Jews (Gentiles) who become Christians do not need to be physically circumcised. Christians are sometimes called the true circumcision, for they have come into a right relationship with God and are now the heirs to the promises of God alongside the believing people of Old Testament times.

Genesis 17; Luke 2:21; Jeremiah 9:25–26; Romans 2:25–29; Galatians 5:2–6; Philippians 3:2–3; Colossians 2:11–15

CITIES
See *Towns*.

CLAUDIUS
The fourth Roman emperor. Claudius reigned AD 41–54. During this time the famine predicted by the Christian prophet Agabus took place. Towards the end of his reign Claudius forced all Jews to leave Rome.

Acts 11:28; 18:2

The Emperor Claudius.

CLAUDIUS LYSIAS

A commander of the Roman garrison at Jerusalem who rescued Paul when an angry crowd of Jews was about to kill him. Claudius Lysias arrested Paul and allowed the Jewish council (the Sanhedrin) to question him, but the session ended in chaos. When he heard about a plot to murder Paul, Claudius Lysias sent him to Caesarea for trial by Felix, the Roman governor.
Acts 21:31–23:30

CLEOPAS

On the day Jesus rose from the dead Cleopas and a friend were walking from Jerusalem to Emmaus. They had thought Jesus was the Messiah and were puzzled about his death and the report that he was alive again. A man joined them. As he explained the Old Testament passages about the Messiah it was as if "a fire burned within them". At Emmaus, Cleopas and his friend invited the stranger to join them for a meal. As he asked God's blessing on the food and broke bread they realized it was Jesus. They went to Jerusalem at once to share the news with the other disciples.
Luke 24:13–53

CLOTHES-MAKING

The main materials used for making clothes were linen (from flax), sheep's wool, goats' hair and animal skins. Cotton was not used in Israel until they began to import it, probably after the exile. The Israelites loved to decorate their clothes with brightly coloured fringes, borders, and tassels. Gold

thread was used to embroider very special clothes —
for example, for the high priest (Exodus 39:3).

Linen In Israel flax grew only on the southern
coastal plain, near Jericho, and in Galilee, though in
New Testament times the amount grown in Galilee
was greatly increased. The Egyptians grew a great
deal of flax and, by soaking the flax in running
water, were able to produce a very soft kind of linen.
The Bible calls this "fine linen". It was a "fine linen
robe" that Pharaoh gave to Joseph when he
appointed him governor (Genesis 41:42). Linen was
used for making clothes and ships' sails. Rahab, in
Jericho (Joshua 2:6), hid the spies beneath flax
spread out on her roof.

After the flax was cut and dried, the seeds were
removed. It was then soaked and dried again in an
oven. The fibres were separated and then it was
ready for spinning and weaving. Linen was not
usually dyed, though occasionally blue threads were
woven in. (The blue linen robe which the high priest
wore was very special — Exodus 28:31.) So, when
the Bible talks about coloured clothes, it usually
means woollen ones.

Wool After being dipped, the sheep were shorn in
the spring. The new wool was washed, or sent to the
fuller to be cleaned of natural oils. He would do this
by treading out the wool on a rock in water. The
wool was then spread out to be dried and bleached in
the sun. We read of the "fuller's field" in 2 Kings
18:17, beside a water supply and — as it often was —
outside the city because of the smell. The fuller also
worked on the newly woven cloth to shrink it, and
sometimes he was responsible for dyeing the wool.

Dyeing In Genesis 30:32 Laban's flock included black and white, striped and spotted sheep! This is a reminder that wool can have many natural colours. So the basic dyes will produce a variety of shades. The colours the Bible refers to most often are blue, scarlet, and purple. These may have been the basic dyes. Purple clothes were a sign of royalty and wealth. A poor quality purple may have been produced by dyeing, first with blue, then with red. The best purple came from Tyre and was very expensive. It was made from molluscs (sea snails) found on the east Mediterranean coast. The industry was firmly in the hands of the Phoenicians, and the Israelites probably had to import all their purple cloths.

Certain places in Israel — where there was a good water supply and good grazing for sheep — became centres for dyeing. Among these were Gezer, Beth-shemesh, Bethzur and Debir. At Debir excavations have shown that about thirty homes had rooms specially designed for dyeing. Each contained two stone vats with small openings on top. Potash and slaked lime were probably put into the vat and dye added later, with more dye in the second vat. The wool was given two baths. The potash and lime fixed the dye, and the wool was laid out to dry. It was then ready for spinning and weaving. Almost every home at Debir also had a loom.

Spinning and weaving After being combed, the wool was spun into yarn. Spinning was usually the women's work. It was probably done on a simple hand spindle, although only the stone, clay and bone whorls of these have been found. Two main types of

A woman using her right hand to twist combed wool into yarn which is then wound onto the shaft of her spindle.

loom were used in Israel: a vertical loom and a horizontal loom.

The weaver stood in front of the vertical loom, with the down-ward threads (warps) attached to a beam across the top (Goliath's spear is said to have been as thick as a weaver's beam — 1 Samuel 17:7) and held down with weights. As the weaver worked, the cross-wise threads were beaten upwards. Five or six warps could be worked on at a time, which made it possible to produce patterns. Because the weaver could move about, he was able to make wide pieces of material. Later a rotating beam was made for the bottom of the loom. The web was begun at the bottom and the finished cloth rolled up. This made it possible to make quite long lengths of cloth.

The horizontal loom was made of two beams, held in place by four pegs in the ground, and the weaver sat in front. The loom could be no wider than the reach of the weaver's arms, although the Egyptians seem to have had a system of two people working this loom. Both wool and linen were woven on this type of loom, and sometimes also the coarser goats' or camels' hair for thick shepherds' cloaks and for tents.

When the Bible talks about embroidered cloth (see Judges 5:30; Ezekiel 26:16) it may refer to different cloths sewn together, or woven patterns, although the Israelites did have embroidery and tapestry.

Shaping clothes There were two main ways of shaping a garment. If the loom was wide enough, the whole garment could be made in one piece (Jesus had a seamless robe — John 19:23). The weaver started at the sleeve edge and worked across to the other sleeve edge, leaving a hole for the neck.

Sleeves could be as long or short as the person wanted, and the striped pattern was easy to make. When cut off, the free warps were twisted into cords which strengthened the sides. Sometimes they were left as tassels at the bottom corners.

If the loom was narrow, the garment was made in three pieces; the main bodice and sleeves; the front skirt; and the back skirt. The neck opening was given a woven binding to strengthen it.

Sometimes circular garments were made. The weaver began in the middle and the web was broadened a warp or two at a time.

See also *Dress*.

COLOSSAE
A town in the Lycus Valley, in the Roman province

of Asia (now south-west Turkey). It stood just a few miles from Laodicea, on the main road east from Ephesus. The Christian message probably reached Colossae when Paul was staying at Ephesus, though he himself never went there. Paul wrote a letter (Colossians) to the church there.
Colossians 1:2

COLOSSIANS

Paul wrote his letter to the Christians at Colossae from prison — probably in Rome about AD 61. Although he had not begun the church in Colossae (in western Turkey) Paul had a great interest in it. Its founder was one of his own converts, Epaphras, and in Rome he had met a runaway slave from the city (see *Philemon*). He heard that false teachers were at work there. They claimed that to know God, people had to worship other spiritual powers — and observe rites and regulations. They were introducing ideas from other philosophies and religions.

Paul clearly sets out the true Christian message (1:1–2:19). Only Jesus — and Jesus alone — can save a person and give new life. Through Jesus Christ, God created the world.

Paul then goes on to show what this new life means in practical terms (2:20–4:6). It affects everything we do and say; feelings and relationships — in the home, at work, and in the church.

He closes with personal news (4:7–18).

COMMANDMENTS
See *Law*.

COMMUNION
See *Lord's Supper*.

COOKING
Food was normally cooked by boiling, in a pot over a fire. Some foods were poached in oil. And bread, of course, was baked. There were several methods of baking bread. The simplest was to scoop out a hole in the ground, make a fire in it, then remove the ash and stick the flat "pancakes" of dough on the sides of the hole. Sometimes stones were put into the fire, and when the dough was ready for baking, the hot stones were taken out and the dough placed on them to cook. Or a large shallow earthenware bowl was placed upside down over the fire, and the dough placed on that.

Wealthier homes had a pottery oven. This consisted of a beehive-shaped funnel. The fire was lit in the bottom of the funnel, and the bread was stuck on the inside towards the top. Not until Roman times was a divided oven invented, with the fire separate from the cooking area. None of these methods of baking was very hygienic.

Many vegetables (such as the cucumber), were eaten raw. Lentils and beans were boiled in water or oil. Corn porridge was made with water, salt and butter.

CORINTH
An old Greek city destroyed by the Romans in 146 BC and rebuilt by them a hundred years later. Corinth stood on the narrow neck of land connecting mainland Greece with the southern peninsula,

between the Aegean and Adriatic seas. It was a good position for trade.

The town attracted people of many nationalities. It was dominated by the "Acro-corinth", the steep rock on which the acropolis and a temple to Aphrodite (goddess of love) was built. Temple prostitutes and a large "floating" population helped to give Corinth a very bad name for all kinds of immoral behaviour.

Paul stayed in Corinth for eighteen months, on his second missionary journey. During that time he founded a church to which he later wrote at least two letters now in the New Testament (1 and 2 Corinthians).

Acts 18

CORINTHIANS

1 Corinthians This is a letter from Paul to the Christians at Corinth. Corinth was a Greek city teeming with people of many different nationalities. It was well known for its trade, culture, its many religions — and its low moral standards.

The church there had been started by Paul during his eighteen-month stay in the city on his second missionary tour. Now he had received bad reports about the church. When some of the members came from Corinth to ask for advice he wrote this important letter. He tried to deal with the main problems in the church: division (chapters 1–4), and problems of morals and family life (chapters 5–7). There were even reports of a case of incest and Christians taking one another to court.

Paul tackled the problem of conscience which

Christians were facing over food (chapters 8–10). Most of the meat sold in the shops had been offered to idols. Was it wrong to eat it?

Chapters 11–14 lay down principles for orderly worship in the church, especially at the Lord's Supper, and discuss the special gifts God gives to his people. The letter gives a clear — not always impressive — picture of the way in which early Christians met and behaved.

Paul also explains the meaning of the resurrection of Jesus, and of all who die trusting him (chapter 15).

In the last chapter he tells the Corinthian church about a collection he is making for needy Christians in Judea. He ends with personal greetings.

Chapter 13, in praise of love — God's best gift to his people — is one of the most famous passages Paul wrote.

2 Corinthians Paul wrote his second letter to Corinth a year or so after the first (about AD 56) when relations between him and the church there were at crisis point. During that year, some of the Corinthian Christians had strongly attacked him. And he had apparently paid a quick visit to Corinth. The letter shows how much he longed to be at one with the church in Corinth.

In chapters 1–7 Paul begins with his relations with the church at Corinth. He explains his previous severe words, and how grateful he was for their change of heart. He looks forward to a third, happier visit.

Paul appeals for a generous response to the needs of the Judean Christians (chapters 8–9).

The last chapters (10–13) are taken up with his defence of his claim to be an apostle. Several Christians at Corinth had questioned his right to the title.

2 Corinthians, with its range of moods, sometimes stormy, sometimes joyful, is one of the most personal of Paul's letters. His loving concern for the church, his suffering and his unshakable faith shine through it all.

CORNELIUS

A Roman army captain (centurion) stationed at Caesarea. He worshipped God and gave generously to poor people. In a dream, an angel told Cornelius to send for Peter, who was at Joppa (see *Peter*). At Cornelius' house Peter found a crowd of the soldier's friends and relatives eagerly waiting to hear him. They believed and were baptized: the first group of non-Jewish converts to Christianity.
Acts 10

COVENANT

The basic meaning of "covenant" in the Bible is summed up in the words of Jeremiah 31:33: "I will be their God, and they will be my people." God enters into a special relationship with men and women. He commits himself to protect his people, and in return he expects obedience from them. Most covenants mentioned in the Bible are between God and man, but there are also "man-to-man" covenants in the Old Testament.

The Bible itself is arranged into two major "covenants", the Old and the New. They are more often called the Old and New "Testaments" (which means the same thing). The old covenant is the one made with Moses on Mt Sinai, when the Ten Commandments were given to God's people as the basic rules for living. This covenant forms the basis of Israel's religion. Some archaeological discoveries suggest that the way the covenant is set out may be based on the pattern of treaties made between certain Near Eastern nations at that time.

There are also other covenants in the Old Testament. There is the one made with Noah after the flood, when God promised never again to destroy the earth with a flood. This is God's general covenant with all people.

Then there is the covenant with Abraham, in which God promised his descendants a land of their own, and urged them to share their blessings with the other nations of the earth. This is God's covenant with his special people, renewed in the covenant with Moses on Mt Sinai.

The New Testament writers show that the new covenant between God and men, to which the Old Testament looks forward, rests on the death of Jesus. Jesus himself spoke of this at the last supper: "This cup is God's new covenant, sealed with my blood." The letter to the Hebrews compares the old and new covenants. The new covenant offers something the old covenant could never secure — release from the power of sin; the freedom to obey God.

See also *Election*.

Exodus 19:3–6; 20:1–17; Genesis 9:1–17; 12:1–3; 15:7–21; Jeremiah 31:31–34; 1 Corinthians 11:25; Hebrews 8:13; 10:4

CRAFTS AND TRADES

In Old Testament times Israel had few if any crafts-men who made beautiful things for their own sake. Even when it came to making places of worship, they often had to bring in foreign artists to complete the decoration. It was a poor country and skills were limited to making strictly useful objects. However, certain trades were regarded as skilled from an early period. These were the crafts of certain families, who probably handed down "trade secrets" from father to son.

Special areas became linked with a particular trade, perhaps because necessary materials were ready to hand. So Succoth became known for the casting of metal utensils; Debir for weaving and dyeing. It is likely that some form of trade guilds came into being fairly early, especially in the cities, where the different crafts seem to have had their special quarters. The Bible mentions the carpenters' quarters, the linen workers', the potters', the gold-smiths' and the perfumers' sections.

In New Testament times trade guilds were well known in the Roman Empire. But they had to have a licence from the emperor to make sure they were not simply a cover for undesirable political activities.

Crafts were held in high regard by the Jews at this time. Craftsmen were exempt from the rule that everyone should rise to his feet when a scholar approached. Most of the scribes probably had a trade. The writings of the rabbis mention a nail-maker, a baker, a sandalmaker, a master builder, a tailor. But some trades were despised: among others, tanning, because "it was dirty"; being a tax collector (publican), because it gave scope for trickery; weaving, because it was women's work. The weavers worked in one of the poorest areas of Jerusalem, close to the Dung Gate.

Leatherwork Bible references to articles made with leather (from sheep- and goatskins) include clothes, belts and footwear. The complete hides of small animals were sewn together to make bottles for wine, water and milk. Tents were originally made of leather covering, but later felt or woven goats' hair was used, as it is today by the Bedouin. Leather was also used as a writing-material. The Isaiah manuscript of the Dead Sea Scrolls, dating from 150 BC, was written on seventeen sheets of leather, the skins sewn together. The details of how leather was processed and worked are not known, but two or three different trades may have been involved.

There was the job of skinning the animals. Knives have been found which may have been used for this.

Then there was the job of tanning. In early times this may simply have been a process of drying the hides in the sun, or perhaps treating them with the juice of certain plants. But tanners were expected to live outside a town because their work was smelly.

Finally there was the work of shaping and sewing the leather. Paul, Aquila and Priscilla are said to have been "tentmakers", but some think that this word may mean "leatherworkers".
Genesis 3:21; 2 Kings 1:8; Ezekiel 16:10; Exodus 26:14; Acts 18:3

Gem-cutting The Israelites used semi-precious stones such as agate, jasper, carnelian and rock-crystal. These were cut and polished to make beads, or engraved with designs, and sometimes the owners' names, to serve as seals. The Bible mentions many different stones, although not all can be identified. Engraving stones and setting them in gold for the high priest's breastplate are described in Exodus 28:9–14.

Glass-making The art of making articles of glass never seems to have been common in Israel. Long before the Israelites entered Canaan the Egyptians and Babylonians had discovered how to make an opaque form of glass and to shape it over a core of sand. By New Testament times the Romans were making transparent glass and "blowing" it into shape. Many of the glass articles which have been found in Israel were clearly imported.

Ivory-carving No list of the crafts in Israel would be complete without a mention of ivory carving, although probably not many craftsmen were involved in it, and those who were may have been mostly foreigners. Ivory was rare. It had to be imported from Africa (or from Syria in the early times). It was a favourite with the kings, but the prophets condemned its use as a symbol of extravagance and idle living.

Solomon probably used ivory carvings and inlay in the temple decorations, but the only detail mentioned in the Old Testament is that he had an ivory throne. King Ahab of Israel built an "ivory house" in Samaria, his capital. It is at Samaria that the largest Israelite collection of ivory has been found. Excavations have shown that the art flourished among all the Near Eastern nations. Objects found

A carved ivory of a man saluting with one hand and holding a lotus tree with the other; from Nimrud, eighth century BC.

consist mostly of small carvings, inlays and sculptures.
1 Kings 10:22; Ezekiel 27:15; Amos 3:15; 1 Kings 22:39
See also *Building, Clothes-making, Mining, Pottery.*

CRANE
A regular migrant and winter visitor to Israel. A large grey bird with a wing-span of 8ft/2.5 metres, the crane feeds mostly on seeds and leaves.

Crane.

CREATION

The Bible teaches that everything was made by God. He was the Creator in the very beginning, and his work continues as he maintains, and occasionally intervenes, in his creation. The Bible has nothing to say about which scientific theory of creation is most likely to be true. This is not surprising, since it was never intended to be a book of science. Its purpose is to tell us about God, and his dealings with men and women and the world they live in.

In Genesis 1 we learn that God created the world perfect. He created plants and animals, able to reproduce themselves. And he placed man and woman at the centre of creation to take care of it. According to Genesis 2 the world as God created it was a delightful place in which to live, especially since the man and his wife enjoyed a free and open relationship with God.

The first perfection of creation is now gone, because people chose to disobey God. But the Bible continues to speak of God as Creator. Again and again it reminds us of his greatness, and the smallness of man in comparison. Yet he cares for people and provides for all his creation. So:

"Fear the Lord, all the earth!
Honour him, all peoples of the world!
When he spoke, the world was created;
At his command everything appeared."

Paul also speaks of a "new creation". By Jesus' death and resurrection God made it possible for people to be forgiven and to share in the new life of the new creation. Christians already know something of this new creation and one day they will be

fully part of it, when the universe spoilt by sin exists no more and all things are made new.
Genesis 1–3; Job 38–42:6; Psalms 8; 33:6–22; 104; Isaiah 40:21–26; Matthew 6:25–33; Acts 14:15–18; Romans 1:18–23; 8:18–23; Colossians 1:15–20; Hebrews 1:1–3; Revelation 21–22

CREEDS AND HYMNS

The New Testament church was a community which believed certain basic truths — "the apostles' teaching", or "the true teaching", or "true words". These beliefs were expressed not only in the New Testament writings, but also in worship, often sung as hymns.

Some of the early Christian creeds were very simple and short. "Jesus is Lord" was the basic one. These were probably words each new convert spoke. Some creeds contain two or three statements of faith. "There is one God, and there is one mediator between God and men, the man Christ Jesus"; "one Lord, one faith, one baptism".

At times, New Testament writers clearly quote early Christian statements of faith. 1 Timothy 3:16 is a creed in the form of a hymn (like the *Te Deum* in later Christian worship):
"He appeared in human form,
was shown to be right by the Spirit
and was seen by angels.
He was preached among the nations,
was believed in throughout the world,
and was taken up to heaven.
An even more detailed confession of the person and work of Christ was used by Paul in Philippians

2:6–11. The hymn ends with the confession of the new convert: "all will openly proclaim that Jesus Christ is Lord". It may have been sung at a baptism service.
Acts 2:42; 1 Timothy 4:6; 2 Timothy 1:13;
1 Corinthians 12:3; 1 Timothy 2:5; Ephesians 4:5

CRETE

Crete is known in the Old Testament and other ancient texts as Caphtor. The Minoan civilization flourished there from 2000 BC, merging with the Mycenaean. It fell in the twelfth century BC. The Cretan scripts Linear A and Linear B represent a local form of writing. Linear B was adopted for an early form of Greek. Caphtor was one of the places from which the Philistines came. Later inhabitants probably supplied David's bodyguard of Cherethites. One Cretan poet — Epimenides — had some strong words to say about the Cretans. But some responded to the Christian message.
Jeremiah 47:4; Acts 18:28; Titus 1:12

CRISPUS

Chief official of the Jewish synagogue in Corinth. He and his family were converted and baptized by Paul.
Acts 18:8; 1 Corinthians 1:14

CROSS

The cross has come to be the universal symbol of the Christian faith, because it reminds us of the most astonishing and important event in the story of Jesus of Nazareth.

It was astonishing because Jesus the Messiah

145

(God's chosen one) was executed like a common criminal. The Jews found it impossible to accept that such a person could really be the Son of God — and many ordinary people just could not understand how the world could be saved by a person who had met such a bizarre end.

Yet to the early Christians the cross had a deep meaning. It was at the heart of all that God had planned for his people. Paul was quite sure that the cross was all-important — so much so that he wrote to the Corinthian Christians: "While I was with you, I made up my mind to forget everything except Jesus Christ and especially his death on the cross."

The New Testament makes it clear that Jesus died on the cross, not because of his own wrong-doing (the charges against him were false), but in the place of ordinary sinful men and women. He experienced the separation from God which they deserved, and so made possible forgiveness and new life for all who will trust their lives to Jesus as the one who died for our sins and rose again from death.

In Jesus' death on the cross we see the depths of God's love. As a result of this, men and women can be reconciled both to God and to each other. In the cross God defeated all the powers of evil.

The cross is also a dramatic symbol of the sort of life Christians ought to live. Jesus called people to "take up their cross" and follow him. He called them to a life of self-sacrifice. They must give up their own claims over their lives, and live in the power of the new life which God gives them. And Paul understood what this meant in his own experience: "I have been put to death with Christ on his cross, so that it is no longer I who live, but it is Christ who lives in me."

See also *Atonement, Reconciliation, Redemption*.
1 Corinthians 1:18–2:5; Romans 5:6–11; Ephesians 2:16–18; Colossians 2:14–15; Galatians 2:20; 1 John 4:7–10

CUMMIN AND DILL
Cummin seeds were used to spice meat, also in eye medicine. Dill (or anise) seed flavours bread or cakes. The Pharisees gave God a tenth of everything, even their seasoning herbs — mint, cummin and dill — but Jesus said they neglected more important things: honesty, justice and mercy.
Isaiah 28:25–27; Matthew 23:23

The herbs cummin and dill.

CUSH (SUDAN)
To the south of Egypt lies the Sudan (Old Testament "Cush", sometimes translated as "Ethiopia"). Pharaoh Tirhakah came from Cush. But usually Egypt dominated, and Cushite soldiers served in her armies. Ebedmelech, who rescued Jeremiah, was a

Sudanese. An independent kingdom existed there in Hellenistic and Roman times, with its capital at Meröe. Queens, entitled Candace, often ruled this state and it was the chancellor of one of these whom Philip met going home from Jerusalem.

2 Kings 19:9; Jeremiah 38:7; Acts 8:27

CYPRUS

The Cypriotes had close links with Syria and Israel/ Judah through trade ("purple from the island of Cyprus", Ezekiel 27:7). In early times the island was known as Elisha or Alashiya, and was a major source of copper. Flourishing cities with colonies of Myceneans from Greece were destroyed by the Sea Peoples (see *Philistines*) about 1200 BC. One city that revived afterwards was Kition, modern Larnaca (Old Testament "Kittim"), whose name was sometimes used for the whole island, and even for the opposite coasts. As a distant place, the name was used to stand for Rome in Daniel 11:30.

Cyprus came under the rule of Rome in 58 BC, and was governed by a proconsul from 27 BC. It was a natural stopping-place for ships passing from the eastern Mediterranean coast to Turkey or Rome.

In the New Testament Cyprus features as the home of Barnabas. It was the first place Paul and Barnabas visited when they set out to take the good news of Jesus to the non-Jewish world. Here they met the governor, Sergius Paulus, and his magician friend. Barnabas later returned to Cyprus with Mark.

Acts 4:36; 13:4–12; 15:39; 27:4

CYRENE

A Greek city on the north coast of Africa, in modern Libya. A man from Cyrene, Simon, was forced to carry Jesus' cross. Jews from Cyrene were among those present in Jerusalem on the Day of Pentecost. Other Cyrenians became involved in the earliest mission to non-Jews, at Antioch.
Matthew 27:32; Mark 15:21; Acts 2:10; 6:9; 11:20; 13:1

CYRUS

The Persian king who captured Babylon in 539 BC. Cyrus allowed the Jews exiled in Babylon to return to Jerusalem to rebuild the temple. He sent back with them all the treasures taken from the temple by Nebuchadnezzar and gave them a large sum of money to help with the work. Isaiah declared that Cyrus was chosen by God to be king and to free the Jewish captives. The later stories about Daniel took place in the reign of Cyrus.
Ezra 1:1ff.–6:14; Isaiah 44:28ff.; Daniel 6:28

DAILY LIFE

In Bible lands there have always been "nomads" — people who move from place to place — as well as those with settled homes.

Abraham exchanged a settled, civilized city life at Ur in Mesopotamia for a semi-nomadic lifestyle when God called him to leave his home. Like the modern Bedouin, he lived in a goats'-hair tent. The black and brown striped material was woven from goats' hair after shearing time, on a loom pegged out on the ground. Wooden rings were stitched along the edge and in the centre to take nine poles in three rows. The middle row of poles was about 6ft/1.8m high, and the two outer rows a little less.

The tent house was made by propping up a long length of goats'-hair cloth about 6ft/1.8m wide, and living in the area underneath it. The women did the hard work, putting up the tent and securing the poles with guy ropes. The area under the curtain was closed in at the back with a screen made of goats'-hair cloth, or reeds and twigs woven together, and the area was then divided into two "rooms". One formed an open porch where visitors could be received, and the remainder was curtained off for the use of the women and for the household stores. The only adult male who could enter this part was the head of the family. Sometimes the ground under the tent was covered with woven matting but more often it was left as bare earth. Tents were pitched in groups for protection. Women very rarely had a tent of their own, unless the family was very rich.

For hundreds of years Abraham's descendants lived in tents: first in Canaan, then in Egypt, then in the desert. When they conquered the Canaanites, they took over the Canaanite cities, patched up the ruins and copied their building style.

House-building The poorer people in Old Testament times lived in very small houses. There was one square room with an outside yard. Houses were built by groups of neighbours, and by skilled builders who went from place to place.

If the house was built on the plain or in a valley, the walls were made of mud brick. Rooms could be added alongside or as another storey as people grew better of, and building skills increased. Mud bricks were quite large — about 21in x 10in x 4in/53cm x 25cm x 10cm — and were made in wooden moulds.

The fathers and grandfathers of the Israelites who settled in Canaan had had plenty of practice at making mud-bricks when they were slaves in Egypt. They began by digging a hole in the ground and filling it with water, chopped straw, palm fibre and bits of shell and charcoal. The workmen then trampled the mixture until they had a soft and pliable mud. Most bricks were laid out to dry in the hot sun. Kilns produced stronger bricks which were used for the foundations. Mud was also used to cement the bricks together and to plaster the finished walls. It is not surprising that in wet weather the houses tended to leak. They were not very strongly built and it was

The type of house owned by wealthy Jews in New Testament times.

easy for a thief to break in just by digging a hole through the wall.

In the mountains, where limestone and basalt were ready at hand, and on the coast where sandstone was found, roughly squared stone was used for the foundations, with rough stone or brick walls nearly 3ft/91cm thick built on top. These thick walls could be hollowed out and alcoves made for storage. In early days the walls were little more than rubble, but as iron tools became available for shaping stone more easily, the stones were roughly squared.

Windows were few and tiny, set high up in the wall for coolness in summer, warmth in winter. There was no glass. Instead, a lattice shutter was put across the hole to keep intruders out. Thick woollen curtains were used in the cold, wet season, to keep the weather out. Doors at first were made of woven twigs. Then, as skills developed, of wood and metal.

The roof was made by laying beams across the width of the walls, and smaller beams at right angles across them. The kind of wood depended on how rich you were: sycamore for ordinary homes, cypress and cedar for those who could afford it. Layers of brushwood, earth and clay were then added and the whole thing made firm by using a stone roller 2ft/ 60cm long, which was kept on the roof.

After the rain the roof often sprouted grass and the smaller animals might be sent up to graze! Gutters took the precious, but not very clean, water to a storage cistern, waterproofed with a mortar made from ashes, lime, sand and water. To have your own stored water was something of a status symbol in Old Testament times. But it cannot have led to very good health.

The roof was a very important part of the house. Poor people probably climbed up by ladder. The better off had a flight of steps built into the walls, leading from the yard to the roof-space. The roof was used for drying fruit and grain (Rahab hid the spies under the flax which was drying on her roof — Joshua 2:6), and was a cool place on a hot evening. Sometimes the family made a tent of branches and slept out on the roof.

As building skills improved, permanent upper storeys became more common. The rich woman at Shunem built on a special guest-room for the prophet Elisha (2 Kings 4:10). Sometimes trellis was put on the roof and vines trained over it. If the house was built into a steep hillside, the roof was sometimes used as a threshing-floor. Householders would shout their news from roof to roof ("from the house-tops") above the noise from the streets below. The roof-space was so much part of the life of the house that the law insisted it must have a railing round the edge for safety (Deuteronomy 22:8). Tiled and pitched roofs began to be built shortly before New Testament times.

Inside the house the floor area was divided into two, like the nomad's tent. The animals were brought into the lower area of the house near the door during winter. This floor area was of beaten earth. The family lived on a raised platform, farthest away from the door. The space underneath may have been for storing tools and jars — and even keeping small animals. Cooking things, clothes and bedding were kept on the platform.

Sometimes stone chippings were worked into the earth floor. But it was only under Greek influence, after about 300 BC, that the art of making mosaic floors was developed. Even then this was frowned on for religious reasons, and the only mosaic floors found in Israel during Bible times were in the palace of King Herod the Great at Masada and rich houses in Jerusalem.

Life in the home What was life like for families living in the ordinary small house? During the hot summer, the house was alive with insects. When the weather grew cold, the house was filled with smoke from the fire. There was no real fireplace. The fire smouldered in a hole in the earth floor. If the family was wealthy enough, they warmed themselves around a brazier. But there was no chimney.

When it rained hard and continuousiy the roof and the walls leaked. The writer of the Old Testament proverb knew just how miserable that was. "A nagging wife," he wrote, "is like water going drip-drip-drip on a rainy day" (Proverbs 27:15). There were no facilities for bathing, and the house of the ordinary person was so dark that a lamp had always to be kept lit. It was placed on a stand, or in a niche in the wall, in the area farthest from the door.

From the time of Solomon, however, a wealthy class began to emerge, and for them life was very different. Rooms were extended around courtyards and gardens which provided shade and cool currents of air in the summer. In winter it was possible to use rooms in a warmer, sunnier position. The whole house was built on a much larger scale, with pillars to support roof beams. Once pillars were used it was possible to have porches and colonnades. The prophet Amos talks about the "winter houses and summer houses" enjoyed by the rich (Amos 3:15).

In the time between the Old and New Testaments wealthy people even began to add special bathrooms, with tubs set into the floor. (Sergius Orata is said to have invented a centrally heated bathroom, with a hot water supply, in about 70 BC!) By New Testament times rich people in Palestine had houses built Roman-style, with two rectangular courtyards, one behind the other, each surrounded by rooms.

Furniture People in the east, even today, have much less furniture than many in western countries. The style, even for the rich, is cool, simple and uncluttered — with just a few mats for the floor, seating, small tables and some kind of heating for winter.

Throughout Bible times the poor possessed very little by way of furniture and furnishings. The "bed" was a thin wool-filled mattress, spread out each evening on the raised part of the floor. The whole family slept there, under goats'-hair quilts. In the morning they rolled or piled up the bed and bedding and stacked it away. The furniture which the woman at Shunem provided for Elisha was better than average: a bed, a table, a chair and a lamp (2 Kings 4:10). The table was often simply a straw mat laid out on the raised floor. In some homes, but by no means all, there were stools to sit on.

Every house had stone or clay storage bins in which they kept fodder for the animals as well as food stores for the family. There were special jars for storing flour and olive oil, earthenware pots for carrying and storing water. There were cooking pots, too, and bowls for serving food.

Cooking things   One of the most important things in the home was the grinding mill. This was made from two circular stones. The larger, lower stone had a spike which pierced the centre of a smaller one, which was turned round on top of it. Corn was poured through the central hole and as two women turned the top stone with a handle, flour ran out at the edge between the two stones. It was hard work! A fire for cooking was made simply in the earth floor, or sometimes in an earthenware pot. Charcoal, thorns or dried animal dung provided the fuel. A convex baking-sheet, which could be put over the fire, and a cooking-pot which could stand in the fire, made up the remainder of the basic cooking things.

Lamps   Because the houses were so dark, one of the most important items in any household was the lamp. Throughout the Old Testament period lamps were simply pottery dishes with a lip at one side. Oil was poured into the dish and a wick laid from it to the lip. Such a lamp might stay alight for two or three hours, then need refilling. By New Testament times potters had learnt how to make lamps in moulds, completely covered over, with a small hole for the oil and a spout for the wick. This was safer and more efficient. The wicks were usually strips of flax or rag. Olive oil or animal fat was commonly used, oil from other seeds and vegetables being introduced by New Testament times. Lamps were small enough for a traveller to carry in his hand. This may have been the picture in the psalmist's mind when he wrote, "Your word is a lamp to guide me and a light for my path" (Psalm 119:105).

Household goods   Brooms for cleaning were made of corn stalks. They were kept with the tools the father needed for his trade. Most of the jars and bowls in everyday use were made by the potter. But in wealthier homes they had things made from metal. By New Testament times glass, moulded on a core, and produced in Egypt, was used. In about 50 BC, the art of glass blowing was developed in Syria. But although this made glass cheaper, it was still beyond the reach of most people. There were no "ornaments" as such in the ordinary home. People used their artistic skills in making and decorating the things they used every day.

The rich   The rich had a good many extra comforts: high beds, tables, chairs and couches. These were often made of fine wood, carved and inlaid with bone or ivory. There were pillows for their beds, and fine wool blankets. Extra clothes and bedding were stored in chests. In New Testament times wealthy people ate their meals Roman-style, reclining on a three-sided couch (*triclinium*) around a square table.

The greatest luxury of all was to be found in the royal palaces, from King Solomon — who built in well-cut stone and lined his walls with cedar — and King Ahab (with a palace at Samaria which boasted beautiful carved ivory inlays and expensive furniture), to Herod the Great. Herod had a summer palace with lovely gardens at Jerusalem, and a winter one at Jericho.

See also *Building*.

DALMATIA

A Roman province on the east coast of the Adriatic Sea, along the coast of modern Yugoslavia. Paul's second letter to Timothy shows him almost alone at the end of his life. His friends have left him for various reasons. Titus has gone to Dalmatia.
2 Timothy 4:10

DAMASCUS

The capital of Syria (see *Aramaeans*). Damascus was already well known in Abraham's day, and is often mentioned in the Old Testament. King David captured the city, but it soon regained its independence. Damascus was the home of Naaman, who came to the prophet Elisha for healing. The prophet later went to Damascus to advise on the king's health.

Isaiah predicted the destruction of Damascus. And after a series of attacks the Assyrians captured the city in 732 BC, carried away its treasures and many of its people, and reduced its power. From 64 BC to AD 33 Damascus was a Roman city.

Paul was on his way to Damascus to persecute the Christians when he met with Jesus himself, and the whole direction of his life was changed. He had to

escape from the city later, when the Jews persecuted him.
Genesis 14:15; 15:2; 2 Samuel 8:5; 1 Kings 20:34; 2 Kings 5; 8:7–15; Isaiah 17; Acts 9

DAN

The land belonging to the tribe of Dan, and a town (Laish) in the far north of Israel. Dan was the northernmost city of Israel, and the expression "from Dan to Beersheba" meant "from one end of the land to the other". When the kingdom was divided, Jeroboam I tried to keep the loyalty of the northern tribes by giving them two golden calves to worship: one was at Dan.
Joshua 19:40–48; 1 Kings 12:25–30

DANIEL

Best-known of several Old Testament Daniels is the high-born Jew who was taken captive to Babylon, probably in his teens. At the court of King Nebuchadnezzar Daniel and his three friends, Shadrach, Meshach and Abednego, were trained to be counsellors to the king. Daniel was determined still to obey God. He refused the rich food he was given and instead grew strong on the simple diet allowed by Jewish food-laws. God gave Daniel great wisdom. Twice he was able to tell Nebuchadnezzar the meaning of strange dreams. Daniel later explained to Belshazzar (who held power after Nebuchadnezzar) the writing that appeared on his wall: the kingdom was about to be overthrown. That same night Belshazzar was killed and the Persians captured Babylon. They made Daniel an important official, but the

159

other leaders were jealous of his power and plotted his downfall. Daniel was thrown into the lions' den, but God saved his life. Daniel also recorded a number of dreams in which God told him of his plans for the future.

The Book of Daniel was written at a time when the Jewish people were being oppressed, perhaps during the persecution of Antiochus Epiphanes in 168 BC. Stories and visions included in the book encouraged them. God would destroy the oppressor and restore his people.

Chapters 1–6 record stories about Daniel and some of his friends in exile at the time of the Babylonian and Persian Empires. Because they trusted and obeyed God no matter what the cost, they triumphed over their enemies.

The rest of the book (chapters 7–12) is a series of Daniel's visions. They describe in picture form the rise and fall of empires. The pagan persecutors will fall, and God's people will be victorious.

DARIUS

1. Darius the Mede is named in the Book of Daniel as ruler after Belshazzar. Darius is not otherwise known from contemporary records (which give a far from complete picture). Cyrus may have made Darius ruler of Babylon, or may even have used the name Darius himself.
Daniel 5:31ff.
2. Darius I of Persia (522–486 BC), who encouraged the Jews to finish rebuilding the temple.
Ezra 4:5; Haggai 1:1; Zechariah 1:1

3. Darius II of Persia (423–408 BC), mentioned in the Book of Nehemiah.
Nehemiah 12:22

DAVID

Youngest of the eight sons of Jesse, a farmer at Bethlehem. David was a shepherd. He was looking after the flocks when Samuel the prophet came to Bethlehem, sent by God to anoint one of the sons of Jesse as king in place of Saul. When David was chosen his brothers were jealous.

David's skill in playing the harp took him to Saul's court, to soothe the king in his fits of madness. Later, when he was sent to take food to his brothers in the army, David took up the challenge to fight Goliath, the giant champion of the Philistines. He killed him with a stone from his shepherd's sling. After the battle the women came out to meet Saul. "Saul has killed thousands, but David tens of thousands," they sang. From then on Saul became very jealous of David and several times tried to kill him. Jonathan, Saul's son and David's close friend, warned him to escape and he became an outlaw. Saul hunted him without mercy, although David twice spared his life.

Saul and Jonathan were killed in battle against the Philistines, and David was crowned in Judah. But it was two years before all Israel accepted him as king. David was a brave soldier and won many victories. He was very popular with the people and ruled them well. When he had captured Jerusalem from the Jebusites David made it his capital. He brought the

The impression made by a tiny cylinder seal of Darius, probably Darius I, showing the king hunting lions.

Covenant Box (the ark) there and planned to build a temple but God forbade it.

David made love to Bathsheba, wife of Uriah, one of his soldiers. When Bathsheba became pregnant David ordered Uriah to the front line and made sure he was killed. David then married Bathsheba. The prophet Nathan denounced his sin and although the king was genuinely sorry and God forgave him, Bathsheba's child died. Their next son, Solomon, was David's heir.

Later there was trouble between David's sons. Absalom, his favourite son, tried to seize the throne. David was forced to leave Jerusalem, but Absalom was defeated and killed, to David's great distress. When he was old, Adonijah, another son, plotted against him.

David was a great king, a great soldier and a great poet, who wrote many beautiful psalms of praise to

God. Although he made mistakes and did wrong, he never failed to repent and ask God to forgive him. The Bible describes him as "a man after God's own heart".
1 Samuel 16ff–1 Kings 2; 1 Chronicles 11–29

DEAD SEA
See *Salt Sea* and *Arabah*.

DEAD SEA SCROLLS
The most exciting discovery from New Testament times has been the Dead Sea Scrolls. No one had expected that ancient papers would last in Palestine. Yet in 1947, in a cave near the north-west shore of the Dead Sea, a shepherd boy happened to find jars containing old leather rolls. He did not know what they were, and sold them for next to nothing. Eventually archaeologists heard about the find and where it had been made. Between them, shepherds and archaeologists collected pieces of over 400 rolls.

These books belonged to the library of a religious commune at Qumran on the edge of the Dead Sea. Their owners had hidden them in caves when the Roman army advanced against the rebel Jews in AD 68. The dry heat of the region preserved them. They are less valuable than the papyri for understanding the text of the New Testament. But the scrolls, mostly written in Hebrew or Aramaic, bring a mass of new information about Jewish religious life in the New Testament period.

Old Testament books were favourites in the library. Every one of them is there, except Esther. Many copies show that the traditional Hebrew text (only available in copies made about AD 900 before this discovery) was current in the first century AD, and earlier. There are also other Hebrew texts amongst the scrolls, though they are in a minority. These have variations, some of which are reflected in the Greek translation (the Septuagint) and in the New Testament (the quotation of Deuteronomy 32:43 given in Hebrews 1:6 is one of them).

The Qumran community Other books are commentaries on sections of the Old Testament. Commentators explained ancient names of people and places in the light of current affairs. They believed the prophets had spoken about them, not about their own days. From these remarks, and from other writings, we learn of the community's early leader, the Teacher of Righteousness. He disagreed with most Jews about the dates of major festivals and withdrew from Jerusalem to set up the strictly ruled community by the Dead Sea.

Enemies were called the "Sons of Darkness"; the people of the Dead Sea community considered themselves "Sons of Light". They looked forward to a day when God's Messiah would lead them to a great victory over their opponents. Then they would worship as they thought right in the temple.

Their hopes were disappointed. Their Messiah did not come, and the Romans broke up their commune. The men of Qumran and the early church were very different. The owners of the scrolls were thoroughly Jewish. They had no direct connection with early Christianity. Some ideas are shared by both — for example, contrasting good and bad, light and darkness — but these are common Jewish ideas of the time. In some cases the similarities — which have been heavily emphasized in recent books — seem striking because there is no other material from Jewish groups of the same date. A study of the attitude to the Old Testament shown in the scrolls has given a clearer view of the way Jesus and his followers treated it.

Jesus attacked Jewish leaders for strict obedience to details of the Law without understanding its real meaning. The Scrolls reveal a Jewish sect as strict as these leaders, if not more so. The "phylacteries" that have been found are an indication of this. In order to obey God's command to remember his laws they actually tied them to their hands and foreheads (see Exodus 13:9, 16). Passages of scripture were written on minute pieces of parchment, bound in leather cases (phylacteries), and strapped on the head and left hand at prayer time. An example from Qumran is ¾ x ½in/20 x 13mm. The parchments, unfolded, are about 1½ x 1½in/40 x 27mm. On one piece Deuteronomy 5:22–6:9 was written in twenty-six lines. Jesus accused the Pharisees and teachers of the Law of showing off by wearing phylacteries for others to see (Matthew 23:5).

DEATH

When Paul was facing possible death, he was able to write in his letter to the Philippian Christians: "What is life? To me, it is Christ. Death then will bring more. I want very much to leave this life and be with Christ." He knew that for a Christian there is a wonderful life beyond death, made possible by the death and resurrection of Jesus. But the Jewish people had not always believed in life after death.

Jewish beliefs   In the early days of the Old Testament, the Israelites believed that when a man died, he went down into a shadowy place under the earth called *sheol*. It was not until much later that people began to ask how a just God could let good people die like this. So they reasoned that *sheol* could not be the end. Surely there would be a resurrection, and a person's final destiny would depend on how he had lived in this life. The prophet Daniel writes: "Many of those who have already died will live again: some will suffer eternal life, and some will suffer eternal disgrace" (Daniel 12:2). In New Testament times, the Pharisees believed in a resurrection but the Sadducees did not.

Funeral customs   The funeral arrangements were much the same as they are today. When someone died, his eyes were closed. The body was washed and wrapped in strips of cloth for a quick burial, because of the hot climate. It was not put in a coffin, but carried on a wooden stretcher (a bier) to the burial-place. Family and friends made a great show of mourning: weeping, wailing, wearing uncomfortable clothes, walking barefoot, putting ashes on their heads, tearing their clothes and shaving off their beards. Sometimes professional mourners were hired to add to the wailing. Mourning normally lasted for seven days, but longer for an important person (seventy days for Joseph; thirty days for Moses). A time of fasting went with the time of mourning. But there was a funeral feast which often took place at the tomb. In countries outside Israel — particularly Egypt — the body was embalmed. The

A decorated limestone ossuary in which the bones of the dead were kept. It dates from about the time of Jesus, and was found in the Jerusalem area.

insides and brain were removed and the space filled with a gummy paste.

Burial   The people of Israel often buried their dead in caves. Some caves were large enough for all the members of a family (Genesis 50:13), but if necessary, they could be enlarged to form corridors with shelves cut out of the rock on which the bodies could be placed. Rich people were able to have tombs specially constructed with a stairway leading down through the solid rock to the burial chamber. A slab of stone was put at the entrance with a boulder against it. In New Testament times a large circular stone was sometimes set in a groove and rolled across to cover the opening. But of course the number of caves, even man-made ones, was limited. So the bones were often removed and stored in chests of wood or stone called "ossuaries".

The poor were buried in shallow graves in open ground. A row of stones was placed round the body and the spaces in between were filled up with small

167

stones and earth. A slab of stone was then put on the top. All graves were painted white to draw people's attention to them. For they must not be touched: any contact with the dead made a person ritually "unclean".

Christian beliefs Throughout the Bible there is a close link between death and sin. Death is part of the judgement that comes to Adam after his disobedience. Paul regards death as the inevitable consequence of the presence of sin in the world. For God is "holy", and cannot tolerate evil. If we die with sin unforgiven, our death is not only physical but spiritual: it is separation from God. The New Testament often speaks of non-Christians as being physically alive, but "spiritually dead because of disobedience and sins".

When Jesus died on the cross he took the ultimate consequences of sin on himself. His resurrection showed that he had defeated death. So although our human fate is to die, by faith in Christ we can have "eternal life". The Christian is already lifted out of spiritual death to new life and looks forward to the end of the age when physical death, "the last enemy", will also be overcome.

See also *Heaven, Hell, Judgement, Life, Resurrection, Second coming of Jesus*.

Psalm 144:4; Deuteronomy 30:15, 19; Psalm 55:4; Genesis 3:19; Romans 6:23; Matthew 7:23; Ephesians 2:1; Hebrews 2:14–15; 1 Corinthians 15:21, 26; 2 Corinthians 5:1–10

DEBORAH

The only woman who was a Judge of Israel. Deborah

encouraged General Barak to fight against Sisera, commander of the army of Jabin, a Canaanite king. The resulting victory ended twenty years of Canaanite oppression.
Judges 4–5

DECAPOLIS (THE TEN TOWNS)
An association of ten Greek towns gave this region its name. The Decapolis was an area south of Lake Galilee, mostly east of the River Jordan. Many of the people living there were non-Jews, but they joined the crowds that followed Jesus. Jewish Christians fled to Pella, one of these towns, before the war with the Romans in AD 70.
Matthew 4:25; Mark 5:1–20; 7:31–37

DEDAN
Within the general area of Midian the city of Dedan (now Al-'Ula) later grew up. This major trading centre was known even to the Babylonians.
Isaiah 21:13; Jeremiah 25:23; 49:8; Ezekiel 27:20

DEER AND GAZELLE
These graceful animals provide the Bible writers with a picture of swiftness and gentleness. Fallow and roe deer, gazelles and ibex, whose sandy colouring makes them difficult to spot, were a major source of meat.
Deuteronomy 12:15; Song of Solomon 2:8–9

DELILAH
A beautiful Philistine woman who betrayed Samson. (See *Samson*).
Judges 16

DEMAS
A Christian who was with Paul when he was a prisoner in Rome. He later deserted Paul and went off to Thessalonica.
Colossians 4:14; 2 Timothy 4:10

DEMETRIUS
1. A silversmith in Ephesus who made souvenirs at the temple of Diana (Artemis) — see below. He was afraid that as a result of Paul's preaching the visitors would no longer buy these models, and so he encouraged other men in the same business to riot.
Acts 19:24ff.
2. A Christian mentioned in John's third letter, of whom everyone spoke well.
3 John 12

DERBE
A city in Lycaonia, in southern Asia Minor (modern Turkey), where Paul preached on his first and second journeys.
Acts 14:20–21; 16:1

DEUTERONOMY
The book of Deuteronomy consists of a number of speeches given by Moses to the Israelites in the plains of Moab, just before they entered the Promised Land.

The name of the book means a "second law-giving". But it is in fact a new statement of the laws God gave at Sinai (recorded in Exodus, Leviticus and Numbers), applying them to the settled life of the land of Canaan.

In the course of his speeches, Moses retells the great events of the last forty years. He repeats and underlines the Ten Commandments, and appoints Joshua as his successor to lead the Israelites.

The great theme of Deuteronomy is that God has saved and blessed his people. They must always remember this, and love and obey him.

The words that Jesus called the greatest commandment: "Love the Lord your God with all your heart, with all your soul, and with all your strength," come from the Book of Deuteronomy (6:4–5; Matthew 22:37).

DIANA
Roman goddess of the moon and hunting, called Artemis by the Greeks. Her magnificent temple at

A statue of the goddess Diana, found at Ephesus.

Ephesus was one of the wonders of the ancient world. (See *Greek and Roman religion*.)
Acts 19

DIBON
A Moabite town east of the Dead Sea and 4 miles/5.5km north of the River Arnon. The Israelites captured it at the time of their entry into Canaan. It was given to the tribes of Gad and Reuben, but changed hands several times in the course of its history.
Numbers 21:30; 32:34; Isaiah 15:2

DIONYSIUS
A member of the Areopagus, a powerful council at Athens set up to hear religious cases. Dionysius was converted to Christianity when Paul was asked to address the council.
Acts 17:34

DISTANCES
New Testament **orgyia** (fathom) = 6ft/1.85m
New Testament **stadion** (furlong) = 202yd/185m
A sabbath day's journey, the maximum distance allowed by the Jewish law, was fixed at 2,000 cubits/1,000 yd/914m
New Testament **milion** (mile) = 1,000 paces (Roman measurement) 1,618 yd/1,478m

DIVORCE
See *Marriage*.

DORCAS/TABITHA

A Christian from Joppa who helped the poor by making clothes for them. When she died her friends sent for Peter, and he brought her back to life.
Acts 9:36–41

DOTHAN

A town on the route from Beth-shan and Gilead to Egypt. Here Joseph's brothers sold him to the Ishmaelite traders. At Dothan, Elisha was rescued from the surrounding Syrian army.
Genesis 37:17–28; 2 Kings 6

DOVES AND PIGEONS

The most common and important of all the Bible birds. Several kinds are native to Israel; others come as winter visitors. They were widely kept as domestic birds, for food. Poor people, who could not afford to sacrifice a sheep or goat would offer two pigeons — which they could buy in the temple courts — instead. It was a dove that brought back to Noah the first green leaf after the flood.
Genesis 8:8–12; Psalm 55:6; Matthew 3:16; 21:12

A Stock Dove (on the left) and Turtle Dove.

DRESS

The Bible covers about 2,000 years of history. But because of the hot climate and the limited number of materials available, dress remained fairly standard in Israel for most of that time.

The main differences in dress were between the rich and poor. The poor peasant had only the woollen or goats'-hair clothes he stood up in. But rich people had clothes for winter and for summer; clothes for working and clothes for leisure; clothes of different materials — fine linen, or even silk. Some of them spent so much time and money on clothes that they needed Jesus' words to remind them of the really important things in life. "Why worry about clothes?" he said. "Look how the wild flowers grow . . . It is God who clothes the wild grass . . . Won't he be all the more sure to clothe you?" (Matthew 6:28–30).

Because the names have changed, we do not know which clothes some Hebrew words mean. We have to make careful guesses.

The first thing a man put on was either a loincloth or a short skirt from waist to knee. This was all he wore when he was doing heavy work.

Over the top of this came a shirt or tunic made of wool or linen. This was like a big sack: a long piece of material folded at the centre and sewn up the sides, with holes for the arms and a slit at the folded end for the head to go through. The shirt was calf-length for a man and coloured, usually red, yellow, black or striped. A woman's tunic came down to her ankles and was often blue. Often it was embroidered on the yoke with a special pattern. Each village had

Israelites shown on the "Black Obelisk" of Shalmaneser III of Assyria. They are wearing pointed caps and shoes and fringed cloaks.

its own traditional pattern of embroidery. Apart from these features a woman's tunic would be very similar to a man's.

The tunic was fastened round the waist with a girdle or belt. This was a piece of cloth, folded into a long strip to make a kind of pocket to hold coins and other belongings. If a man was rich he might have a leather belt with a dagger or an inkhorn pushed into it. When a man needed to be able to move more freely, to work, he would tuck his tunic into this belt to make it much shorter. This was called "girding up the loins". It meant getting ready for action. A woman could lift up the hem of her long dress and use it as a large bag, even for carrying things like corn.

Out of doors, a rich man would wear a light coat over his tunic. This came down to his knees and was often gaily striped or woven in check patterns. Rich people wore lightweight coats indoors as well, perhaps made from imported silk. In Joseph's time, a long-sleeved coat of many pieces was worn by the future leader of the clan (see the story of Joseph, Genesis 37:3).

There was also a thick woollen coat or cloak to keep out the cold, called a *himation* in New Testament times. This was made from two pieces of material, often in stripes of light and dark brown, stitched together. The joined material was wrapped round the body, sewn at the shoulders, and slits were then made in the side for the arms to go through. The shepherd lived in his. It was his blanket when he slept in the open at night. It was also thick enough to make a comfortable seat. A poor man's cloak was so important to him that if it was handed over to guarantee repayment of a debt, it had to be returned to him at sunset.

Headgear In Israel the sun was so hot that some covering was needed to protect the head, neck and eyes. This was usually a square of cloth folded diagonally, with the fold across the forehead. A circle of plaited wool held it in place over the head, and the folds protected the neck. A cap was sometimes worn, and a fine wool shawl or *tallith* over it, especially during prayer. Women put pads on their heads to steady the jars of water and other things they carried.

Footwear Although many poor people probably went barefoot, sandals were the normal footwear. The simplest design was a piece of hide the same size as the foot, with a long leather strap which passed between the big and second toe, and was then tied round the ankle. Sandals were cool to wear, but people's feet got very dusty. Sandals were always taken off before going into someone else's home. It was the lowliest servant's job to take off the visitor's sandals and wash his feet. Sandals also were removed before entering a holy place. According to custom the right sandal was always put on and taken off before the left. A man selling property took off his sandal and gave it to the buyer as a token that he gave up his right to the property (as Boaz' relative did in the story of Ruth — Ruth 4:7).

It is interesting that despite the strict rules against all work on the sabbath the Jewish law book allowed for a man to take certain clothes from a burning house on the sabbath day. Most people had few clothes, and they had to make them last. They were carefully washed with soap made from olive oil, and rinsed in fast-flowing water so that the current could run through the material and loosen the dirt. If someone tore his clothes as a sign of mourning, it was out of real grief!

There were no nightclothes. At night people simply lay down and loosened their day clothes.

These basic clothes were influenced to some extent by styles from other countries. But fashions did not change much. A painting of Asiatic nomads who visited Egypt, can be seen on the wall of a tomb at Beni-Hasan (about 1890 BC). They have cloaks of coloured wool which reach below the knee, with a loose end thrown over the shoulder. This was probably the type of clothing worn by Abraham.

See also *Clothes-making, Hair, Jewellery, Make-up*.

DRINK

Although water was the basic liquid used in cooking, it was not very good for drinking. Water from the local well or spring was generally safe enough. It was collected in porous earthenware jars in which the water remained cool by a process of slow evaporation. Water from the family cistern, a conical shaped pit in the ground with a waterproof lining, was far from safe. Because the water came from the roof and ran down into the cistern through gutters, it was often dirty and full of germs. In Roman times when water was brought to the towns by aqueduct (as it was to Caesarea and Bethlehem) or mixed with olive oil to clean and heal wounds. (The Good Samaritan poured oil and wine on the wounds of the injured man — Luke 10:34.) by pipeline (as it was to Jerusalem), the water was still not fit to drink. For this reason other liquids made better drinks.

There was milk, often straight from the family goat, or brought to the door by the "milkman". But wine was the commonest drink. At the time the grapes were picked, there was fresh grape juice, pressed straight from the bunch into a cup. But most of the juice had to be fermented so that it would keep. The first wine of the year was made from the juice extracted when the grapes were trodden in the press. A second batch was made by squeezing the remainder in a press. Wine was sometimes mixed with gall or myrrh to relieve pain. (This was offered to Jesus at the crucifixion — Matthew 27:34.)

Although wine was the normal drink — Jesus himself provided wine for the wedding at Cana, and drank enough to be called a "tippler" ("wine-bibber") by the Pharisees — people under a vow to God, or engaged on special service, sometimes gave up drinking it (Leviticus 10:9; Numbers 6:3). And any drunkenness or excess was always condemned. The Rechabites avoided drinking wine as part of their calling to keep the nomadic way of life. Planting vineyards and producing wine was considered part of a settled life.

Wealthy homes in New Testament times had cellars of fine wines from all over the Mediterranean world. They were kept in narrow jars (*amphorae*) with a pointed end, so that they could be pushed deep into earth or sand to keep the wine cool. But wine was usually stored in leather bottles (wineskins).

DRUSILLA
The youngest daughter of Herod Agrippa I and wife of the Roman governor Felix. (See *Felix*.)
Acts 24:24

EAGLES AND VULTURES

The word usually translated "eagle" also includes the Griffon-Vulture. From a distance both look alike. Isaiah and the Psalmist both speak of the eagle's strength and vigour. The "eagle" was the badge of the Roman legions. Matthew probably had that in mind when he described the eagles waiting for Jerusalem to fall.

Isaiah 40:31; Psalm 103:5; Matthew 24:28

A Golden Eagle (on the left) and Griffon Vultures; two birds of prey — forbidden foods for the Israelites.

EBAL

A rocky mountain in Samaria, opposite the wooded height of Mt Gerizim, close to ancient Shechem and modern Nablus. Here Joshua carried out a command given him by Moses before the conquest of the land. He built an altar on Mt Ebal and gave the people a choice — to obey God and enjoy his blessing, or to disobey and be punished. Some of the people stood on Mt Ebal, whose bare, scorched height represented God's curse, and others on Mt Gerizim.

Deuteronomy 11:29; 27; Joshua 8:30, 33

EBED-MELECH

An Ethiopian who was one of King Zedekiah's palace officials (sixth century BC). Because he saved Jeremiah's life God promised that Ebed-melech would not be killed when Jerusalem was destroyed.

Jeremiah 38; 39:16–18

ECCLESIASTES

This book gathers together the "wisdom" — wise observations, thoughts and sayings — of "the Philosopher" (Qoheleth). This kind of writing was popular in the ancient Near Eastern countries at the time.

The writer looks at human life. He finds it short and meaningless, and concludes that it has no point. He cannot understand the purpose of it all. But he ends by recommending hard work and enjoyment of pleasure while it lasts. Much of the book seems depressing and destructive, because it looks at "life under the sun" — from a purely human viewpoint. Life without God lacks purpose and meaning. But wisdom and justice inject at least some nobility into man's existence.

EDEN

The garden God made, in the beginning, as a place for his people to live in. After they had disobeyed him, God sent Adam and Eve out of the Garden of Eden. Two of the rivers in it were the Tigris and the Euphrates.
Genesis 2:8–14

EDOM

The land of Edom lay south of Moab, stretching down to the Gulf of Aqaba. The Edomites lived here, ruled by kings, from an early date. Some Edomites travelled as traders; others worked at copper mining and farming. Like their neighbours they were hostile to Israel. They were conquered more than once, but often broke free again. Their Red Sea port, Ezion-geber (Elath) was used by Solomon and later kings. Many Hebrew prophets spoke bitter words against Edom. The Edomites took advantage of the exile to occupy much of southern Judah. This area, known later as Idumaea, was the home of the Herod family who ruled Judea in New Testament times.
Genesis 36:1–19, 36–39; 1 Kings 9:26; 22:48; 2 Kings 14:22; Amos 1:11–12; Jeremiah 49:7–22; Obadiah

EDUCATION

As far back as Abraham's time certain nations were developing education. In Sumer, Abraham's homeland, there were schools to train future secretaries for work in the temples, palace and business life. This education was voluntary. The pupil's family had to pay and so it was usually only the privilege of the rich. But the range of subjects was wide. Botany, geography, mathematics, grammar and literature were all studied.

Excavations have unearthed many clay tablets containing exercises to be copied, while others record the pupils' attempts and their teachers' corrections. In the palace of Mari, two schoolrooms with benches and desks have been found. School staff included a professor (often called "the school father", with pupils called the "school sons"), an assistant who prepared the daily exercises, specialist teachers, and others responsible for discipline (one called "big brother").

There was a similar system in Egypt, where schools were often attached to the temples. After the beginners' course pupils transferred to a government department where they studied composition, natural science and the duties of office. There was special training in letter-writing and "model letters" have been found. If they were being trained to be priests, they studied theology and medicine. Discipline was strict: no wine, no music, no women.

Systems like these must have influenced the people of Israel at certain points in their history. Abraham may have been a man of some learning. Joseph would have relied on secretaries for his work as a chief minister of Pharaoh. And Moses had an Egyptian education — so it was a man with a trained mind who was chosen to teach God's law to the people of Israel. But education in Israel itself took a very different course.

The basic idea in Israel and all through the Bible is that all knowledge comes from God. He is the greatest of all teachers. All wisdom and learning should begin with "the fear of the Lord". Its aim is to understand the Creator and his work better. So learning leads to praising God (as in Psalm 8). It is not enough simply to satisfy human curiosity. It also helps people to use their God-given abilities to the full. So elementary mathematics was needed for surveying land and calculating the harvest, and for large building works. Studying the movements of the sun, moon and stars helped in working out the calendar. Many of these things were learnt by experience, or, as in other crafts, in an apprenticeship.

At the same time, the education of children was given an important place. It was every parent's duty to make sure that his children were taught. But the content of this teaching was almost entirely religious.

They were to be taught the story of God's dealings with Israel.

They were to be instructed in God's laws. God is holy and requires holiness from his people. Children must therefore be taught how to "keep the ways of the Lord".

They were to be given instruction in wise dealing. The Book of Proverbs is full of maxims on the subject of "how to get along with people" and is written for "sons". This type of teaching Israel had in common with other nations.

Exodus 20:4; Proverbs 1:7; 9:10; Job 28:28; Deuteronomy 4:9–10; 6:20–21; Exodus 13:8–9; 12:26–27; Joshua 4:21–22; Leviticus 19:2; Genesis 18:19; Proverbs 1:8; 4:1

How education developed Education began at home. Abraham was instructed to teach his children. It was important that the truth of God's acts for his people was passed from father to son, from generation to generation. Mothers also probably shared in this when the children were young.

Opinions differ about how many people could read and write in Old Testament times. Some think that only the nobles could. But, on the other hand, Joshua expected written reports on the land of Canaan; Gideon expected a young passer-by to be able to read; and in the time of Hezekiah it was presumably a workman who wrote on the wall of the tunnel dug to bring water into Jerusalem (see *Building*). Enough other examples of ancient Hebrew writing have been found to show that there was widespread knowledge of the skill.

It it not known when schools for children started. They are not referred to until 75 BC, when the country came under Greek influence and there was an attempt to enforce elementary education. But there may have been voluntary schools before this. The boy Samuel was handed over to the priest's keeping and was presumably taught by him. This kind of thing may have been a regular practice. The "Gezer calendar" (see *Farming*) may also be evidence of a more formal type of education. Certainly the young men had the chance to become pupils of the prophets, and probably also of the priests and Levites. Isaiah gave private teaching to a group of disciples and Elisha was very concerned for the welfare of his pupils and their families. But none of this was "education" either in the modern sense, or in the way we find it in Egypt or ancient Babylon. It was learning about religion in order to serve God better.

After the people returned from exile, a specialized class of Bible scholars, known as "scribes", came into being. This term had been used earlier to mean secretaries, but some of the Levites were scribes, and even before the exile they were recognized as experts in God's law. According to Jewish tradition, after the exile these scribes were the equivalent of the earlier prophets, and were called "men of the great synagogue". They came to be known as "lawyers", "doctors of the law" and "rabbis". Simon the Just, Shammai, Hillel and Gamaliel were some of the most famous. They taught and explained the written Law of God, and they applied the Law to contemporary life. These teachings built up into large collections of rules. At first they were taught by word of mouth, but eventually they were written down to form the *Mishnah*, about AD 200. They were regarded as having the same authority as the Old Testament itself.

It was during these last centuries before Christ that the group later known as the Pharisees seems to

A Greek vase-painting showing a teacher hearing a boy read.

have organized a school system. Children first went to school in the synagogue, "the house of the book". Further education then took place in "the house of study". Many of these were under the direction of famous rabbis.

We can only guess at educational methods. Isaiah may throw some light on this. He writes that the people think his message is only for babies: "He is trying to teach us letter by letter, line by line, lesson by lesson." This may reflect the practice of teaching a little at a time, or it may represent the first letters of the alphabet being learnt by repetition. Most instruction was given by word of mouth, and various devices were used to make it easy to memorize. Jesus himself used catchwords, repetition, and parables. Psalm 78:3–6; Proverbs 31:1; 1:8; 6:20; Joshua 18:4, 8–9; Judges 8:14; Isaiah 8:16; Jeremiah 36:26; 1 Chronicles 24:6; Jeremiah 8:8; Mark 7:6–9; Isaiah 28:10; Proverbs 1:8; Mark 9:42–50; Matthew 6:2–18

Adult education Education in the Bible was not only for children. Abraham was told to teach the whole of his household. Moses taught the people of Israel the Law of God, and the Levites were commanded to pass on this teaching. The kings sent Levites throughout the land to teach, though the prophets complained that this duty was often done badly, and regarded as a way of making money. The custom of regular teaching of the people probably developed only after the exile.

Ezra was a priest and scribe "with a thorough knowledge of the Law". He "devoted his life to studying the Law of the Lord . . . and to teaching all its laws and regulations to the people of Israel."

Nehemiah 8 pictures him standing in a wooden pulpit, with all the people gathered to hear him.
Genesis 18:19; Leviticus 10:11; 2 Chronicles 17:7–9; 35:3; Micah 3:11; Malachi 2:7–8; Ezra 7:6, 10

Greek education By the time of Jesus Greek education had become world-famous. Body, mind and soul, it was thought, needed room for expression, so the syllabus included athletics, philosophy, poetry, drama, music and rhetoric. Boys would attend elementary school between the ages of seven and fifteen. They would then go to a "gymnasium" for a wider education (not just for athletics). Members of the public were welcome to come and join in the students' discussions. Standards in the gymnasia had declined by the time of Jesus, but these schools still represented the best of Greek culture. They were set up wherever Greeks came to live, and one was started in Jerusalem in 167 BC.

Most Jews thoroughly disapproved of the Greek view of education. The gymnasia were also condemned because Greek athletes practised and competed naked. Foreigners, were, however, welcome, and since Paul's home-city of Tarsus was also famous for its gymnasium we may wonder if Paul ever went there. He certainly refers to the Greek games, and shows a knowledge of Greek culture in his letters.
1 Corinthians 9:24–27
See also *Writing*.

EGLON

1. A king of Moab in the time of the Judges. He defeated Israel and captured Jericho, keeping the

Israelites subject for eighteen years. He was murdered by Ehud.
Judges 3:12–26

2. One of a group of Amorite cities conquered by Joshua in his first vigorous campaign. It was probably Tell el-Hesi near Lachish, in the Shephelah, the low hill-country west of Jerusalem.
Joshua 10; 12:12; 15:39

EGYPT

The huge Sahara Desert sweeps across North Africa from the mountains of Morocco in the west to the Red Sea in the east. From the lakes and highlands of tropical East Africa, the River Nile flows north across the dry deserts all the way to the Mediterranean Sea. For the last 600 miles to the sea, the river flows through a valley bordered by cliffs on either side. Then, 100 miles from the sea, it splits into two streams. They enclose a great triangle of flat land called the Nile Delta, because its shape is like the Greek letter "D", *delta*, a triangle.

The Nile flood Every year, tropical rains in East Africa cause the river to flood its banks, bringing down masses of mud in the flood-waters. Until modern times, that fertile mud was deposited fresh each year along the valley and in the great Delta triangle, which was entirely formed of this mud. This is Egypt: rich green crops on black soil along the narrow ribbon of valley and river, and across the broad Delta. On either side, the yellow-brown deserts stretch away beyond the cliffs. Nowadays, great dams control the Nile floods, and hold back the mud. In ancient times, there was no control. A small flood meant no water for crops, and so nothing to eat. Too big a flood swept away villages and farm animals. To spread the water as far as possible, the ancient Egyptians cut canals and irrigation channels among the fields.

Transport The Egyptians quickly learned to make boats. At first, they made canoes out of papyrus-reeds, then larger boats of wood. With these they could travel easily on the River Nile along the whole valley, or through the Delta. Going north, they simply rowed with the current. Going south, the north wind would fill their sails to travel against the river's flow. So the Nile has always been Egypt's "main road".

The other parts of the country were also important. The deserts and the Sinai peninsula contained valuable metals (copper, gold), and stone that was used for building the giant pyramids and the temples in the Nile Valley.

A land of history To begin with there were two kingdoms in Egypt: the Nile Valley (Upper Egypt) and the Nile Delta (Lower Egypt). But before 3000 BC a king of the Valley managed to defeat the king of the Delta and become the king of all Egypt. To rule both lands, he built his capital city, Memphis, at the point where the valley widens into the Delta. Menes, this first king of all Egypt, began a line of kings or "pharaohs". For the next 3,000 years, thirty such families of kings (dynasties) ruled Egypt, mainly following one after the other. During that long span of time, Egypt enjoyed three periods of greatness.

The Pyramid Age The first great age in Egypt was

the "Old Kingdom" (about 2600–2200 BC), or "Pyramid Age", from the huge, pointed stone tombs that the kings built. After the strong kings of the Pyramid Age, Egypt became poorer under less able leaders. Once more rival kings came to power in south and north, until a prince from Thebes again re-united Egypt.

The Middle Kingdom This prince's family, and the one after it (the 12th Dynasty) were Egypt's "Middle Kingdom" (about 2060–1786 BC). Its new, strong pharaohs took over the river valley and deserts of Nubia, south of Egypt, to obtain gold and other African products. By improving the use of the Nile-waters for farming, these kings also increased the crops grown, and the wealth of the people. It was probably about this time that Abraham visited Egypt because of famine in Canaan. Many others like him came from Canaan into Egypt. Some stayed, and were even promoted to important posts in the government of Egypt; others were less fortunate and became servants or slaves.

After the 12th Dynasty, from about 1780–1550 BC weaker kings ruled. This was perhaps the time when Joseph was sold as a slave into Egypt, to be followed some years later by his family. From amongst the foreigners living in the east Delta, princes arose who made themselves kings of all Egypt. They are known as the Hyksos, or 15th Dynasty. But it was not long before Egyptian princes from Thebes in the south again came north, to expel the Hyksos rulers and re-unite Egypt once more.

The Empire These pharaohs also won control over

King Tutankhamun and his queen. The scene is created in gold, silver and coloured glass on the back-rest of his throne.

Canaan, to the north of Egypt, as well as Nubia to the south. This period, the "New Kingdom", is often called the "Empire". It includes the 18th–20th Dynasties, and covers the period from about 1500 to 1070 BC. These kings fought many battles in Canaan and Syria. In Egypt, they built many huge temples, the most important at Memphis (their capital) and Thebes (their sacred city).

In the meantime the Hittites in the far north conquered part of Egypt's empire in Syria. A new line of pharaohs tried to win back the lost provinces, especially kings Sethos I and Ramesses II (19th Dynasty, thirteenth century BC). These kings were great builders. Being a Delta family, they built a new royal city, Pi-Ramesse — the Raamses (Rameses) of

Exodus — in the east Delta. This was the climax of the "oppression" of the Hebrews — who were used as slave-labour by the pharaohs — and the time when Moses was sent to lead the Hebrews out of Egypt (the "Exodus"). Shortly before 1200 BC another pharaoh, Merenptah, sent soldiers to Canaan and defeated several groups of people there. One of these was the Israelites, who obviously must have been in Canaan by that date.

Soon after 1200 BC, the ancient world had much trouble. The "peoples of the sea" and others overthrew the Hittite Empire and most of the kingdoms in Syria and Canaan. Ramesses III pushed the invaders back from Egypt's borders in two fierce battles on land and sea. One of these peoples was the Philistines. After Ramesses III, Egypt's 20th Dynasty and empire lost power under weak kings. They governed badly and low Niles brought famines.

The Late Period From about 1070 BC to 330 BC, Egypt went through her "Late Period". Egypt was never again as powerful as in earlier times. In 925 BC, Shoshenq I (Shishak) subdued King Rehoboam of Judah and King Jeroboam of Israel. The Egyptians recorded this victory in their temple of Karnak. But their power did not last long: 200 years later neither So nor Tirhakah could help the Hebrew kings against Assyria. Nor did Hophra in 588 BC really help Zedekiah against the Babylonians.

From 525 BC Egypt, like her neighbours, was part of the Persian Empire, sometimes rebelling and becoming free again (28th–30th Dynasties), until finally Alexander the Great took over (332–323 BC).

193

After him, the Greek Ptolemies ruled Egypt until the coming of the Roman Empire.
Genesis 12:10–20; 37–50; Exodus 1:11 and chapters 1–14; 1 Kings 14:25–27; 2 Kings 17:4; 19:9ff.; Jeremiah 37:5–7 and 44:30

Life in ancient Egypt The pharaoh was supreme ruler of Egypt. He was assisted by his great men, including wise men like those the king sent for to explain his dreams. The land was divided into provinces. Each had its chief city for local government and supplies. Most Egyptians were farmers, growing grain, keeping cattle, depending on the Nile. These are all features of the dreams of Joseph's pharaoh.

A jackal representing Anubis, the Egyptian god of embalming, on a funerary chest.

Dreams mattered to all classes (prisoners as well as kings) and the Egyptians even wrote textbooks to interpret dreams.

Egyptian writing began as pictures ("hieroglyphs"), used to write the sounds of their language. An owl was *m*, a mouth was *r*, and so on. For use on papyrus sheets (an early form of paper), flowing forms of script were used ("hieratic", "demotic"). The Egyptians wrote stories, poetry, books of wisdom (like the Bible book of Proverbs), as well as everyday things like lists, letters and accounts.

Both Egyptians and foreigners had to work as labourers on building sites, especially making bricks. For these, straw was needed to mix with the clay to make better bricks. The papyri also mention straw, and fixed work-targets. Like Moses, many young foreigners were brought up at court, were well educated, and had all kinds of jobs. Like Moses and the Hebrews, others, too, tried to escape from Egypt. The papyri mention slaves who ran away to gain their freedom.

Genesis 40 and 41; Exodus 1–14

EGYPTIAN RELIGION

The Egyptians had many gods. Some came from nature: Re, the sun-god; Thoth, Khons, moon-gods; Nut, the sky-goddess; Geb, the earth-god; Hapi, the god of the Nile-flood; and Amun, the god of hidden life-powers in nature. Some stood for ideas: Maat was goddess of truth, justice, and right order. Thoth was also the god of learning and wisdom. Ptah was the god of craftsmanship. Most Egyptians turned to Osiris for hope of a life after death. Osiris was said to have been slain by his brother and then made king of the underworld.

Animals noted for special qualities were treated as sacred to particular gods. They could act as "live images" for their gods. So the Apis-bull was sacred to Ptah, the ibis-birds to Thoth, falcons to Horus, cats to the goddess Bastet. A god was sometimes shown wearing the head of his sacred animal, to make him easier to recognize.

With so many different gods controlling their world, the Egyptians tried to link these to one another. They produced "myths" (stories about the gods), in which gods were often grouped as "families". There would be a chief god and goddess as husband and wife, with a lesser god or goddess as their son or daughter.

In the fourteenth century BC, Pharaoh Akhenaten tried to make all his subjects worship the sun-god only (as seen in the sun's disc — Aten). But he failed, and after about ten years the Egyptians returned to the gods they had worshipped before.

Worship at the great temples The life the Egyptians imagined for the gods was modelled on their own daily life. The huge stone temple, hidden behind great brick walls, was the home of the god. The priests were his servants. Each morning, they woke him up with a morning hymn, broke the seal on his shrine, redressed his image, and gave him food and drink offerings for "breakfast". These offerings were then placed before statues of Pharaoh's ancestors (earlier kings of Egypt and the great men of Egypt) before being finally eaten by the priests. At midday, a shorter service and offerings made up the god's "lunch". An evening hymn sent him to rest, after a third offering ("supper"). On special festival days, smaller images of the gods were carried in procession from temple to temple. These were days on which the gods "went visiting", sometimes to celebrate events mentioned in the stories about them. People believed that the "spirit" of the god lived in his image in the temple.

In theory, Pharaoh himself was high priest of all the gods. In real life, his deputies were high priests in the various temples, assisted by other priests. Only the king, priests and higher officials could go beyond the first sunlit court into the dim, pillared halls and the darkness of the sacred inner room of the temple. Akhenaten's sun-god religion worked in the same way, but in open-air temples. There is a famous hymn, praising the Aten as the creator who provides for the world. People have compared it with Psalm 104. But there are no links between the Egyptian hymn and the psalm, or the Hebrew worship of one holy God.

The religion of the people Pharaoh was the go-between for gods and people. Through his deputy priests he made offerings to the gods on behalf of the people in order that, in turn, the gods might shower their gifts on Egypt (good Nile-floods, rich crops). He also appeared as the representative of the gods to the people. He directed the building and upkeep of the temples which were always built in his name.

The mass of the ordinary people could not enter the great state temples. They only saw the great gods on festival days, when their veiled images were carried in procession in small sacred boats by the priests. Instead, ordinary people worshipped at small, local shrines, or the chapels at the gateways of the great temples. Their worship was mostly to present offerings, following certain set rituals. The people were allowed to make merry at the great festivals. They also sometimes got time off to worship their own god (this was what Moses asked Pharaoh's permission to do, Exodus 5:1, 3). When troubles such as illness struck them, the Egyptians sometimes thought this was punishment from the gods for wrong-doing. They then confessed their sins and prayed for healing and help. If healing came, they often set up little inscriptions, with a short hymn to the god or goddess, to record their thanks.

Like most peoples, the ancient Egyptians had a moral sense of right and wrong. Murder or theft were wrong then, as now. But magic was used to grasp at supernatural power. Good or "white" magic was designed to ward off life's troubles. Harmful or "black" magic was a crime, and was punished as such. Magic usually meant the exact reciting of spells, often over small images or drawings connected with the subject of the magic. People often wore lucky charms, or amulets. The symbol of life, or the scarab-beetle for renewal, was popular.

Life after death The early Egyptians buried their dead along the edges of the dry deserts that bordered the Nile Valley. The dry sand and hot sun often dried up and so preserved the bodies of those early people in their shallow graves. The Egyptians came to believe that the body was a home for the soul, and that the soul needed its personal belongings in a life after death something like earthly life. So, when tombs became too big and deep for the sun's heat to dry the body, the Egyptians did this artificially. They packed the body in salt to dry it up, stuffed it and bandaged it (mummification). The mummy was then buried in a coffin in the tomb with the other belongings. Joseph was embalmed in this way, and put in a coffin in Egypt (Genesis 50:26).

Most Egyptians hoped to have a pleasant after-life in the kingdom of Osiris. They had papyrus-roll books of magical spells to help them pass the judgement of the dead. This by-passed the moral test of that judgement. The most famous collection of spells is the *Book of the Dead*.

Souls of dead kings spent their after-life with the sun-god, crossing the sky in his heavenly boat by day. Then, at night, they passed through the realm of Osiris, providing for their dead subjects. The emphasis on mummification, magic, and richly furnished tombs led to very materialistic views of the after-life.

Egyptian religion and the Bible Egyptian religion was very different from that of the Hebrews. Israel's God dealt with his people in actual history. He required obedience to his just laws more than rituals or sacrifices (1 Samuel 15:22). Ritual without right living was useless. (The Egyptians also admitted this sometimes.) Unlike the gods of Egypt (who needed three meals a day), the God of Israel had no personal need of food or of anything that human hands might provide (see Psalm 50:11–13). Egyptian rituals were symbols, and magical acts. The rites which took place in the Hebrew tabernacle and temple were intended to instruct the people in the nature and purity of their God. Egyptian rites were complicated and for the special few. The Hebrew ones were far simpler, designed mostly for the instruction of people as well as priests.

EHUD

A left-handed Israelite from the tribe of Benjamin. Ehud thought up a cunning and daring plot to kill King Eglon of Moab who had oppressed part of Israel, including the eastern section of the land belonging to Ehud's tribe, for eighteen years. With Eglon dead, Ehud gathered an army to defeat the Moabites and free his people.
Judges 3:15–30

EKRON

One of the five main cities of the Philistines. It was given to the tribe of Judah in the early years of conquest. But the Philistines on the coastal plain were too strong for them to keep it. When the Philistines defeated Israel and captured the Covenant Box (ark), plague broke out in each of the Philistine cities to which the ark was taken. When the plague reached Ekron, the Philistines finally decided to send the ark back to the Israelites.
Joshua 15:11, 45–46; Judges 1:18; 1 Samuel 5:10–6:17; 7:14; 17:52; 2 Kings 1:3–6; Amos 1:8, etc.

ELAH

1. Best-known man of this name in the Old Testament is the son of King Baasha. Elah was an evil king who reigned over Israel for less than two years

(886–885 BC). While drunk he was killed by Zimri, a general in his army.
1 Kings 16:8–14

2. A valley south-west of Jerusalem. The Philistines marched through the Valley of Elah to invade the land of Israel. Here David fought the Philistine champion Goliath.
1 Samuel 17:2

ELAM

The Elamites were an isolated nation whose chief city was Susa. They had lived there from prehistoric times. Their culture, shared with the Sumerians (see *Babylonians*) in the earliest cities and writing. Their king, Chedorlaomer, joined the attack on cities in the Jordan Valley, and was defeated by Abram. The Elamites were often under the thumb of their western neighbours. The Assyrians sent some of the

An Elamite archer of the Persian royal guard; from the palace at Susa built in the fifth century BC.

citizens of Samaria to Elam and Elamites were sent to Israel to replace them. Elam became part of the Persian kingdom.

Jews from "Elam", the semi-independent kingdom called Elymais in Greek, heard Peter in Jerusalem on the Day of Pentecost.
Genesis 14:1; Ezra 4:9; Isaiah 11:11; 21:2; Jeremiah 25:25; Acts 2:9

ELATH/EZION-GEBER
A settlement (later a town) at the head of the Gulf of Aqaba on the Red Sea. The Israelites camped there on their way from Egypt to Canaan. King Solomon based a Red Sea trading fleet there. King Jehoshaphat later tried to revive this, but his ships were wrecked. The town eventually came under Edomite control.
Numbers 33:35–36; Deuteronomy 2:8; 1 Kings 9:26–27; 22:48; 2 Kings 16:6.

ELEAZAR
The most important of several Eleazars was Aaron's third son. Eleazar's two elder brothers were killed, so he became high priest when Aaron died. He was in charge of the Levites and supervised everything to do with the worship tent (tabernacle).
Exodus 6:23; Leviticus 10; Numbers 3ff.; Joshua 14, etc.

ELECTION
"You did not choose me; I chose you", said Jesus. These words sum up the Bible's teaching on election (choice). Because God is the all-powerful Creator he

is the one who makes the ultimate decisions — not man.

The Old Testament records how God chose people. He chose Abel and not Cain; Isaac and not Ishmael; Jacob and not Esau; Joseph and not his brothers. They were not chosen for their own goodness or greatness. Moses tells the people of Israel, "The Lord did not love you and choose you because you outnumbered other peoples ... But the Lord loved you." "Do not say to yourselves that he brought you in to possess this land because you deserved it." The reason for God's choice is hidden within his own mind and no human being can understand it.

It is clear, however, that those who accept the challenge of God's choice are expected to obey him and give their lives in his service. This was so for Abraham and the people of Israel. It is now true of Christians: "You are the chosen race, the king's priests, the holy nation, God's own people, chosen to proclaim the wonderful acts of God, who called you out of darkness into his own marvellous light."

For God's choice of individuals, see *Call*; see also *Covenant, Grace*.
John 15:16; Deuteronomy 7:7–8; 9:4–5; Romans 9:18–29; 1 Peter 2:9

ELI

A Judge and priest in Israel. Samuel's mother (see *Hannah*) took her son to Eli to be trained in the shrine at Shiloh. Eli's two sons, Hophni and Phinehas, were a disgrace. They would not listen to their father, and God warned Eli of their terrible fate.

Later, they were both killed in a battle against the Philistines and God's Covenant Box (the ark) was captured. When Eli heard the news he collapsed and died.
1 Samuel 1–4

ELIAH
Jesse's eldest son, the brother of David.
1 Samuel 16:6ff.; 17:13, 28

ELIAKIM
The most important man of this name was the son of Hilkiah, King Hezekiah's chief palace official. When King Sennacherib of Assyria threatened to besiege Jerusalem Hezekiah sent Eliakim, along with Shebna and Joah, to hear the Assyrian spokesmen.
2 Kings 18:18ff.; Isaiah 36–37:6

ELIEZER
Abraham's chief servant. Before Abraham had a son, Eliezer was his heir. It was presumably Eliezer who was trusted with the task of going to Mesopotamia to choose a wife for Isaac.
Genesis 15:2; 24

ELIHU
The angry young man in the story of Job who wrongly insisted that the reason for Job's suffering must be Job's own sin.
Job 32–37

ELIJAH

A prophet who lived in Israel during the reign of King Ahab. Ahab and his foreign queen, Jezebel, sinned against God by worshipping Baal and killing God's prophets. Because of this, Elijah was sent to tell Ahab that God was sending a drought. Then Elijah went into hiding by the Brook Cherith, where ravens brought him food. When the brook dried up, he went to Zarephath in Sidon and stayed with a widow and her household. She shared the last of her food with Elijah, but God renewed her supply of flour and oil until the famine was over. When the widow's son died, God answered Elijah's prayer and brought him back to life.

In the third year of the drought Elijah went back to Ahab. The king accused him of causing Israel's troubles. "I'm not the troublemaker," Elijah replied. "You are — you and your father. You are disobeying the Lord's commands and worshipping the idols of Baal." He told Ahab to send the prophets of Baal and Asherah to Mt Carmel. There Elijah challenged them to prove that their god was real. If Baal could set fire to their sacrifice then the people should worship him; but if God sent fire to burn up Elijah's sacrifice, that would prove he was the true God. The prophets of Baal danced, prayed, and cut themselves all day, but nothing happened. When Elijah prayed to God the fire fell and burnt his sacrifice. All the people shouted, "The Lord, he is God." The priests of Baal were killed — and that same day the drought ended.

Jezebel was furious when she heard her prophets had been killed. Elijah ran away south into the desert to save his life. He felt alone and near to despair. But God spoke to him. He told Elijah there was work still to do. He was to anoint a new king and train Elisha to take over his work.

Later, when Ahab had Naboth killed in order to seize his vineyard, Elijah warned the king that God would punish his whole family. Ahab was killed in battle, but God protected Elijah. When his work was finished, God took him to heaven in a chariot of fire.

The prophet Malachi foretold that Elijah would return: much later he appeared with Moses when the disciples saw Jesus' glory (the transfiguration). 1 Kings 17–2 Kings 2; Malachi 4:5–6; Luke 9:28ff.

ELIMELECH
See *Naomi*.

ELISHA
Elisha carried on Elijah's work as God's prophet in Israel for more than fifty years. Before Elijah was taken up into heaven, Elisha asked for the share of his power that would make him Elijah's successor. This request was granted. Elisha worked a number of miracles. He brought the Shunammite woman's son back to life and healed Naaman, the Syrian general, of leprosy. Elisha lived through the reigns of six kings of Israel.
1 Kings 19:16ff.; 2 Kings 2–9; 13:14ff.

ELIZABETH
Wife of Zechariah, the priest. Elizabeth had been unable to have children. But to her joy, in old age she became the mother of John the Baptist. Mary,

Jesus' mother, was a relative of Elizabeth and visited her before the babies were born. Elizabeth knew at once that Mary's child was the long-awaited "Lord" (Messiah).
Luke 1

EMMAUS
A village within 8 miles/13km of Jerusalem. It was probably modern El-Qubeibeh. On the day of his resurrection Jesus appeared to two of his followers who were on their way to Emmaus.
Luke 24:13

ENDOR
A place in northern Israel, near Mt Tabor. King Saul made a secret journey to Endor on the night before his last battle. He wanted to ask the witch (or medium) there to call up the spirit of the dead prophet Samuel, to advise him. Saul and his son Jonathan were killed next day in the disastrous defeat at nearby Mt Gilboa.
1 Samuel 28

ENGEDI
A spring to the west of the Dead Sea where David hid out.
Joshua 15:62; 1 Samuel 23:29, etc

ENOCH
A descendant of Adam's son, Seth. He lived in such close friendship with God that the Bible says he did not die. Instead "God took him away".
Genesis 5:22; Hebrews 11:5

EPAPHRAS

A Christian who founded the church at Colossae. Epaphras visited Paul when he was in prison in Rome and gave him news about the Colossian Christians. As a result Paul wrote his letter to them. Colossians 1:7–8; 4:12; Philemon 23

EPAPHRODITUS

A Christian from the church at Philippi. When Paul was in prison in Rome, members of the Philippian church sent Epaphroditus to Rome with a gift. Philippians 2:25–30; 4:18

EPHESIANS

The letter from Paul to the Ephesians was probably a "circular" to a group of churches in what is now western Turkey. The church at Ephesus — the main city of the whole region — was most important of the group. Paul wrote this letter (as he did Philippians, Colossians and Philemon) from prison — probably in Rome in the early sixties.

The theatre is one of the splendid remains of the major Hellenistic city of Ephesus; here Paul and his companions were taken by the angry mob.

The great theme is "God's plan . . . to bring all creation together, everything in heaven and on earth, with Christ as head" (1:10).

The letter opens up this idea of unity (chapters 1–3). God the Father has chosen his people. Jesus, the Son, has freed them from their sins and broken down the barriers of race, religion and culture. God's Spirit is at work in their lives leading them from strength to strength.

The second part of the letter (chapters 4–6) calls on Christians to live so that their oneness in Christ may be seen in their love for each other. We must come out of the dark, and walk in the light!

Paul uses a series of pictures to illustrate this oneness with Christ: the body, the building, the relationship of husband and wife. Everything in human life and experience is seen in the light of Christ: his love, his death on the cross, his forgiveness and his purity. Paul ends by encouraging Christians to put on the "whole armour of God, ready to do God's will and stand firm against evil".

EPHESUS

The most important city in the Roman province of Asia (western Turkey). Ephesus was a bridgehead between East and West. It stood at the end of one of the great caravan trade routes through Asia, at the mouth of the Cayster River. By Paul's day the harbour was beginning to silt up. But the city was magnificent, with streets paved in marble, baths, libraries, a market-place and theatre seating more than 25,000 people. The temple to Diana at Ephesus was one of the seven wonders of the ancient world, four times the size of the Parthenon at Athens. There had been a settlement at Ephesus since before the twelfth century BC. But by New Testament times the population had grown to something like a third of a million, including a great many Jews.

Ephesus soon became an important centre for the early Christians, too. Paul made a brief visit on his second missionary journey, and his friends Aquila and Prisca stayed on there. On his third journey he spent over two years at Ephesus, and the Christian message spread widely throughout the province. Sales of silver images of Diana began to fall off. People's incomes were threatened and there was a riot.

Paul wrote his letters to Corinth from Ephesus. And some of his letters from prison (Philippians, etc.) may have been written from Ephesus. Timothy stayed behind to help the church when Paul left. Paul later wrote a letter to the Christians at Ephesus. One of the letters to the seven churches in Revelation was also addressed to them.

There is a tradition that Ephesus became the home of the apostle John.
Acts 18:19; 19; 20:17; 1 Corinthians 15:32; 16:8–9; Ephesians 1:1; 1 Timothy 1:3; Revelation 2:1–7

EPHRAIM

The younger of Joseph's two sons, born in Egypt. Ephraim was adopted by Jacob, his grandfather, and received a greater blessing from him than Manasseh, his elder brother. The tribe which descended from

him was an important one. Israel is sometimes called Ephraim by the prophets.
Genesis 41:52; 48

ERASTUS

1. An assistant of Paul who went with Timothy to work in Macedonia (Greece) while Paul stayed on in Asia Minor (Turkey).
Acts 19:22; 2 Timothy 4:20
2. The city treasurer at Corinth. Erastus was a Christian and sent his greetings to the church in Rome.
Romans 16:23

ERECH

One of the great Sumerian cities, in southern Babylonia, about 40 miles/64km north-west of Ur. It is mentioned in Genesis in the list of nations.
Genesis 10:10; Ezra 4:9

ESARHADDON

Son of Sennacherib. He became king of Assyria (680–669 BC) when his father was murdered. Manasseh, king of Judah, was one of many minor kings who were subject to Esarhaddon.
2 Kings 19:37; Ezra 4:2

ESAU

The (elder) twin brother of Jacob, son of Isaac and Rebekah. He became a hunter, and cared so little about the promises of God that one day when he came in hungry Esau "sold" Jacob the rights of the elder son in return for food. When Jacob also gained

Isaac's blessing by a trick, Esau was angry. Afraid of what he might do, Jacob left home. In the years that Jacob was away, Esau settled in the area around Mt Seir and became rich. When they met again Esau greeted his brother warmly and accepted his gift of livestock. Esau went back to Seir and founded the nation of Edom, while Jacob went into Canaan. But there was continued trouble between their descendants.
Genesis 25:21ff.; 27–28:29; 32–33; Hebrews 12:16–17

ESHCOL
A valley near Hebron. The name means "a cluster of grapes". When Moses sent spies into the Promised Land they brought back samples of the fruit of the country, including a huge bunch of grapes from this valley.
Numbers 13:23–24; 32:9; Deuteronomy 1:24

ESHTAOL
A place about 10 miles/16 km west of Jerusalem, on the borders of the land belonging to the tribe of Dan. This was the home district of Samson. Here he grew up, and the Spirit of God first moved him to go out against the Philistines in the lowlands to the west. In spite of Samson's exploits, the Danites never occupied their inheritance.
Joshua 15:33; 19:41; Judges 13:24–25; 16:31; 18

ESSENES
The Essenes were a small and fairly exclusive sect, never numbering more than a few thousand. They

had grown up in the second century BC as a protest movement — against Greek influence on the Jewish religion; against corrupt kings; and against the growing carelessness among Jewish people about keeping the Law. They were even stricter than the Pharisees, whom they denounced as "givers of easy interpretations"! They were so disgusted with Jewish society that many of them opted out of it and went to live in monastic communities.

The community at Qumran, the people who wrote the Dead Sea Scrolls, probably belonged to the Essene movement. See *Dead Sea scrolls*.

ESTHER

A Jewish girl who became queen of Persia. Esther was an orphan brought up in Susa, capital of Persia, by her cousin Mordecai. After King Ahasuerus (Greek Xerxes) had divorced Vashti he chose Esther as his new queen. Esther kept secret the fact that she was a Jewess. When Haman, the king's chief minister, planned to wipe out all the Jews because he so hated Mordecai, Esther pleaded with the king and uncovered the plot. Instead of being destroyed, the Jews were allowed to kill all their enemies. This event is remembered at the annual Feast of Purim.

The book of Esther records this story and shows how, once again, the Jewish nation was saved from being destroyed.

ETHIOPIA

This is Sudan, not modern Ethiopia, and is called Cush in many translations of the Old Testament. See *Cush*.

EUCHARIST
See *Lord's Supper*.

EUNICE
Mother of Timothy.
Acts 16:1; 2 Timothy 1:5

EUPHRATES
In the Old Testament this great river is often referred to simply as "the river". It is 1,200 miles/1,931km long. It rises in eastern Turkey and flows south east to the Persian Gulf. Its course through the Babylonian plains has moved west, leaving many of the ancient cities which once stood on its banks now 3–4 miles/5–6km to the east. The route to Syria followed the Euphrates north to Carchemish, then turned south towards Damascus, Israel and Egypt. The Euphrates is mentioned as one of the four rivers of Eden.
Genesis 2:14; 15:18; etc; Revelation 9:14; 16:12

EUTYCHUS
A young man who went to hear Paul preach in Troas. It was late and Eutychus went so sound asleep that he fell to his death from the third-floor window where he was sitting. Paul went down and brought him back to life.
Acts 20:7–13

EVE
The first woman, and companion to Adam. She and Adam disobeyed God's command not to eat the fruit of the "tree that gives knowledge". Because of this,

death came into the world and God sent them out of the Garden of Eden. Genesis names three sons of Eve: Cain, Abel and Seth.
Genesis 2:18–4:2; 4:25

EVIL-MERODACH
King of Babylon 562–560 BC. When he came to the throne he released King Jehoiachin of Judah from prison in Babylon.
2 Kings 25:27–30; Jeremiah 52:31–34

EXILE
The Jewish exile began in 597 BC when the Babylonians first took thousands of Jews captive to Babylon. Ten years later they destroyed Jerusalem completely and the kingdom of Judah ceased to exist. The Jewish people were exiles in a foreign country.
Israel They had long been warned that this would happen. Even before the people entered Canaan Moses told them that if they did not listen to God and keep his laws they would lose their land. For 200 years before Jerusalem fell, the prophets had been repeating the warning. In the eighth century BC Amos and Hosea told the northern kingdom of Israel how they would suffer if they did not keep their promise to obey God. They ignored the warning, and in 721 BC the Assyrians captured Samaria, their capital city. The people were deported and scattered in other provinces of the empire. Foreigners were settled in the land and it became the Assyrian province of Samaria. The ten tribes of Israel were never heard of again.

Deuteronomy 8:19–20; 2 Kings 17; Amos 2–9; Hosea 9

Judah In the south Judah, too, was threatened by the Assyrians. The Assyrian King Sennacherib took many Judean cities and besieged Jerusalem. But King Hezekiah trusted God and obeyed God's laws. He listened to the prophet Isaiah's messages from God. When the Assyrians called on him to surrender he turned to God for help and God saved them from defeat.

The people of Judah learned only half the lesson. The idea grew that Jerusalem, the city of God, was unconquerable. With the city and the temple they were safe from any enemy. It did not matter what they did. For a time they were safe because they paid tribute to the Assyrians who were fighting other enemies, and at the end of the seventh century BC that empire broke up.

But a new danger loomed — from Babylon. In the reign of King Josiah, the prophet Jeremiah began to warn the people of Judah. Only if they gave up their selfish ways and obeyed God would they be safe. But no one listened.

In 604 BC the Babylonians took control of Syria and the land to the south. King Jehoiakim of Judah was one of the kings who had to pay tribute to them. The Babylonian King Nebuchadnezzar also took hostages back to Babylon. Before long King Jehoiakim thought he would be better off on the side of the Egyptians, and he rebelled against Babylon. He died before the Babylonians reached Jerusalem. After a short siege the new king, his son Jehoiachin, surrendered, on 16 March 597 BC. Nebuchadnezzar stripped Jerusalem of its treasures and took the king and many leading citizens to Babylon. The exile had begun.

Isaiah 36–37; Jeremiah 7; Daniel 1

The fall of Jerusalem   Nebuchadnezzar left Zedekiah, the king's uncle, as a vassal king in Judah. Jeremiah told the people again and again that to be safe they must accept Babylonian rule. But false prophets said Babylon would soon fall and encouraged Zedekiah to rebel. Quickly the Babylonians marched against Judah and again besieged Jerusalem. Other cities fell until only Jerusalem was left. It held out for eighteen months. Food supplies were used up and people were starving when Nebuchadnezzar's army broke through the walls in the summer of 587 BC. Zedekiah tried to escape by night but was captured. The Babylonians looted the city and left it and the temple a burnt-out ruin. Many important men from Jerusalem were executed. Other survivors were taken to Babylon to join the earlier exiles.

A city under siege, with a battering-ram against its walls, and refugees with their possessions leaving in carts drawn by oxen, is depicted on this Assyrian relief.

Very little remained of the kingdom of Judah. Settlers from Edom were already taking over the land south of Hebron and Beth-zur. Nebuchadnezzar appointed a governor, Gedaliah, to rule the rest of the country in the name of Babylon. The Book of Lamentations describes the horror of it all. The cities were in ruins. Apart from the thousands exiled to Babylon many people had died in the fighting. Many more died of starvation and disease in the siege. Now few remained to farm the land the invaders had ruined.

Gedaliah made his headquarters at Mizpah and tried to rule well. But some still refused to accept the Babylonian rulers. They plotted against Gedaliah and murdered him. His supporters were afraid and fled to Egypt, taking the prophet Jeremiah with them. The Babylonians carried off still more of the people in 582 BC, and joined the land to the province of Samaria.

Jeremiah 27–28; Lamentations; 2 Kings 25:22–26; Jeremiah 40–43

The exiles In Babylon the Jews lived in their own settlements in the capital and other towns. They were free to build houses, earn a living and keep their own customs and religion. They could not go back home but they were not ill-treated. King Jehoiachin and his family were "guests" in the king's household. Some Jews, like Daniel, rose to high positions in government service. Skilled Jewish craftsmen were among the workmen Nebuchadnezzar employed. Many became so much at home in Babylon that when the opportunity came to rebuild Jerusalem they did not want to go. But some Jews longed to return to Judah and in exile they clung to their religion and their way of life.

Ever since Solomon had built the temple it had been the centre of Jewish faith and worship. Now it was gone. There was nowhere to offer the temple sacrifices. So the people began to lay new stress on those parts of their religion that they could observe. Keeping the day of rest, the sabbath, became very important. So also did circumcision, the sign of God's covenant with them, and the laws about what was clean and unclean. And they began to value the written records of God's message as never before. Some of the priests, such as Ezra, began to study the law of God in every detail (they were called "scribes"). Many of the books that make up our Old Testament were given their present form during the time of the exile.

Return from exile   In 539 BC, nearly fifty years after King Nebuchadnezzar of Babylon had captured Jerusalem, Cyrus king of Persia conquered Babylon. The Babylonian Empire passed to the Persians. They put a Persian governor (a satrap) in control of each province of their new empire. But they gave the people of these provinces much more say in their own affairs. They were encouraged to keep their own customs and religion — and nations exiled by the Babylonians, including the Jews, were allowed to go back home if they wanted to.

In 538 BC Cyrus issued a decree saying that the Jews could "go to Jerusalem and rebuild the Temple of the Lord, the God of Israel". They were to be given money and all the supplies they needed. Cyrus gave them back the gold and silver bowls and other things that Nebuchadnezzar had taken from the temple. The first party of exiles made the long journey back home.

EXODUS

The word Exodus means a "going out". The Book of Exodus tells how the people of Israel left Egypt, where they had been slaves, and how they emerged as a nation. They are set free and given hope for the future.

The book centres on Moses, the great champion of Israel. He is called by God to lead the people of Israel out of Egypt.

Exodus falls into three parts.

Chapters 1–19: the Hebrew people are freed from slavery in Egypt. Moses leads them through the desert to Mt Sinai.

Chapters 20–24: God makes a binding agreement with his people at Sinai. He gives them rules which they must live by, both while in the desert and when they reach the Promised Land. These rules are summed up in the Ten Commandments in chapter 20. God's laws affect the whole of life: how people behave towards one another; how they are to live together, and how they must behave towards God himself.

Chapters 25–40: God instructs the people of Israel to build and furnish a movable tent (the tabernacle) where they can worship him. Laws are drawn up for the priests and for the worship of God.

The Exodus The "going out" of Egypt, the exodus, was the key event in the history of Old Testament Israel. All future generations were to look back to it. Annual religious festivals commemorated it. Parents were to make sure their children learned what it meant. Through Moses God led the Hebrew slaves out of Egypt and began to make them into the nation of Israel. The date was probably early in the thirteenth century BC, about the time when Ramesses II was pharaoh of Egypt.

When Moses first asked the Pharaoh to free the Hebrew slaves, his reply was not encouraging. Pharaoh was not moved by the signs Moses did or by anything his brother Aaron could say. He immediately tightened his grip on the discontented workers. But then God took direct action. In the course of some eight or nine months ten disasters (the "plagues") struck the country. Some of these troubles had been experienced before in Egypt, but not all, and never one after the other in such a short space of time.

The plagues Under God's direction Moses warned Pharaoh when each disaster was going to strike — and at the expected time it happened. Some came to an end when Moses prayed. Several times the Hebrews living in the Nile Delta region escaped, so that when Egyptian cattle died of disease the Hebrew slaves lost none of their animals. When hail destroyed crops and herds alike, when it stayed dark for three long days, again the people of Israel were not affected.

In all this, too, the Egyptians saw their gods defeated. When the God of the Hebrews took action the Nile-god, for example, who should have made the land fertile, brought only ruin. Even the powerful sun-god Ré was overwhelmed in unnatural darkness. The king's magicians could do nothing about it. Nine plagues came and went: the Nile water was polluted; then came frogs, gnats and flies; animals died; the people had boils; hail was followed by locusts, and after that a terrible darkness.

But it was the tenth "plague" that gained Israel's freedom, and this was something different. "All through Egypt," Moses announced, "on a certain night, the firstborn sons in every household will die." The firstborn sons of the Hebrews would be safe if the people carefully followed the instructions Moses gave them. They must mark their doorposts with the blood of a lamb killed in sacrifice. They must cook that lamb (again as instructed) and eat it that night, with bitter herbs and bread made without yeast. They must pack their belongings and get dressed, ready for a journey. It all happened as God said.

Every year afterwards the people of Israel kept the anniversary of this event as the Festival of the Passover: for after this (when death "passed over" the families of Israel) Pharaoh let them go.

At midnight the firstborn died. Before morning the king ordered the Hebrews out of his country. With gifts of gold and jewellery from their neighbours — and anything else they asked for — the Hebrews began to move. But their troubles were not yet over. As the long, straggling line of families with their goods and cattle began the slow journey eastwards, Pharaoh summoned his charioteers and set out to bring them back. He sighted the runaway slaves camped by the sea, at a point the Old Testament calls "the Sea of Reeds". It was probably a part of Lake Menzaleh near present-day El Qantara on the Suez Canal. The sea blocked the way of escape. They were trapped between it and an armed, fast-moving enemy.

Again God intervened. He opened a path for them across the sea. When the Egyptians tried to follow, the waters returned and drowned them. The people of Israel were safe on the other side.
Exodus 5–15

The commandments at Mt Sinai With no more to fear from the Egyptians, the refugees turned south-east towards Sinai and the planned meeting with God. After travelling for nearly three months they camped before Mt Sinai, one of the mountain peaks in the south of the Sinai peninsula. There, in an awe-inspiring setting, God completed what he had begun when he rescued the people from Egypt. He made his agreement (covenant) with them. He formally declared that the rabble of ex-slaves were his people, the nation of Israel.

For their part they must listen to him and obey his laws, summed up in the Ten Commandments which he gave to Moses on two stone tablets. They set out the basic principles that would govern the people's

An Egyptian pharaoh stands in his chariot, firing arrows at the enemy.

lives. Their promise to obey was confirmed in a solemn ceremony under the shadow of the mountain. Animal sacrifices were offered and the blood was sprinkled on the people and on the altar. So the agreement was sealed. God then told them how to build a special tent (the tabernacle) that would be the sign of his presence with them all the rest of their journey.

They spent almost a year at Sinai. Then they turned north to go through the Wilderness of Paran until they came to Kadesh-barnea. There they camped on the southern borders of Canaan.

There were problems all the way. Very soon after they left Egypt their food supplies began to run out and it was obvious that the desert scrub land could not supply them. More than once they had no water because there was no oasis anywhere near, or because the spring they found was polluted. Each time the people turned on Moses and blamed him and Aaron for leading them to their deaths. Soon, too, they looked back at the slave-ghetto in Egypt through a rosy glow — "At least we had plenty to eat there"! Yet each time God met their need. He fed them with "bread from heaven" (manna) every day throughout the long years until they came to Canaan, and he supplied water even in unlikely places.

Exodus 16–40; Numbers; Deuteronomy

On the borders of Canaan At Kadesh-barnea the people's grumbling had serious results. Spies were sent into Canaan and they came back with reports of the great and powerful people who lived there. When they heard this the frightened Israelites rebelled. Moses' life was threatened and some began calling for a leader to take them back to Egypt. The trouble was eventually overcome. But they had to spend another thirty-eight years of aimless wandering in the desert — until the people who were afraid to go on into Canaan had died. Only then did the nation again come in sight of their Promised Land.

They made their way through the wilderness of Zin, bypassing the country of Edom. They defeated other kings who would not let them pass and finally camped opposite Jericho ready to cross the River Jordan into the land God had promised to give them. Moses, on the point of death, appointed his assistant, Joshua, as the people's new leader. "There has never been a prophet in Israel like Moses; the Lord spoke with him face to face. No other prophet has ever done miracles and wonders like those that the Lord sent Moses to perform against the king of Egypt." The people mourned his death.
Deuteronomy

EZEKIEL
One of the great Old Testament prophets. Ezekiel was the son of a priest called Buzi and lived in Jerusalem until Nebuchadnezzar invaded the city in 597 BC. Along with King Jehoiachin and other important citizens he was taken captive to Babylon. There he was allowed to have his own house and lived in a settlement of Jewish exiles at Talabib on the River Chebar. After about four years he was called by God to be a prophet. Until Jerusalem was completely destroyed in 586 BC his main message was a call to repentance. The Jews had disobeyed

God and must seek forgiveness. After the Babylonians had overthrown Jerusalem Ezekiel looked forward to the day when God would allow the Jews to rebuild the city and God's temple.

The book   Ezekiel was called to be a prophet at the age of thirty. He gave God's message both to the exiles in Babylonia and to his people still living in far-off Jerusalem. When his call came to be a prophet he was also given a vivid vision of the holiness of God (chapters 1–3). This affected his whole life.

Chapters 4–24 consist of warnings to Israel of God's judgement. Jerusalem will be destroyed.

Ezekiel also brought a message of God's judgement on the nations who were threatening his people (chapters 25–32).

When Jerusalem finally fell in 587 BC Ezekiel's message took on a new note (chapters 33–39). He brought comfort to the people, and a promise of hope for the future. God would restore his people.

Finally Ezekiel described his visions of the time to come, when God's people would offer his perfect worship in a new temple (chapters 40–48).

Ezekiel underlined that each individual has a responsibility towards God. He stressed the need for people to be made new from the heart. He was a dedicated prophet. Holiness is his constant theme. He gives his message in pictures, much more than most other prophets.

EZION-GEBER
See *Elath*.

EZRA

A priest and teacher of the Law at the time of the exile. Ezra was given permission by King Artaxerxes to lead a large group of Jewish exiles back from Babylon to Jerusalem. The temple had been rebuilt, but when Ezra arrived he was distressed to find that the people no longer obeyed God's laws, even after all that had happened. Many Jews, including priests, had married women from nations that did not worship God. Ezra put an end to these mixed marriages. He taught the people God's laws and they turned to God again with new joy.
Ezra 7–10; Nehemiah 8–9

BOOK OF EZRA

The Book of Ezra follows directly on from Chronicles. It describes the return of some of the Jews from exile in Babylon. They brought back life and worship to Jerusalem. The account covers roughly the years 538–433 BC. Some of the book may consist of the leader Ezra's own writings.

The return to Jerusalem is presented in three stages:

Chapters 1–2: the first party returns, with Zerubbabel, on the orders of Cyrus, emperor of Persia.

Chapters 3–6: the temple is rebuilt and worship at Jerusalem begins again, despite local opposition.

Chapters 7–10: Ezra leads another group back to Jerusalem. He helps restore the religion and way of life of Israel.

FAIR HAVENS

A small port on the south coast of Crete. Paul's ship called in at Fair Havens on the voyage to Rome. Here Paul conferred with the centurion Julius and the owner and captain of the ship, who wanted to reach a more attractive harbour in which to spend the winter. In spite of Paul's advice they put out to sea, and were caught in the violent wind which drove them to shipwreck on Malta.
Acts 27:8–12

FAITH

Paul carefully explains in his letters to the Christians in both Rome and Galatia that a person can find a right relationship with God, not through his own good deeds (as people often think), but only through faith or believing.

"Faith" means having confidence and trust in God. It is not a "leap in the dark" which a man must take without thinking. It is trust in a God whom we believe to be trustworthy. Confident in this knowledge, a person can believe and entrust his life to Jesus Christ. As sinful people we can do absolutely nothing to save ourselves. We have to depend totally on what God has already done for us through Jesus.

This is the start of a "life of faith". No one can be certain of living aright by his own efforts. We need to continue to trust wholly in Jesus and the Spirit he gives to help us live in a way that pleases God. This life of dependence on God goes right back to the beginning of God's dealings with man, as Paul shows when he traces it back to Abraham.

The New Testament also refers to "the faith", meaning the basic teaching about Jesus on which our trust is grounded.

1 John 5:1–5; John 1:12; 3:16; 5:24; Romans 1:17; 5:1; 10:9–10; Galatians 3; Ephesians 2:8–9. See also Genesis 15:6; Psalm 37:3–9; Proverbs 3:5–6; Jeremiah 17:7–8; Habakkuk 2:4; Hebrews 11; James 2; 1 Timothy 3:9; 5:8

FALL

Sin is present in the world because mankind has rebelled against God. There has never been a person (except Jesus) who was not a sinner. The Bible traces this back to the very beginning of history. The story of Adam and Eve depicts the dramatic "fall" of men and women from the high place they once had as friends of God and the crown of his creation.

Adam and Eve originally lived in full and open fellowship with God and each other. There was no sin to spoil their lives. This was how God meant it to be. But in Genesis 3 we learn that all this changed drastically. The couple listened to the serpent and decided to rebel against God by doing what he had forbidden. As a result of this disobedience Adam and Eve were banished from God's presence. They were told that from then on life would be hard work. They would know sorrow, and life would end in death.

Since the fall of Adam and Eve the whole creation

has been affected by their rebellion against God. "Sin came into the world through one man, and his sin brought death with it. As a result, death has spread to the whole human race because everyone has sinned."

Every part of the universe is affected by sin — both people and the natural world in which we live. Although we still have much of the original nature God gave us, and we still know and search for God, yet we have an inbuilt bias towards sin.

See also *Death, Judgement*.
Genesis 1–3; Romans 1:18–32; 5:12–19; 7:14–25

FAMILY LIFE

The "family" of Abraham's time was what those of us who live in small family units would call the "extended family". It consisted not just of parents and children, but grandparents, aunts, uncles and cousins — and servants, too. It could be very large. Abraham was able to take 318 fighting men with him when he went to rescue Lot from the raiding kings who had taken him prisoner (Genesis 14:14).

In this kind of family group the grandfather had complete authority, not just in practical matters but in religious ones, too. When he died, his eldest son took over by right of birth. The leader's word was law. Abraham's family clan accepted the fact that God had made himself known to Abraham in the silence of the desert. His God was their God, even though they did not always share the kind of faith he had.

God had made a promise to Abraham. He made the same promise again to Isaac and to Jacob. He would be their God, caring for them and protecting them. In return they must live by his rules. Those rules were spelt out in detail to a later generation, when God gave the "commandments" to Moses at Mt Sinai. So, from the very beginning, ordinary life in Israel was bound up with religious life. The two were one and could not be separated. Everything the family did was based on God's law. If they treated one another badly, they broke God's law. Things had to be put right between them, and a sacrifice was needed to put them right with God (Leviticus 6:1–6).

Parents and children   Religion and family life were woven together in the way parents brought up their children. Children were encouraged to ask questions and find out about their religion and history (Exodus 13:14). Places where God had done something special for his people were marked with large stones. When the children asked what they were for, the parents would explain (Joshua 4:5–7).

The regular weekly rest-day (the sabbath) was intended also to be a day when God could be remembered and worshipped (Exodus 31:15–17). In early Old Testament times parents and children would

The inside of a simple peasant house, with women grinding corn and spinning.

visit the local shrine. There they would offer a sacrifice and the priest would teach them. In New Testament times the sabbath day began on the Friday evening with the best meal of the week. Then came a visit to the meeting-house ("synagogue") to hear the law explained by the teacher.

Parents taught their children the laws of God. They also learned by heart other parts of the Bible. David's great poem on the death of Saul and Jonathan was a favourite. In the evenings, members of the family recited many of the stories now written down in the Bible.

Festivals The meaning of the great religious festivals was clearly shown by special ceremonies. At Passover, for example, the eldest child was asked by the father, "Why do we have this service?" And the child explained how it had come about, as he had been taught. There was the Day of Atonement, followed by the Harvest Festival (Tabernacles), when everyone lived in tents made of branches to remind them of the way their ancestors lived in the desert. Later in Israel's history the children acted the story of Esther at the Festival of Purim. All the festivals were so full of life and action that children wanted to know what they were about. In this way they learned the history of their nation as the people of God.

Teaching There were no schools as such in Old Testament times. The children were taught at home, first by their mother, then by their father. In addition to religion and history, which was learned through stories and by question and answer, and memorized, the girls learnt homemaking skills —

baking, spinning, weaving — from their mother, while the boys learned a manual trade from their father. The Jews had a saying "He who does not teach his son a useful trade, is bringing him up to be a thief". The father's work, tools and (in later Old Testament times) fellow members of his trade guild, were all important for a boy's education. (See *Education*.)

Land and animals Everyone owned some land so both boys and girls had outdoor work to do. There was always plenty to do in looking after the vines, ploughing and threshing.

The children also looked after any animals the family kept — usually sheep and goats. Every family, even the poorest, hoped to be able to buy two lambs at Passover time. One was killed and eaten, but the other became a playmate for the children, giving its wool for their clothing. In a poor home there was no separate shed for the animals, and the lamb often slept with the children and fed from the same dishes (2 Samuel 12:3). At the end of summer it was killed and the meat was preserved in the fat from the sheep's tail. Most families would also have at least one goat which was kept for milk. Some of the milk was allowed to go sour to produce goats' milk cheese.

Although some households had dogs they were not common and were regarded as scavengers.

The donkey (ass) was the most common form of transport. It could carry heavy loads as well as people. Richer farmers used oxen for farm work and camels for transport.

Nomads and settlers In the early days of the Old

Testament — before the years in Egypt — the people lived in tents. Abraham left a settled, civilized city life in Ur on the far-off River Euphrates to obey God's call. For the rest of his life he was, at least from time to time, on the move. His son Isaac and grandson Jacob also lived in tents — like the Bedouin today. Water was scarce, particularly in the summer or during a time of drought, and the people who lived in Canaan defended their wells against these wanderers, who took water not only for themselves, but for their animals as well. The dispute between Abraham and Abimelech over the well at Beersheba is one example (Genesis 21:25–31).

Although they had no permanent home, Abraham and his family were settled enough to grow crops. And they never moved far from the big centres of population. After the time of Moses the people of Israel wanted to settle more permanently, and then for some years there was war. When the Israelites had won their land, other groups of nomads wanted to settle there too. So the Israelites in their turn had to learn to deal kindly with these landless strangers, who soon came to form the working class of the population.

The pattern of each day did not vary much. The basic pattern of family life changed little over many centuries. It was interrupted now and then by invading armies, but otherwise peaceful. The people lived close to the land. Each family looked after its own small farm. There were always some animals to care for. Then there was the daily cleaning, baking, spinning, weaving and dyeing, as well as the work of the farm itself.

Family relationships Family life grew more important during the course of Israel's history. When the clans began to settle in permanent homes the normal family unit became smaller.

The father Within this smaller unit, as before, the father had complete authority. He could, if he wished, even sell his daughter into slavery. In early Old Testament days it was possible for a father to have disobedient children put to death. He could divorce his wife without any reason and without providing for her. And he could arrange the marriages of his sons.

Women The woman was *owned* by her husband, and looked up to him as her master. This attitude was still found even in New Testament times. Though women did much of the hard work, they had a low position both in society and in the family. But the law did protect a divorced woman, and her children were taught to respect her.

Jesus' dealings with women — for example, his readiness to speak to and help the Samaritan woman (see John 4) — contrast strongly with prevailing attitudes. And Christian teaching is clear: "There is no difference . . . between men and women: you are all one in union with Christ Jesus" (Galatians 3:28). There are no second-class citizens in Christ's kingdom.

Inheritance Normally only sons could inherit — and the eldest son in a family had a special position. He had the right to a double share of his father's property. Only if there were no sons could daughters inherit. If there were no children at all, the property passed to the closest male relative.

Respect and discipline The Book of Proverbs speaks of family relationships more freely and directly than any other Bible book. For their own good, children were expected to respect their parents and pay attention to their teaching and advice. Parents who really love their children will discipline and correct them, especially when they are young. "A good spanking will teach them how to behave." "If a child has his own way, he will make his mother ashamed of him." The happiness of parents and children are bound up with one another. And reverence for God is the starting-point.

The New Testament builds on the same foundation. It is the Christian duty of children to obey their parents, and of parents to bring their children up with Christian discipline and teaching.

Some Bible passages on family relationships: Exodus 20:12; 21:7–11; Deuteronomy 21:15–21; 24:1–4 (compare with Matthew 19:8–12)

The teaching in Proverbs on parents and children: 1:8–9; 4 and 5; 6:20ff.; 10:1; 13:1; 24; 17:21, 25; 19:13, 18, 27; 20:11; 22:6, 15; 23:13–16, 19–28; 28:7, 24; 29:15, 17; 30:11, 17

In the New Testament see especially: Ephesians 5:21–33; 6:1–4; Colossians 3:18–21

Worship in the home At home every Jew was expected to pray the "Eighteen Benedictions" every morning, afternoon and evening. Each benediction begins, "Blessed art thou, O Lord, king of the universe". They all praise God — for the promise of a redeemer, or the resurrection of the dead, or the gift of repentance, or healing the sick, and so on.

Before every meal the father of the household said

a blessing: "Blessed art thou, our God, king of the universe, who createst the fruit of the vine" (or, "who bringest forth food from the earth"; or, "who createst the fruit of the tree").

A new baby "Children are a gift from the Lord; they are a real blessing.

The sons of a man when he is young are like arrows in a soldier's hand. Happy is the man who has many such arrows."

These words from Psalm 127 show how the people of Israel felt about children. A big family was a sign of God's blessing. If no children came, people thought God must be displeased — and this could be very hard on a couple who had no children (see for example the story of Hannah in 1 Samuel).

Children were important for a number of reasons. Boys were the most valued. It was so important to have a son that the woman's name was changed to "Mother of . . ." when her first son was born. As they grew up boys were able to help work the family's land. Girls were much less important, but still useful workers. A wedding-gift had to be paid to the parents to make up for the loss of the daughter's work when she left to be married. Sons were also needed to carry on the family name. In the earliest times, before people were sure that there was a life after death, they liked to think they would live on through their children, so without children there was no future. This was why, if a man died without a child, it was the duty of his closest relative to marry the wife. Their first son would then take the dead man's name and inherit his land (the "Levirate law" — Deuteronomy 25:5–6).

Family life

Customs   The new-born baby was washed and rubbed over with salt (it was thought this made the skin firm). Then it was wrapped in "swaddling cloths". The mother or her helper placed the baby on a square of cloth. Then she folded the corners over its sides and feet, and wrapped bandages (often embroidered) round the whole bundle to keep the baby's arms straight by its sides. The bandages were loosened several times a day and the skin was rubbed with olive oil and dusted with powdered myrtle leaves. This went on for several months. The wrappings made it easy for the mother to carry her baby in a woollen "cradle" on her back. At night the cradle was hung from a beam in the house, or between two forked sticks.

Babies were normally breast-fed for two or three years. But there was a very high death-rate amongst babies because of the poor conditions in most houses.

In Old Testament times the baby was named when it was born. The name always had a meaning. It might say something about how the baby was born, his character, or the family's feelings towards God. For example, Jacob's wife, Rachel, who had waited so long for her first son, called him Joseph — "may God add sons". The name Barak means "lightning"; Elijah means "the Lord is God"; Isaiah means "God is salvation".

Ceremonies   In New Testament times a baby boy was not named until the eighth day after birth. At the same time he was "circumcised" (the loose skin was cut off the top of his penis). In many other nations boys were circumcised when they were recognised as adult members of the clan. But as far back as the days of Abraham God had made circumcision on the eighth day after birth the physical sign of the promise he had made to Abraham and his descendants for all time. This ceremony reminded them that every child in Israel was one of God's own people. Sadly, the real meaning of the ceremony was often forgotten, and by the time of the exile to Babylon it was looked on simply as a sign of being a Jew.

Two other ceremonies sometimes took place at the same time. If the baby was the "firstborn" in the family he belonged to God in a special way and had to be bought back (redeemed). This was because at the time of the exodus, when all the firstborn children of the Egyptians had died, God saved the firstborn sons of Israel. From then on the firstborn belonged to him. "You must buy back every first-born male child of yours." "This observance will be a reminder . . . it will remind us that the Lord brought us out of Egypt by his great power" (Exodus 13:13ff.). The first generation after the exodus were redeemed by dedicating the Levites for God's service. After that each family paid five pieces of silver to the priest to buy back their firstborn.

The other ceremony was a sacrifice made by the mother for her "purification" (see Leviticus 12). According to the law of Moses a person had to be ritually "clean" to worship God. Certain things, — contact with a dead body, for example, or having a baby, or eating forbidden foods which might carry disease — barred people for a time from joining in worship. To be "clean" again the mother had to sacrifice first a pigeon and then a lamb. If, like Jesus' parents, Joseph and Mary, they were too poor to afford a lamb, they could offer a second pigeon instead. In New Testament times money was put into the offering boxes of the temple to pay for the sacrifices, and the women gathered on the steps near the altar for the ceremony.

In New Testament times, too, a boy became a man on his thirteenth birthday. This was marked by a special service called the Bar Mitzvah ("son of the law"). In the months before his birthday he learned to read the passages from the Old Testament Law and Prophets that were to be read in the synagogue that day. He had to recite them at the service. The minister ("rabbi") then spoke to the boy and asked God's blessing on him in the beautiful words of Numbers 6:24–26:

"May the Lord bless you and take care of you;
May the Lord be kind and gracious to you;
May the Lord look on you with favour and give you peace."

The boy was now a grown-up member of the community. Sometimes his parents took him to watch a service like this the year before his own thirteenth birthday.

FARMING

In the main, the people of Palestine have always been farmers, although the nature of the soil, the climate, and other factors made farming a life of constant toil and hardship. A large part of the land was desert and rock, and could not be farmed. When the Israelites first settled in the Promised Land each household was given a plot of land and also, perhaps, grazing rights on land held in common. But, as time passed, those who were well off tried to "buy out" the small farmers (see Isaiah 5:8), and it was a constant struggle for poor people to hold on to their land.

A typical Israelite farmer did not live on his farm but in a nearby village or town, which was often close to a fortified city. It was important to be within reach of water supply and protection, in case of enemy invasions. He owned no more land than he and his family could manage by themselves, perhaps with the help of a few servants or hired labourers. Everyone in the farmer's family shared in the work. He might grow arable crops, as well as grapes and olives. He might possess a few sheep and goats, with one of his sons or a hired shepherd to care for them. Or a farmer might decide to specialize.

The farmer had four main problems: drought; strong winds from the east (the "sirocco") which could take away his dry soil; locust plagues; and invading armies.

A farmer using a simple plough: a wooden stake with a metal tip at the bottom.

Farming

The main crops were grain, grapes (for wine) and olives (for oil). These three are mentioned together over and over again in the Bible (for example, Deuteronomy 7:13; Nehemiah 5:11; Hosea 2:8). But this list of crops can be expanded.

Grain In the few fertile valleys, the Philistine plain, the Jordan Valley, and the Plain of Jezreel, a valuable crop of wheat was grown. Barley was grown more widely, as it needed a shorter growing season and flourished on poorer soil. Spelt and millet were also grown. Bread was the basic item of diet for everyone, and every available valley and lowland area was used for these crops. The many rocks and stones lying about were built into terraces on the hillsides to keep the precious soil from being lost.

Vegetables There were small harvests of vegetables — lentils, peas, beans, onions, cucumbers, garlic and herbs. These were grown near the house or between the vines.

Fruit Wine and raisin cakes were made from grapes. Other fruits included melons, figs, dates, pomegranates and nuts. Many of these provided a useful source of water during the six-month summer drought from May to October. The oil from olives was used for cooking, lighting, medicine and washing. Vines and olives grew on the hillsides.

Flax Some flax was grown for making linen cloth.

The farmer's year Some time ago a limestone plaque was discovered dating from about the time of King Solomon, on which was written a kind of schoolboy rhyme. It is called the Gezer calendar.

The two months are (olive) harvest
The two months are planting (grain)

The two months are late planting
The month is hoeing up of flax
The month is harvest of barley
The month is harvest and feasting
The two months are vine tending
The month is summer fruit

Here is the farmer's year at a glance.

Olive harvest From September or October to November there was time for the olives to be picked and pressed for oil. Olive-trees can stand long periods of drought and can grow in very shallow soil. They take two years to mature and, because the fruit ripens slowly, the farmer could pick them whenever he had time. They were carried in baskets to the vats and, in earlier times, the oil was squeezed out by treading, or pounding with a pestle. Later, a mill-stone was developed. The olives were placed on a grooved stone wheel, and another stone was turned over them, worked by a beam. The pulp was then pressed under weights.

Large olive presses have been found from the time of David, consisting of a beam which would press on the baskets of olives. The upper end had weights attached, while the lower end was fixed in a hole in the wall. The oil ran into stone vats, where it was left for some time to settle and clear.

Ploughing and planting In October/November came the precious "early rain" after the long summer drought. From then till January was the time for ploughing and planting. The plough was usually a simple wooden stake with a handle and a point of iron (bronze before the time of David). It was attached to a yoke, and drawn by one or two oxen.

The farmer could hold the plough with one hand while the other held a stick for beating the oxen. Since it was light the plough could easily be lifted over any large stones. It left a furrow 3–4ins/80–100cms deep. The seed (wheat, barley, flax) was scattered by hand and then the plough was sometimes used again to cover the seed with earth. Occasionally branches were dragged along to smooth the ground, and a hoe used to remove weeds.

Late planting From January to March the winter rains fell and planting continued — millet, peas, lentils, melons and cucumbers.

Flax and grain harvests In March and April the later rains came. These developed the grain to the point where harvesting could begin.

Flax was harvested first, in March and April. The plant was cut with a hoe near to the ground and the stalks were dried, ready to be made into cord and linen cloth.

Then in April, May and June came the harvests of barley and wheat. The stalks were cut with sickles (a small wooden handle with a curved iron or copper blade) and the bundles were tied into sheaves. These were loaded on to donkeys or carts and taken to the "threshing-floor". This seems to have been common property and a centre of village life at this time of year. It was usually a rocky outcrop, or clay-covered patch, in a windy spot outside the village. Stones were put around the edge and the sheaves were spread out on the floor about a foot deep.

Threshing was done by beating with a stick, or by driving animals round, or by using a threshing-sledge. This was simply a board, or a board on wheels, with bits of stone or iron fixed to it. The stalks were chopped and the grain loosened.

The farmer would then "winnow", tossing the stalks in the air with a wooden fork or shovel. The straw was blown aside (and in winter used to feed the animals), but the heavy grain fell back on the floor. This was probably then sifted and stored in large earthen-ware jars, in dry cisterns (silos) dug in the floor, or in "barns". There seem to have been large national silos, and the farmer probably paid his "income tax" (and debts) in grain at this time.

Vines In June, July and August the vines were pruned and tidied up. Isaiah 5 and Mark 12 provide pictures of how a new vineyard was prepared. A boundary trench was dug, and posts driven in to support a hedge or fence. The young vines were planted in rows and the branches raised up on supports. Then the pruning was done. When the fruit began to form, a shelter of branches or a stone tower was put up, and the household kept watch against thieves, or raiding foxes or jackals.

Fruit harvest In August and September the summer fruits were harvested — figs, sycomore figs, pomegranates and grapes. Baskets of grapes were taken to small vats, whose floors sloped towards jars. The grapes were trodden to squeeze out the juice. Great numbers of these vats have been found in the "Shephelah" (the foothills of Judah).

The picking and the treading of the grapes was all done in holiday mood. The fruit could be eaten at the same time. "When you walk along a path in someone else's vineyard", says Deuteronomy 23:24, "you may eat all the grapes you want, but you must not carry any away in a container." Forty days were needed for the "lees" or sediment to settle. Then the fermenting wine was stored in new goat-skin bags or pottery containers.

In some places wine-making became something of an industry. At Gibeon, fifty-six jar handles have been discoverd inscribed with the name of the town and the vineyard owners. In addition there were sixty-three bell-shaped vats used as wine cellars during the time of the kings, together with fermenting-vats and wine presses.

Animals "Cattle" in Hebrew includes sheep, goats, oxen and asses, but not pigs. Asses were kept for carrying loads, and oxen for ploughing. Only on special occasions were oxen killed for meat. Sheep and goats were always kept together. Sheep mainly provided wool for clothes. They were occasionally eaten as meat — in Israel their distinctive fat tail was considered a rare delicacy. They also provided milk in the form of curds for the very poor. Goats were valuable for meat and milk. Their hair made coarse cloth and their skins made bottles.

The life of the shepherd seems to have altered little from the time of Abraham to that of Jesus. The shepherd led his sheep, knew each one, and watched over them night and day (see John 10:1–6). Despite the rough stone enclosures which served as folds, there was constant danger from thieves and wild beasts — lions, leopards and bears (until they became extinct), wolves and hyenas, jackals, snakes and scorpions. The shepherd carried a staff to catch hold of any sheep which fell, and was armed with a wooden club. If sheep were stolen he had to repay his master. If they were attacked by wild beasts he had to bring back evidence (see Exodus 22:12–13).

New Testament times Farming changed little in the land of Israel throughout the Bible period, though in other Mediterranean countries notable progress was made. Pharisees often referred to those with no religious education as "people of the land", which perhaps suggests that the farmer was not held in very high regard. However, the country was being farmed more intensively. A writer of the time described Israel's fruit as being better than that of any other land. Fertile Galilee was producing more flax, and probably some attempts were being made at irrigation. It had, by then, become quite common to keep poultry.

FASTS

Only one day in the year is set apart for a national fast in the Old Testament laws. That is the Day of Atonement, on the "tenth day of the seventh month" (end of September/beginning of October). During the exile in Babylon, special fasts were also held in the fifth and seventh months to mourn the destruction of the temple and the murder of Gedaliah, governor of Judah.

After the exile two other regular fasts were held: in the tenth month, to remember the start of the siege of Jerusalem, and in the fourth month, marking the final capture of the city. Fasts were also kept by the nation and by individuals at times of special need.

Prayer and fasting often went together. People fasted as a sign of genuine repentance. During the time of fasting they did not eat or drink. Other customs were to tear their clothes, dress in coarse sackcloth, throw dust and ashes on their heads, and leave their hair uncombed and their bodies unwashed. But the prophets, and Jesus himself, made it plain that these outward signs of fasting were not enough. A real change of heart was what mattered most.

Leviticus 16:29; Zechariah 7:5; 8:19; Judges 20:26; Nehemiah 1; 2 Samuel 12:16, 20; Esther 4:16; Isaiah 58:3–5; Joel 2:13; Jonah 3:5; Matthew 6:16–18

FEASTS AND FESTIVALS

The sabbath and most of the great festivals of the Jewish religion were kept from the very earliest period of Israel's history. But two of the festivals described here began to be observed much later — Purim (from the time of the Persian Empire, fifth century BC) and Dedication/Lights (from the time of the Maccabees, second century BC).

Israel's main religious festivals were connected with the seasons and the farmer's year in Canaan. They were held in the spring, the early summer, and the autumn. On each occasion the men were expected to go to their local shrine and present their offerings to God. After the seventh century BC these "pilgrim" festivals were held only in Jerusalem. By the time of Jesus, the city's normal population of 40,000 or so was swollen to about 150,000 by the pilgrims who came for the Passover. Festivals were times of thanksgiving to God for harvests, occasions for remembering outstanding events in Israel's history, and opportunities for great rejoicing and feasting.

Passover and Unleavened Bread Passover was one of the most important annual festivals. It took place the evening before the fourteenth of Nisan. On that night every family sacrificed a lamb. It was a reminder of the first such sacrifice, which took place just before God rescued the Israelites from Egypt. On that occasion God "passed over" the Israelite houses where the blood of the lamb had been sprinkled on the door-posts and lintel, and he spared the lives of their firstborn.

Bread, made quickly and without yeast ("unleavened bread") was eaten at the Passover meal and all through the following week. This, too, was a reminder of the hurried preparations made when Pharaoh finally allowed the Israelites to leave Egypt. It also recalled the first bread baked from new corn, four days after the Israelites entered Canaan.

The sound of the ram's-horn trumpet, the "shofar", announced the start of all the religious festivals in Israel.

At first the Passover was held in people's homes, but by New Testament times it was the main "pilgrim" festival celebrated in Jerusalem. It remains one of the most important Jewish festivals today.
Exodus 12; Joshua 5:10–12; Mark 14:1–2

Firstfruits This ceremony was held on the last day of the Festival of Unleavened Bread. The first sheaf of the barley harvest was presented to God. The main harvest festival (Weeks) came later.
Leviticus 23:9–14

Weeks (later **Pentecost**) At the end of the grain harvest the priest offered two loaves of bread made from the new flour, along with animal sacrifices. This took place fifty days (or seven weeks plus one day) after Passover and the start of the harvest. The festival later came to be known as "Pentecost", from the Greek word meaning "fiftieth". It was a time of great rejoicing and thanksgiving for God's gifts at harvest.
Exodus 23:16; Leviticus 23:15–21; Deuteronomy 16:9–12

Trumpets (later **New Year**) The beginning of every month, as well as every festival, was signalled by a blast of trumpets. But on the first day of the seventh month the trumpets sounded for a special celebration. It was a day for rest and worship, more important even than the sabbath, judging by the offerings made. It marked out the seventh month as the most solemn month in the year. After the exile it was treated as a religious New Year festival (*Rosh Hashanah*), but the months were still counted from Nisan (March/April).
Numbers 10:10; 28:9; 29:1–2

Day of Atonement   On this day (*Yom Kippur*) the whole nation of Israel confessed their sin and asked for God's forgiveness and cleansing. The high priest, dressed in white linen, first offered a sacrifice for his own sin and the sin of the priests, and then offered another sacrifice for the sin of the people. It was the only day in the year when the high priest went into the "holy of holies" — the inner, most sacred part of the tabernacle (worship tent) or temple. There he sprinkled blood from the sacrifice. Then he took a goat, known as the "scapegoat", and, after laying his hand on its head, sent it off into the desert as a sign that the people's sins had been taken away.

See also *Atonement, Priests and Levites, Sacrifices.* Leviticus 16

Ingathering/Tabernacles/Booths/Shelters   This was the most popular and joyful of all the festivals. It was held in the autumn when all the fruit crops had been harvested. The celebrations included camping out in gardens and on roof-tops in tents or huts made from the branches of trees. These tents (or "tabernacles") were a reminder of the time when Israel had lived in tents in the desert.

This festival included a ceremony in which water was poured out and prayers made for good rains for the coming season. It was at this festival, perhaps following this particular ceremony, that Jesus stood up and declared: "Whoever is thirsty should come to me and drink. As the scripture says, ' Whoever believes in me, streams of life-giving water will pour out from his heart.' "

Exodus 34:22; Judges 21:19–21; Nehemiah 8:14–16; Leviticus 23:39–43; John 7:37–38

Dedication/Lights This festival commemorated the cleansing and re-dedication of the second temple by Judas Maccabaeus in 165 BC, after it had been defiled by the Syrian ruler Antiochus IV Epiphanes. It was also called "Lights", as each evening lamps were placed in houses and synagogues. This festival, called Dedication in John 10:22, is celebrated today as *Hanukkah*.
1 Maccabees 4:52–59

Purim An excited and noisy celebration, traced back to the time when Esther and her cousin Mordecai saved the Jewish people from massacre during the reign of the Persian King Xerxes ("Ahasuerus"). Purim means "lots" and the name refers to the lots cast by Haman, the king's chief minister, to decide on which day he should massacre the Jews.
Esther 3; 7; 9:24, 26

The sabbath The sabbath was Israel's most distinctive festival. Other nations had their harvest festivals and new moon rituals. Only Israel had the sabbath, which cut across the rhythm of the seasons. Every seventh day was set aside for rest. This was the "sabbath" and it belonged to God. The fourth commandment instructed the people of Israel to stop work on this day. The pattern of six days' work followed by a day of rest was also traced right back to creation, when God "rested" on the seventh day. On the sabbath people were to remember all that God had done, especially in rescuing them from slavery in Egypt.

"If you treat the Sabbath as sacred," God said through the prophet Isaiah, "and do not pursue your own interests on that day; if you value my holy day and honour it by not travelling, working or talking idly on that day, then you will find the joy that comes from serving me."

By New Testament times, keeping the sabbath had become so complicated with rules and regulations that Jesus had to remind people that "the Sabbath was made for the good of man; man was not made for the Sabbath".
Genesis 2:2–3; Exodus 20:8–11; 31:12–17; Deuteronomy 5:12–15; Isaiah 56; 58:13–14; Matthew 12:1–14; Mark 2:23–27

New Moon   The day of the new moon signalled the start of each month. Trumpets were blown and special sacrifices made. The arrival of the new moon was understood as a reminder that God had created an orderly world. No work was done on this day, but there were special meals and religious teaching.
Genesis 1:16; Numbers 10:10; 28:11–15; Psalm 104:19; 1 Samuel 20:5, 24; 2 Kings 4:23

Sabbatical year   Just as every seventh day was to be a day of rest, so every seventh ("sabbatical") year was "to be a year of complete rest for the land, a year dedicated to the Lord". Obviously the whole land could not lie fallow at the same time. Probably each field lay fallow every seventh year after it was first sown. Anything which did grow in this year could be harvested free by the poor. This arrangement was a sign to the Israelites that the land was not their own. It was "holy" (belonging to God). Also, each seventh year all Israelite slaves were set free and all debts cancelled.
Leviticus 25:1–7; Exodus 23:10–11; 21:2–6; Deuteronomy 15:1–6

Jubilee year   The law said that in every fiftieth year — the year after seven "sabbatical" years — land and property (except for town houses) was to be returned to its original owners. Israelite slaves were to be set free, debts cancelled and the land allowed to lie fallow. The jubilee law may have proved too difficult to keep, so it was looked forward to as a time that only God could introduce. It was the "year" promised by Isaiah, and announced by Jesus. Leviticus 25:8–17; 23–55; Isaiah 61:1–2; Luke 4:16–21

FELIX
The Roman governor before whom Paul was brought for trial at Caesarea. He kept Paul in prison for two years, hoping for a bribe.
Acts 23:24; 24:1–27

FELLOWSHIP
The "sharing" companionship which is at the heart of Christian experience. Man was made to live in "fellowship" with God. Man's disobedience broke this friendship. Jesus came to restore it by dying to deal with the sin which separates us from God.

So Christians can begin to know the companionship with God for which every man and woman was created. A Christian shares, with Jesus, in the love of God himself, "the fellowship that we have with the Father and with his Son Jesus Christ". Jesus pictures the closest possible "sharing" between himself and his followers. "I am the vine," he said, "and you are the branches."

Just as we share Jesus' life, so we share in the lives

of our fellow-Christians. The Christian is not just an individual joined to Christ, he also shares a new life with fellow-Christians and with Christ himself. "We are all joined to each other", and the hallmark of this Christian "fellowship" is love.

This sharing and love which characterizes the Christian church shows itself in action. The early church in Jerusalem showed their oneness by sharing all their possessions with one another. The non-Jewish churches showed their love for the needy church in Jerusalem by sending money.

See also *Body, Church*.

1 John 1:3; John 15:1–17; Romans 12:4–13; John 13:34–35; Acts 2:44–47; 4:32–37; Romans 15:25–27

FESTUS

The Roman governor of Palestine after Felix. He listened carefully to Paul and called him to defend himself before King Herod Agrippa II and Bernice. He agreed with them that Paul was innocent of any crime. But Paul had appealed to Caesar, and would have to go to Rome for trial.

Acts 25–26

FIG AND SYCOMORE FIG

The fig was an important fruit in Bible times. The ideal of peace and prosperity was summed up as "everyone able to sit down under his own vine and fig-tree". Figs are slow-growing trees, bearing fruit for about ten months of the year. The large leaves make useful wrappings. Cakes of dried figs made excellent food — compact "iron rations" which were easy to carry. Amos the herdsman and prophet also

"took care of fig-trees". The tree Zacchaeus climbed to get a better view of Jesus was a sycomore — another kind of fig-tree.
Amos 7:14; Luke 19:4

FISHING

The Israelites were not much involved in the fishing trade until New Testament times. There is only one Hebrew word for fish — to cover everything from the smallest "tiddler" to the great fish that swallowed Jonah. The main fishing industry in Old Testament times was in the hands of the Phoenicians, though the presence of a "Fish Gate" is probably an indication of a market for imported fish in Jerusalem.

By the time of Jesus, however, a flourishing industry seems to have developed on the inland Sea of Galilee. The name of the lakeside town, Tarichaea ("pickling"), probably indicates that it was a centre for salting and preserving fish. The Gospels describe

A fisherman casts his net.

the fishermen working in family groups, and often using hired helpers. They mended nets and sails, repaired boats and often fished by night. This was dangerous, for storms could quickly blow up on the lake.

Bone or iron fish-hooks were used from early times. Isaiah refers to a hook and line (no rod was used) and Job mentions a spear, but fish were usually netted. There were two kinds of nets. One was a net thrown by hand while the fisherman stood on the shore. The other was a large net (dragnet) used from the boats, with floats and weights attached so that it moved vertically through the water, bringing the fish to the boats or to shallow water in smaller and smaller circles. The fish were brought to the shore and sorted before being sent to market.
Nehemiah 13:16; Mark 1:20; Isaiah 19:8; Job 41:7; Ecclesiastes 9:12; Matthew 13:47–48

FLAX
Linen cloth is made from this pretty blue-flowered plant which grows about 1½ft(45cm) high. After the plants are pulled up, the stem fibres are separated by steeping them in water (retting). They can then be combed and woven like threads. The fibres are also used for string, nets and lamp-wicks. Linen was used for sails. It was also wrapped round dead bodies, and made into fine clothes, in Egypt and Israel.
Exodus 26:1 Joshua 2:1, 6; Proverbs 31:13; Ezekiel 27:7; Mark 15:46

The attractive flowers of the flax plant ripen into seeds used to produce linseed oil.

FLESH

The word "flesh" in the Bible is often used to refer to people as physical beings — "mortal flesh". In this sense it can be used to show the weakness of man, who is "only human", in contrast with the strength of God. When Jesus' disciples fell asleep in the Garden of Gethsemane he told them to watch and pray: "the spirit is willing, but the flesh is weak".

Paul used the word "flesh" ("lower nature" or "human nature" in some recent translations) to refer to the life non-Christians live under sin's domination.

The Christian, on the other hand, is both "in the flesh" and "in the Spirit". He is caught in a battle between his own inborn bias to sin and the presence of God's Spirit in his life, working to make him more like Christ. He has to say "no" to the sinful desires which are part of his fallen nature, and allow the "fruit" of the Spirit to grow in his life.

See also *Body*.

Psalm 78:39; Isaiah 40:5; Mark 14:38; Romans 7:13–25; 8; Galatians 5:16–24

FLOOD

The flood was a tremendous disaster from which only Noah's family and the birds, animals and reptiles he took with him into the "ark" (the boat God had instructed him to make) were saved. The flood was sent by God because the human race had become so wicked that he was sorry he had made men and women. The flood waters covered everything for a whole year.

Rain fell for forty days. The floods were swollen by water released from underground sources. For five months (150 days) the waters went on rising. It was nearly eight months before any dry land was seen again. The growing population and civilization described in the early chapters of Genesis were destroyed.

Noah, his wife, his three sons and their wives were saved in the ark. God gave Noah the plan for this gigantic basket-boat which would float on the rising waters. The measurements given are enormous: about 450 x 76 x 45ft/137 x 23 x 14m.

It had a wooden framework bound with reeds and sealed with a thick layer of tar to keep out the water. It was roofed and had an opening to let the light in all around, just below the roof. The people and the animals went in through an opening in the side. There were three decks and presumably some means of separating the various creatures. Noah took on board one pair of all living creatures — seven pairs of the ones used for sacrifice and for food — and stocked the ark with food for them all.

When the flood began to go down the ark grounded on one of the mountains in the country of Ararat (Urartu) in eastern Turkey. But the land dried slowly. It was over two months before Noah could see the mountain tops. Forty days later he sent out a raven, and after another week a dove, to try to get some idea of the situation further away. The raven never came back. The second time the dove went out it returned with a fresh green leaf. The plants were beginning to grow again. A week later the dove flew off again and did not return. Still Noah waited. In another month the water had gone, but it was nearly two months more before God told them they could safely set foot on dry land again.

As soon as they left the ark Noah built an altar and expressed his thanks to God by offering sacrifices. God promised that he would never again destroy the earth and its inhabitants in such a flood. He made the rainbow a sign of his promise, to reassure them. "Whenever I cover the sky with clouds and the rainbow appears, I will remember my promise," God said.

Genesis 6–9

Other stories Besides the Bible account of the flood, there are many other fascinating stories of an ancient flood from various parts of the world. Folk tales of a great flood are worldwide.

In one Babylonian story the gods sent the flood in order to get some rest from the noise of mankind. The god who made man warned the hero, and he built a boat in which he and his family and animals escaped. After seven days the gods missed the food supplied by sacrificial offerings and called a halt.

The Genesis flood story is set against a Mesopotamian background and in view of the similarities may well look back to the same event.

Archaeologists have found evidence of floods in southern Mesopotamia, but these were only local disasters. They came much later (about 3000 BC) than the flood described in Genesis.

FOOD

For ordinary people, food and clothing have always been two of the main concerns. "Don't start worrying," Jesus said. " 'Where will my food come from? or my drink? or my clothes?' " He knew how easy it is to worry when there is only just enough to live on. In Bible times this was how most of the people in Israel lived. For this reason their enemies attacked during the growing season. If the crops were destroyed, the people could not survive. In Gideon's time, "wherever the Israelites sowed any seed, the Midianites would come . . . and attack them . . . and destroy the crops" (Judges 6:3–4). Unreliable rainfall, drought, and pests such as locusts, made the crops uncertain. Famines were expected as a normal part of life. It is not surprising that the Israelites saw the golden age of the future as an age of plenty with more than enough for all.

There were a number of sources of food: mainly cereal crops, fruit and vegetables. Bread was the basic item of everyone's diet. The word "bread" in the Lord's prayer stands for food in general. And

Jesus called himself "the Bread of Life", meaning "the food of life".

Bread Barley bread — the bread the boy with the five loaves and two fish gave to Jesus (John 6:9) — was probably the most common. Wheat gave the best flour and was also quite common, and spelt, too, was sometimes used.

The grain was first sorted in a shallow basket, to remove poor grain and any poisonous seeds such as darnel ("tares"), weeds which grew with the corn and looked very similar. Then it was ground. In early days this was done by rubbing between a small stone and a larger one. Later it was ground between two small millstones. The lower one was fixed; the upper one turned round on top of it.

For each baking, forty litres of flour (Matthew 13:33) were mixed with water (or sometimes olive oil) to form a dough. People seldom had fresh yeast, so a piece of fermented dough ("leaven") from the previous baking was kneaded into the new dough and the whole left to rise. Before it was baked, part of the dough was put aside for the next day's "leavening". The bread was baked as a flat cake. This was appetising when fresh, but soon went dry. "Parched" corn — fresh ears put on a metal sheet over the fire and "popped" — was a popular alternative. For special occasions cakes and pastries were included in the baking.

Fruit and vegetables Fruit was another important food. The grape vine did more than produce juice. Many grapes were eaten fresh at harvest time, and many more were dried and used as raisins. Figs, too, were eaten fresh, and also dried and pressed together

to make fig cakes. When Abigail gave David supplies for his men they included "a hundred bunches
of raisins and two hundred cakes of dried figs" (1
Samuel 25:18). They were specially useful for taking
on a journey. The prophet Isaiah prescribed a paste
made of figs to heal King Hezekiah's painful boil
(Isaiah 38:21).

Dates are not mentioned by name in the Bible, but
they were certainly grown. The crowd waved date
palm branches to welcome Jesus to Jerusalem, the
week before he died. Dates were also used in the
special sauce (*charoseth*) in which everyone dipped
their bread at the Passover meal. The sauce was
made from dates, figs, raisins and vinegar.

Olives were also eaten — some fresh, in October,
and others after pickling in salt water. The most
important produce of the olive was its oil, which was
used in cooking. Pomegranates, almonds and pis-
tachio nuts were also available, and citrus fruits were
just coming in in New Testament times.

There were fresh vegetables in season. Beans,
lentils and peas were dried and stored in jars. There
were also onions and leeks, melons and cucumbers.
Vegetables were used to make soups. Esau
exchanged his birthright for a bowl of red lentil soup
(Genesis 25:29–34). Farm products were also available. Butter was not much used because it would not
keep in the hot weather. But cheese and yoghurt
were popular, and in New Testament times people
kept hens and poached the eggs in olive oil.

Meat and fish   Not much meat was eaten. Mutton
and meat from the goats was the most common, and
birds were caught for food, although the wealthy,

even in Old Testament times, fed on lamb, veal and beef. Meat was normally boiled. The lamb roasted for the Passover Festival was an exception. Ordinary people ate meat only on special occasions such as a celebration party, or when entertaining guests at a religious festival, or special sacrifice at the local shrine. On this occasion the family gathered together to eat some of the animal that had been sacrificed at the shrine, as a sign of their renewed friendship with God.

Fish was certainly an important food in New Testament times. (At least seven of Jesus' twelve disciples were fishermen.) Small fish were dried and salted and eaten with bread, as at the feeding of the 5,000. Or they could be cooked over an open fire and eaten fresh, as at the breakfast Jesus prepared for his followers (John 21).

Sweetening and seasoning The Israelites had no sugar. Honey from wild bees was the main sweetener (see the story of Jonathan in 1 Samuel 14:25–27 and of Samson in Judges 14:8). But another kind of "honey" may have been produced by boiling dates and locust beans to make a syrup.

Seasoning was important, too. There was plenty of rock salt on the south-west shores of the Dead Sea. Salt was also obtained by evaporation. The outer layer of rock salt was often impure and hard. It had no flavour and was used to spread on the temple courtyards in wet weather to make them less slippery.

Salt was used for seasoning food, but it was much more important for preserving it. In New Testament times the main industry at Magdala, on the Sea of

Galilee, was the salting of fish. Mint, dill (anise) — and cummin (seeds like caraway but used in place of pepper) were also used to give food the strong flavouring which everyone liked. They also helped give variety and interest to an otherwise boring diet. Rarer spices, imported from Africa and Asia, were used only by the wealthy.

See also *Meals*.

FOOD LAWS

Strict laws about diet are laid down in the Old Testament saying what may, and what may not, be eaten. The general rule was that animals which chew their cud and have divided hoofs could be eaten. This ruled out the pig. Fish were allowed, but only those with fins and scales. Many birds were not to be eaten, particularly if they were scavengers. It was also laid down that the blood must be drained from a carcase before it was cooked and that meat and milk dishes were not to be cooked or eaten together.

These two rulings meant that a Jew could not eat at the home of a non-Jew, where these restrictions were not normal. They resulted in a division between Jewish and non-Jewish Christians in New Testament times. Paul needed to teach the Christians at Corinth about their Christian freedom in this respect. In New Testament times, too, a family which followed the teaching of the Pharisees was not allowed to buy or eat food which had been killed in a pagan temple as an offering. For three days before a festival they were not allowed to buy any food at all from a non-Jew.

The reason for these strict laws on diet was never

explained. They may have been God's way of protecting the health of the people. They may have been intended to avoid cruelty to animals: for example, the law which forbade the boiling of a kid in its mother's milk; and the draining of the blood, which prevented the practice of cutting a limb off a live animal for meat. Or they may have been given for more strictly "religious" reasons. This was certainly the reason for forbidding meat which had been offered to an idol. And boiling a kid in its mother's milk may have been a Canaanite religious practice which the Israelites were to avoid. We cannot always be sure in any particular case whether one or all of these reasons holds good.

Leviticus 11; 17:10–16

FORGIVENESS

It is one of the most extraordinary things that God loves sinful human beings and delights to forgive them.

"If you kept a record of our sins,
who could escape being condemned?
But you forgive us,
so that we should stand in awe of you."

Yet from start to finish the Bible makes it clear that when we repent and turn from our sinful past to God, he will forgive us.

As Christians we enter a new life; we become children of God; we have been forgiven. Christians will forgive others because they have been forgiven, and although there may still be times when they fall into sin, they have only to turn to God in repentance and God will forgive and restore them.

See also *Repentance*.
Exodus 34:6–7; Psalm 51; Psalm 130:3, 4; Isaiah
1:18; 55:6–7; Hosea 14; Matthew 6:12–15; 26:26–
28; Luke 7:36–50; Acts 2:38; Ephesians 4:32; 1 John
1:9

FOX AND JACKAL
These are smaller cousins of the wolf. The fox, who
hunts alone, likes fruit and often damages the low
vines. Jackals go about in packs, scavenging at
night. The foxes in the story of Samson were probably jackals.
Judges 15:4

A fox (in the foreground) and jackal.

FRANKINCENSE
Gum collected by peeling back the bark of the
frankincense-tree (*Boswellia*) and cutting into the
trunk. The resin gives off a sweet scent when
warmed or burned, and was used as incense in Bible
times. Frankincense was one of the gifts brought to
Jesus by the three wise men.
Exodus 30:34–38; Leviticus 2:1, 15–16; Matthew
2:11

FREEDOM
In any society where some men rule harshly over

others one of man's greatest longings is for physical freedom. So it is not surprising that this idea has a large place in the Bible. Freedom is the central theme in the quotation from Isaiah which Jesus used to describe his own work. "The Spirit of the Lord is upon me . . . he has sent me to proclaim liberty to the captives."

Many hoped that Jesus had come to set Israel free from the Romans. But he made it plain that his first concern was to deal with a far more cruel slavery. He had come to set men free from the power of evil, and he demonstrated this by releasing people from the grip of evil spirits, and healing the sick.

In his letters to Rome and Galatia Paul is anxious to show how important this freedom is. It is freedom from the penalty of our sin, and freedom from the effort of trying, and failing, to please God. The Christian knows he is saved by God's grace, not by anything he can do himself.

Paul saw two main ways in which Christians abused this precious gift of freedom. Some hankered after the rules and regulations of the old Jewish religion. This was happening in the churches of Galatia, and Paul wrote his letter to them to show how Christian faith was entirely different from a religion of rules. Others thought that because Jesus had set them free they could do what they liked, even sin as much as they wanted. This was quite wrong: they were freed *from* sin, not to go on sinning. They gladly serve a new master — Jesus Christ. True freedom is found in serving God and in serving others.

Luke 4:18; John 8:31–36, 41–44; Mark 3:22–27;

5:1–13; Luke 13:10–16; Romans 6:16–23; 8:2, 21; Galatians 3:28; 5:1, 13; Romans 1:1; 6; Matthew 11:28; James 1:25; 2:12; 1 Peter 2:16

FURNITURE
See *Daily Life*.

FUTURE DESTINY

Apart from the certainty of judgement at the second coming of Jesus, the Bible says very little about what happens after death.

The Old Testament writers generally expected a continued existence in *Sheol*. This was simply a place of rest and silence when the blessing of life had been taken away. But as time went on people began to understand more clearly that God had a glorious future in store for them beyond *Sheol*. God does not abandon his people in *Sheol* but will lead them into life and joy. Job and Daniel both express confidence about the future. Job is certain he will see God. And Daniel speaks of the dead living again.

Hades is the New Testament equivalent of *Sheol*. Peter, speaking of the death of Jesus, said that David "spoke about the resurrection of the Messiah when he said, 'he was not abandoned in the world of the dead (*Hades*); his body did not rot in the grave'." In another context Peter says that Jesus went to preach to the dead, "the imprisoned spirits", presumably in the time between his crucifixion and his resurrection.

The New Testament often talks of death as a sleep. "Paradise" is the word used by Jesus to describe the pleasant existence of those who die at peace with God. And Paul was confident that when a Christian dies he is in the presence of Jesus. It is impossible for us to imagine an existence outside time; but the New Testament writers were confident that Christian believers, whether dead or living, would meet with Jesus, and enter into the glory of heaven, being given new "resurrection" bodies no longer subject to death.

See also *Death, Heaven, Hell, Judgement, Second coming of Jesus.*
Psalms 94:17; 16:9–11; Job 19:25–27; Daniel 12:2, 3; Acts 2:31; 1 Peter 3:19–20; Matthew 9:24; 1 Corinthians 15:20, 35–58; Luke 23:43; 1 Thessalonians 4:13–17; Revelation 20:11–22:5

G

GABRIEL

An angel who was God's special messenger. Gabriel was sent to Daniel twice: once to tell him the meaning of a dream and later to predict what was going to happen to Jerusalem. Gabriel was also sent to announce the birth of John the Baptist to Zechariah, and of Jesus to Mary.

Daniel 8:16; 9:21; Luke 1:11–20, 26–38

GAD

1. Seventh son of Jacob, who gave his name to the tribe of Gad.

Numbers 32

2. The land belonging to the tribe of Gad. Part of the former Amorite kingdom, east of the River Jordan (south Gilead).

Joshua 13:8–13

GAIUS

1. A Macedonian Christian who was with Paul on his third missionary journey. Gaius was dragged into the amphitheatre during the Ephesian silversmiths' riot. (See *Demetrius*.)

Acts 19:29

2. A Christian from Derbe who travelled with Paul to Jerusalem.

Acts 20:4

3. One of the few Christians Paul baptized at Corinth.
1 Corinthians 1:14
4. The Christian friend to whom John addressed his third letter.
3 John 1
These may not all be different people.

GALATIA

A Roman province in central Asia Minor. Its capital was Ancyra (now Ankara, the capital of modern Turkey). Several cities visited by Paul — Pisidian Antioch, Iconium, Lystra and perhaps Derbe — were in the southern part of Galatia, and Paul's letter to the Galatians was probably addressed to them. Galatia was also one of the areas of which 1 Peter was sent.
Acts 16:6; 18:23; Galatians 1:1; 1 Peter 1:1

GALATIANS

This letter is the earliest of Paul's New Testament letters, written in about AD 47–48. It was sent to a group of churches in the Roman province of Galatia (central Turkey), some of which, at least, Paul had visited. He had taught, simply, that God's gift of new life is for all who believe. And many people had responded. But since then Jewish teachers had come, arguing that Christians must keep the Old Testament laws.

So Paul's letter answers a vital question. Did non-Jews have to obey the Jewish law of Moses to be true Christians?

He begins by defending his claim to be an apostle who speaks with God's authority, and with a special mission to non-Jews (chapters 1–2).

Paul then puts forward his argument (chapters 3–4). People are put right with God by faith in Christ on its own. New life is God's gift to all who believe. We can do nothing to *earn* it.

Paul finishes his strongly-worded letter by showing that the way Christians behave springs from the love that comes from belief in Christ (chapters 5–6).

His letter is a great defence of Christian freedom: "Christ has set us free. Stand, then, as free people, and do not allow yourselves to become slaves again" (5:1).

GALILEE
The name of an area and large lake in northern Israel. The home area of Jesus and a number of his disciples. When his public work began, Jesus spent much of his time here.

Galilee is mentioned occasionally in the Old Testament. It was surrounded on three sides by other nations and strongly influenced by them. Most of Galilee is hilly, but the land falls steeply to 600ft/184m below sea level around the lake.

At the time of Jesus several major roads of the Roman Empire crossed Galilee. Farming, trade and the lakeside fisheries were the main industries. Many of the towns and villages mentioned in the Gospels were in Galilee, including Nazareth (where Jesus grew up), Capernaum, Cana and Bethsaida. The lake, which is liable to sudden fierce storms as the wind funnels through the hills that ring it round,

is also a focal point in the Gospel stories.
1 Kings 9:11; 2 Kings 15:29; Isaiah 9:1; Luke 4:14;
5:1 and following; 8:22–26; John 21, etc; Acts 9:31

GALLIO

The Roman governor of Achaia, about AD 51–53.
Gallio was the Emperor Nero's tutor and the brother
of Seneca, the philosopher. While Gallio was governor of Achaia he was based at Corinth. When Paul
was in Corinth Jews who were worried about the
success of his preaching tried to persuade Gallio to
condemn him. However, Gallio refused to get
involved with Jewish laws, and as a result Paul was
able to continue his work.
Acts 18:12–17

GAMALIEL

A famous Pharisee, Paul's teacher, and a member of
the supreme Jewish council, the Sanhedrin. When
the apostles were arrested and questioned, some of
the council wanted to put them to death. But Gamaliel advised caution. "Leave them alone!" he said.
"If what they have planned and done is of human
origin, it will disappear, but if it comes from God,
you cannot possibly defeat it."
Acts 5:34ff.; 22:3

GAMES AND SPORTS

Children's games seem to have changed very little.
We know that children in Bible times had toys which
made a noise — such as rattles and whistles. These
have been found in many places by archaeologists.
Some rattles were shaped like boxes with small holes

in each side, others like dolls and birds, though they were rather heavy to handle.

Girls played with dolls' houses, too. Miniature cooking pots and furniture, made out of pottery, have been found dating from between 900 and 600 BC. Some dolls had jointed arms and legs, and hair of beads and mud. They had holes in their shoulders for puppet strings. But whether these were really used for play, or in religious ceremonies, is not quite certain.

Israelite children, like children everywhere, also played "imitating" games, copying the grown-ups. Matthew 11:16–17 describes groups of children in the market-place, playing at weddings and funerals.

The game played by the soldiers at the trial of Jesus was also a dice game. As a four-sided dice was used, they moved a skittle from a central mark to positions where it could be "robed", "crowned" and "sceptred", and the soldier whose move completed the "ceremony" called "king" and collected the stakes which had been put down. In this instance the prisoner was used as a human skittle (Matthew 27:28–29). Although dice games were so popular amongst the people, the religious leaders strongly disapproved of gambling, and Jewish law disqualified a gambler from testifying before a court of justice.

As time went on some people began to make a living by entertaining others. This kind of entertainment — what Paul calls a "spectacle" in 1 Corinthians 4:9 — became very popular in Greek times. It was one of the areas of disagreement between the Sadducees, who enjoyed it, and the Pharisees, who

A Greek discus-thrower.

believed it to be wrong. King Herod built a stadium (for fights between gladiators — who were trained captives taken in war, or criminals — and between men and animals) and an amphitheatre (for chariot-racing) in Jerusalem. He built theatres at Caesarea and Sebaste which can still be seen.

Greek-style athletics were also performed in the stadium and in the gymnasium. The Greeks believed that exercise of this kind was necessary for a healthy body. But Greek athletics were not very popular with the Jewish people. They found it offensive that the athletes competed naked. And the close link with Greek religion was a further obstacle. The sporting events mentioned in Paul's letters are all linked to the Greek games. He uses the strict training of the athlete as an example (1 Corinthians 9:24–27), and writes of runners competing to win a crown of laurel, pine or olive leaves. He also refers to boxing, with arms and hands bound with studded leather, so that a blow must be avoided rather than parried! Philippians 3:13–14 pictures a race, and Hebrews 12:1–2 reflects the long-distance foot race, where weight has been lost in training and clothes are shed for the race.

GATH

One of five Philistine strongholds in Old Testament times. When the Philistines captured the Covenant Box (ark) it was taken to Gath, but plague followed. Goliath came from Gath, the home of other "giants", too. Later, when David was on the run from King Saul, he escaped to Gath. Soldiers from Gath helped him when his son Absalom led a rebellion against him. The city was subject to the kingdom of Judah for some time and eventually fell to the Assyrians in the eighth century BC. The site is still not certain.

Joshua 11:22; 1 Samuel 5; 17:4; 21:10–22:1; 27; 2 Samuel 15:18; 2 Kings 12:17; 2 Chronicles 11:8; 26:6

GATH-HEPHER

A place in Galilee on the borders of the lands belonging to the tribes of Zebulun and Naphtali. It was the birth-place of the prophet Jonah. It lay close to the later town of Nazareth.

Joshua 19:13; 2 Kings 14:25

GAZA

One of five Philistine strongholds in Old Testament times, on the coastal plain. Joshua conquered and then lost the city. The town features in the story of Samson. He was put in prison here, and finally died when he brought about the collapse of a great building Gaza suffered with the other Philistine cities when they captured the Covenant Box (ark).

The town was an important one on the trade route to Egypt. It was conquered by King Hezekiah of Judah, and later by the Assyrian armies and the Egyptian pharaoh.

In the New Testament, Philip was on the road from Jerusalem to Gaza when he met the Ethiopian official.
Joshua 10:41; Judges 16; 1 Samuel 6:17; 2 Kings 18:8; Jeremiah 47; Acts 8:26

GEBA

Modern Jeba', opposite Michmash, 6 miles/10km north of Jerusalem. A city belonging to the tribe of Benjamin. Saul's army camped here in front of his capital at Gibeah when the Philistines held Michmash. Later Geba became the northern limit of the southern kingdom of Judah, and was fortified by King Asa. Like Michmash, it was on the route of the Assyrian approach to Jerusalem, and was resettled after the exile.
Joshua 18:24; 21:17; 1 Samuel 13:16; 1 Kings 15:22; 2 Kings 23:8; 1 Chronicles 6:60; Isaiah 10:29; Ezra 2:26; Nehemiah 7:30; Zechariah 14:10

GEBAL

A very ancient Phoenician city, often known by its Greek name Byblos. It was on the coast of modern Lebanon, north of Berytus (Beirut). "There is still

much land to be taken," God told Joshua in his old age. Gebal was one of the areas included on the list. Later, workmen from Gebal helped to prepare the timber and stone for building Solomon's temple. Ezekiel prophesied against Tyre and other Phoenician towns, including Gebal.
Joshua 13:5; 1 Kings 5:18; Psalm 83:9; Ezekiel 27:9

GEDALIAH
Best-known of several Gedaliahs is the man appointed governor of Judah by King Nebuchadnezzar of Babylon after he had captured Jerusalem. After seven months he was murdered by Ishmael, a member of the royal family. The Jews still living in Judah were afraid that the Babylonians would treat this murder as a rebellion, and fled to Egypt.
2 Kings 25:22–26; Jeremiah 39:14–41:18

GEHAZI
Servant of the prophet Elisha. When Naaman came to Elisha to be cured of leprosy, Gehazi took the gift which the prophet refused. He lied to Elisha and as punishment became a leper himself. He continued as Elisha's servant and spoke to King Jehoram about the wonderful things Elisha had done.
2 Kings 4–5; 8:4ff.

GENESIS
Genesis, the first book of the Bible, is a book of beginnings. The name Genesis itself means "origin".

The book tells about the creation. God made the universe. Genesis also tells of the origins of man and woman, how things began to go wrong, and God's good purpose for his creation.

There are two main parts to the book. Chapters 1–11 tell the story of the creation of the world and of the human race. We read about Adam and Eve, Cain and Abel, Noah and the flood, and the tower of Babel.

God's good creation is gradually spoilt by the selfishness, pride and wickedness of men and women. The book tells of the beginnings of sin and suffering — and God's promise of hope.

Chapters 12–50 narrow down from the general story of the human race to one person — Abraham — and his family. Abraham trusted and obeyed God: God chose him to found the nation of Israel. The following chapters tell the stories of his son, Isaac, his grandson, Jacob (also known as Israel), and of Jacob's twelve sons, the founders of the twelve tribes of Israel.

The story then focuses on one of Jacob's sons, Joseph. He is imprisoned in Egypt, and later his whole family comes to live there. The book ends with God's promise to care for his people. All through its chapters, God is active, judging and punishing people who do wrong; guiding and keeping his people, moulding their history. Genesis tells the stories of some of the great men of faith.

GENNESARET
A place on the western shore of Lake Galilee. The name is also used of the lake itself.
See also *Galilee, Chinnereth*.
Mark 6:53; Luke 5:1

GEOGRAPHY OF ISRAEL

The land of Israel is very small. From north to south — "from Dan to Beersheba" as the Bible puts it — it is less than 150 miles, barely 230 kms, long. The northern end of the Dead Sea is only 50 miles/80 kms from the coast (though about 1,300ft/400 metres below sea level). The land is, in fact, rather like the roof of a house. It rises gently from the Mediterranean to about 3,200ft/1,000 metres above sea level, and then plunges steeply down to the great gash of the Jordan rift valley. There the earth's surface has cracked and dropped to form a trench which we can trace south all the way into East Africa. East of the Jordan and north of Galilee the mountains rise to greater heights — to nearly 6,500ft/2,000 metres in Edom on the eastern desert fringe, and over 9,800ft/3,000 metres in Lebanon and Mt Hermon to the north.

To surrounding nations, therefore, the people of Israel in their land seemed like hill tribes. "The gods of Israel are mountain gods", say King Benhadad's officials. The heart of their kingdoms lay along the mountain spine between the coast and the Jordan rift. In these mountains they could hold off attacks from the Philistines on the coast. But they themselves never really conquered the coastlands. From time to time (especially under King David) they expanded north into Syria or east beyond the Jordan where, at different times, they took control of Moab and Edom. But the Judean hills were their first base — and their last.

Geology Geologically, most of the materials making up these lands are young. Limestones or chalk occupy a large part of the surface. The structure is important in helping us understand the Bible.

There are certain characteristic landscape features wherever limestones occur. Water sinks through them (they are permeable), and there is little surface drainage. But they usually develop underground streams and the water can be tapped by sinking wells. Limestones contain many caves. And on the surface they often develop a kind of stony pavement which makes cultivation difficult and yields only a patchy soil. All these features are found in the hills of Palestine and all of them figure in the Bible story.

The desert climate also has its effects on the landscape and its structures. In the desert, regardless of rock type, there is usually a surface covering of sand, flintstone or salt. Much of the southern part of the land is covered by these infertile deposits. Wind and water are the forces which shape the desert rock. The wind scours the desert rocks into fantastic shapes. The force of water, made all the more powerful and dramatic because it is so rare, gouges out steep-sided valleys and overhanging crags. Occasional "flash" floods can fill a dry valley several metres deep with water in a few minutes.

The rift The long, straight gash of the Jordan Valley, deepening at the Dead Sea, is one of several signs that the earth's surface is unstable. Volcanic activity and changes in the structure are still going on. The Jordan rift has slipped down between two parallel "faults" to produce the deepest natural depression in the world. The shore of the Sea of Galilee is 660ft/200 metres below sea level. The deepest point of the Dead Sea is more than 2,600ft/

800 metres below sea level, despite the deposits brought down by the River Jordan for thousands of years. Hot springs and mineral-stained rocks along the sides of the rift show that the area is still geologically active.

Climate The lands on the Mediterranean coast have a climate which is midway between temperate and tropical. The winters are wet, like those of northern countries. The summers are hot and dry, influenced by the tropical deserts that lie beyond the sea's southern rim. Thanks to this seasonal contrast, snow will lie on the coastal mountains but tropical fruits will ripen in the plain.

The climate varies a good deal in the different areas of the Middle East. But there are a few general factors.

Rainfall The amount of rainfall generally depends upon height above sea level. The mountains attract more rain than the lowlands. They also tend to cut off rain-bearing winds and prevent them reaching inland. In Israel/Syria, the result is more rain in the high mountains north of Galilee (29–60in/750–1,500mm each year) than in the hills of Judea (20–29in/500–750mm). The rainfall total lessens rapidly going south. By the time we reach Beersheba it is less than 8in/200mm. South again, desert conditions apply all the way into the Sinai peninsula.

The fall-off in rainfall going *both* inland *and* downhill to the Jordan Valley is even more rapid. The average rainfall for Jerusalem is about 20in/500mm, whereas at Jericho, 15 miles/25kms to the east but 3,200ft/1,000 metres lower, it is barely 4in/100mm. It then rises again on the east side of the Jordan, so that there is a tongue of desert extending north up the Jordan Valley from the Dead Sea, but a tongue of well-watered hill country extending south on the east side of the Jordan all the way from Lebanon to Edom. No wonder that two and a half of the original twelve tribes decided that the land on the east side of the Jordan Valley was as good for their cattle as the land on the west, and asked if they could settle there rather than across the river in the land God promised (Numbers 32). In later years, this land — the land of Gilead — became famous for its fertility. Its hills brought as much rain as that of the hills of Judea, which are nearer the coast but not as high.

Although the northern part of Palestine seems to have a good amount of rainfall (similar to that of southern Britain, for example) the average is very deceptive. There are in fact great variations in the total from year to year. In Jerusalem, where the average is 20in/500mm, there have been years with as little as 10in/250mm and as much as 42in/1,075mm during the past century. This means that the margin of the desert is not fixed. In some years the margin withdraws east and south. In other years it overruns the area and there is drought and famine. These exceptionally wet and exceptionally dry years play a great part in the Bible story. They constantly remind God's people that they depend on him.

Dew In places where there is not much rain, the dew may play an important part in watering the land. Most of the areas with heavy dews are on the coast. The moisture comes in from the Mediterranean during the summer days, then falls to the ground as dew when it is cooled at night. Some coastal areas may have dew on 200 nights each year, and it can give them as much as a quarter of their moisture. So it is not difficult to see why the dew plays so large a part in the life of Bible peoples. Elijah the prophet, for example, predicting a drought, says "there will be no dew or rain" (1 Kings 17:1).

Winter rains   In the Near East and northern Africa most of the rain for the year comes in the winter season. Between the middle of June and September, rain is unlikely to fall. The weather conditions are stable and predictable, dominated by a flow of air from the east. For example, for thirty years Tel Aviv, on the coast, has never recorded rain in June, July or August.

After such a dry summer, the coming of the rains is especially important for the farmer. They should begin in mid-September, but the start of the rainy season is sometimes delayed. This gives the farmer less time for ploughing, and there is also less time for the wells to fill up again after the summer's use. So the Bible pictures the farmer watching and waiting for the autumn rain (James 5:7), to begin work.

Once the rains really start, the winter months are wet. December, or January, has most rain. The rain blows in from the Mediterranean for two to three days at a time, followed by drier and brighter conditions. This pattern continues until, in late March or early April, drier weather sets in. But this is a very important time for the farmer. Plants are beginning to grow after the winter cold. It is vital that the rains continue for long enough into the spring for his crops to be watered during their growing period. He therefore looks for the "later" rain in April, as well as the "early" rain in October.

Temperature   The temperature range in lands with seasonal rainfall is often very large. There are great contrasts — for example between a summer's day by the Dead Sea, with temperatures reaching 40 degrees C as a matter of course, and a wet winter's day a hundred miles away in Upper Galilee, where a freezing rain is falling. Winter weather on the uplands can be very unpleasant. There are 45–60 days of rain, and snow often falls in winter in Jerusalem. The daily changes can be trying in low-lying areas, too. Jericho has a January average temperature of 15 degrees C. But this is made up of high daytime temperatures and freezing nights.

Temperatures in summer on the coast and in the uplands average a pleasant 22–25 degrees C. They are affected generally by height above sea level and, from time to time, by the winds. In the daytime, in summer, cooling breezes blow in from the Mediterranean to make the heat less intense. But the effect of the *hamsin* is much less pleasant. This fiercely hot and dry wind blows from the south, out of Arabia, bringing a breath from the desert which can sometimes be felt even near the coast. It is well known to the people who live in Israel. "When you feel the south wind blowing," Jesus said, "you say that it is going to get hot — and it does" (Luke 12:55).

The climate today does not seem to be very different from the time when Israel occupied the Promised Land, or when Jesus lived there. The landscape has certainly changed but this is not because of a change in climate.

Vegetation In an area with this sort of climate we would expect to find the following kinds of vegetation — starting in the heart of the desert and moving outwards to the coast and the mountains: desert scrub — steppeland with shrubs and grasses — grassland — transitional forest — forest at higher levels. We would also expect many of the plants to be specially adapted to store water from the wet to the dry season — plants with shiny, smooth, non-evaporating surfaces. All these types of vegetation are, in fact, found in the land of the Bible and its surroundings, the forests in Lebanon to the north, and the desert scrub to the south. The steppe and grassland forms just a narrow band around the uplands of Judea and east of the Jordan at middle levels. However, on the coastal slopes most of the original grassland has long since been ploughed and sown. And some of the desert was cultivated by irrigation agriculture in Roman times just as it is in modern Israel.

Changes But there have been great changes over the centuries. When Israel entered the Promised Land, most of the upland area was covered by forest. Even in the time of Jesus there seems to have been widespread tree cover. Many kinds of hardwoods and softwoods are referred to in the Old Testament, and the Romans laid out forest areas. Today, the landscape is quite different, and almost all the forest and woodland has disappeared.

Felling trees for building and firewood and to clear land for ploughing led to soil erosion. This meant that new trees could not grow, and the forest was gradually replaced by the kind of thorny scrub (*maquis*) which is so common in long-settled Mediterranean lands. This scrub clutters the ground and is quite useless (for example, for building). It contains few trees of any size, is a serious fire risk in summer and today may represent all that remains of once-splendid forests. In Israel there has also been deliberate destruction of trees in war after war and destructive grazing by goats. The same has happened on the now-bare hills of Moab, east of the Jordan, which was once a densely-settled woodland area.

Only in the past half-century have we begun to reverse this process of deforestation. This was just in time to save a few of the famous cedars of Lebanon and some of the mountain forest of the north. Landscape changes over the same time have been even more dramatic, because they have happened so much more quickly than those taking place in the long and dreadful period of destruction. Marshes have been drained and cultivated. Groves of fruit trees have been planted in place of the old oak forests. And irrigation has been extended into the desert, in some cases to the same areas once farmed under Roman rule in the time of Jesus. It is well known that some desert soils are fertile when watered. And the southern fringe, together with the lower Jordan Valley, is an area of oasis agriculture — for example at Jericho and Engedi.

The resources of the land God promised Israel a fertile land. In addition "its rocks have iron in them, and from its hills you can mine copper" (Deuteronomy 8:9). Copper has been mined from very early times. Mining for iron came later, after the Hittites had discovered how to smelt it. The Philistines brought the secret with them. But not until the time of David and Solomon were the Israelites able to make their own iron tools. The copper mines just north of the Gulf of Aqaba were in full production in Solomon's time.

The country's other main resorces are building stones, pitch, sands and clays, with a variety of chemical salts in the Dead Sea area where evaporation has left them bedded in thick layers. Today phosphate rock is extensively worked, and the waters of the Dead Sea themselves yield potash, bromine and magnesium.

The regions of Israel The Jews in the time of Jesus had a very precise idea of what was, and what was not, "the land". Their "regional geography" was based on a scale which worked from the most sacred to the least sacred area. The Holy of Holies in Jerusalem came highest on the scale and, at the other end, the very touch of the dust of areas outside "the land" was considered defiling. The heart of the country consisted of Judea and Galilee on the west side of the Jordan, separated by Samaria (which did not belong to it) but linked on the east bank by Peraea. The approved route from north to south without leaving "the land" (avoiding Samaria) involved crossing the Jordan twice. Surrounding this core area was a kind of inner belt of lands which had once belonged to Israel. They were thought to be not quite as defiling as the heathen lands that were completely outside the boundaries.

The more usual regional geography, however, recognizes seven major natural divisions in the land.

The central highlands The core area of the Jewish kingdoms lay in the "hill country" along the watershed — with the land sloping away to the coast on one side, and away to the Jordan Valley on the other. This upland rises to just over 3,280ft/1,000 metres at its highest points, near Hebron. The western slope is gentle, the eastern abrupt. The forest cover has long since gone and it has become a region of bare limestone slabs and poor soils. Cultivation is on terraces and in very small fields, much of the area is used for raising stock. The fortified towns of this hill-country made good defence points. The capitals of the southern and northern kingdoms (Judah and Israel) were both in this area. The northern kings of Israel used several different strongpoints before building the capital at Samaria.

At the northern end of this region a number of isolated hills look down on the neighbouring region, the Plain of Esdraelon. But the hill country continues north-westwards to the coast in the jutting promontory of Mt Carmel. The 1,970ft/600 metre ridge cuts the coastal plain in two, breaking the general north–south pattern of the regions. On the northern edge of Carmel lies the modern port-city of Haifa.

Even today the "hill country" has few roads apart from the main Hebron–Jerusalem–Nablus (ancient Shechem) highway. The main highways of both the ancient and modern worlds pass north of the hills or run parallel with them along the coast. So, although this region contains Jerusalem, it has always stood a little apart from the everyday comings and goings through the land.

The Plain of Esdraelon Some distance back from the Mediterranean coast, mountain ranges run in a continuous line from Lebanon to Sinai. But there is one important break where a fault in the underlying rock has caused a section of mountain to drop to a height of 300ft/100 metres or less. This break divides the central highlands from Galilee and the northern mountains. It extends from Haifa Bay, north of Mt Carmel, to the valley of the Harod, a tributary of the Jordan. The watershed itself is cut through by the Valley of Jezreel.

The central plain forms a rough triangle, with each side about 15 miles/24kms long. Originally, the floor of the valley was marshy. It was here that Sisera lost his chariots and had to escape on foot — Judges 4:15. But it has been drained and today forms the most fertile agricultural area in the modern state of Israel.

Although the plain was infertile for many centuries before Jewish settlers began to reclaim it in 1911, it has always had great strategic importance. The principal north–south route of the ancient world (which the Romans called *Via Maris*, "the way of the sea") cut through it on the way from Egypt to Damascus and Mesopotamia. It was an obvious route for trade — or for invasion. This may account for the long list of battles which have been fought in the plain, right up to modern times, in the Israeli War of Independence (1948). Megiddo lies at the western edge of the plain so the Hill of Megiddo, or "Armageddon", became a symbol of the great battle in Revelation 16.

Galilee North of the Plain of Esdraelon, the

upland ranges begin again. They stretch away north-wards, gradually rising as they come nearer to the high mountains of Lebanon. They rise in a series of steps, with scarp edges facing generally south or south-east. The lower steps in the "staircase" were and are fertile basin lands, separated from each other by the barren limestone edges. In the time of Jesus, these basins were known for their grain, fruit and olives. They formed a prosperous, well-populated area. But the higher steps rise to a bleak and wind-swept upland. This is isolated and infertile, and lacks the forests of the higher mountain slopes further north.

This whole area forms the region of Galilee, some-times divided into Lower and Upper Galilee. The southern and eastern edges of the region are clearly drawn, but to the north, it merges into the moun-tains. In the past this northern boundary area was always the part of "the land" where foreign influ-ences were strongest. The Israelites seldom really had it under control. And the great trade routes which passed across it brought in many strangers. This was the region where Jesus spent his childhood years. It was a busy area, full of coming and going, with a very mixed community. Along its trade routes it was in touch with the outside world and aware of non-Jewish ideas. It lived off its fertile farmlands and its lake fisheries. And it was far more alert to the realities of life in the Roman Empire than the aloof Jews of Jerusalem — who despised their northern cousins as country bumpkins and because they were racially mixed.

The coastal plain   When Israel occupied the Promised Land, they captured the central highlands and then made sporadic attempts to spread their control down to the Mediterranean coast. But this region was occupied by the powerful nation of the Philistines. And although, under David, Israel was able to gain control for a while, more often in Israel's history the Philistines were exerting pressure from their five cities on the coastlands up into the hills.

The coastlands were not, at this time, a particularly attractive area. They consisted of a belt of coastal sand dunes backed by forest, lagoons and swamp. There were no large natural harbours south of Carmel. The Philistines were not seafarers, and the first major port on this coast was the artificial harbour at Caesarea, built by King Herod the Great, not long before Jesus was born.

South of Mt Carmel, the plain was known as the Plain of Philistia and the Plain of Sharon. North of Carmel, it became the Plain of Asher. Going north, it narrows, but is much better provided with natural harbours. It was from here that the sea-going Phoenicians traded.

The "Shephelah" or Piedmont Between the coastlands and the upland is an area of low foothills formerly covered by forests of sycamores. When the Philistines fought the Israelites the hills formed a kind of no-man's-land, where there were constant skirmishes. For either side to attack the other, it was necessary to pass through the Shephelah. Most of the routes through it were therefore fortified or guarded. Today, much of it is cultivated.

The Jordan Valley The River Jordan rises near Mt Hermon and flows south through Lake Huleh (now largely drained) and into the Sea of Galilee. At the southern end of the Sea it enters a deep valley known as the Ghor. Not only is the valley itself steep-sided but the river has cut into the floor and has created a winding, cliff-lined "valley within a valley", filled with dense, jungle-like vegetation. This made crossing the river very difficult before the first modern bridges were built.

The Jordan valley is a geological rift. The sides follow parallel faults in the earth's crust. These faults carry on the line of the valley down to the Dead Sea and beyond it, through the depression known as the Arabah, which eventually leads to the Gulf of Aqaba. The faults are the reason why the valley is so deep. The shore of the Dead Sea is 1,270ft/388 metres below sea level. The distance from the mountain rim on one side of the valley to that on the other is 9–12 miles/15–20kms. But no major road follows the valley. One reason for this is the broken and difficult ground created by the Jordan and its tributaries. Another is the fact that inside the Ghor, the summer temperatures are so high that travellers are glad to cross as quickly as they can from the heights on one side to the heights on the other.

The land east of the Jordan (Transjordan) Here there are uplands, like those to the west, but higher. They are well-watered and provide good pasture for the huge flocks of sheep and herds of cattle formerly raised in Moab. At one time the king of Moab paid 100,000 lambs and the wool from 100,000 sheep every year to Israel as tribute (2 Kings 3:4). The mountains here rise from 1,900–2,300ft/600–700 metres east of Galilee to almost 6,560ft/2,000 metres south and east of the Dead Sea. They attract a rainfall which increases with their height and makes them a fertile belt between the dry valley on one side and the Arabian Desert on the other.

The fertility of parts of the region, such as Bashan and Gilead, the prosperity of the sheep raisers of Moab, and the success of the traders of Edom made all these areas powerful rivals of the Israelites west of the Jordan. It was, perhaps, just as well for Israel that the Jordan made it so difficult for these people to move into their land from the east. It almost completely separated two similar regions which lay within sight of each other across the valley.

GERAR

A place in the Negev, between Beersheba and Gaza, where both Abraham and Isaac stayed. For safety, Abraham said that his wife Sarah was his sister. Abimelech, king of Gerar, wanted to take Sarah as his wife. But God prevented this.
Genesis 20:26

GERIZIM

The mountain of God's blessing, in Samaria, opposite Mt Ebal (see *Ebal*). Gerizim later became the Samaritans' sacred mountain, the place where they built their temple. It was the mountain which the woman of Samaria mentioned as the place where her ancestors worshipped. The site of the ancient Samaritan temple has recently been found on a spur of Mt Gerizim.
Deuteronomy 11:29; 27; Joshua 8:33; John 4:20

GERSHON

Levi's eldest son. Gershon and his descendants formed one of the three groups of Levites.
Exodus 6:16–17; Numbers 3:17ff.

GESHUR

A region and town in southern Syria. King David married the king of Geshur's daughter. Their son, Absalom, fled to Geshur after he had killed his half-brother Amnon in revenge for the rape of his sister Tamar.
Joshua 12:5; 2 Samuel 3:3; 13:38, etc.

GETHSEMANE

A garden across the Kidron Valley from Jerusalem, close to the Mount of Olives (the name means "olive press"). Jesus and his disciples often went there. So Judas knew where to take the soldiers on the night of the arrest.
Matthew 26:36–56; Mark 14:32–51; Luke 22:39; John 18:1–12

GEZER

One of the Canaanite towns Joshua campaigned against. It was in the low hills, on the road from Joppa (on the coast) to Jerusalem. Gezer belonged to Egypt for a while until one of the pharaohs gave it to his daughter, King Solomon's wife. Solomon fortified the town, with Hazor and Megiddo. It is the place where archaeologists discovered the "Gezer calendar" (see *Farming*).
Joshua 10:33, etc.; 1 Kings 9:15–17

GIBEAH

A hill-top town 3 miles/4km north of Jerusalem, which became famous as the home and capital city of King Saul. The place had been tragically destroyed as a result of a crime committed by its people during the time of the Judges. The site is at Tell el-Ful, overlooking the suburbs of Jerusalem.
Judges 19:12–20:48; 1 Samuel 10:26, etc.; Isaiah 10:29

GIBEON

A town about 6 miles/10km north-west of Jerusalem. After the fall of Jericho and Ai the Gibeonites tricked Joshua into a peace treaty. Saul later broke this. David's men fought the supporters of Saul's son Ishbosheth at the pool of Gibeon, to decide which should be king. The tent of worship (tabernacle) was kept at Gibeon, and King Solomon worshipped there. The people of Gibeon helped Nehemiah to rebuild the walls of Jerusalem.

Archaeologists have discovered a huge pit at Gibeon, with a stairway leading down to water. Inside it there were handles of a great many storage jars, each one inscribed with the name "Gibeon" and the owner's name. The town seems to have been an important centre for wine-making in the seventh century BC.
Joshua 9; 2 Samuel 2:12–29; 20:8; 21; 1 Kings 3:4; 1 Chronicles 21:29; Nehemiah 3:7

GIDEON

The "Judge" of Israel who defeated the Midianites, one of Israel's greatest enemies at that time. Gideon was secretly threshing his crop when God's angel messenger called to him to rescue Israel from the Midianites. To make sure that the call was from God he put it to the test. Twice God gave him the sign he asked for.

Gideon chose 300 men from the thousands who followed him. These were divided into three groups. Armed with an empty pitcher, a torch and a trumpet, they surprised the enemy at night with a tremendous shout, "the sword of the Lord and of Gideon". Panic broke out in the army of Midian. They turned on each other and then fled, with the Israelites in hot pursuit. Victory was complete and Gideon gave the land peace for forty years until his death.

Judges 6:11–23, 36–39; 7:1–23

GIHON

The name of one of the four great rivers which flowed out of the Garden of Eden.

Gihon was also the name of a spring at the foot of the hill on which the first city of Jerusalem stood. It was then the main source of water for the city. Solomon was anointed king at this spring by the command of his father David, to forestall the attempt of his rival Adonijah to seize the throne. The Gihon spring water was vitally important to the safety of the city and, later, King Hezekiah cut a tunnel to bring the water right through the hill and inside the walls. This tunnel still exists. The water comes out at the Pool of Siloam (see *Siloam*).

Genesis 2:13; 1 Kings 1; 2 Chronicles 32:30; 33:14

GILBOA

A mountain and range in the north of Palestine, overlooking the deep Valley of Jezreel which runs down to the River Jordan. King Saul and his army took their last stand against the Philistines on Mt Gilboa. Saul, Jonathan and his other two sons were all killed there.
1 Samuel 28:4; 31:1, 8; 2 Samuel 1; 21:12; 1 Chronicles 10:1, 8

GILEAD

A large area east of the River Jordan, extending north from the Dead Sea. The tribes of Reuben, Gad and Manasseh each occupied part of Gilead. The region was good grazing-land, famous for its flocks and herds. It was also famous for a gum or spice known as the "balm" of Gilead. This was used to heal wounds, and also as a cosmetic. Jair, Jephthah and the prophet Elijah all came from Gilead.
Genesis 37:25; Joshua 17:1; Judges 10:3; 11; 1 Kings 17:1; Song of Solomon 4:1

GILGAL

A place between Jericho and the River Jordan. The Israelites camped at Gilgal after crossing the river, and set up stones to mark the event. From Gilgal they set out to conquer Canaan. It became the site of an important shrine, and was on Samuel's circuit as a Judge. Gilgal is mentioned in the stories of Elijah and also of Elisha, who dealt with a pot of "poisoned" stew there. The prophets Hosea and Amos condemned the worship at Gilgal as empty ritual.
Joshua 4:20; Judges 3:19; 1 Samuel 7:16; 10:8, etc.; 2

Samuel 19:15; 2 Kings 2:1; 4:38–41; Hosea 4:15; Amos 4:4

GLORY

When the word "glory" is applied to people in the Bible, it usually refers to their wealth or position. But the "glory of God" refers to his unique power and greatness: "the King of kings and the Lord of lords. He who alone is immortal; he lives in the light that no one can approach. No one has ever seen him; no one can ever see him." Though people cannot see God, they are sometimes allowed to catch a glimpse of his "glory".

In the Old Testament God's glory is seen in history, especially perhaps in the two major events of the exodus and exile. The Israelites were led through the desert by the glory of God seen in the cloud and fire which guided them on their journey. When Moses went up the mountain to receive the law of God the cloud of God's glory covered the mountain. Again, during the exile the prophet Ezekiel saw some amazing visions which showed the "glory" of God.

The New Testament suggests that Jesus was the glory of God made visible on earth. God's glory was seen by the shepherds when they heard that Jesus was born. And those who saw Jesus recognized God's glory in him. "We saw his glory," writes the apostle John (see also *Transfiguration*). Jesus' way of life and his miracles "revealed his glory". But the glory of God was seen above all in Jesus' death on the cross. Jesus went to the cross, not as a defeated man but as the conqueror of sin and Saviour of the world.

His resurrection was the living proof. Because of this there is a "future glory" promised to all God's people as they share in the glory with which he will return to earth.

1 Timothy 6:15–16; Exodus 16:7, 10; 24:15–18; 40:34–38; 2 Chronicles 7:1–3; Ezekiel 1:26–28 and other passages; Luke 2:8–14; 9:28–36; John 1:14; 2:11; 17; Romans 8:18–30; Mark 8:38; 13:26

GOD

In the Bible, God is the all-powerful, personal, spiritual being who is beyond our understanding, but who has revealed himself to mankind in his work of creation and in his continuing activity in history. He created all life — and he is the one who keeps it going. We see him at work time and again in the Old Testament as he helps his people Israel. In the New Testament we see him at work especially in the life, death and resurrection of Jesus. He also continues to work in a personal way in the lives of Jesus' followers.

The Bible tells us what God is like by telling us what he does. It does not give us abstract philosophical descriptions of God's nature. But it is clear that he is all-seeing and all-knowing, present everywhere. His nature is both holy and just, loving and forgiving. The Bible takes the existence of God as a fact which needs no proof. It begins with the simple statement, "In the beginning God created . . ."

People have always had many ideas about God. They have worshipped many different gods. One of the concerns of the Old Testament is to show that *Yahweh* (the Hebrews' name for God) is the only true God. He is the Creator, and King over all there is; the one who is "light", who is utterly holy — and utterly loving.

The word *Yahweh*, the personal name for God in the Old Testament, is sometimes spelt Jehovah in English, and in many translations of the Bible is written LORD. The ordinary Hebrew word for "God" is *Elohim*. The name *Yahweh* means "the one who exists eternally", though the Jews have always referred to him by the Hebrew word *Adonai*, which means "my Lord".

In the Old Testament God was sometimes referred to as the "father" of the people of Israel. Jesus gave this a new importance. God has made us for a parent–child relationship, made possible through faith in Jesus. God delights to work in the world through the people he has made for friendship with himself. He works with them through their prayer and action so that the whole world might come to know him.

See also *Trinity* and the many words which describe what God does.

The "otherness" of God: the eternal spirit; the Creator: Genesis 1; Deuteronomy 33:26–27; 1 Kings 8:27; Job 38ff.; Psalms 8; 100; 104; Isaiah 40:12–28; 55:9; John 4:23–24; Romans 1:19–20; Revelation 1:8

The power of God: Genesis 17:1; Exodus 32:11; Numbers 24:4; Job 40–42:2; Isaiah 9:6; 45–46; Daniel 3:17; Matthew 26:53; John 19:10–11; Acts 12; Revelation 19:1–16

— *his knowledge:* Genesis 4:10; Job 28:20–27; Psalm 139:1–6; Daniel 2:17–23; Matthew 6:7–8; John 2:23–25; 4:25–29; Ephesians 1:3–12

— *his presence everywhere:* Genesis 28:10–17; Psalm 139:7–12; Jeremiah 23:23–24; Acts 17:26–28

The character of God — his holiness and righteousness: Exodus 20; Leviticus 11:44–45; Joshua 24:19–28; Psalms 7; 25:8–10; 99; Isaiah 1:12ff.; 6:1–5; John 17:25–26; Romans 1:18–3:26; Ephesians 4:17–24; Hebrews 12:7–14; 1 Peter 1:13–16; 1 John 1:5–10

— *his love and mercy:* Deuteronomy 7:6–13; Psalms, e.g., 23; 25; 36:5–12; 103; Isaiah 40:1–2;, 27–31; 41:8–20; 43; Jeremiah 31:2–4; Hosea 6; 11; 14; John 3:16–17; 10:7–18; 13:1; 14:15–31; 15:9, 12ff.; Romans 8:35–38; Galatians 2:20; Ephesians 2:4–10; 1 John 4:7–21

God the "father": 1 Chronicles 25:10; Psalms 68:5; 103:13; Matthew 5:48; 6:1–14; 28:19; Romans 8:14–15

GOG

Described in the Book of Ezekiel as the ruler of Magog and the prince of Meshech and Tubal. He and his army invade from the north and Israel wins a great victory over them. In Revelation, Gog and Magog, led by Satan, are totally destroyed by God himself.

Ezekiel 38–39; Revelation 20:7–9

GOLIATH

The 9-ft (3-metre) Philistine giant from Gath who was killed by David. The stone from David's sling stunned the giant and he fell to the ground. David then drew Goliath's sword and cut off his head. The Philistine army fled.

1 Samuel 17

A shepherd-boy using his sling.

GOMER
Unfaithful wife of the prophet Hosea. (See *Hosea*.)
Hosea 1–3

GOMORRAH
One of five cities probably now beneath the southern end of the Dead Sea. Gomorrah was violently destroyed with Sodom for deliberate, persistent and vicious sin. Throughout the Bible, Sodom and Gomorrah are used as examples to warn God's people of his judgement. Jesus says that any town which refuses to hear his messengers is in a worse situation than Sodom and Gomorrah.
Genesis 14; 19; Isaiah 1:9–10; (Ezekiel 16:48–50); Matthew 10:15

GOSHEN
A fertile area of the eastern Nile Delta in Egypt. When Jacob and his family went to join Joseph, they settled in Goshen. It was a good place for their flocks and herds, and it was close to Pharaoh's court. In the time just before the exodus, the Israelites in Goshen escaped the plagues suffered by the rest of Egypt.
Genesis 45:10; Exodus 8:22, etc.

GOSPEL

The word "gospel" means "good news". This good news, as far as the Bible is concerned, is the fact that we need not be cut off from God because of sins, for Jesus has come to bring forgiveness.

Mark's Gospel describes itself as "the good news of Jesus Christ", and at its simplest Jesus himself *is* the good news, the "gospel". The facts of the gospel are simple: "That Christ died for our sins, as written in the Scriptures; that he was buried, and that he was raised to life three days later, as written in the Scriptures." We can have forgiveness and new life because of the death and resurrection of Jesus.

In fact the gospel is so simple that some sneered at it. It was not as complex as they thought it should be. Paul made it clear that it is never difficult to find God. The good news of Jesus Christ was not a system of philosophy, but the plan of God himself. Paul had proved in his own experience that it was "God's power to save *all* who believe".
Luke 2:10–11; Mark 1:1, 14; Luke 4:18–21; 1 Corinthians 15:3–4; 1:17–23; Ephesians 1:6–13; Romans 1:16–17

GOVERNMENT

The Bible does not put forward any one form of government as the right way to organize society. In fact the Bible reflects many different forms. The "patriarchs", Abraham, Isaac and Jacob, lived in family clans. The nation of Israel was at first ruled by Judges, then by kings. And Christians in the New Testament accepted the Roman system of government under which they lived.

From the beginning Israel was meant to be a "theocracy" — a nation with God as its king. But because of the sinful nature of men and women, it was soon clear that society also needed its human rulers to make laws and enforce them. The nation of Israel discovered this during the period of the Judges when there was no central government. "There was no king in Israel at that time. Everyone did just as he pleased."

God delegates authority to governments to uphold justice. "Everyone must obey the state authorities, because no authority exists without God's permission, and the existing authorities have been put there by God." God's people should pray for the government and support it as it tries to rule justly.

At the same time, the Bible shows that God expects rulers to uphold justice, not to pervert it. The Old Testament prophets — especially Amos — spoke out plainly against the injustices and tyrannical rule of many of the kings of Israel and Judah. And when governments oppress their subjects, the people of God must stand up fearlessly and condemn them. If it comes to a straight choice between what the government says and doing God's will, Christians "must obey God".

Judges 21:25; Romans 13:1–7; 1 Timothy 2:2; 1 Peter 2:11–25; Isaiah 56:9–12; Jeremiah 21:11–22:19; Daniel 3; Amos and many other passages from the prophets; Matthew 22:15–21; Acts 5:27–29

GOZAN

Israelites from Samaria were taken captive to Gozan by the Assyrians. The town is modern Tell Halaf on

the River Khabur in north-east Syria.
2 Kings 17:6; 19:12

GRACE

Both the Old and New Testaments teach that God is good and kind to men and women. There is no need for God to be like this. We certainly do not deserve it. God is good to us because he loves us — this is the "grace" of God.

The Old Testament is full of reminders of God's goodness, his constant love. But the grace of God is seen most clearly in the coming of Jesus. In the cross God has shown us how much he loves us — it was "while we were still sinners that Christ died for us". The human race did not deserve salvation, but God freely gave it. This is what the New Testament means by "the grace of our Lord Jesus".

But the New Testament also suggests that the Christian life, from start to finish, depends on God's grace. We obey God out of gratitude for his "grace". "My grace", God says in answer to Paul's prayer for healing, "is all you need, for my power is strongest when you are weak." Paul's letters often begin or end with a prayer for God's grace.

See also *Covenant, Justification.*
Deuteronomy 7:6–9; Psalms 23:6; 25:6–10; 51:1; Jeremiah 31:2–3; Romans 5:8; 16:20; 3:19–24; 6:14; Ephesians 2:8–9; 2 Corinthians 12:9; 1 Timothy 1:2; 1 Peter 5:5–7; 2 Peter 3:18

GREAT SEA

The Bible often uses this name for the Mediterranean Sea.

GREECE

The Greeks   Until modern times the beginnings of Greece were a puzzle. *The Iliad* and *The Odyssey*, two great poems said to have been written by a blind Greek poet called Homer, about 800 BC, give hints of an even older way of life. Now modern discovery has built up a surprising picture of that early civilization. The Minoans in Crete had built great palaces long before, and traded with Egypt. But their empire fell suddenly, to earthquake or invasion. Its last rulers spoke Greek: tablets with the oldest known Greek language have been found in their palace.

The *Iliad* tells part of the story of the ten-year war when the Greeks attacked the city of Troy. We now know that there was a real Troy, and an early Greek civilization centred on Mycenae on the mainland of southern Greece. Homer echoes memories of what had really taken place long before.

Early history   Greek-speaking people had entered Greece from the north. Greece is a poor and rocky land. The people lived in small towns separated by the mountains. After the great days of Mycenae, the land was never united. Town fought against town. It was often easier to travel by sea than by land. There was too little fertile land to support the people and the Greeks became adventurous sailors. The regular summer winds and the shelter of the many islands helped them to voyage across the Aegean Sea to Asia (modern Turkey). They imported food, and founded new cities on many parts of the Mediterranean coast, especially in Asia Minor. Greeks in Bible times lived over a far larger area than the land we now call Greece.

Alexander the Great riding to the rescue of a subject king. A detail from his tomb at Sidon.

The "golden age" In the fifth century BC the most famous of the Greek cities was Athens. The Athenians took a leading part in defeating two great attacks on Greece by the Persians in 490 and 480 BC. They became rich and powerful, and built many beautiful temples, including the Parthenon, which can still be seen today. Athens also became the home of some remarkable leaders, thinkers, writers and poets. The names of Pericles, Socrates, Plato, Sophocles, Euripides and others are still famous. These men have had great influence on the world.

Athens was the perfect example of the Greek way of life. It was a "democracy". That is a Greek word for a very Greek idea. To an Athenian it meant that every citizen ought to play his part in the affairs of the "city" (Greek *polis*). The Greeks were a very gifted people, clever and active, quick to argue, with a great love of freedom, and a feeling for beauty in art and writing. Although they were so divided, they were all very proud of being Greek. They thought of themselves as different from other races, whom they called "barbarians". Every four years all the cities met at Olympia in southern Greece for the Olympic Games, and wars between them stopped for that time.

Alexander   Greece was divided and weakened by these bitter local wars. And after 336 BC Alexander the Great, king of Macedon (to the north), conquered the whole country. Alexander's people were Greeks, but had never been important until then. Alexander proved to be a brilliant soldier. He overthrew the great empire of Persia, and made conquests as far east as India. But he was also more than a conqueror. He aimed to spread Greek language and civilization through all this area.

Alexander's hopes were never fulfilled, for he died young, and his generals disputed his empire. It was divided from the start. Ptolemy won Egypt, and founded a line of Greek kings there. Seleucus tried to hold the East, and his line, the Seleucids, made their capital at Antioch in Syria. They struggled for Palestine with the Ptolemies. One of their kings, Antiochus Epiphanes (175–163 BC), became the bitter enemy of the Jews. In Asia Minor, Macedonia and Greece the situation was confused, as rival kings fought for power.

Greek influence   The high point of Greek civilization belongs to the period before Alexander. The later period is known as the Hellenistic age (from *Hellen*, meaning "Greek"). During this time Greek became an international language for the eastern Mediterranean and beyond. It was the language of trade, and of education and writing, even for people who still usually spoke their own languages. Even the Jews were influenced by it. In the second century BC the Old Testament was translated into Greek at Alexandria in Egypt, for the Greek-speaking Jews there.

This translation, called the Septuagint, was the version of the Old Testament best known to the first Christians.

As the power of Rome increased, the Romans became involved in the affairs of Greece. In 146 BC they destroyed Corinth, which had resisted them. This was the end of Greek political freedom. But their Roman conquerors took over Greek ways of thinking. Greek was established as the official language of the eastern half of the Roman Empire. It was natural for the New Testament to be written in Greek.

The New Testament The New Testament often mentions Greeks. It sometimes means simply non-Jews (Gentiles), Greek-speaking people of the Roman world. Very little of its story takes place in the land of Greece. Yet Paul, though a strict Jew, wrote in Greek and understood Greek ways of thinking. He knew, for instance, of the Greek interest in athletics, and pictured the Christian life as a race and a boxing match (1 Corinthians 9:24–27). Most of his work was in cities of the Greek kind, especially in Asia Minor (Turkey), which at that time contained some of the largest and richest Greek towns, such as Ephesus. These cities still had their rights, and lived a busy public life. There were meetings, markets, committees, elections, debates, sports, and theatres. They had trade-unions, and even strikes and demonstrations. But the real power belonged to the Roman governor.

Christian meets Greek The classic meeting of Christian with Greek took place in Athens itself. It was still a university town, though now living on its past glory. Paul found it a city full of religious images. He began to argue with those whom he met in the public square, and was called before the "Court of the Areopagus" to present his new ideas. Paul spoke in terms they would understand. He quoted their poets. He dealt with the arguments of the Stoics and Epicureans, two leading parties among their thinkers. But he was deeply in earnest, and had more than this to say. For all the cleverness of their scholars they did not know God. He said boldly that God does not "live in man-made temples" (Acts 17:24) like the beautiful ones that stood all around them. God called all people to change their way of life. He would judge all by Jesus, whom he had raised from the dead.

Most of the Athenians were unwilling to receive these teachings. Greeks, said Paul, looked for "wisdom", but his message was foolish to them (1 Corinthians 1:22–23). Their thinkers took a different view of life after death. They were proud and did not care to open their minds to the evidence for such a disturbing challenge to their ways.

GREEK AND ROMAN RELIGION

The Roman Empire covered a very large area, and included peoples with many different beliefs. Those living in the eastern Empire were the ones whom the early Christians first met. They were often influenced by eastern ideas which had been handed down from long before Greek civilization came to them.

The Minoans of Crete and the oldest peoples of Greece worshipped a fertility goddess. Like Baal in the Canaanite myths her consort-god was believed to die and rise again, like the seasons of the year. The details of this kind of religion varied from place to place, but many of these ideas were common throughout the eastern Mediterranean lands. They remained especially strong in country districts, where people's living depended on their herds and crops.

The gods of Greece and Rome   The first Greeks brought with them a new group of gods. Their supreme god was Zeus. He ruled over the other gods who lived on Olympus, the highest mountain in Greece. The Greeks were a logical people, and tried to build complete family histories of the gods and fit all the older beliefs and local stories into the system. So these gods were pictured vividly. They were like people in the way they behaved — often jealous or vengeful, or immoral — but of course they were far more powerful.

Roman religion was really quite different. But when the Romans conquered the Greeks they took over all their gods and gave them Roman names. So Zeus became the Roman god Jupiter. His wife Hera became the Roman Juno, and his brother Poseidon, god of the sea, was given the name Neptune. Among the other gods were Ares (Mars), god of war; Hermes (Mercury) the messenger of the gods; Hades or Pluto (Dis), god of the dead; Hephaestus (Vulcan) the lame craftsman; and Apollo, god of wisdom. The best-known of the other goddesses were Artemis (Diana), the huntress and twin sister of Apollo; Athena (Minerva), patroness of art and war; Aphrodite (Venus), goddess of love; and Demeter (Ceres), goddess of the harvest. These names were remembered long after people ceased to believe in these gods. Some of them are still in use as the names of planets.

Festivals   Greek religion was based on the city. There were great festivals in which everybody took part together, and social events were based on religion. The Olympic Games were first held as a religious event to honour Zeus. The plays in the theatre at Athens, tragedies and comedies, were performed at the festival of the god Dionysus. And the greatest works of Greek art all had a religious meaning.

Yet this religion did not satisfy people. It offered no real answers to the problems of good and evil, life and death. Life was uncertain. These gods had no power to save their cities from sudden disaster. People looked for purpose in life. Why should they live good lives if the gods could not give them justice?

The philosophers   Many thoughtful people turned to philosophy. Plato wrote down the discussions of his master Socrates, about subjects like justice and life after death, and built up a noble system of

The Maison Carrée at Nîmes in France was built as a Roman temple in 16 BC.

thought. Later the Stoics advised people to live in harmony with reason. And the Epicureans believed the world had come about by the chance meeting of atoms. They thought that men should live quietly without fear. Others made new moral lessons from the old stories of the gods. But many were near despair. They worshipped Tyche ("Chance"), and hoped that then the chances of life might favour them. Or they turned to astrology or magic.

New religions   Others found hope in new religions, often from the East, which promised a personal "salvation" to the worshipper. This idea was a very important one, but it meant very different things to people — being saved from evil or death, or from trouble or danger, or being given success in life. It was a fashionable word, rather as people speak of "security" today. A victorious king was often honoured as the "saviour" of his people. He was the one who could give them what they needed. It was only a matter of time before some of his less sophisticated subjects began worshipping him as a god.

The Romans   Little is really known about the earliest Roman religion, but it was clearly then very different from that of the Greeks. The early Romans felt that a divine power (*numen*) existed in nature, and they wanted to harness it to their needs. So there were "gods" for every area of life: gods of the house and of its doorway, of the fields, and so on. Most of these seem to us to have had a vague kind of existence. Only a few of the official gods of the state, like Jupiter, were clearly pictured as persons. But then Greek influence came, and the old Roman gods were fitted into the Greek system. Roman beliefs merged with Greek ideas in such a way that it is hard to separate out what is purely Roman.

Religion and the ordinary man   Many things were always common to both Greeks and Romans. Both worshipped many gods, but their religion had little effect on the way the worshipper lived. Neither belief nor behaviour was really important. A person might believe what he wished, as long as he did what was expected of a good citizen, and remained loyal to the state. There was no great stress on a search for truth, nor was there any powerful body of priests. The gods were distant. They were to be paid due honour. But they were not deeply interested in human affairs.

Educated Romans in the time of Julius Caesar (first century BC) often had little regard for these gods. They would use the forms of religion for their own ends when there was some personal advantage or a political point to gain. But if they thought seriously about life they turned, like the Greeks, to philosophy or new religions.

The emperor   Augustus (27 BC–AD 14) tried to revive Roman religion in a more splendid form. His chosen title, "Augustus", had a sense of religious awe. He wanted to use religion to bind people in loyalty to his own government. In the East he was worshipped as a god in his lifetime, for he had brought peace and good government to a world torn by war. A great temple was built to Rome and Augustus at Pergamum (near the west coast of modern Turkey).

The mysteries   Those who wanted a more personal faith went to the "mystery" religions. Here the worshipper was admitted step by step into the secret inner spiritual knowledge of the faith. The mysteries at Eleusis in Greece had been known since early times. But many new foreign cults became popular in the Greek and Roman world of the first century AD. The Egyptian goddess Isis had many priests and an impressive ritual, and was thought to answer prayer. The Persian Mithras was the soldier's god. Men advanced from rank to rank in his service in the fight againt evil. For a time Mithraism was one of the most serious rivals of Christianity.

Rome and the Christians   Rome usually allowed these different beliefs to flourish. But groups which might not be loyal to the state were always banned. Judaism was specially allowed and, at first, Christianity was too, because it seemed to be a kind of Judaism. But, as time went on, the Romans began to use emperor worship as a test of loyalty. The Emperor Domitian (AD 81–96) required people to worship him as "lord and god". So the position of Christians changed and they had to be ready to suffer for their faith. That was the situation when the Book of Revelation was written.

The New Testament accounts of other religions are mostly set in the East (especially in modern Turkey). At Lystra, Paul and Barnabas were mistaken for Hermes and Zeus (Acts 14:12–13). At Ephesus the famous temple of Artemis was one of the "seven wonders of the world" (Acts 19). She was really an eastern fertility goddess fitted to a Greek name. Paul answered these ideas at Lystra and at Athens: God creates, supplies, loves and judges all men.

Gnosticism Most of these religions easily became mixed. And about the time of the New Testament there arose a kind of thinking called "Gnosticism". Gnostics believed that "spirit" was good and that material things were evil. Gnosticism came to be mixed with Christian and other ideas. But because it put other beings between God and man it denied the special place of Christ. Gnosticism, like the mystery religions, appealed to people who boasted of having a special inner knowledge (*gnosis*) that was better than the simple "trust" that Christians talked of. Paul opposed the beginnings of this kind of thinking at Colossae. It became a serious problem for the church in the second century.

HABAKKUK
A prophet to Judah who lived at the end of the seventh century BC, the time of Jeremiah. The Chaldaeans were becoming more and more powerful and Habakkuk found it hard to understand how God could use this wicked nation to punish his people. The answer came that God would one day judge all who were proud and wicked, including Judah's enemies.

HABOR
The River Khabur in north-east Syria. A tributary of the River Euphrates. The town of Gozan was on the Habor River.
2 Kings 17:6

HADADEZER/HADAREZER
A king of Zobah in Syria. Three times King David defeated Hadadezer's troops. After the third defeat the people of Zobah became David's subjects.
2 Samuel 8–10; 1 Chronicles 18–19

HAGGAI
A prophet who probably returned from Babylon to Jerusalem in the party led by Zerubbabel. His message, recorded in the Book of Haggai, was given in 520 BC. Haggai was concerned to find that the people had built houses for themselves and were

living in comfort while God's temple was still in ruins. He urged the people to rebuild it.

HAGAR

Sarah's servant. Abraham took her as his secondary wife (concubine) when it seemed God's promise that his descendants would become a great nation could not come true because he had no children. Hagar became pregnant and ran away into the desert because Sarah treated her unkindly. An angel told Hagar to return and promised that her son Ishmael would be the founder of a nation. Ishmael was about fourteen years old when Sarah's son, Isaac, was born. When Ishmael made fun of Isaac Sarah asked Abraham to send Hagar and her son away. Hagar travelled through the desert until all her water was gone. Death seemed near, but instead an angel showed her a well and repeated God's promise about Ishmael.
Genesis 16; 21

HAIR

The Israelites in the Old Testament normally grew their hair long. (See for example the stories of Samson and Absalom.) The Asiatic nomads shown as visitors to Egypt on the Beni-Hasan painting have long hair which came over their foreheads and hung down their backs. They also have beards which are neatly trimmed. Many years later, Assyrian inscriptions show the Israelites wearing beards. To shave off the beard was a sign of mourning. But by New Testament times, under the influence of the Greeks

A Roman lady, with her hair kept in place by a net.

and Romans, hair was worn short and many men were clean shaven.

Grey hair was to be respected, as a sign of old age. "One who had been living for ever" — presumably God himself — is pictured with white hair in Daniel 7:9. Men sometimes plaited their hair. At other times it was trimmed by the barber. The hair at the sides of the head, by the ears, was never cut. Leviticus 19:27 forbids it, as a pagan practice, a law still observed. Women plaited, braided or curled their hair. It was often kept in place by beautiful ivory combs. In Roman times the hair was piled on top of the head and kept in place by a net. The rich had nets of gold thread.

HAM

Noah's second son. Ham was the founder of the Egyptian, Ethiopian, Libyan and Canaanite nations. Genesis 5:32; 6:10; 10:6–20

HAMAN

The chief minister of King Ahasuerus of Persia. He hated the Jew Mordecai for refusing to bow down to

him, and plotted to kill Mordecai and all the Jewish people in Persia. Haman was hanged when Queen Esther revealed his plot to the king.
Esther 3–9

HAMATH
Modern Hama, on the River Orontes in Syria. In Old Testament times Hamath was an important town, capital of a small kingdom, and on a main trade-route from Asia Minor (Turkey) south to Israel and Egypt. Hamath Pass, some distance to the south, was the "ideal" northern limit of Israel. In the reigns of David and Solomon, Israel had a peace treaty with King Toi of Hamath. The town fell to the Assyrians and many of its people were moved into Israel. First Pharaoh Neco (before the Battle of Carchemish) and then King Nebuchadnezzar of Babylon made it their headquarters for a time.
Joshua 13:5; 2 Samuel 8:9–11; 1 Kings 8:65; 2 Chronicles 8:4; 2 Kings 17:24; 18:34, etc.

HANANI
Best-known of several Hananis is the man who travelled to Susa to tell Nehemiah that Jerusalem was still in ruins, even though the Jewish exiles had returned. When Nehemiah had rebuilt the walls of Jerusalem he made Hanani governor.
Nehemiah 1:2; 7:2

HANNAH
The wife of Elkanah and mother of Samuel. For several years Hannah had no children. While she was making her annual visit to the shrine at Shiloh

Hannah made a vow. She promised God that if he gave her a son, she would give him back to serve God. When Samuel was old enough Hannah took him to Shiloh where he helped Eli, the priest. Mary, the mother of Jesus, echoed Hannah's wonderful prayer of thanks in her great song of praise to God before Jesus was born. Hannah became the mother of three other sons and two daughters.
1 Samuel 1–2

HAROD
The spring where Gideon chose his fighting-force by watching how the men drank from the stream. The 300 who showed their alertness by stooping and lapping the water were chosen. The place was in northern Palestine, probably by a stream which flows down the Valley of Jezreel.
Judges 7:1–8

HARRAN
A town in what is now south-east Turkey, on the River Balikh, a tributary of the River Euphrates. This was the place where Abraham's father, Terah,

Simple mud "beehive" houses at present-day Harran.

settled after leaving Ur, and where Jacob worked for Laban. Harran was on the main road linking Nineveh with Aleppo in Syria, and on south to the port of Tyre. It was fortified by the Assyrians as a provincial capital. For three years after the fall of Nineveh it was Assyria's capital city. Then in 609 BC it fell to the Babylonians.
Genesis 11:31; 12:4–5; 29:4, etc.; 2 Kings 19:12; Ezekiel 27:33

HASIDIM

The name "Hasidim" means "pious ones". This group was not an organized sect. It is the name given to those Jews who resisted the inroads of Greek culture (Hellenism) into Jewish life and culture. In the second century BC some of them joined the Maccabees in the armed struggle against the Greek rulers (1 *Maccabees* 2:42). Others were pacifists. All certainly were faithful followers of the Law, and many of them joined the sects of the Pharisees and the Essenes.

HAZAEL

An officer at the court of Benhadad II whom God told Elijah to anoint as king of Syria. Elisha wept when God showed him what Hazael would do to the Israelites. Hazael killed Benhadad and seized the throne. He made war against the kings of Israel and Judah.
1 Kings 19:15–17; 2 Kings 8ff.

HAZOR

A Canaanite city in the north of Israel. King Jabin of

A bronze plaque of a Canaanite, found at Hazor.

Hazor organized an alliance against Joshua. But he was defeated, and the city was burned. Another king of Hazor was defeated by Deborah and Barak. King Solomon rebuilt and fortified Hazor, with Megiddo and Gezer. In the eighth century BC the Assyrians destroyed the city.

Archaeologists have uncovered an upper and a lower city, which at its greatest may have housed as many as 40,000 people. The lower part was destroyed in the thirteenth century BC (about the time of Joshua). A city gate and wall from Solomon's time match others of the same design at Megiddo and Gezer. Hazor is mentioned in Egyptian and Babylonian texts, and in the Amarna Letters, as well as in the Bible itself.
Joshua 11; Judges 4; 1 Kings 9:15; 2 Kings 15:29

HEALING
One of the results of evil in the world is illness.

People become sick, age and die as a result of the "fall", the coming of sin into the world.

This does not mean to say that a person is ill because he has sinned. This idea was commonly held in Jesus' day, but he did not agree.

Jesus came to announce a whole new creation in which sin and sickness and death would be no more. The new creation has already begun, with the resurrection of Jesus, but it remains to be completed in the future. Those who believe in him will share in it.

So the power of Jesus to heal sickness as well as to forgive sins was a way of showing what the new kingdom was like, and that it was real. He applied to himself the prophecy of Isaiah: "The spirit of the Lord is upon me, because he has chosen me to bring good news to the poor. He has sent me to proclaim liberty to the captives and recovery of sight to the blind." His healing of the sick in mind and body was a sample, a foretaste, of the coming age.

Christ's healing work has been continued by his disciples ever since. Paul describes a gift of healing given to every church. James considers it natural to call in the elders of the church to pray for a sick person. He advised Christians: "confess your sins to one another, so that you will be healed." The salvation Jesus brings is for the whole person.

But until "all things are made new" at the end of time, the church cannot reverse the whole process of sickness, ageing and death. Healings will still be the occasional demonstration of the kingdom, of God's love and power, until the spiritual reality of the kingdom reaches its complete fulfilment.

Genesis 3:14–19. *Some Old Testament healings:* Numbers 21:4–9; 1 Kings 17:17–24; Deuteronomy 7:12–15; 28:20–23; 2 Kings 4:18–37; 5. *Some of Jesus' healings:* Matthew 8:5–13, 28–34; 9:32–33; 17:14–18; Mark 7:31–37; 10:46–52; Luke 4:18–19; 7:11–15; 8:41–42, 49–56; 17:11–19; John 9; 11. Acts 3:1–10 and other passages; 1 Corinthians 15; James 5:14–16; Revelation 21:1–5; 22:1–2

HEAVEN
The Hebrews used the word "heaven" to refer to the sky. The phrase "the heaven and the earth" means the same as our word "universe".

Heaven can also refer to where God is. So Jesus taught his disciples to pray, "Our Father in heaven . . ." God is not alone in "heaven". He is surrounded by the "angels of heaven" who serve him. Christians are promised a place "in heaven" after this life. Jesus promised his disciples that he was going there to prepare a place for them. So "heaven" is the experience in which all the angels and all the believers who once lived on earth join in unending worship of God.

What is heaven like? We are told that it will be "home", where there will be rest, but also a share in God's work. In "heaven" we shall be safe and happy in God's presence, with nothing to spoil things. In "heaven" we shall meet all who have trusted Jesus in life — and we shall know them, as Jesus' disciples recognized him after the resurrection. "Heaven" is a "treasure-house", where more important things than money are kept for us. In heaven there are no tears, there is no pain, no weakness, no night or need for sleep. In God's presence there is joy for ever.

See also *Angel, Future destiny, Resurrection, Second coming of Jesus.*
Matthew 6:9; Nehemiah 9:6; Mark 13:32; Luke 6:21–23; 1 Peter 1:4; John 14:2; Romans 8; 1 Corinthians 15; Philippians 1:21–23; 3:12–21; 1 Peter 1:3–5; Revelation 4; 21–22

HEBREWS

A letter written to a group of Christian Jews, some time in the first century. They seemed to be in danger of giving up their Christian faith.

The writer sets out to strengthen their faith. He shows Jesus as the one who truly and finally reveals God to man.

The writer shows that Jesus is far greater than the angels, or the great men of the Old Testament, Moses and Joshua (1:1–4:13). He shows that Jesus, as priest "for ever", is far greater than the priests of the Old Testament (4:14–7:28). He shows that Jesus provides a better agreement between God and man, and a final once-for-all sacrifice, to which the Old Testament writers pointed forward (chapters 8–10). Jesus is the perfect priest, offering the perfect sacrifice, reconciling God and man.

The writer looks at the shining example of faith given by the great men and women in Israel's history (chapter 11). He urges his readers not to turn back, but to stay faithful to Jesus despite suffering and persecution (chapters 12–13).

It is not known who wrote the letter.

HEBRON

A town high in the Judean hills (3,040ft/935m above

sea level). The old name for Hebron was Kiriatharba. Abraham and his family often camped near Hebron. He bought the cave of Machpelah from the Hittites at Hebron (see *Machpelah*). Moses' twelve spies came to Hebron, and it was later given to Caleb. Hebron was a city of refuge, and one of the Levites' towns. It was David's capital before he captured Jerusalem. Absalom staged his rebellion from Hebron. Much later, after the exile, Jews returned to live there.

Genesis 13:18; 23; 35:27; 37:14; Numbers 13:22; Joshua 14:6–15; 2 Samuel 2:1–4; 15:9–10; Nehemiah 11:25

HELIOPOLIS
See *On*.

HELL
The teaching of Jesus is clear about the fact of hell as an eternal punishment for those who do evil. Jesus uses very vivid imagery to describe it — a rubbish tip; outer darkness; fire which never goes out; a fiery furnace where people will cry and grind their teeth; and the place where God destroys both body and soul.

These phrases are not to be taken as a literal description. They are meant as warnings. They emphasize the absolute and final nature of God's judgement and it is a mistake to draw exact meanings out of them. But it is also a mistake to dismiss the idea of hell as some medieval idea about little devils with pitchforks. Hell is an essential part of Jesus' own stern warnings about sin and its power.

In fact Jesus said that he himself will pronounce sentence on the day of judgement — "Away from me, you that are under God's curse! Away to the eternal fire which has been prepared for the Devil and his angels!"

In English (for example in the Apostles' Creed) the word "hell" has sometimes been used with a different meaning to describe the Hebrew word *Sheol* (Greek *Hades*). In this case it means, not the place of eternal punishment but the place of the dead.

See also *Death, Future destiny, Judgement*.
Matthew 18:8–9; 3:12; 13:42; Mark 9:48; Matthew 10:38; 25:41; Revelation 20:10–15

HERMON

A mountain on the Lebanon/Syria border. It is over 9,000/2,750m high. It is also called Sirion in the Bible. It is topped with snow almost all the year round. The melting snow and ice form a major source of the River Jordan. Mt Hermon is close to Caesarea Philippi and may be the "high mountain" where Jesus' disciples saw him in his glory.
Joshua 12:1, etc.; Psalm 42:6; 133:3; Matthew 17:1, etc.

HEROD

1. Herod the Great. Son of Antipater, who was made procurator of Judea by Julius Caesar in 47 BC. Antipater appointed Herod to be governor of Galilee. After the death of his father and brother Joseph, who was governor of Jerusalem, the Romans gave Herod the title "king of the Jews". He reigned from

37–4 BC. Herod was hated by the Jews, although he spent large sums of money on the temple. He was not a Jew by birth and murdered members of the Jewish Hasmonaean family whom he saw as a threat to the throne. When the wise men came to worship the baby Jesus he again felt threatened and ordered the murder of all male children in Bethlehem under two years old. After his death his kingdom was divided amongst three of his sons: Archelaus, Antipas and Philip.
Matthew 2; Luke 1:5

2. Archelaus, called Herod the Ethnarch, ruled Judea 4 BC–AD 6. When Mary and Joseph returned with Jesus from Egypt and heard that Archelaus was ruler of Judea they decided to settle in Galilee instead. Archelaus treated the Jews and Samaritans so cruelly that they complained to the Romans, who sent him into exile.
Matthew 2:22

3. Antipas, called Herod the Tetrarch, ruled Galilee 4 BC–AD 39. He imprisoned John the Baptist and as a result of a rash promise agreed to his wife's request to have him beheaded. Pilate handed Jesus over to Antipas for trial because he came from Galilee. Antipas treated Jesus with scorn and then sent him back to Pilate.
Matthew 14; Mark 6; Luke 23:7ff.

4. Agrippa I, called Herod the King, was son of Aristobulus and grandson of Herod the Great. He became ruler of Galilee, Judea and Samaria. To please the Jews he persecuted the Christians. He killed James, the son of Zebedee, and imprisoned Peter. Luke, the writer of Acts, records that Agrip-

pa's death in AD 44 was a result of his pride.
Acts 12

5. Agrippa II was the son of Agrippa I. When he went to Caesarea to visit the Roman governor, Festus, he heard Paul's case. His verdict was that Paul could have been released if he had not appealed to Caesar.
Acts 25:13–26:32

HERODIAS

The wife of Herod Antipas. Herod married Herodias while Philip, her first husband, was still alive. Because John the Baptist condemned the marriage, Herodias had him beheaded.
Matthew 14; Mark 6; Luke 3:19

HEZEKIAH

King of Judah 716–687 BC (co-regent from 729) after his father, King Ahaz. As soon as he became king, Hezekiah re-opened and repaired the temple. He organized a national campaign to destroy everything to do with idol worship. Hezekiah rebelled against the Assyrians and refused to pay taxes to them. During his reign the northern kingdom of Israel was completely conquered by Assyria. Hezekiah realized that his country was also threatened. He cut a rock tunnel to ensure Jerusalem's water supply in the event of siege. King Sennacherib of Assyria captured several cities in Judah and surrounded Jerusalem. Judah was saved when death struck the Assyrian army overnight. Soon after this, Hezekiah became very ill but God answered his prayer and gave him another fifteen years to live.

2 Kings 18–20; 2 Chronicles 29–32; Isaiah 36–39

HIERAPOLIS
A city in the Roman province of Asia, now in western Turkey. Paul mentions the Christians at Laodicea and Hierapolis in his letter to nearby Colossae. Over the centuries the hot-water springs at Hierapolis (modern Pamukkale), have "petrified" to form amazing waterfalls of stone.
Colossians 4:13

HILKIAH
Best-known of several Hilkiahs is the high priest who lived in the reign of King Josiah of Judah. While the temple was being repaired he found an old scroll with God's laws written on it. This discovery led to a great reform in the worship at the temple.
2 Kings 22–23; 2 Chronicles 34

HINNOM
The name of a valley on the south side of Jerusalem, forming the boundary between the tribes of Judah and Benjamin. Here the kings Ahaz and Manasseh set up a shrine for the god Molech, and children were offered to him in sacrifice. It was destroyed by Josiah. Jeremiah denounced the evil of this place. Later, rubbish from the city was burned in the Valley of Hinnom. So it became a picture of hell. The word "Gehenna", meaning "Valley of Hinnom", became a word for "hell".
Joshua 15:8; 18:16; 2 Kings 23:10; 2 Chronicles 28:3; 33:6; Jeremiah 7:31; 19:2; 32:35

HIRAM

1. A king of Tyre who was a friend of King David and King Solomon. He sent cedar-wood from Lebanon to Jerusalem for the building of David's palace and later for Solomon's temple.
2 Samuel 5:11; 1 Kings 5; 9–10
2. A craftsman sent by King Hiram to help King Solomon build his palace and the temple.
1 Kings 7

HISTORY OF ISRAEL

The Near East before 3000 BC had two quite separate centres of civilization. Each had its own culture, crafts and system of writing. One was in Mesopotamia, the land around the Tigris and Euphrates rivers, part of the "fertile crescent". The other was Egypt. The story of mankind begins in Eden, placed somewhere in Mesopotamia. Abraham came from the south Mesopotamian city of Ur. Some of his family settled at Harran in the north while he went on to Canaan.

So the world of Israel's early ancestors was one of rich and powerful kingdoms in the river valleys of Egypt and Mesopotamia. In the lands between were many walled cities and tiny kingdoms. These strongholds protected the settlers who farmed the country around. But there were also nomadic tribespeople who moved from place to place in search of good grazing for their flocks and herds. Abraham and his family were just one group among many on the move in the area.

This was the pattern in Canaan when Abraham arrived to set up camp at Shechem. The coastal plain and the Jordan Valley, where there was good farm-land, were already settled. This looked attractive to Abraham's nephew Lot, who moved down from the hills to camp near Sodom. But life there had its dangers. Lot was only one of many who suffered when rebel kings tried to throw off the control of their distant overlords (Genesis 14).

Drought and famine often struck Canaan. So it was natural for the nomads to move down to the fertile land of Egypt. On one occasion (Genesis 12) Abraham was among them. A later famine took the brothers of Abraham's great-grandson, Joseph, to Egypt to buy corn. Soon the whole family of Israel (Jacob's twelve sons) were settled in Goshen, in the eastern Nile Delta.

The Exodus For nearly 400 years Jacob's people remained in Egypt. During that time they had grown into a nation — the nation of Israel. The

Semitic people arriving in Egypt. Part of a wall-painting at Beni-Hasan, Egypt, from about 1890 BC.

Egyptians, now ruled by a less friendly dynasty of kings, began to see these people as a threat. They tightened their control, forcing the Israelites to work as slaves in the brickfields. To reduce their growing numbers, newborn Hebrew boys were drowned in the Nile. The people cried out to God — and he sent them a leader: Moses.

It took a series of terrible plagues before the king of Egypt would agree to let the Israelites leave his country. At the last minute he changed his mind and sent his army in pursuit — but the Israelites escaped across the "sea of reeds" to Sinai. The "exodus" had begun.

See *Exodus*.

Exodus 1–14

The conquest of Canaan Joshua took over leadership of the people as they entered the land across the Jordan. In front of them was the walled city of Jericho. The whole land God had promised them was waiting to be possessed. Canaan at this time was divided into a large number of small independent states, each centred on a fortified town with its own ruler.

Joshua took Jericho, and struck fear into the hearts of the Canaanites. At the second attempt, Ai fell. Men from Gibeon lost no time in sueing for peace. They tricked the Iraelites into a treaty and this led to the next stage in the war. Joshua won a series of victories in the south and then turned north to defeat the king of Hazor's alliance. The Philistines remained in their cities on the coastal plain. And the Canaanites still controlled many inland towns. But it was possible for the Israelites to settle.

Lots were cast to share out the land among the tribes. Two and a half tribes settled east of the Jordan. The rest shared the land of Canaan. The Levites had no tribal land, but were given certain towns to live in. Six towns were set aside as cities of refuge, where people guilty of manslaughter were safe from revenge.

Joshua

The Judges The tribes settled into the areas allotted to them. They were scattered now, and surrounded by hostile neighbours. Joshua was dead. It began to seem impossible to gain full control of the land. Gradually the Israelites lost sight of the fact that God was fighting for them. They began to compromise with the nations around, and with their gods, for the sake of peace. Their enemies took advantage of their evident weakness. The Book of Judges relates the sad story.

The surrounding nations returned to the attack: the king of Mesopotamia from the north; Moabites and Ammonites from across the Jordan; Midianites from the east. The Canaanites at Hazor grew strong enough to make a second attack on the settlers. And from the coastlands the Philistines pushed the Israelites further and further into the hills.

As at so many times in their history, the Israelites cried to God for help in their need. Each "Judge" won at least a temporary respite. The most famous of these freedom-fighters are Deborah and Barak, Gideon, Jephthah and Samson.

Israel's first kings The last and greatest of the Judges was Samuel — prophet and king-maker. When Samuel grew old, the people asked for a king to rule them, like the other nations. Samuel warned them that a king would mean conscription to the army, forced labour and oppression. But the Israelites insisted. And at last Samuel did as they asked.

The first king was a tall, handsome Benjaminite called Saul. To begin with all went well. But power went to Saul's head and he began to disregard God's clear instructions. Because of Saul's disobedience, his son Jonathan did not inherit the throne. Instead, during Saul's lifetime, God sent Samuel to anoint David as Israel's next king.

While still just a shepherd-boy, David killed the Philistine champion, Goliath. His popularity made Saul jealous, and for a number of years David was forced to live as an outlaw, in danger of his life. Then Saul and Jonathan were killed in battle against the Philistines. David became king.

David united the kingdom, captured Jerusalem, the Jebusite stronghold, and made it his capital. He was a soldier-king. During his lifetime he expanded the kingdom and drove off old enemies. His legacy to his son Solomon was peace and security.

David wanted to build a temple for God in Jerusalem, but he had to be content with getting materials together. It was Solomon who built the temple, and many other fine buildings. A strong, secure kingdom made it possible for Solomon to prosper through trade alliances. His wisdom was legendary. At Solomon's court there was leisure for culture and beauty. His reign was Israel's golden age.

1 Samuel 8–1; Kings 11

The two kingdoms Under King Solomon Israel became a rich and powerful kingdom, but the people

King Jehu of Israel paying homage to Shalmaneser III of Assyria: from Shalmaneser's "Black Obelisk".

were oppressed and burdened with heavy taxes and forced labour. When Solomon's son Rehoboam came to the throne they appealed to him to lighten their burdens. He refused. The ten northern tribes rebelled. They set up a new kingdom, the kingdom of Israel, with Jeroboam I ruling as king from his capital at Shechem. In the south, Rehoboam ruled the kingdom of Judah (the tribes of Judah and Benjamin) from Jerusalem.

Jeroboam also had to set up a new centre of worship for the northern kingdom, now cut off from Jerusalem. He chose Dan, in the north, and Bethel, an important centre when Samuel was alive. But pagan practices quickly became part of the worship. The historians who wrote Kings and Chronicles classified the kings as "good" or "bad" depending on whether they reformed religion or let the pagan practices continue.

Uzziah and Hezekiah were two of the reforming kings of Judah. King Ahab of Israel had one of the worst records. He and his foreign wife Jezebel opposed Elijah and persecuted those who worshipped God. The remains of his "ivory house" at Samaria can be seen today. Assyrian annals record that he brought 10,000 men and 2,000 chariots to the Battle of Qarqar, where he joined forces with the Egyptians to resist the Assyrian King Shalmaneser (853 BC).

The rise of the northern powers Israel and Judah, in their strategic position between Egypt and the Mesopotamian powers, were very vulnerable to aggression. David and Solomon were successful partly because none of the larger nations were powerful enough to attack during their reigns. But after the division of the kingdom the nations were immediately around — Syria, Ammon, Moab — gave the subsequent kings of Israel and Judah increasing trouble. However, it was the growth of the major powers farther north-east that proved decisive.

The Assyrian Empire had an earlier period of power under Tiglath-pileser I. But the ruthless aggression for which Assyria was so much feared reached its peak in the period between 880 and 612 BC. The empire was based on three great cities: Asshur, Calah and Nineveh.

From the mid-ninth century BC, the time of Ahab

in Israel, the kings of Assyria repeatedly attacked Israel and Judah. Soon King Jehu of Israel was paying tribute to Shalmaneser III of Assyria. A hundred years later Ahaz of Judah asked Tiglath-pileser III of Assyria to help him fight Syria and Israel (Isaiah 7; 2 Kings 16). He did so and defeated them both, but Judah had to become a subject kingdom of the Assyrians in return for their help.

When Israel refused to pay their yearly tribute, the next king of Assyria took Samaria, exiled the people and destroyed the northern kingdom (722/1 BC; 2 Kings 17). Soon after this, Egypt was defeated by the Assyrians. In 701 BC the powerful King Sennacherib besieged Jerusalem, but because of King Hezekiah's trust in God the city was saved (2 Kings 19).

The Assyrians had to fight many battles to defend their empire. In the next century several provinces regained their freedom. The empire lasted until Asshur fell to the Medes in 614 and Nineveh was destroyed by the Medes and Babylonians in 612.

Invasion and exile   If Assyria in the Bible meant oppression, Babylon meant power. Nabopolassar, governor of the area around the Persian Gulf, freed Babylon from the Assyrians and in 626 BC was made king. He continued to gain victories over the Assyrians and in 612 BC the Babylonians and Medes captured the Assyrian capital of Nineveh. They were not content with taking over Assyria itself but set out to conquer the whole Assyrian Empire.

The Assyrians retreated to Harran but were soon driven out. The Egyptians, realizing that their own country might be in danger, marched north to support them. King Josiah of Judah intercepted the Egyptian army at Megiddo. In the resulting battle he was killed and Judah became subject to Egypt (2 Kings 23:29). Four years later, in 605 BC, the Babylonian army led by Nebuchadnezzar defeated the Egyptians at Carchemish (Jeremiah 46:1–2). The Babylonian Empire was spreading. Jehoiakim of Judah was one of the many kings who now had to pay tribute to Nebuchadnezzar.

After a fierce battle with the Babylonians in 601 BC the Egyptians encouraged Judah to rebel. Nebuchadnezzar sent troops to crush the rebellion and in 597 BC, shortly after Jehoiachin had become king, Judah submitted. The king and many of the country's leaders were taken into exile in Babylon. The policy of the invaders was not just to plunder and destroy, but also to weaken the subject nations and prevent further rebellions by deporting their leading citizens (2 Kings 24:10–17).

Despite this, ten years later Zedekiah, a puppet king placed on the throne of Judah by Nebuchadnezzar, appealed to the Egyptians for help. The Babylonians invaded Judah and laid siege to Jerusalem. The siege lasted eighteen months. Finally, a breach was made in the walls. In 586 BC the city was taken. King Zedekiah was captured and blinded. Valuable objects including the temple treasure were taken to Babylon. Jerusalem and its temple was destroyed and the citizens deported. Only the very poor were left to cultivate the land (2 Kings 25:1–21).
See *Exile*.

Return to Jerusalem   In the first half of the sixth

century BC Babylon appeared all-powerful. But the prophets spoke of a God to whom kings were as puppets, and who could use even pagan powers to fulfil his purposes.

Cyrus the Persian united the two kingdoms of Media and Persia to the east of Babylon. He conquered lands as far east as India. Then he attacked Babylon. The city fell in 539 BC and he took over the whole empire.

The Persian kings extended their borders even further than the earlier empires. They took Egypt and all of what is now Turkey. When Babylon fell, Cyrus began to reorganize the empire. He divided it into provinces, each with its own ruler, called a "satrap". These were mainly Persians, but under them were local rulers who retained some power. The different peoples were encouraged to keep their own customs and religions.

As part of this policy, Cyrus sent the Jews back to Jerusalem to restore the city and rebuild the temple, as told in the books of Ezra and Nehemiah. Jews also settled in many other parts of the empire. In Susa, one of the Persian capitals, a later king, Xerxes I, even made a Jewess his queen, as told in the book of Esther. The "dispersion", as Jews living in other lands came to be called, was significant later, in New Testament times. Because they were away from the temple, these Jews developed the local synagogue as a centre of teaching and worship. And this laid the basis for the later rapid spread of the Christian churches, which were formed on this model.

King Darius I (522–486), builder of the great new capital, Persepolis, and conqueror of western India, also pushed the empire westwards. In 513 he took Macedonia in northern Greece. In 490 the Persians were defeated by the Greeks at Marathon, and the stage was set for some of the greatest stories of Greek classical antiquity. Xerxes I (486–465) invaded Greece, even occupying Athens, but was defeated in the sea battle of Salamis. Artaxerxes, Darius II, and the kings that followed, took up the struggles. The fortunes of Persia and Greece, Media and Egypt ebbed and flowed until finally, in 333 BC, the Greek soldier Alexander of Macedon crossed the Hellespont to begin his meteoric career.

Alexander was only twenty-two when he set out on a campaign which swept across the ancient world. He "liberated" Egypt from the Persians (founding the port of Alexandria), then marched east, to the heart of the Persian Empire. He pressed on as far as India, conquering all who stood in his way and founding Greek city-states wherever he went. His title "Alexander the Great" was well earned. He died, when only thirty-three, in 323 BC.

Following his death, the great Greek Empire was divided up among his four generals. The Seleucid rulers, based on Antioch in Syria, controlled Palestine. The Ptolemies, based on Alexandria, ruled Egypt. Culturally, however, the Greek or "hellenistic" world continued as a unity, with Greek as a common language and with a common pattern of civilization. This background played a vital part in events which were to follow: the events of the New Testament.

Israel in the New Testament By New Testament times the Jewish people had lived under foreign occupation for some 500 years since returning to their own land. Under Greek rule they had paid tribute to Ptolemy of Egypt and adopted Greek as the language of the empire. In 198 BC the Seleucid Greek ruler of Syria, Antiochus the Great, defeated the Ptolemies and took Palestine. But he in turn was defeated by the Romans at Magnesia in 190 BC.

The Romans taxed the Seleucid Empire harshly, and they in turn took any opportunity to loot cities and temples. Antiochus Epiphanes used the opposition of loyal Jews, the "Hasidim" or "pious ones", as an excuse to plunder the Jerusalem temple. Later he built a pagan Greek centre in the heart of the city and in the temple an altar to Zeus on which pigs (forbidden under Jewish food laws) were sacrificed.

This final affront resulted in the Maccabean Revolt. The Jews succeeded in freeing themselves for a time and were able to cleanse and rededicate the temple in 165 BC. The high priest Aristobolus, a late member of the Hasmonaean family which had led the revolt, declared himself king in 104 BC. But before long, rivalries among the Jews gave the Romans the chance to intervene. The last high-priest king was executed in 37 BC.

Judea became subject to Rome under the governor of the province of Syria. But the Jews kept the freedom to practice their religion and had their own ruler: from 37 to 4 BC an Idumaean Jew named Herod. Despite his ambitious building projects — including a new temple in Jerusalem — the Jews hated Herod the Great, and he is chiefly remembered for his tyranny and cruelty.

This was the background to the birth of Jesus.

Luke records the fact that Jesus was born in the time of the first Roman Emperor, Augustus. He was succeeded by Tiberius in AD 14. Herod's act in putting the male children of Bethlehem to death was wholly in character with what we know of him otherwise. When he died, the kingdom was divided among three of his sons. One ruled so badly that the Romans removed him and appointed a "prefect" for Judea. Pontius Pilate, who passed the death sentence on Jesus, was prefect AD 26–36.

The Jewish council, the Sanhedrin, tried to keep the peace with the Romans to protect its own position. Others, such as the hated tax collectors, profited from the Roman occupation to line their own pockets. Many looked forward to the day when they would be delivered, when they would be free. Like Simeon, who was in the temple when Jesus' parents came to present their baby, they were "waiting for Israel to be saved". So Jesus had to be careful to play down any claim to be the promised Messiah, the deliverer, for fear of raising people's hopes that he would lead a revolt against the Romans. The spirit of resistance was strongest among the Zealots (a guerilla group): and it was this spirit that led eventually to the disastrous events of the Jewish War, and the destruction of Jerusalem in AD 70.

But the time when the Jewish temple was destroyed and the Jewish nation scattered was also a time of a new beginning. After the death and resurrection of Jesus, it was made plain to his followers that the new kingdom was not just for the Jews but for all who believed in him. It offered a completely new start, not just for the Jewish people but for all who were to enter into the promises given to Abraham, which were based on faith. It was to mean liberation from sin and guilt and from the petty-fogging legalism of the Jewish Law. Jew and non-Jew ("Gentile") alike could begin a new life, filled with God's Spirit. The dynamic of this message was to turn the Empire upside-down, and change the world.

HITTITES

Before the time of the Israelites and Aramaeans, Syria was controlled by the Hittites from Turkey. They were an Indo-European race who built up an empire which was very powerful from about 1600–1300 BC. Their capital city was Hattusha (now Bogazköy), near Ankara, the modern capital of Turkey. In its ruins the royal archives have been found. They are written in the Babylonian cuneiform script on clay tablets, but in the Hittite languages. Amongst the important documents are many treaties made with subject states. These follow a set pattern — the same pattern followed in Exodus and Deuteronomy, where God's treaties with his people, Israel, are set down.

The Hittites also developed a hieroglyphic writing of their own. In 1286 BC the Hittites fought the Egyptians at the Battle of Qadesh. Neither side won, so they drew up a treaty to agree a border. This was roughly the line followed by the northern boundary of Israel's Promised Land (see Joshua 1:4). About 1200 BC the Hittite Empire disappeared under the attacks of the Sea Peoples (see *Philistines*). Their culture was lost, except in a few outposts. These included some places in northern Syria (Carchemish, Hamath), where descendants of the Hittites mingled with other peoples. Hittite kings and Hittite women are still mentioned in the time of Solomon and even of Elisha — 1 Kings 10:28ff.; 11:1; 2 Kings 7:6. (The Hittites living in Canaan very much earlier — at the time of Abraham, Genesis 23 —may have been migrants from the north, or a separate group with a similar name.)

HOLINESS

The basic idea of holiness is "separate (set apart) for God". In the Old Testament, places, things, people and seasons were called holy when they were set apart for God. For that reason the seventh day, the sabbath, was holy.

The character of God himself shows what holiness is. He is different. He is the one who is absolutely separate from creation, and from all that is evil. Nothing compares with him. His very nature is different from our own: he is "holy". Because of this we should stand in awe of him. When someone realizes how holy God is, as Isaiah did, he is intensely conscious of his own sin that separates him from God.

The people of God have always been expected to reflect the holiness which they see in God. God wants his people to share his holiness. So in the New Testament the common word for Christians is "saints". This did not then mean an especially devout Christian. It meant "the holy ones", those who are set apart and dedicated to God's service. And "saints" are meant to grow in holiness and likeness to God — a process sometimes called "sanctification".

Genesis 2:3; Exodus 20:8; 30:22–33; Leviticus 19:1 Isaiah 6:1–5; 40:18–28; 10:20; Psalm 33:21; Isaiah 8:13; 6; Hebrews 12:10; Ephesians 5:25–27

HOLY SPIRIT

The Spirit of God is one with God the Father and Jesus Christ (see *Trinity*). He is active throughout the history of God's work and God's people. But it is not until the new Testament and the "age of the spirit" that we see the details of his work.

The Spirit of God was active in the creation of the world. As God, he is present everywhere — there is nowhere in the whole of creation outside his domain. Again and again we read of the Spirit of God giving people the power needed for special service. The Spirit of God gave the prophets their inspiration and communicated the word of God through them. But the Old Testament looked forward to the day when the Spirit of God would be poured out on all people.

When Jesus came, he was born by the power of the Holy Spirit. The Holy Spirit descended upon him at his baptism in the River Jordan. He was led by the Spirit into the desert where he was tempted by the devil. And at the beginning of his public work Jesus declared that he would carry it out through the power of the Spirit. John the Baptist declared that Jesus would baptize people with the Holy Spirit. And Jesus himself promised his disciples that after he had left them he would send the Holy Spirit to be with them all the time. After Jesus had returned to his Father, the Holy Spirit would teach and guide the followers of Jesus and give them power. "He will give me glory," Jesus said, "because he will take what I say and tell it to you."

The disciples were baptized with the Holy Spirit, as Jesus promised, on the Day of Pentecost. This was obvious to everyone because of a new note of praise and boldness, because they spoke in other languages, and because of their powerful preaching. As Peter told his listeners on the Day of Pentecost, the prophecy of Joel had come true. God had poured out his Spirit on all believers.

When someone becomes a Christian he or she receives the "gift" of the Holy Spirit. The Holy Spirit lives within the Christian giving new understanding and direction, and making him aware that he really is a child of God. The Spirit is a guarantee of a future with God in heaven.

The Holy Spirit helps Christians to realize their oneness in Jesus Christ. He works to reproduce the character of Jesus in the life of every Christian — the qualities of "love, joy, peace, patience, kindness, goodness, faithfulness, humility and self-control". And he gives Christians the power and gifts needed to serve God.

See also *Trinity, Church*.

Genesis 1:2; Psalm 139:7–12; Judges 3:10; 14:6, and many other passages; Isaiah 11:1–3; 2 Samuel 23:2–5; Ezekiel 36:26–27; Joel 2:28–29; Micah 3:8; Luke 1:35; 3:22; 4:1–18; 3:16; John 14:16–17; 16:7–15; Acts 2; Romans 8; 1 Corinthians 12; Galatians 5:22–23

HOPE

The Christian's hope is a confident looking forward to a future beyond this world, promised by God. It is something that keeps him joyful in troubles.

He has learned that God's promises can be trusted, and so he is confident about the future. "I alone know the plans I have for you," says God to Jeremiah, in the dark days of exile, "plans to bring you prosperity and not disaster, plans to bring about the future you hope for."

The resurrection of Jesus is the great foundation of the Christian's hope. "Because of (God's) great mercy he gave us new life by raising Jesus from death," wrote Peter. "This fills us with a living hope." This is confirmed by the gift of the Holy Spirit, who is the guarantee of the Christian's own future resurrection.

See also *Future destiny*.
Romans 4:18; 5:1–5; 8:24–25; 12:12; 15:4; Jeremiah 29:11; 1 Corinthians 15:19–20; Colossians 1:15; 1 Peter 1:3–6; 2 Corinthians 5:1–5

HOPHNI AND PHINEHAS

Eli's two sons, priests at Shiloh. Because they showed open contempt for God, he forewarned Eli of their death. Hophni and Phinehas carried God's Covenant Box (the ark) into battle against the Philistines. It was captured and they were both killed.
1 Samuel 2:12ff.; 4

HOREB

Another name for Mt Sinai.

HORSE

In Bible times horses were owned only by the rich. They were not kept in Israel until David's day. The country's geographical position made Solomon a convenient middleman, trading in chariots from Egypt and horses from Turkey (Cilicia). The horse was a "weapon" of war and stood for power.
Exodus 14:23; Joshua 11:4; Esther 6:8, 10, 11

HOSEA

Hosea lived at about the same time as Isaiah, the eighth century BC. But he lived in the northern kingdom of Israel. He prophesied during the troubled forty years before the fall of Samaria in 722 BC. Israel had six kings in just over twenty years, and was often turning to pagan religions.

Hosea was greatly concerned about this idol worship. He pictures the faithlessness of Israel in terms of his own marriage to an unfaithful wife (Hosea 1–3). Although God's judgement would come, his love would win his people back in the end.

Chapters 4–13 record his messages to Israel. They show how angry God was, and yet how he could never forget his love for his people. The final chapter pleads with the people to return to God. They would then be able to enjoy his promise of new life.

HOSHEA

The last king of Israel. Hoshea made himself king by killing King Pekah. He was defeated by King Shalmaneser V of Assyria and as a result had to pay him tribute. When Hoshea rebelled he was imprisoned by Shalmaneser. Three years later Samaria, the

capital of Israel, was captured and the people taken away to Assyria.
2 Kings 17

HULDAH
A prophetess who lived in the reign of King Josiah. When Hilkiah the priest found an ancient scroll of God's Law in the temple Josiah asked her advice.
2 Kings 22:14ff.; 2 Chronicles 34:22ff.

HUNTING
Esau, we are told, hunted "venison" (deer). The people of Israel had laws on the subject of hunting — particularly which animals and birds could be eaten

An Assyrian hunter; from a relief in the palace of King Sargon II at Khorsabad, eighth century BC.

and how they were to be killed. Israelite kings may have hunted for sport, as the Mesopotamians and Egyptians did, since "deer, gazelles, roebucks and poultry" were brought to the table of Solomon. People hunted when hunger, or the attacks of wild animals on their flocks, drove them to it. But we do not know whether men regularly hunted for a living. The Old Testament references to catching animals are few.

However, the country lies on a main migration route for birds, so it is not surprising to find frequent mentions of the "fowler" with his nets and snares.

Genesis 25:27; Deuteronomy 14:4–5; Leviticus 17:13; 1 Kings 4:23; Proverbs 1:17; Hosea 7:11–12; Proverbs 6:5; Psalm 124:7

HURRIANS

One group which became part of the Hittite Empire was the Hurrian people. They are known from 2500 BC in Babylonia. But their origin is uncertain and their language — recorded in cuneiform texts — is not properly understood. Groups of them settled throughout the Fertile Crescent. They appear in Edom (the Horites, Genesis 14:6), in Shechem and in Gilgal (the Hivites, Genesis 34:2; Joshua 9:3–7). Hurrian names occur on cuneiform tablets of about 1400 BC found in Canaan, and Egyptian texts refer to Canaan as "Huru". At that time there was an important Hurrian state in upper Mesopotamia (Mitanni). These kings wrote letters to the pharaohs of Egypt. Among their gods they worshipped Mithra and others well known in India. The Hurrians had a strong influence on the Hittites, and they carried Babylonian culture wherever they went.

HUSHAI

A trusted friend of King David. During Absalom's rebellion Hushai pretended to go over to Absalom's side. His misleading "advice" won time for David and he enabled him to escape by informing David's spies of Absalom's plans.
2 Samuel 15:32–17:15

HYMENAEUS

A man who was thrown out of the church by Paul because he taught things which were not true and weakened the faith of some Christians.
1 Timothy 1:20; 2 Timothy 2:17

HYMNS

See *Creeds and hymns*.

HYSSOP

On the cross, Jesus was given vinegar in a sponge passed to him on a bunch of hyssop. In the Old Testament it was used in sprinkling the blood of the sacrifice, and on the eve of the Passover. It was

A sprig of marjoram, possibly the plant called "hyssop" in the Bible.

obviously a bushy plant, and must therefore have been different from the herb we call by the same name today, and may have been either marjoram or caper.

Exodus 12:21–22; John 19:29

I

IBLEAM
A Canaanite town in the north of Israel, about 10 miles/14km south-east of Megiddo. Here Jehu killed King Ahaziah of Judah.
Joshua 17:11–12; 2 Kings 9:27; 15:10

ICONIUM
Present-day Konya in south-central Turkey. Paul preached at Iconium, then a town in the Roman province of Galatia, on his first missionary journey. He met with violent opposition.
Acts 13:51; 14:1–6, 19—22; 2 Timothy 3:11

IDUMAEA
The Greek name for the Old Testament Edom. By New Testament times many Idumaeans had settled west of the Jordan, in the dry country in the south of Palestine. This district was then called Idumaea. King Herod was an Idumaean. People came even from this area in the far south to see Jesus in Galilee.
Mark 3:8

ILLYRICUM
The Roman name of a land stretching along the eastern shore of the Adriatic Sea. It covered much the same area as modern Yugoslavia. The southern part was also called Dalmatia (see *Dalmatia*). When Paul wrote to the Romans, he said he had preached

the gospel from Jerusalem as far west as Illyricum. There is no other mention of Paul's work in this land.
Romans 15:19

ISAAC

The son God promised to Abraham and Sarah. He was born when his parents were very old. A few years after Isaac's birth God tested Abraham's faith even more. He told Abraham to sacrifice his son. Just as he was about to kill Isaac, an angel stopped him. God rewarded Abraham and again promised that his descendants would be a great nation. When Isaac was forty he married Rebekah, a girl chosen for him from Abraham's family in Harran. After many years God answered Isaac's prayer for a son and the twins, Esau and Jacob, were born. God gave Isaac the same blessing he had given Abraham. When Isaac was old and nearly blind he was tricked into passing the blessing on to Jacob instead of Esau, the older twin. Jacob left home but returned several years later in time to see his father before he died.
Genesis 21–22; 24–28:9; 35:27–29

ISAIAH

Isaiah lived in Jerusalem in the eighth century BC. The book named after him is one of the most powerful books of prophecy in the Old Testament. It has a strong picture of God's power and a message of hope for his people. Isaiah's own call to be a prophet is recorded in chapter 6. He continued to prophesy for more than forty years.

Chapters 1–39 belong to the period when the

southern kingdom of Judah was under threat from Assyria — the great power of the biblical world of that time. But Isaiah warned the people that the real danger to the nation was their own sin and disobedience to God. They had failed to trust God. Isaiah called the nation to return to God, and restore justice and right action. If they did not respond, destruction would follow. Isaiah also looked forward to a time when there would be peace throughout the world. A descendant of King David would become the ideal king who would do God's will.

Chapters 40–55 picture the exile of Judah in Babylon. They are often thought to be the work of another prophet who was a follower of Isaiah. The people were without hope. But the prophet spoke of a time when God was going to free his people and restore them to Jerusalem. He emphasized that God controls history. He spoke of God's plan to use the nation of Israel to bring hope to all the nations. This section of the book includes a number of passages in which the prophet looks forward to the coming of the "Servant of the Lord" who would bring hope to the nation.

Chapters 56–66 form a separate section and are mainly addressed to the Jewish people back in Jerusalem. The prophet reassures the people that God will keep his word. But he calls them, also, to justice and right living, and instructs them to keep God's sabbath, to offer sacrifices, and to pray.

ISHBOSHETH/ISHBAAL
One of King Saul's sons. When Saul was killed by the Philistines, Ishbosheth was crowned by Abner,

the commander of Saul's army. He reigned in Israel while David was king of Judah. For two years Judah and Israel were at war. Then Ishbosheth was murdered by two commanders of his army, and David became king of both Israel and Judah.
2 Samuel 2–4

ISHMAEL
Son of Abraham and Hagar. (See *Hagar*.)
Genesis 16; 21

ISRAEL
The new name God gave to Jacob after he had wrestled all night with the "man" at the River Jabbok. Israel means "the man who fights with God". The twelve tribes descended from Jacob were known as the children of Israel. For a full description of the other aspects of the life, land and religion of Israel see separate entries, especially *History of Israel, Religion of Israel, Geography of Israel*.

ISSACHAR
1. Son of Jacob and Leah, who gave his name to one of the twelve tribes of Israel.
Genesis 35:23
2. The land belonging to the tribe of Issachar, south of Lake Galilee and west of the River Jordan.
Joshua 19:17–23

ITHAMAR
Aaron's youngest son. Ithamar was the priest who supervised the making of the worship tent (the tabernacle). He was in charge of two groups of

Levites and founded one of the important families of priests.

Exodus 6:23; 38:21; Numbers 3ff.; 1 Chronicles 24:1

ITURAEA

A name mentioned only in Luke's careful dating of the time when John the Baptist began to preach. Herod Philip was then ruler of Ituraea and Trachonitis. The Ituraeans were probably the descendants of the Old Testament people called Jetur. They were a wild tribal people in the hills west of Damascus, north of the headwaters of the River Jordan. See also *Trachonitis*.

Luke 3:1; compare 1 Chronicles 5:19

J

JABBOK
Now the Zerqa, a river that flows into the Jordan from the east, between the Dead Sea and Lake Galilee. Jacob wrestled with an angel beside the Jabbok. Adam — the place where the Jordan was dammed, allowing the Israelites to cross into the Promised Land — stands at the confluence of the Jabbok and the Jordan. The river is also mentioned in the Bible as a boundary.
Genesis 32:22–30; Numbers 21:24; Deuteronomy 3:16; Judges 11:13

JABESH-GILEAD
A town on the east of the Jordan. When the wives of the Benjaminites were killed in a civil war at the time of the Judges, the town of Jabesh provided replacements. Saul answered an appeal for help when Jabesh was besieged by the Ammonites. Men from Jabesh later risked their lives to remove his body from Beth-shan.
Judges 21; 1 Samuel 11; 31:11–13

JABIN
1. King of Hazor defeated and killed by Joshua.
Joshua 11:1–11
2. A Canaanite king, also from Hazor, who oppres-

sed the Israelites for twenty years. His army was defeated by Barak and Deborah.
Judges 4

JACOB

Son of Isaac and Rebekah; Esau's (younger) twin. When Esau was hungry after hunting, Jacob persuaded him to give up his rights as the elder son in exchange for a bowl of stew. Later Jacob gained his father's special blessing by pretending to be Esau. After that, Esau hated Jacob and planned to kill him. Jacob escaped north to his Uncle Laban in Harran. On the way he had a dream. He saw a staircase reaching from earth to heaven, with angels moving up and down it. God promised him and his descendants the land where he was sleeping. "I will not leave you until I have done all that I have promised you."

Jacob worked for Laban as a shepherd for twenty years. He loved Laban's daughter, Rachel, but was tricked into marrying her sister, Leah, first. While he was in Harran, Jacob became the father of eleven sons and one daughter. He waited long years for his first son by Rachel: Joseph. Later Rachel died giving

Nomads still use camels to travel across the desert, as Jacob did.

birth to a second son, Benjamin. Laban cheated Jacob but in the end was outwitted. Jacob built up his own large flocks of sheep and goats, and then left for his own country. On the way he had a strange all-night wrestling-match with an unknown "man", and would not let him go until he had been blessed. God gave him the new name of Israel which means, "the man who fights with God".

To Jacob's great relief Esau gave him a warm welcome. But afterwards they went their own ways. Jacob lived in the land of Canaan until Joseph invited him to settle in Egypt. Before Jacob died he blessed his sons, the ancestors of the tribes of Israel. Genesis 25:21–34; 27–35; 37:1; 42–49

JAEL
A woman from the nomadic Kenite tribe. After Sisera, commander of the Canaanite army, had lost his battle against the Israelites he ran away and hid in Jael's tent. While he was asleep she murdered him. Deborah praised Jael in her victory song. Judges 4; 5:24–27

JAIRUS
The synagogue official at Capernaum who asked Jesus to heal his twelve-year-old daughter. By the time Jesus reached Jairus's house she was dead. But, to the amazement of her parents, Jesus brought her back to life. Mark 5:22ff.

JAMES
1. The son of Zebedee and a disciple of Jesus. Like

his brother John, James was a fisherman. Jesus nicknamed the two stormy brothers "men of thunder"! When Jesus called him to be one of his special followers James went with him at once. James was present when Jesus brought Jairus's daughter back to life, and at Jesus' glory (the transfiguration). He was killed for his faith by Herod Agrippa I.
Matthew 4:21ff.; 17:1ff.; Mark 5:37; 10:35ff.; Acts 12:2

2. Another apostle, the son of Alphaeus. He was probably the man called "James the younger".
Matthew 10:3; Mark 15:40; Acts 1:13

3. One of Jesus' brothers. James did not believe that Jesus was the Messiah until he saw him after the resurrection. He became a leader of the church in Jerusalem and probably wrote the Letter of James. The Jewish historian Josephus records that he was stoned to death in AD 62.
Matthew 13:55; Acts 12:17; 1 Corinthians 15:7; James

JAMES, LETTER OF

A letter full of practical instructions for "all God's people". We are not sure who wrote it, to whom, or exactly when, though it is often thought that it may have been James, Jesus' brother.

The writer uses colourful word-pictures to set out the behaviour and attitudes which should mark out Christians. The letter comments on faith and wisdom, property and wealth, testing and tempting, hearing and doing. We are to treat everyone with equal respect. Christians must guard their tongues and watch their attitudes towards the world around them. The writer emphasizes that without actions to match, faith is not faith at all. Genuine faith will affect the way we live.

JAPHETH
One of Noah's three sons. He survived the flood to become the founder of several nations.
Genesis 5:32; 9:18ff.; 10:1ff.

JASON
1. A Christian with whom Paul and Silas stayed when they were in Thessalonica.
Acts 17:5–9
2. A Jewish Christian mentioned by Paul.
Romans 16:21

JAVAN
One of the sons of Japheth. Javan is named as the father of a group of peoples, probably including those who lived in Greece and Asia Minor in early times. The name may be connected with the Greek "Ionia", in western Turkey, and it is used in later parts of the Old Testament for Greece or the Greeks.
Genesis 10:2; 1 Chronicles 1:5; Isaiah 66:19; Ezekiel 27:13

JEBUS
An early name for Jerusalem.

JEHOAHAZ
1. King of Israel 814–798 BC, after Jehu, his father. He led his subjects away from the worship of God

and was defeated by Hazael and Benhadad, kings of Syria.
2 Kings 13:1ff.
2. Son of Josiah and king of Judah for three months in 609 BC. He was captured and taken prisoner to Egypt by Pharaoh Neco.
2 Kings 23:31–34

JEHOIACHIN

King of Judah for three months in 597 BC. He was taken prisoner to Babylon by Nebuchadnezzar. Many years later a new king of Babylon released Jehoiachin from prison and gave him a place at court.
2 Kings 24:8–16; 25:27ff.; 2 Chronicles 36:9–10; Jeremiah 52:31ff.

JEHOIADA

The most important man of this name was chief priest in Jerusalem during the reigns of Ahaziah, Queen Athaliah and Joash. Jehoiada was married to Jehosheba, sister of King Ahaziah. Athaliah, the queen mother, seized the throne when her son died and gave orders for all the royal family to be killed. But Jehoiada hid his nephew Joash, one of Ahaziah's sons. After six years he made Joash king and Athaliah was killed. Jehoiada ruled as regent until Joash was old enough to govern the country himself.
2 Kings 11–12; 2 Chronicles 23–24

JEHOIAKIM

Son of Josiah and king of Judah 609–597 BC. He was made king by Pharaoh Neco and had to pay taxes to

Egypt. Jehoiakim undid all the good of his father's reign and was greedy and cruel. He burnt the scroll of Jeremiah's prophecies. When he rebelled against Babylon Judah was invaded.
2 Kings 24:1–7; 2 Chronicles 36:4–8; Jeremiah 22:18ff.; 26; 36

JEHORAM/JORAM

1. Son of King Ahab. Jehoram was king of Israel 852–841 BC, after the death of his brother, King Ahaziah. He ended Baal worship but did not wholly reform and was murdered by Jehu, who wiped out all Ahab's descendants.
2 Kings 3; 8–9
2. King of Judah 848–841 BC (co-regent from 853) after his father Jehoshaphat. Elijah warned that he would die from a terrible disease because he had murdered his six brothers and encouraged his subjects to worship idols.
2 Kings 8:16ff.; 2 Chronicles 21

JEHOSHAPHAT

Best-known is the son of King Asa who became king of Judah 870–848 BC (co-regent from 873). He was a good king who destroyed idols and made sure his subjects learned God's laws. He improved the legal system and appointed judges in the major towns. But he made the mistake of forming an alliance with King Ahab and became involved in Israel's wars.
1 Kings 22; 2 Kings 3; 2 Chronicles 17–21:1

JEHOSHEBA/JEHOSHABEATH

The sister of King Ahaziah of Judah. Jehosheba was

married to Jehoiada, the priest. (See *Jehoiada*.)
2 Kings 11:1–3; 2 Chronicles 22:11–12

JEHU

A commander in the army of King Jehoram of
Israel. He was king 841–814 BC. He was anointed
king by Elisha and told to wipe out all King Ahab
and Jezebel's descendants as punishment for their
wickedness. This he did. Later in his reign King
Hazael of Syria invaded Israel. Shalmaneser III of
Assyria includes Jehu in a list of subject kings. Jehu
may have asked Assyria to help him defeat Syria.
2 Kings 9–10

JEPHTHAH

One of the "Judges" of early Israel. Before he went
into battle against the Ammonites Jephthah vowed
that if he was successful he would sacrifice whatever
came out of his house when he returned. Jephthah
returned from defeating the Ammonites to be
greeted by his daughter, an only child. Despite his
grief Jephthah kept his vow. He ruled as a Judge for
six years.
Judges 11–12

JEREMIAH

The prophet Jeremiah lived about one hundred
years after Isaiah. He was called to be God's prophet
in 627 BC and died some time after 587 BC. While
he was writing, the power of Assyria, the great
empire to the north, was crumbling. Babylon was
the new threat to the kingdom of Judah.

For forty years Jeremiah warned his people of

God's judgement to come on them for their idol worship and sin. Finally, his words came true. In 587 BC the Babylonian army, led by Nebuchadnezzar, destroyed Jerusalem and the temple. Nebuchadnezzar took the people into exile. Jeremiah himself turned down the offer of a life of comfort at the Babylonian court. He probably finished his days in Egypt.

The chapters in the book do not follow the order in which events happened. The book opens with a description of Jeremiah's call to be a prophet. The first twenty-five chapters consist of messages from God to Judah during the reigns of the last kings — Josiah, Jehoahaz, Jehoiakim, Jehoiachin and Zedekiah.

Israelites being taken prisoner: from an Assyrian relief.

Chapters 26–45 are made up of the events in the life of Jeremiah and additional prophecies.

Chapters 46–51 record God's messages to several foreign nations. The final chapters describe the fall of Jerusalem and the exile to Babylon.

Jeremiah became very unpopular. He was labelled a traitor because he urged his people to give in to Babylon. But he loved his own people, and hated telling them of judgement. He had little self-confidence, but never softened the message God gave him. Although he is remembered as the by-word for pessimism, he also brought hope. He promised that God would restore his people to their homeland after the dark time of exile.

The book contains all sorts of writing — some poetry, some prose, acted parables, history and Jeremiah's own life-story.

JERICHO

A town west of the River Jordan, 820ft/250m below sea level, about 5 miles/8km from the northern end of the Dead Sea. Jericho's freshwater spring makes it an oasis in the surrounding desert — the "city of palm trees". The town guarded the fords of the Jordan, across which Joshua sent his spies. It was well fortified, and the first main obstacle facing the invading Israelites. Joshua gained his first victory in the land when Jericho fell.

At the time of the Judges Ehud killed King Eglon of Moab at Jericho. At the time of Elijah and Elisha it was the home of a large group of prophets. After the return from exile, men from Jericho helped rebuild the walls of Jerusalem.

In the New Testament Jesus gave Bartimaeus his sight, and Zacchaeus became a changed man, at Jericho. The story of the Good Samaritan is set on the road from Jerusalem to Jericho.

Jericho has a very long history covering thousands

of years. The first town was built here some time before 6000 BC. At the time of Abraham, Isaac and Jacob, life in Jericho was a civilized affair. In tombs from about 1600 BC, fine pottery, wooden furniture, basket-work, and boxes with inlaid decoration have been found. Some time after this Jericho was destroyed, but a small settlement remained.
Joshua 2; 6; Judges 12:13; 2 Kings 2; Nehemiah 3:2; Mark 10:46; Luke 19:1–10; 10:30

JEROBOAM I

A man from the tribe of Ephraim who became first king of Israel, the breakaway northern kingdom (931–910 BC). During Solomon's reign the prophet Ahijah predicted that Jeroboam would be the ruler of ten tribes. After Solomon's death his son, Rehoboam, succeeded him, but all the tribes except Benjamin and Judah rebelled against him and made Jeroboam their king. Jeroboam introduced idol worship and ordered two golden calves to be made. He put these in Dan and Bethel to stop his subjects returning to Jerusalem to worship. His bad example was followed by other kings of Israel and led eventually to Israel's total defeat and dispersion by Assyria in 721 BC.
1 Kings 11:26–14:20

JEROBOAM II

Became king of Israel after his father, Joash, and reigned for forty-one years, 793–753 BC. He reconquered land which Israel had lost and during his reign the country became wealthy. Israel grew confident and careless. Neither king nor people took

notice of the warnings of the prophets, Hosea and Amos. They continued to worship idols and to disregard God's covenant agreement.
2 Kings 14:23–29; Amos 7

JERUBBAAL
Another name for Gideon.

JERUSALEM
Capital of Israel's early kings, later of the southern kingdom of Judah, and one of the world's most famous cities. Jerusalem stands high (2,500ft/770m) in the Judean hills with no access by sea or river. The ground drops steeply away on all sides except the north. To the east, between Jerusalem (with its temple) and the Mount of Olives, is the Kidron Valley. The Valley of Hinnom curves around the city to the south and west. A third, central valley cuts right into the city, dividing the temple area and city of David from the "upper", western section.

Jerusalem as it may have looked in Jesus' time. The temple is in the foreground; Herod's palace is on the far side of the city.

Jerusalem is probably the "Salem" of which Melchizedek was king in Abraham's day. It was certainly in existence by 1800 BC. It was a Jebusite stronghold (called Jebus) when King David captured it and made it his capital. He bought the temple site and brought the Covenant Box (ark) to Jerusalem. Solomon built the temple for God, and from that time on Jerusalem has been the "holy city" — for the Jews, and later for Christians and Muslims, too. Solomon added fine palaces and public buildings. Jerusalem was a political and religious centre, to which the people came for the great annual festivals.

The city declined to some extent after Solomon, when the kingdom became divided. In the reign of King Hezekiah (Isaiah's time) it was besieged by the Assyrians. The king had the Siloam tunnel built, to ensure his water supply. On several occasions powerful neighbouring kings were pacified with treasures from the city and its temple. The Babylonians besieged Jerusalem in 597 BC and in 586 they captured and destroyed both the city and the temple. The people were taken into exile.

In 538 BC they were allowed to return. Under Zerubbabel's leadership, the temple was rebuilt. With Nehemiah in charge they rebuilt the city walls. In 198 BC, as part of the Greek Empire, Jerusalem came under the control of the Syrian Seleucid kings. One of these, Antiochus IV Epiphanes plundered and desecrated the temple. Judas Maccabaeus led a Jewish revolt and the temple was rededicated (164 BC).

For a time Jerusalem was free. Then, in the

middle of the first century BC, the Romans took control. Herod the Great, made king by the Romans, repaired Jerusalem and undertook new building work, including a magnificent new temple.

It was to this temple that Jesus' mother brought him as a baby. His parents brought him again when he was twelve, to attend the annual Passover Festival. When he grew up, Jesus regularly visited Jerusalem — for many of the religious festivals, and to teach and heal. His arrest, trial, crucifixion and resurrection all took place in Jerusalem.

Jesus' followers were still in the city several weeks later, on the Day of Pentecost, when the Holy Spirit made new men of them. So the Christian church began life in Jerusalem — and from there, spread out far and wide. The Christians at Jerusalem played a leading role in the early years. The Council that met to consider the position of non-Jewish Christians was held at Jerusalem.

In AD 66 the Jews rose in revolt against the Romans. In AD 70 the Romans regained Jerusalem. They destroyed its defences — and the temple. In the fourth century — the reign of Constantine — the city became Christian, and many churches were built.

In 637 the Muslims came — and Jerusalem remained under their control for most of the time until 1948, when the modern state of Israel came into being. Jerusalem was then divided between the Jews and the Arabs — Israel and Jordan. In 1967 the Jews won control of the whole city.

Genesis 14:18; Joshua 15:63; 2 Samuel 5; 1 Kings 6; Psalms 48; 122; 125; 1 Kings 14:25–26; 2 Kings

Jesse

12:18; 18:13–19:36; 20:20; 25; Ezra 5; Nehemiah 3–6; Luke 2; 19:28–24:49, etc.; John 2:23–3:21; 5; 7:10–10:42, etc.; Acts 2; 15

JESSE
Grandson of Ruth and Boaz, and father of King David.
1 Samuel 16–17

JESUS
The name (Old Testament "Joshua") means "saviour". At the time when Herod was king of Judea and the whole country was under Roman occupation the angel Gabriel came to Mary in Nazareth. God had chosen her to be the mother of the promised Messiah. Mary's fiancé, Joseph, was told in a dream that they were to call him Jesus "because he will save his people from their sins". A census took Mary and Joseph to Bethlehem, where Jesus was born, in the town of King David, his ancestor. Herod was afraid that Jesus would be a rival king and plotted to kill him, but God guided his parents to take him to Egypt. After Herod died they went back to their home town of Nazareth. Here Jesus grew up and probably worked as a carpenter.

When he was thirty years old, Jesus was baptized by John the Baptist in the River Jordan. He chose twelve followers as his close companions to share his life and work. For three years Jesus taught the people and worked miracles, healing all kinds of diseases. Crowds followed him. But the Jewish leaders were afraid of his power and of his claim to be the Son of God. They wanted to kill him. Judas, one of the twelve, accepted a bribe and helped Jesus' enemies to capture him without the people's knowledge. Soldiers arrested Jesus in the Garden of Gethsemane, close to Jerusalem. He was tried and condemned by a Jewish court before dawn. Pilate, the Roman governor, had to ratify all death sentences. He found no fault in Jesus, but was afraid of a riot if he let him go free. So Jesus was crucified. He was buried in the tomb of Joseph of Arimathaea, a secret follower.

At dawn on the third day after Jesus' death a group of women found the tomb empty. Angels told them Jesus was alive again. His followers and many other people saw him during the next forty days. Now they knew he really was the Son of God. Then from the Mount of Olives Jesus returned to heaven. While the disciples were still looking at the sky an angel told them that one day Jesus would come back. Matthew, Mark, Luke, John, Acts 1:1–11

The Bible's teaching about Jesus is summed up in several titles used to describe him.

Jesus, the "Servant of God". Matthew gives Jesus this title, which comes from the prophecies of Isaiah. The character of the lowly, gentle servant of God who comes to bring justice was perfectly lived out in the person of Jesus. When Jesus said that he "came to serve and to give his life to redeem many people", he was living out the work of the Servant of God, suffering to bear the sins of mankind, just as Isaiah describes him.
Matthew 12:15–21; Isaiah 42:1–4; 52:13–53; 12 and other passages; Mark 10:45

Jesus, the "Son of David". The angel who

announced his birth told Jesus' mother that God would make her son a king "as his ancestor David was". By human birth Jesus was a descendant of King David. This title shows Jesus as the fulfilment of the hopes of the Jewish nation. It is the one used to describe Jesus in the opening sentence of Matthew, the most Jewish of all the Gospels. It was the title that the Jews used when they acknowledged Jesus as the Messiah. "Praise to David's Son! God bless him who comes in the name of the Lord! Praise God!"
Luke 1:32; John 7:42; Matthew 1:1; 21:9

Jesus, the "Son of man". This is the title Jesus most often used of himself, and it tells us much about him. He borrowed the phrase from Daniel's vision of someone who "looked like a human being", yet had God's authority for ever. "His kingdom," Daniel says, would "never end". The Bible teaches clearly that Jesus was a real man. He identified himself completely with mankind. As the "Son of man" he came to serve men and women and to give his life to save them. "The Son of man must suffer . . . He will be put to death, but three days later he will be raised to life." As the Son of man Jesus defeated sin and death and will come again "with great power and glory".
Daniel 7:13–14; Mark 10:45; 9:21–22; 21:25–28

Jesus, the "Son of God". At Jesus' baptism in the River Jordan a voice from heaven declared, "You are my own dear Son. I am pleased with you." Again, on the mountain, when Jesus' glory was seen, the voice came, "This is my Son, whom I have chosen —

listen to him." John's Gospel explains what this phrase means. Jesus is God's "only Son". His whole life and purpose is to carry out the Father's work. "The Father and I are one," Jesus says. He was with the Father before the world was made. They are one for ever. Because Jesus shares God's nature and is free from sin, he was able to pay in full for the sins of the whole world for all time. And we now "have someone who pleads with the Father on our behalf — Jesus Christ, the righteous one".
Mark 1:11; Luke 9:35; John 1:14; 10:30; 17; Romans 1:3–4; Hebrews 1; 1 John 1–2:2

Jesus, the "Lord". In the Gospels Jesus is often called "Lord" in the everyday sense of "master". But after the resurrection the word took on a new meaning. "My Lord and my God," declared Thomas when he saw the risen Jesus with his own eyes. This was the way in which Jews often referred to God, and the first Christians publicly declared their faith in the words, "Jesus Christ is Lord". Paul, in his letter to the Philippians, looks forward to the time when Jesus will return as Lord, when "all beings in heaven, on earth, and in the world below will fall on their knees, and all will openly proclaim that Jesus Christ is Lord, to the glory of God the Father".
Luke 5:8; John 20:28; 1 Corinthians 12:3; Philippians 2:6–11
See also *Trinity, Judgement, Justification, Kingdom of God, Messiah, Redemption, Salvation,* and the events of Jesus' life: *Resurrection, Second coming of Jesus, Transfiguration.*

JESUS' TEACHING

Many people today think of Jesus' teaching as basically the Sermon on the Mount, summed up in the "Golden Rule": "Do for others what you want them to do for you" (Matthew 7:12). But the centre of Jesus' message was his announcement that the "kingdom of God" had arrived.

The kingdom of God The "kingdom of God" meant the rule of God breaking into human history, the new creation which would supercede the old creation spoilt by sin and death.

For a long time Jews had looked forward to the time when God would come in power to be their King. He would set his people free and judge the nations. "No king but God" was in fact the slogan of the fanatical Zealots who hoped to drive the Romans out of their land by force. But the kingdom that Jesus announced and brought with him did not "belong to this world". It would not be brought about by brute force. The kingdom of God had in fact already arrived with the coming of Christ — for he was the first who fully obeyed the will of God. So he could say to the Pharisees: "The kingdom of God is among you." It was present in the words and works of Jesus.

Yet there is another sense in which the kingdom of God has not come, even yet. "May your kingdom come", Jesus taught his followers to pray in the Lord's Prayer. So far the kingdom of God is still only partly in operation. In the future it will come "with power". Yet the future coming of the kingdom will not be a joyful event for everyone. For all who believe the good news of the kingdom there is "salvation", a new life. But for many the coming of God's rule will be a judgement.

Jesus often used parables to explain what the kingdom of God is like. The kingdom turns the world's values upside down. It is the humble, the poor and those who mourn who are really happy. God's kingdom belongs to them. Rich people cannot buy their way in. For the first time in their lives they may find their riches a hindrance. Beggars are invited in — and they accept God's invitation when respectable people refuse and find themselves shut out.

Jesus' parables show God at work in the world, quietly, almost secretly. Yet "the kingdom" goes on growing and spreading from small beginnings. It is like the tiny mustard seed which becomes a tree, or the yeast which makes a great batch of dough rise.

The "Sower" goes out, making God's message known to people everywhere. Much of the "seed" is wasted. People close their minds to what they hear. Or other things crowd in and they forget. But some listen, and their lives are changed. The seed comes to harvest.

John 18:36; Luke 17:21; Matthew 3:2; Mark 1:15; Matthew 6:10; Mark 9:1; 14:25; Luke 13:23–30; 14:15–24; Matthew 20:1–16; 19:23–24; 13:31–33; Mark 4:3–8

"Repent and believe" "The kingdom of God is near!" said Jesus. "Turn away from your sins and believe the Good News!" People must "repent", have a total change of heart, if they are to accept the rule of God in their lives. They must *believe* the good news Jesus came to bring.

God offers new life to all who believe, who will leave their old way of life and follow him. This is worth everything anyone has. Finding it is like finding treasure hidden in a field — and selling everything to buy the field. It means giving up all we have clung to for security, and trusting God. It also means being sorry for our sins. This is not something we can manage just by trying hard enough. God actually comes to find the sinner. In the parables of the lost sheep and the lost son Jesus emphasizes the joy of being found by God.
Mark 1:15; Matthew 13:44–46; Luke 15:1–7, 11–32

Jesus' teaching about himself   Jesus knew that he was very close to God. He encouraged his disciples to call God their father, but he was God's Son in a unique way. John's Gospel especially presents us with this aspect of Jesus' teaching. He even said "the Father and I are one". So believing in God means believing in Jesus also. He is so close to God that people may rely on him as they do on God. But he said nothing to make himself more prominent than God. He was the "way" to God. He did nothing of his own accord, but only as the Father directed him. He was mankind's "bread" that the Father had sent down from heaven.

The way to "eternal life" — the vital life of God that can be shared by human beings also — is to believe in (put our trust in) Jesus the Son of God. That is the same as true belief in the Father who sent him. It brings a person from "death" to "life".
John 10:30; 14:1; 14:6; 5:19–20, 30; 6:32–33; 3:16, 18, 36; 5:24

Joy   A note of joy runs all through the teaching of

Jesus. The kingdom of God frees people and releases them to live a full life. Even when Jesus' disciples fast, he tells them they must make a festival out of it, anointing themselves with oil, not going about with dismal faces like most people. Among the Jews of Jesus' day, being good and obeying God's law was often a gloomy business. The religious leaders grumbled because Jesus enjoyed himself, and became angry when he was greeted with shouts of joy in Jerusalem. They were like the bitter elder brother in the parable of the lost son. But the boy's father says: "We had to celebrate and be happy, because your brother was dead, but now he is alive; he was lost, but now he has been found." God himself rejoices over every man and woman who comes back home to him, every "sinner who repents".

John 10:10; Matthew 6:16–18; 11:19; 21:15; Luke 15:11–32

The "Beatitudes" Jesus pronounced blessings ("beatitudes") on the "humble" — those who realized that spiritually they were "poor". In fact all those mentioned in the Beatitudes are "poor" and "humble" in one way or another. ("Blessed" means "happy".) These are the people God declares "happy". They will receive what God has promised. His kingdom belongs to them. They have nothing in the world, but they can expect everything from God.

Those who are "hungry and thirsty for righteousness", "whose greatest desire is to do what God requires", have their lives centred on God. They know they cannot survive without him. The "merciful" are dealing with other people in the way God deals with them. Those who work for peace have no worldy power. They depend on the love of God which can change two enemies into friends. The persecuted are hunted out of the world of men.

It is to people like this that God's "kingdom" belongs. They are the ones God will reward. All these are praised by Jesus. And so the Beatitudes turn the world's idea of "happiness" upside down. They also set a standard. They represent a challenge, the demand the kingdom makes upon God's people. Matthew 5:1–12; Luke 6:20–26

Jesus' followers To be a "disciple" of Jesus, one of his students, was a great privilege. Unlike other teachers he did not lay great burdens on his followers. "The yoke I will give you is easy," he said, "and the load I will put on you is light." Yet he taught that "the gate to life is narrow and the way that leads to it is hard". His disciples must be like their master, ready to put themselves and their own interests last. Even family ties must not stand in the way of wholehearted obedience to him.

Jesus told his disciples to expect persecution. But they need not be anxious. God would give them the words they needed when they were on trial. Jesus called his followers to a life of service for others, yet he treated them as friends. They shared his confidences. They shared his sufferings. They would also share his life, his joy and his future glory. Matthew 13:16–17; 11:30; 7:13–14; Mark 8:34; Luke 9:57–62; Matthew 10:16–25; John 13:4–17; 14–17

God and worship Jesus spoke of God as "Father" in a new, more personal way than anyone before him. He taught that God was, in a special way, his own Father. But he also taught his followers to pray: "Our Father in heaven". He taught them to come to God as children to a loving, forgiving and wise Father. He gave his followers "the right to become God's children".

This teaching was new and revolutionary to many people. "Religion" for many was a burdensome system of rules and ceremonies. Jesus showed that the basis of religion was a loving relationship with God himself. God, as Father, was concerned about every detail of life. He cared. This changed people's attitude to prayer.

As a result of what Jesus said and did, greater changes were to come. When the woman at the well asked where people should worship God, Jesus answered: "The time will come when people will not worship the Father either on this mountain or in Jerusalem . . . by the power of God's Spirit people will worship the Father as he really is, offering him the worship that he really wants." In the Book of Acts we see this beginning to happen, as the "good news" is preached to non-Jewish as well as to Jewish people.

Jesus himself went regularly to the local synagogue and attended the festivals in Jerusalem. He did not set up a new system of religious ceremonies. He expected his disciples to follow his example, to meet to study the Bible, to pray and to fast. And he commanded them to baptize new believers and remember his death for them by sharing bread and wine together, as he had done with his disciples at the last supper.

Matthew 6:6–18, 31–32; 7:7–11; John 1:12–13;

Matthew 9:14–17; John 4:19–24; Matthew 28:19; 1 Corinthians 11:23–25

JETHRO/REUEL
A priest in the land of Midian and father-in-law of Moses. When Moses brought the Israelites to Sinai, Jethro came to see him, bringing Moses' wife and sons. He advised Moses to choose capable men to share the burden of leadership.
Exodus 2:16ff.; 2:1; 4:18–19; 18

JEWELLERY
The people of Israel were not as skilled at making jewellery as some of their neighbours — particularly the Egyptians. But jewellery has been worn from earliest times. Quite apart from its beauty, in the days before banks, a necklace was easier to carry from place to place than a bag of coins. It was certainly less trouble than a herd of cattle! Even before coins, jewels were a form of wealth which could be exchanged for other things — and taken as booty in war.

Bracelets, necklaces, pendants, anklets and rings — for ears and noses as well as fingers — were all worn. They were made from gold, silver and other metals, and set with precious or semi-precious stones, or even coloured glass. the stones were smoothed and polished, engraved and sculptured. Ivory was beautifully carved. It was often used for panelling and inlay in furnitue-making, and also for hair-combs, brooches and plaques, and vases and flasks for cosmetics.

The jewellers and goldsmiths of Egypt were

master-craftsmen. They produced some of the most colourful and beautiful jewellery the world has ever seen. Elaborate pendants (pectorals) hung on bead chains were made from semi-precious stones — deep blue lapis lazuli, turquoise, red carnelian, quartz — and coloured glass in dazzling blues and reds set in gold and silver. These pectorals were originally intended to give protection against evil spirits. The carved scarab beetles which decorate Egyptian rings and bracelets represent the belief that Re', the sun-god, took the form of a beetle, and are a symbol of eternal life.

When the Israelites left Egypt (the exodus), they took with them gold and silver jewellery as well as clothes. Gold ear-rings were melted down to make a gold bull to worship at Mt Sinai. But the people were soon sorry for this disloyalty to God, and "both men and women brought decorative pins, ear-rings, rings, necklaces and all kinds of jewellery and dedicated them to the Lord", (Exodus 35:20ff.). Skilled

A Roman gold necklace from the first century AD.

Israelite craftsmen used the gold and jewels to beautify the tent of worship (tabernacle). The sacred breastplate worn by the high priest was set with precious stones, one for each of the twelve clans of Israel.

The jeweller's skill was also used in making and engraving personal seals, sometimes worn as rings. These were impressed on lumps of clay to secure and authenticate documents. Poor people had roughly engraved seals of terracotta. But the rich often had beautiful seals cut from carnelian, agate, jasper, rock crystal and other semi-precious stones.

Jewellery was worn in Israel for special occasions — such as a wedding. But to be obsessed with jewels and clothes was wrong and a sign of pride, condemned in both Old and New Testaments (Isaiah 3:16–24; 1 Timothy 2:9).

JEZEBEL
The princess from Sidon who married Ahab, king of Israel. Jezebel worshipped the weather and fertility gods Baal and Asherah. She persuaded Ahab and forced his subjects to accept her religion. She had God's prophets killed and replaced them with prophets of Baal. But the prophet Elijah escaped to challenge and defeat the prophets of Baal on Mt Carmel. After this Jezebel was determined to kill Elijah and he was forced to go into hiding. Jezebel signed her own death warrant when she urged Ahab to have Naboth killed so that he could take over Naboth's vineyard. Elijah predicted her violent death, and some time later she was thrown from an upstairs window at the command of Jehu.

1 Kings 16:31; 18:4, 13, 19; 19:1–2; 21; 2 Kings 9:30ff.

JEZREEL
A town in the north of Israel and the plain in which it stood, close to Mt Gilboa. Saul camped at the spring in the Valley of Jezreel before the Battle of Gilboa. King Ahab of Israel had a palace at Jezreel. It was here that the sad story of Naboth's vineyard took place. King Joram of Israel went to Jezreel to recover from his wounds. Queen Jezebel was thrown down from the palace window and died here.
1 Samuel 29:1; 1 Kings 18:45–46; 21; 2 Kings 8:29; 9:30–37

JOAB
King David's nephew and commander of his army. He was fearless but violent. Joab helped David become king of all the tribes of Israel. He remained loyal to David during Absalom's rebellion, but towards the end of David's reign supported Adonijah's revolt. After David's death King Solomon ordered Joab to be executed for taking part in the revolt and for the murders of Abner and Amasa, two other army leaders.
2 Samuel 2–3; 10–11; 14; 18–20; 24; 1 Kings 1–2; 1 Chronicles 11ff.

JOANNA
The wife of an official of Herod Antipas. Joanna was healed by Jesus. She gave money to Jesus and his disciples. On the resurrection morning she was one

of the women who found Jesus' tomb empty.
Luke 8:1–3; 24:10

JOASH/JEHOASH

1. Son of King Ahaziah, made king of Judah when he was seven years old. While he was a baby his life was saved by Jehoiada, the priest. In the early part of his forty-year reign (835–796 BC) he was guided by Jehoiada. He obeyed God's laws and repaired the temple. After Jehoiada's death he introduced idol worship and murdered Zechariah, Jehoiada's son. He stripped gold from the temple to appease the invading Syrians. Joash was murdered by his officials (see *Jehoiada*).
2 Kings 11–12; 2 Chronicles 24

2. King of Israel for sixteen years (798–782 BC) after King Jehoahaz, his father.
2 Kings 13–14

JOB

The Book of Job is about a good man — Job — who meets complete disaster. The meaning of suffering is looked at from many angles.

The Book of Job stands alone in the Old Testament. We do not know who wrote it, or when, but its hero belongs to a "patriarchal" society. The beginning and end are in prose, but most of the book is poetry.

Job, a prosperous and truly good man, loses all his children and possessions and is struck with a hideous disease. Job and the three friends who come to comfort him try to understand his terrible suffering (chapters 3–37). Job's friends assume that he must have sinned to have brought such suffering on himself. Job himself cannot understand how God can allow a good man to suffer like this.

Finally God responds to Job's challenge by appearing to him in power and wisdom. Job recognizes him humbly (chapters 38–42). He realizes at last that God is bigger than the religious thinking of his day allowed. The story has a happy ending as his health and his wealth are restored.

JOEL

A prophet; the son of Pethuel. In his book Joel describes a plague of locusts and a terrible drought. These are pictures of God's coming judgement on those who disobey him — the "Day of the Lord". He called for repentance and spoke of a new age when God would send his Spirit upon all people.

Joel used the picture of a locust-plague to describe God's judgement.

JOHANAN

A Jewish leader who stayed in Judah after Jerusalem

was captured by King Nebuchadnezzar of Babylon. Johanan warned Gedaliah, governor of Judah, about the plot to murder him. Afterwards, against Jeremiah's advice, he led the people to Egypt.
Jeremiah 40–43

JOHN THE APOSTLE

Like his father, Zebedee, and his brother James, John was a fisherman. He was probably a follower of John the Baptist before Jesus called him to become his disciple. Jesus nicknamed John and James "sons of thunder" because they were quick-tempered. Peter, James and John were especially close to Jesus. John was with Jesus when he brought Jairus's daughter back from the dead. He saw Jesus' glory at the transfiguration, and was with him in the Garden of Gethsemane just before his death. John's name is not mentioned in the Gospel of John, but he is almost certainly "the disciple whom Jesus loved", the one who was close to Jesus at the last supper and to whom Jesus spoke from the cross, and told to look after his mother. After Jesus had ascended into heaven John, with Peter, became a leader of the church in Jerusalem. He was still in Jerusalem fourteen years after Paul was converted. There is a tradition that John lived in Ephesus until he was very old. If he is the same John who wrote the Revelation he must also have been exiled to the island of Patmos. The Gospel of John was written to bring men to faith. Three New Testament letters also bear John's name.
Matthew 4:21ff,; 10:2; 17:1ff.; Mark 3:17; 5:37;

10:35ff.; 14:33; Luke 9:49ff.; John 19:26–27; Acts 3–4; Galatians 2:9

JOHN THE BAPTIST

The prophet sent by God to prepare people for the coming of Jesus, the Messiah. In their old age his parents Zechariah and Elizabeth, were told by an angel that they would have this special son. John was related to Jesus and just a few months older. He lived in the desert of Judea until God called him to be a prophet. Crowds of people came to hear his fiery preaching. "Turn away from your sins and be baptized," he said, "and God will forgive you." Although Jesus had not sinned, he asked John to baptize him, too, in the River Jordan, to show his obedience to God.

Later John was put in prison by King Herod for his outspoken criticism. From prison he sent some of his disciples to Jesus to ask if he really was the person they were expecting. "Tell John how I heal the sick and preach Good News to the poor," Jesus answered. Then he told the crowds, "John the Baptist is more than a prophet. He is greater than any man who has ever lived." Not long after this, Herod's wife tricked him into having John beheaded.

Luke 1; 3; 7:18ff.; Matthew 3; 11; 14:1–12; Mark 1; 6

JOHN'S GOSPEL

John's Gospel — the fourth New Testament account of Jesus' life — stands apart from the other three. It was probably written last, possibly around AD 90. It is more concerned with the meaning of events than with the events themselves, which were presumably well known by that time.

John's Gospel begins with Jesus as the "Word" of God, existing before time itself, yet born in time as man.

In Jesus (the Word) God speaks to man. The Gospel was written "in order that you (the reader) may believe that Jesus is the Messiah, the Son of God, and that through your faith in him you may have life" (20:31).

The Gospel probably contains the reminiscences of John, the brother of James and one of the closest of Jesus' twelve friends. In the Gospel John is not mentioned by name. He appears only as "the disciple whom Jesus loved". It may have been actually written down by a secretary.

After the opening passage presenting Jesus as the "Word" of God (1:1–18) the Gospel goes on to describe a number of miracles which show that he really is the promised Saviour (chapters 2–12). The story of his preaching and teaching is arranged so that each miracle is followed by an explanation and discussion. John also shows how some people believed, but others rejected Jesus. He does not recount any of Jesus' parables.

Chapters 13–19 tell of Jesus' last days with his disciples in Jerusalem. They recall his words of encouragement and teaching to his followers before his death on the cross. Chapters 20–21 describe some of the times when Jesus was seen by his followers after he rose from the dead.

John understands the miracles as "signs" showing

who Jesus was. He also uses a series of common things to point to hidden truths about Jesus: water, bread, light, the shepherd and the vine. The famous "I am . . ." statements come in John's Gospel. He presents Jesus as the way, the truth and the life.

JOHN'S LETTERS

1 John   A letter written towards the end of the first century AD, probably by the apostle John, then living at Ephesus (in modern Turkey). His purpose was to encourage Christians to live in fellowship with God, and to warn against false teachers.

John was particularly concerned to counter the ideas of a group who believed they had special "knowledge" about God (the "Gnostics"). They also believed that the physical world was evil, and therefore that Jesus, the Son of God, could not have been a real man.

John writes as someone who knew Jesus, as the Son of God and also as a real man. Anyone who claims to know God must live as Jesus did (chapters 1 and 2). Christians are the children of God. They have his nature and cannot go on persistently sinning. Those who believe in Jesus will love each other, too (chapter 3). In chapter 4 John contrasts the true and the false. "God is love," John declares. "We love because God first loved us." Chapter 5 speaks of victory over the world, and of God's gift of eternal life.

2 John   This letter is probably also by the apostle John. The "lady" to whom it is addressed is probably a local church. The writer appeals to his Christian readers to love one another. He warns against false teachers and teachings.

3 John The third letter by "the Elder" (John) is a private letter to a church leader named Gaius. The writer praises Gaius for his help to fellow Christians. He warns against a man called Diotrephes, who is behaving like a petty dictator in the church.

JONAH

Unlike the other books of prophecy, Jonah is written as a story.

The Book of Jonah describes the adventures of a prophet who tried to disobey God's orders. God told Jonah to go to Nineveh, the capital of Assyria — the great enemy nation — to denounce its people. Jonah finally delivered his message — and then sulked when God did not carry out his threat to destroy the people.

The book shows God's love and care. He would rather forgive and save than punish and destroy.

JONATHAN

Eldest son of King Saul and a great friend of David. He was a brave warrior and distinguished himself in several battles against the Philistines. Although Jonathan knew David might become king in his place he was a loyal friend and saved him from being killed by Saul. Jonathan and Saul were both killed in battle when the Israelites were defeated by the Philistines. David was deeply grieved and wrote a lament in praise of Jonathan.

1 Samuel 13–14; 18–20; 23:16–18; 31:2; 2 Samuel 1

JOPPA

The only natural harbour on the coast of Israel south of the Bay of Acre (Haifa): modern Jaffa, close to Tel Aviv. Joppa was the port for Jerusalem, 35 miles/56km away. The town has a long history and was mentioned about 1400 BC in the Egyptian Amarna Letters. Jonah set sail for Tarshish (Spain) from Joppa. Dorcas (Tabitha), the woman Peter restored to life, came from Joppa. Peter was there when he had his dream about the "clean" and "unclean" animals. He went from Joppa to the house of the Roman officer, Cornelius, and saw God at work amongst non-Jews.

2 Chronicles 2:16; Jonah 1:3; Acts 9:36–43; 10

JORAM

See *Jehoram*.

JORDAN

The main river of Israel, constantly referred to in the Bible. The Jordan flows from Mt Hermon in the far north, through Lake Huleh, and Lake Galilee to the Dead Sea. It is 75 miles/120km from Lake Huleh to the Dead Sea, but the river winds about so much that it is more than twice that length.

The name "Jordan" means "the descender". It flows through the deepest rift valley on earth. Lake Huleh is 230ft/71m above sea level. Lake Galilee is nearly 700ft/215m *below* sea level, and the north end of the Dead Sea 1,290ft/397m below.

The northern part of the Jordan Valley is fertile; the southern end, approaching the Dead Sea, is desert, but dense jungle grows on the banks. The main tributaries of the Jordan are the Yarmuk and Jabbok rivers, both of which join it from the east. Many smaller tributaries dry up completely through the summer.

Joshua led the people of Israel across the Jordan from the east into the Promised Land near to Jericho. At the time of Absalom's rebellion, David escaped across the Jordan. Elijah and Elisha crossed the Jordan just before Elijah was taken up to heaven. Elisha told the Syrian general Naaman to wash himself in the Jordan and he would be healed. John the Baptist baptized people — including Jesus — in the Jordan.

Joshua 3; 2 Samuel 17:20–22; 2 Kings 2:6–8, 13–14; 5; Jeremiah 12:5; 49:19; Mark 1:5, 9, etc.

JOSEPH

1. Jacob and Rachel's first son after many years of waiting. Joseph was marked out as his father's favourite by the gift of a special coat. Joseph's brothers became jealous of him, especially when he told them his dreams, in which they bowed down to him. They planned to kill him but Reuben persuaded them to delay and Judah suggested that instead they should sell him as a slave. Joseph was taken to Egypt, and the brothers told Jacob he had been killed by wild animals.

In Egypt Joseph was bought by Potiphar, a high official, and put in charge of his household. Potiphar's wife claimed that Joseph had tried to rape her, and he was put in prison. There he was able to tell the butler and baker of the Pharaoh (king) of Egypt the meaning of their dreams. Two years later

Pharaoh had dreams he could not understand. The butler remembered Joseph and Pharaoh sent for him. Joseph told him he must prepare for a long famine. Pharaoh made Joseph his chief minister and put him in charge of the preparations.

Joseph saw his brothers again when they came to Egypt to buy corn during the famine. He pretended to think they were spies and told them to come back with his younger brother, Benjamin, to prove their story. Then he tested them to see if they could be as cruel to Benjamin as they had been to him. When Joseph realized they really cared about Benjamin, he told them who he was.

Joseph invited his father and his brothers' families to live in Egypt. Jacob was overjoyed to see Joseph again. Their descendants lived in Egypt for four centuries.
Genesis 30:24; 37–50

2. Husband of Mary and foster-father of Jesus. Although Joseph was not Jesus' father physically, he was his legal father. Before Jesus was born an angel told him that Mary's child was God's Son. Joseph took Mary and the baby to Egypt when he was warned in a dream that King Herod planned to kill Jesus. After Herod's death Joseph brought his family back and they settled in Nazareth, where Joseph worked as a carpenter. When Jesus was twelve Joseph and Mary took him to the temple for the Passover. Nothing more is known about Joseph. He may have died before Jesus was grown up.
Matthew 1–2; Luke 1:27; 2

3. Joseph of Arimathea. A member of the Jewish Sanhedrin council and a secret disciple of Jesus.

After the crucifixion he asked Pilate for Jesus' body and placed it in his own unused tomb.
Luke 23:50–53; John 19:38–42

Egyptian officials measuring grain for tax purposes. An Egyptian tomb-painting from about 1400 BC.

JOSHUA

1. Leader of the Israelites after Moses' death. His name means "God is salvation". Joshua was chosen to lead the army while the Israelites were in the desert. Of the twelve spies sent by Moses to bring back a report on Canaan, only Joshua and Caleb believed the Israelites could conquer the land with God's help. God rewarded their faith. Of all the Israelites born in Egypt they were the only ones who lived to occupy Canaan. After Moses' death Joshua led the Israelites into Canaan. When the land had been conquered he divided it up amongst the twelve tribes. Before Joshua died he urged the Israelites to love and obey God. "As for my family and me," he said, "we will serve the Lord." And the people replied, "We also will serve the Lord, he is our God."
Exodus 17:9ff.; Numbers 13–14; Joshua
2. High priest immediately after the Jews returned

from exile in Babylon. He started rebuilding the temple, but the work ground to a halt. When the prophets Haggai and Zechariah spurred the people into action, Joshua once again took charge.
Haggai; Zechariah 3

JOSHUA, BOOK OF JOSHUA

The Book of Joshua tells how Israel invaded Canaan, led by Joshua, Moses' successor. It is the first of the twelve "books of history" in the Old Testament.

Chapters 1–12 tell of the conquest of Canaan, probably after 1240 BC. The stories may first have been written down during the lifetime of Samuel, though the book as a whole forms part of the great "Deuteronomic history" that runs from Joshua to 2 Kings. It is not known who wrote the book. The account includes the crossing of the River Jordan, the fall of the city of Jericho and the battle of Ai.

Chapters 13–22 tell how the Israelites divided up and settled the lands they had conquered. The book ends with Joshua's farewell speech and the renewing of God's agreement and promise to his people at Shechem (chapters 23–24).

JOSIAH

Crowned king of Judah at the age of eight after the assassination of his father, Amon, in 640 BC. Josiah grew to be a strong, good king who led the nation back to God. He ordered the repair of the temple and while this work was being carried out a scroll was found on which were written the laws God gave to Moses. Josiah studied these laws and had them

read to the people. Many reforms were made including the keeping of the Passover Festival. When Josiah was thirty-nine years old he was killed in battle against the Egyptians. Jeremiah the prophet mourned Josiah's death.
2 Kings 21:24–23:30; 2 Chronicles 33:25–35:27; Jeremiah 22:15–16

JOTHAM
King of Judah 750–732 BC, after his father King Uzziah. He began to reign while his father was still alive but suffering from leprosy. Jotham worshipped God. He fortified Judah and defeated the Ammonites.
2 Kings 15:32–38; 2 Chronicles 27:1–6

JOY
Joy in the Bible is not an occasional emotional experience; it is a basic part of a personal relationship with God. As the Scottish *Shorter (Westminster) Catechism* says, "The chief end of man is to glorify God and to enjoy him for ever."

Living with the presence of God in one's life is a continuous experience of joy. And as this joy is a gift of God, it is possible for Christians to rejoice even in times of persecution. "Rejoice in the Lord always," wrote Paul to his readers at Philippi.
Psalms 16:11; 30:5; 43:4; 51:12; 126:5–6; Ecclesiastes 2:26; Isaiah 61:7; Jeremiah 15:16; Luke 15:7; John 15:11; 16:22; Romans 14:17; 15:13; Galatians 5:22; Philippians 1:4; 1 Thessalonians 2:20; 3:9; Hebrews 12:2; James 1:2; 1 Peter 1:8; Jude 24

JUBILEE YEAR
See *Feasts and Festivals*.

JUDAH
1. The fourth son of Jacob and Leah. Judah persuaded his brothers to sell Joseph to passing traders on their way to Egypt, instead of killing him. Jacob's last words to Judah promised him a future kingdom.
Genesis 29:35; 37:26–27; 38; 49:9–10
2. The Judean hills south of Jerusalem and the desert bordering the Dead Sea. The land belonging to the tribe of Judah. Later the name of the southern kingdom, with Jerusalem as its capital.
Joshua 15; 1 Kings 12:21, 23, etc.

JUDAS/JUDE
There are several people with this name in the New Testament. Best-known are:
1. Judas, the son of James. He was one of the twelve apostles and was with the others after Jesus' ascension.
Luke 6:16; Acts 1:13
2. One of Jesus' brothers. Judas did not believe Jesus was the Messiah until after his death and resurrection. He may have written the letter of Jude.
Matthew 13:55; John 7:5; Acts 1:14
3. Judas Iscariot. The disciple who betrayed Jesus to the Jewish leaders. He looked after the disciples' money. He probably hoped Jesus would lead a rebellion against the Romans. When Jesus turned out to be a different kind of leader, Judas sold him to his enemies for thirty pieces of silver. Judas led the soldiers to arrest Jesus at night in the Garden of

Gethsemane. When he realized how wrong he had been, he returned the money to the priests and committed suicide.

Matthew 10:4; 26:14ff.; 27:3ff.; John 12:4–6; 13:21–30; Acts 1:18–19

JUDE

A letter "From Jude". He is sometimes identified as Jesus' younger brother, but we know nothing certain about him. The reason for writing was alarming news of false teachers. Jude describes their activities, and God's judgement on them. He refers again and again to the Old Testament and other Jewish writings. He encourages his Christian readers to keep the faith.

Almost the whole of this short letter is included word-for-word in 2 Peter 2:1–3:3.

JUDEA

The Greek and Roman name for Judah. Usually it refers to the southern part of the country, with Jerusalem as capital. But it is sometimes used as a name for the whole land, including Galilee and Samaria. The "wilderness of Judea" is the desert west of the Dead Sea.

Luke 3:1; 4:44 ("the whole country" in *Good News Bible*), etc.

JUDGEMENT

Because God is Ruler of the universe he is also the Judge. The ruler makes laws and carries them out. This is what the Bible means by judgement.

Judgement in the Old Testament often meant "good government". The "Judges" were national leaders before Israel had a king. God was the supreme Judge, the Ruler of all things.

So the "last" judgement, as taught by Jesus, will be the final sorting out of good from evil. Because the Judge is God himself there will be no injustice. We can be confident that the Judge of all the earth will act fairly. God has given to Jesus the actual task of judgement.

Everyone will be judged according to what they know. Those who have never heard the written laws of God will be judged by what they know of God from creation, and what their own conscience tells them about right and wrong. But it is a fact that we all fail to live up to what we know of God and his standards, and we all stand condemned on the basis of the life we have led.

On the great day of judgement everything will depend on a person's relationship to Christ. Jesus himself said so. The early Christians were certain that the only way to be sure of life on the day of judgement was by believing in Christ. "Whoever believes in the Son has eternal life," wrote John, "whoever disobeys the Son will not have life, but will remain under God's punishment."

See also *Future destiny, Heaven, Hell, Second coming of Jesus.*

Psalm 96:10; Genesis 18:25; Romans 3:3–4; 1:18–2:16; 3:9–12; Matthew 10:32–33; John 3:18; 5:24–30; Acts 4:12; 10:42; 2 Corinthians 3:10–15; 5:10; 2 Thessalonians 1:5–10; Hebrews 12:22–27; Revelation 20:12–15

JUDGES

The Book of Judges is a collection of stories from the two lawless centuries from the time of the Israelite conquest of Canaan to just before the crowning of King Saul, roughly 1200–1050 BC.

The "Judges" were local heroes of the tribes of Israel, usually military leaders, whose exploits are retold in the book. They include such figures as Deborah, Gideon and Samson. During this period only their shared faith in God held the tribes of Israel together. When they turned to local gods they became divided and weak, and a prey to the Canaanites. But even when they turned their backs on him, God was prepared to step in and save his people if they returned to him.

JULIUS

The Roman centurion in charge of Paul on his voyage to Rome to be tried before Caesar.
Acts 27:1, 3, 42–44

A Roman centurion.

JUSTIFICATION

There is nothing a person can do to get right (be justified) with God. Sin cuts us off from a holy God. However "good" we try to be, we cannot escape its grip.

Therefore if a person is to be made right with God it can only come about by God's own action: by "grace". This is the point made by the doctrine of "justification". God accepts us as his children because of Jesus' death on the cross. "Christ was without sin, but for our sake God made him share our sin in order that in union with him we might share the righteousness of God." Christ took on himself the sentence on sin so that we could be acquitted. God now looks upon the Christian as "in Christ" — a new person acquitted because of Jesus' obedience, and given the power to be obedient himself.

The Christian is therefore put right with God ("justified") by "grace" on the basis of the death of Jesus. And his acquittal comes through faith in Christ.

See also *Atonement, Grace*.
2 Corinthians 5:21; Romans 3:24; 5:1, 9

KADESH-BARNEA

An oasis and settlement in the desert south of Beersheba. It is mentioned in the campaign of Chedorlaomer and his allies at the time of Abraham. It was near Kadesh that Hagar saw an angel. After the escape from Egypt, most of Israel's years of desert wandering were spent in the area around Kadesh. Miriam died there, and Moses brought water out of the rock. From Kadesh he sent spies into Canaan. It is later mentioned as a point on the southern boundary of Israel.

Genesis 14:7; 16:14; Numbers 20; 13; 33:36; Deuteronomy 1:19–25, 46; Joshua 10:41; 15:23 (Kedesh)

KEDESH

A Canaanite town in Galilee conquered by Joshua and given to the tribe of Naphtali. It was the home of Barak. Kedesh was one of the first towns to fall to the Assyrians when Tiglath-pilezer III invaded Israel from the north (734–732 BC).

Joshua 12:22; 19:37; Judges 4; 2 Kings 15:29

KIDRON

The valley which separates Jerusalem and the temple from the Mount of Olives, on the east. For most of the year the valley is dry. The Gihon Spring, whose

The Kidron Valley, just east of the city of Jerusalem.

water King Hezekiah brought inside the city walls through the Siloam tunnel, is on the west side of the Kidron Valley.

David crossed the Kidron when he left Jerusalem at the time of Absalom's rebellion. Asa, Hezekiah and Josiah, kings who reformed the nation's worship, destroyed idols in the Kidron Valley. Jesus and his disciples crossed it many times on their way to the Garden of Gethsemane.
2 Samuel 15:23; 1 Kings 15:13; 2 Chronicles 29:16; 2 Kings 23:4; John 18:1

KINGDOM OF GOD
"God is King" is one of the constant themes of the Old Testament. And in one sense it was true. But it was only partially true and it was obvious that God would need to act decisively if the evils that man's sin had brought were to be put right. God promised that this would happen.

"The right time has come," Jesus declared when he began to preach in Galilee, "and the Kingdom of

God is near! Turn away from your sins and believe the Good News." God had sent Jesus to establish his new rule, to put an end to the evil mess into which the world had fallen, and to make a fresh start, a new age. God's rule is what the "kingdom" means, rather than a *place* where God rules. The presence of God's rule was seen in Jesus' miracles and in the fact that he could drive out demons. Jesus was putting right both physical and spiritual illnesses to show the power of the new kingdom, in which evil would be completely destroyed.

The life and teaching of Jesus show that the kingdom of God has already arrived. He died for the sins of the old, sinful creation and rose again in the eternal life of the new creation, the life of the kingdom. But it is not yet fully established. This awaits the return of Jesus at the end of the age, when all things will be made new.

Jesus used parable stories to teach about the "kingdom of God". The Jews thought that it was going to be deliverance from the Romans. But Jesus made it clear that it was to be a slow growth of something which would eventually affect the whole world. It is worth all we have to enter it. It is not for the proud or self-centred, but for people who humble themselves before God — for sinners who repent.

People who believe in Jesus have his new life already. In the future, they will know the "new heavens and the new earth", their bodies will be made new, when the new age, the kingdom, is completed.

Micah 4:6–7; Mark 1:15; Luke 7:18–23; Matthew

5:1–20 ; 6:10; 13; Mark 4; 9:45–47; Luke 8; 14:16–24

KINGS

The two books of Kings cover 400 years of Israel's history: from the death of David to the destruction of Jerusalem in 587 BC.

It is not known who wrote these two books. But it is certain that, like 2 Samuel, they contain information that has been extracted from court records contemporary with the events they describe. They probably went through a number of editions and revisions, reaching their final form some time during the exile in Babylon (587–539 BC).

1 Kings can be divided into two parts:

Chapters 1–11: Solomon succeeds his father, David, as king of Israel and Judah. His golden reign includes the building of the temple in Jerusalem.

Chapters 12–22: the nation divides into northern and southern kingdoms. We are given the stories of the kings ruling each area, including Jeroboam (Israel), Rehoboam (Judah), Ahab (Israel), Jehoshaphat (Judah) and Ahaziah (Israel).

The prophets of God stand out as brave spokesmen, at a time when the people are turning to other gods. Elijah is the greatest of them all. His contest with the prophets of Baal on Mt Carmel is recorded in 1 Kings 18.

2 Kings continues the history of the two Israelite kingdoms where 1 Kings leaves off. It also has two parts:

Chapters 1–17: the story of both kingdoms from the mid-ninth century until the defeat of the northern kingdom by Assyria and the fall of Samaria in 722 BC. During this time the prophet Elisha, Elijah's successor, stands out as God's messenger.

Chapters 18–25: the story of the kingdom of Judah, from the fall of the kingdom of Israel until the destruction of the city of Jerusalem by King Nebuchadnezzar of Babylon in 587 BC. This includes the reigns of two great kings, Hezekiah and Josiah.

In the two books of Kings, the rulers of Israel are judged by their faithfulness to God. The nation succeeds when the king is loyal. When they turn to other gods, they fail. The northern kings are all failures according to this standard, but for a time the kings of Judah did a little better. The fall of Jerusalem and the exile of many Israelites was a major watershed in the history of Israel.

KING'S HIGHWAY

The road by which Moses promised to travel peacefully through the land of Edom and the land of Sihon, king of Heshbon. Both refused his request, and so the Israelites were forced to avoid Edom and to fight and defeat Sihon. The King's Highway was probably the main route north to south along the heights east of the Jordan, between Damascus and the Gulf of Aqaba.
Numbers 20:17; 21:22; Deuteronomy 2:27

KIRIATH-ARBA

An earlier name for Hebron.

KIRIATH-JEARIM
A hill-town a few miles east of Jerusalem. It was one of the towns of the Gibeonites, who tricked Joshua into a peace treaty. The Covenant Box (ark) was kept at Kiriath-jearim for twenty years before King David took it to Jerusalem.
Joshua 9; 1 Samuel 6:20–7:2; Jeremiah 26:20; Nehemiah 7:29

KISHON
A small stream which flows across the plain of Megiddo (Esdraelon) and into the Mediterranean Sea just north of Mt Carmel. In the story of Barak heavy rain raised the water level so high that the surrounding ground turned to mud and bogged down Sisera's chariots, giving Israel victory. The prophet Elijah killed the prophets of Baal by the River Kishon after the contest on Mt Carmel.
Judges 4; 5:21; 1 Kings 18:40

KITTIM
One of the sons of Javan in the Genesis "table of the nations", and so the name of Cyprus and of its early city of Kition (modern Larnaca). See *Cyprus*.
Genesis 10:4; 1 Chronicles 1:7; Numbers 24:24; Isaiah 23:1, 12; Jeremiah 2:10; Ezekiel 27:6

KOHATH
A son of Levi and grandfather of Moses. His descendants were known as the Kohathites and formed one of the three groups of Levites.
Exodus 6:16ff.; Numbes 3:17ff.

KORAH

1. A Levite who led a rebellion against Moses and Aaron. He did not see what right they had to be leaders and was angry because the people had not reached Canaan quickly enough. Korah and the others died because they rejected God's chosen leader and rebelled against him.
Numbers 16
2. A son of Levi. His descendants were singers in the temple.
1 Chronicles 6:37; Psalms 44–49

L

LABAN

The brother of Rebekah, Isaac's wife. He lived in Harran and welcomed his nephew Jacob when he had to leave home. Laban had two daughters — Leah and Rachel. Jacob agreed to work for Laban for seven years to marry Rachel. But Laban tricked him into marrying Leah and he had to work another seven years for Rachel. Jacob in turn outwitted Laban and as a result his flock of sheep and goats became larger and stronger than his uncle's. When Laban discovered that Jacob had secretly left for Canaan he chased after him. God warned Laban in a dream not to harm Jacob. They agreed to go their own ways and Laban returned to Harran.
Genesis 24:29ff.; 29–31

LACHISH

An important fortified town in the low hills about 30 miles/48km south-west of Jerusalem. Lachish has a long history. It was a military stronghold before the sixteenth century BC.

The king of Lachish joined with four other Amorite kings to fight Joshua. But Joshua won. He attacked and captured Lachish and put everyone there to death. Solomon's son, King Rehoboam, rebuilt Lachish as a defence against the Philistines and Egyptians.

Lachish

King Sennacherib's attack on Lachish; a relief commemorating his victory from his palace at Nineveh.

The town had an outer and inner wall, 19ft/6m thick. These walls were strengthened with towers. So too was the gateway. A well 144ft/44m deep ensured a good supply of water. Lachish had a palace and store-rooms approached by a street lined with shops.

King Amaziah of Judah fled to Lachish for safety. But his enemies followed and killed him there.

When the Assyrian King Sennacherib attacked Judah he besieged Lachish, cutting Jerusalem off from possible help from Egypt. He sent envoys from Lachish to demand Jerusalem's surrender. Lachish fell, and Sennacherib had the siege pictured on the walls of his palace at Nineveh. Archaeologists have also discovered at Lachish a mass grave from this time, holding 1,500 bodies.

The Babylonian army attacked Lachish at the time of the final siege of Jerusalem (589–586 BC). The "Lachish Letters", written by an army officer to his superior, belong to this period. Lachish fell and the Babylonians burnt it. After the exile it was resettled, but was never again an important place. Joshua 10; 2 Chronicles 11:5–12; 2 Kings 14:19; 18:14–21; Isaiah 36–37; Jeremiah 34:7; Nehemiah 11:30

LAMECH

1. A descendant of Cain.
Genesis 4:18ff.
2. Son of Methuselah and father of Noah.
Genesis 5:28–31

LAMENTATIONS

The Book of Lamentations is a collection of five poems. They mourn the fall of Jerusalem in 587 BC, and the exile which followed. God's temple had been destroyed, and the nation saw this as a sign that God had given them over to their enemy. The prophet was mourning the sin of his people.

Although the book is mainly a lament, there is also the promise of hope. The author is not known. The poems are still read aloud in Jewish synagogues each July, when the Jews remember how the temple was destroyed in 587 BC and again in AD 70.

LAODICEA

A town in the Lycus Valley of present-day western Turkey (the Roman province of Asia in New Testament times). Laodicea stood at the junction of two important main roads. It grew prosperous from trade and banking. The region produced clothes made of glossy black wool, and also medicines.

Water for the town was piped from hot springs some distance away. A number of these points are reflected in the letter to the church at Laodicea in the Book of Revelation. Paul's letter to the Colossians was intended for Laodicea, too, although he had not been there. The Christian group there may have been started during the time when Paul was staying at Ephesus.
Colossians 2:1; 4:13–16; Revelation 1:11; 3:14–22

LAW

After their escape from slavery in Egypt, God led the Israelites through the desert to Mt Sinai. They camped at the foot of the mountain, while God gave Moses the laws his people were to obey. The promise (covenant-treaty) God had previously made with individuals — Abraham, Isaac, Jacob — he now renewed with the whole nation. They were his people; he was their God. He had rescued them and he expected them to respond by obeying his laws. These were not just rules for worship or religious occasions. They covered every aspect of life. And they are summed up in the Ten Commandments.

The Ten Commandments God spoke, and these were his words:

I am the Lord your God who brought you out of Egypt, where you were slaves.

Worship no god but me.

Do not make for yourselves images of anything in heaven or on earth or in the water under the earth. Do not bow down to any idol or worship it, because I am the Lord your God and I tolerate no rivals. I bring punishment on those who hate me and on their

descendants down to the third and fourth generation. But I show my love to thousands of generations
of those who love me and obey my laws.

Do not use my name for evil purposes, because I, the
Lord your God, will punish anyone who misuses my
name.

Observe the Sabbath and keep it holy. You have six
days in which to do your work, but the seventh day
is a day of rest dedicated to me. On that day no one is
to work — neither you, your children, your slaves,
your animals, nor the foreigners who live in your
country. In six days I, the Lord, made the earth, the
sky, the sea, and everything in them, but on the
seventh day I rested. That is why I, the Lord,
blessed the Sabbath and made it holy.

Respect your father and your mother, so that you
may live a long time in the land that I am giving you.

Do not commit murder.

Do not commit adultery.

Do not steal.

Do not accuse anyone falsely.

Do not desire another man's house; do not desire his
wife, his slaves, his cattle, his donkeys, or anything
else that he owns."

This is the best known collection of Israel's laws.
It clearly has a special sigificance: in Exodus it is the
first set of laws given on Mt Sinai, and in Deuteronomy it is said at the end of the Ten Commandments: "These words the Lord spoke to all your
assembly . . . and he added no more" (Deuteronomy
5:22), that is, there were no others of equal importance.

The Ten Commandments are addressed to the

An ancient scroll containing the Pentateuch, the first five books of the Bible.

whole nation of Israel, not just to a particular group like the priests, and to every Israelite as an individual. All the same, though these Ten Commandments are unique as a collection, each one of them is found again in other places in the Hebrew laws.

The Ten Commandments were written on two stone tablets. This probably means two copies. The reason for having two copies of the Ten Commandments has only recently been understood. When a written covenant was made in the world of the Bible, each party making the covenant had a copy of its contents. If the covenant was between two nations, for instance the Hittites and the Egyptians, the two copies would be kept far apart, in the temple of a god of each land. In Israel, though, the covenant was between God and his people. Both copies of the Ten Commandments were kept in the Covenant Box (ark). This was the centre of Israel and it was also the place of God's presence. So God's copy and Israel's copy could be kept together. The Ten Commandments, then, were the terms of the covenant that God had made with his people. At Sinai, in response to all that God had done for them, the people of Israel accepted these terms.

The penalty for breaking any of the Ten Commandments is not mentioned. But if we compare these commandments with similar ones, it seems that the penalty was death (compare Exodus 20:13 with Exodus 21:12). This does not mean that the penalty was always carried out.

Other collections of laws Of course in any society many more detailed rules and laws are necessary. The basic laws need to be expanded. If the commandment says that you are not to do any work on the sabbath, who is meant by "you" and what counts as "work"? Already in Exodus 20:10 the simple command has to be spelled out in detail. It has to be made clear that "you" is not just the father of the Israelite family, but also "your children, your slaves, your animals . . . the foreigners who live in your country" (Deuteronomy 5:14). (We must assume and hope that "your wife" was also included!) Later, the Jewish rabbis spent much time on defining exactly what was "work". Jesus was criticized by some because he and his disciples healed and picked grain on the sabbath (Luke 14:3–4; Matthew 12:1–2). This was against the Pharisees' definition of "work".

The Ten Commandments are God's "covenant-law" for Israel. In addition to these, Israel's law-books (Exodus to Deuteronomy) contain many "case-laws", some of them similar to those of other nations. There are three major collections of laws.

The first follows on from the Ten Commandments, in Exodus 21–23. It is sometimes called the "Book of the Covenant". It contains moral, civil and religious laws. Instructions about worship are followed by laws dealing with the rights of slaves; manslaughter and injury to human life; theft and damage to property; social and religious duties; justice and human rights. At the end come instructions for the three great religious festivals:
Unleavened Bread, Firstfruits and Harvest. The laws show God's concern that life as a whole should be just and fair. They show his concern to protect the rights of those least able to help themselves — slaves, the poor, widows and orphans, foreigners.

Leviticus 17–26 contains a second collection of laws (the "holiness" laws). These mainly concern how the Israelites should worship God, the rituals connected with the tabernacle. But they also deal with everyday behaviour. The keynote of the teaching is the command, "Be holy, because I, the Lord your God, am holy" (Leviticus 19:2). Israel is to be "holy" because the nation belongs to God.

The third collection of detailed laws is set down in Deuteronomy 12–25. They cover many of the same matters dealt with in Exodus and Leviticus. But they come in the form of a sermon given by Moses to the Israelites before they went into the Promised Land. They include frequent encouragements to keep the Law, and warnings of what will happen if the people disobey. Deuteronomy 17:14–20 is the only part of the Law which spells out the duties of the king.

The purpose of the commandments The Law

was intended to be a guide to good relationships — with God and with other people. In it, God, the maker and rescuer of his people, tells them how they are to live — for their own good and well-being. The Hebrew word which is usually translated "law" (*torah*) actually means "guidance" or "instruction". These laws were never intended to be a long list of dos and don'ts to make life a burden.

The Law reflects God's character — his holiness, justice and goodness. It expresses his will. It gives his people the practical guidance they need in order to obey his command to "Be holy, as I am holy."

How far does the Old Testament Law still apply? Are Christians today bound by it as the Law of God? On the one hand, we have the sayings of Jesus. He has not come to abolish the Law; he has come to "fulfil" it (that is, to fill it with fuller meaning). Until heaven and earth pass away, he says, not the least portion will pass from the Law. Whoever disobeys the least important of the commandments shall be called least in the kingdom of heaven.

On the other hand, Paul states that Christ "has brought the Law to an end". He sees the Old Testament Law as something that was "introduced" at a certain point in history and was intended to be valid only till the time of the coming of Christ.

How do these two attitudes fit together? Some have thought the difficulty can be solved by distinguishing between the moral laws, which are still in force, and the ritual, ceremonial, and social laws of the Old Testament, which applied only to the Israelites. But for one thing it is impossible to say which laws are which, and, for another, although

Paul acknowledges that the law is from God and is "holy, just, and good", he speaks of even the moral law as "cancelled" by the work of Jesus Christ. Christians are "free" from the Law and are not subject to it — and in these passages Paul is thinking of the law as a whole, not just the moral law.

For Christians, then, Jesus Christ has taken the place of the Law. He has not put the Law aside or rejected it, but has summed it up. When Paul says that he is under Christ's law, he does not mean that he has accepted a new set of laws. Rather, he is a follower of Jesus and is filled with his spirit. By being linked with Jesus, sharing his new life and the power of his Holy Spirit, Christians are able to follow his example and obey his law. Christ's law is not a law that enslaves people because they are unable to keep it. It is the "perfect law that sets people free".

Deuteronomy 6:5; Leviticus 19:18; Matthew 5:17–20; Romans 10:4; 5:20; Galatians 3:19; Romans 7:6, 12; Colossians 2:14; Galatians 5:18; 1 Corinthians 9:21; Galatians 6:2; 5:1; James 1:25

LAZARUS

1. Brother of Martha and Mary who lived in Bethany. When Lazarus became ill his sisters sent for Jesus. Although he loved them all, Jesus delayed until he knew that Lazarus was dead. (See *Martha.*) Jesus went with the weeping women to the cave tomb — and wept himself. He told people standing by to roll away the stone which blocked the door and then cried, "Lazarus, come out." Lazarus came, with the grave clothes still wrapped around him.

Jewish leaders who saw this happen believed in Jesus. When the chief priests and Pharisees heard of Jesus' power over death they were afraid the whole nation would follow him, and plotted to kill him and Lazarus, too.
John 11–12:11
2. The name of the beggar in Jesus' story of the rich man and the beggar at his gate.
Luke 16:19–31

LEAH
Elder daughter of Laban, married to Jacob through Laban's trick. She and Jacob had six sons, ancestors of the tribes of Israel, and a daughter.
Genesis 29:16–33:7

LEBANON
The modern country of that name and its mountain range. Lebanon in the Old Testament was famous for its forests, especially its great cedar-trees. The Bible refers also to the snows of Lebanon, and to the country's fertility. All kinds of fruit grow on the coastal plain and lower hill slopes: olives, grapes, apples, figs, apricots, dates and all kinds of green vegetables.

The great Phoenician (Canaanite) ports of Tyre, Sidon and Byblos were all on the coast of Lebanon and grew rich exporting its products. King Solomon sent to the king of Tyre for cedar and other wood from Lebanon to build the temple and royal palace at Jerusalem.
1 Kings 5:1–11; Hosea 6:5–7; Ezra 3:7; Psalm 72:16; Isaiah 2:13; 14:8; Ezekiel 31, etc.

LEOPARD

Isaiah and Jeremiah both mention the leopard, which was well known in Israel in Bible times. Its spotted coat helps it to creep up on its kill unseen, even in the open.
Isaiah 11:6; Jeremiah 13:23

LEVI

1. Third son of Jacob and Leah. His descendants formed the tribe of Levi. The Levites were chosen to serve God in the tent of worship and, later, the temple.
Genesis 29:34; 34:25ff.; 49:5ff.; Numbers 3:5–20
2. See *Matthew*.

LEVITICUS

Leviticus is basically a rule-book. It contains the laws about religious ceremonies, worship and daily life which were designed to keep the people of Israel in a right relationship with God.

Leviticus gets its name from the priests (the members of the tribe or clan of Levi) who had the job of carrying out the rules for worship. It is always coming back to the theme of God's holiness — his utter goodness, so different from man. When Jesus summed up the law, he quoted from Leviticus: "Love your neighbour as yourself" (19:18).

Leviticus contains the following sections of teaching:

Chapters 1–7: laws about sacrifice and offerings, and their meaning.

Chapters 8–10: laws about the men who could be priests, and how they were set apart for their work.

Chapters 11–15: laws for daily living. These concentrate on "pure" and "impure" things which barred people for a time from joining in God's worship.

Chapter 16: the Day of Atonement — an annual occasion when offerings were made to make the people "clean" from sin.

Chapters 17–27: laws about holy living and worship, with promises for those who obeyed and warnings for those who disobeyed.

LIBNAH

A fortified lowland town not far from Lachish, taken by Joshua. In the reign of King Jehoram of Judah Libnah rebelled. The town survived a siege by the Assyrian King Sennacherib when plague hit his army.
Joshua 10:29–30; 2 Kings 8:22; 19:8, 35

LIFE

Life was "breathed into man's nostrils" by God and he "began to live". God is in all the natural processes that keep us alive; and it is he who determines when life shall end. Life is a person's most valued possession, and one of his greatest desires is for God to bless him with a long life.

But there is more to life than just physical existence. A relationship with God enables people to live life on a new level. This is the full, abundant life that Jesus came to bring. It is "eternal life", which Jesus offers as a free and permanent gift. Eternal life is life in a new dimension, "God's life". "Whoever has the Son", says John, "has this life." It begins when a person becomes a Christian, and survives death. It is an eternal relationship with God.

See also *Death, Resurrection.*
Genesis 2:7; Psalm 104:29; Job 2:4; Psalm 91:16; Deuteronomy 8:3; 30:15–20; John 10:10, 28; 1 John 5:12; John 11:25–26; Romans 6:4–13, 22–23 and many other passages

LIGHT

The Bible often uses the contrast of light and darkness to show the absolute difference between God and the forces of evil. "God is light, and there is no darkness at all in him." God is altogether good. His holiness is so utterly pure that he is said to "live in the light that no one can approach". In contrast to this the forces of evil are called "the cosmic powers of this dark age". John describes the spiritual battle between "light" (God and goodness) and "darkness" (Satan and everything evil). "The light shines in the darkness, and the darkness has never put it out." In the life, death and resurrection of Jesus light won its victory over darkness.

Jesus calls himself "the light of the world" and promises "the light of life" to all who follow him. Men and women need no longer walk in darkness, ignorant of the truth, cut off from God, and blinded by sin. They can "live in the light — just as he is in the light". To become a Christian is to move out of darkness into light. God's people are "like light for the whole world". They must let that light shine out to others.

At last, in the new heaven and earth, the light of God's presence will be a constant reality. There will be no darkness, no night, no lamps, not even sunlight. All God's people will be with him, and he will be their light.

1 John 1:5; 1 Timothy 6:16; Ephesians 6:12; John 1:4–9; 8:12; 1 John 1:7; Matthew 5:14–16; Revelation 21:23–24; 22:5

"LILY OF THE FIELD"

In the Old Testament the lily may have been the wild blue hyacinth, or the madonna lily (the bulb was also considered a delicacy to eat). When Jesus spoke of the lilies of the field he was probably thinking of wild flowers in general, rather than one in particular. In spring the hillsides of Galilee are ablaze with brightly coloured flowers: anemone, crocus, poppy, narcissus and yellow chrysanthemum.

Song of Solomon 5:13; 6:2; Matthew 6:28

LION

The lion is mentioned many times in the Bible — although by New Testament times it was rare in Israel. Assyrian kings kept lions in pits, and enjoyed lion-hunts with their nobles. Lions lived in the thickets of the Jordan Valley and could be a danger to flocks and to humans. The strength and courage of the lion made him a symbol of power, so that Jesus himself is called "lion of the tribe of Judah".

Daniel 6:16–24; Revelation 5:5

LORD's SUPPER

Jesus instituted this communal meal at Passover time, at the last supper with his disciples before his death. At the Passover Festival people looked back to the deliverance from Egypt, and forward to the coming kingdom of God. The Lord's Supper, too, looks back. It reminds us, by the bread and wine, of the past event of Jesus' death. And it looks forward to the time when Jesus will come again. "You proclaim the Lord's death until he comes," says Paul.

The Passover meal began with a blessing — thanking God for the bread. Then pieces of the loaf were passed round to the guests. The same action in the Christian service was a reminder of the fact that Jesus' body had been "given for you". The meal ended with a shared cup of wine. In the Christian ceremony the wine was a token of the blood (the death) of Christ. His death was a sacrifice that sealed the new covenant agreement between God and man, just as the old covenant was sealed by the blood of sacrificial oxen (Exodus 24:5–8). So Jesus says, "This is my blood . . . which seals God's covenant."

Those who share in this sacred meal declare their loyalty to the Lord who has created the new covenant. The wine also points to the future kingdom of God, pictured as a banquet. Jesus said, "I will never again drink this wine until the day I drink the new wine in the Kingdom of God."

In Acts, the Lord's Supper is called "the breaking of bread" ("fellowship meal"). This was the name used by the Jews for the blessing said over the bread. Originally it was part of an actual meal. The Christians at Corinth brought their own provisions for just such a meal together. Paul saw a further meaning in sharing the loaf. Christians share in Christ as they share the bread, and they also share in the "body of Christ", the church. Division and disunity in the church denies the truth for which the one loaf stands.

Eventually the Lord's Supper moved from the homes of individual Christians to a special building, and was no longer part of an actual meal. Christian prayers and praises that had developed from the synagogue services were added to the ceremony. The earliest account we have of the prayers at the Lord's Supper (or Eucharist) come from the *Didache* ("The Teaching") written late in the first or early in the second century AD.
Matthew 26:26–30; Mark 14:22–26; Luke 22:14–20; Acts 2:46; 20:7; 1 Corinthians 11:20–34; 10:16–17

Bread and wine, shared by Christians at the Lord's Supper.

LOT

Abraham's nephew. He went with Abraham from Harran to Canaan but they parted after their herdsmen quarrelled. Lot went to live at Sodom in the fertile plain. Abraham rescued him from raiding kings. Later, when Sodom was destroyed for its wickedness, Lot just escaped. His wife, stopping to look back at the city, was caught in the disaster. Genesis 11:31–14:16; 19

LOVE

"God is love". This has always been the character of God. It is a mistake to think that the God of the Old Testament could not be described in this way. One of the most moving testimonies to God's love in the whole Bible is by the prophet Hosea. God's love was the reason why he chose and cared for the people of Israel. In return, God's people were expected to love him with their whole being, and show a similar love to their fellow men.

In the New Testament "love" sometimes translates the usual Greek word for love, *philia*. This means "intimate affection". Far more important, however, is the word *agape*. This is not a sex word, although the Bible regards sex very highly. *Agape* is used to describe self-giving love, seen above all in Jesus Christ. It is in his death that we see the true depths of this love.

It is far greater than human love. It is the love that unites the Father and the Son. It is the love that God has for the world, and it becomes part of a Christian's life through the gift of God. It is in fact the mark of God's presence in the life of every Christian. "If you have love for one another," Jesus says, "then everyone will know that you are my disciples." 1 John 4:8; Hosea 11:1–4; 7–9; Deuteronomy 7:7–8; 6:5; Leviticus 19:18; Romans 5:5, 8; John 3:16, 35; 1 Corinthians 13; Galations 5:22; John 13:34–35; see also John 14:15, 21–24; 15:9–14; 1 John 4:7–5:3

LUD

Lud, a son of Shem, gave his name to a people known later as the Lydians. They lived in the west of Asia Minor (Turkey) around Sardis.
See *Lydians*.

LUKE

A Greek-speaking doctor who wrote the Gospel of Luke and the Acts of the Apostles. He was a friend of Paul and travelled with him on some of his journeys, so he was able to describe at first-hand some of the things Paul said and did. On these journeys Luke was also able to learn about Jesus' life and the beginnings of the church from the apostles and first Christians. He sailed to Rome with Paul and stayed with him while he was a prisoner there.
Colossians 4:14; 2 Timothy 4:11; Philemon 24

LUKE'S GOSPEL

Luke's Gospel — third of the four accounts of Jesus' life in the New Testament — has by far the most detail. The story of the growth and spread of Christianity after Jesus returned to heaven is continued by the same writer in the Book of Acts (see *Acts*). Both books were written for a Roman official called Theophilus.

The Gospel writer has been careful to get his history and facts right. He sets out to tell what happened in Palestine during Jesus' life. Tradition suggests it was written by Luke, the doctor who went with Paul on some of his journeys.

Luke's Gospel presents Jesus as the promised Saviour of Israel — and as the Saviour of all people.

It emphasizes how he preached this Good News to the poor.

The Gospel opens with the story of the birth and childhood of John the Baptist and Jesus (chapters 1 and 2). Many of these details are found only in Luke.

Chapters 3–9 deal with the baptism and testing of Jesus, and his preaching and teaching in Galilee.

His journey from Galilee to Jerusalem is covered in 9:51–19:46. Some of Jesus' parables, recorded in these chapters, are found only in Luke: for example the good Samaritan, the prodigal son and the rich fool.

His last week in Jerusalem is covered in 19:47–23:56.

Finally, chapter 24 tells how Jesus came back from death and returned to heaven.

Luke's Gospel is full of joy. It also stresses the need for prayer, the power of the Holy Spirit in Jesus and his followers, and God's forgiveness of sins. It is marked by a warm interest in people.

LUZ
The older name of Bethel.

LYCIA
A small, mountainous land in the south-west of Asia Minor (Turkey). The ports of Patara and Myra, at which Paul landed, were in Lycia.
Acts 27:5

LYDDA
A town about 10 miles/16km inland from Joppa.

Peter healed a lame man, Aeneas, when visiting the first Christians here. The place is now again called by its Old Testament name, Lod.
Acts 9:32–35, 38

LYDIA
A "dealer in purple cloth" who came from Thyatira in Asia Minor (Turkey). She heard Paul preach in Philippi (Greece) and became a Christian.
Acts 16:14–15, 40

LYDIANS
On the west coast of Turkey lived an Indo-European people, the Lydians. Inscriptions and objects unearthed in their capital, Sardis, are beginning to reveal their culture and history. Gyges (Gog), who was king about 650 BC, was used by the prophet Ezekiel as a figure standing for a distant ruler. Obadiah refers to Sardis (Sepharad) as one of many places of exile. Lydia had rich deposits of gold. It was here that coinage began and the wealthy Croesus ruled. He was defeated by Cyrus the Persian in 546 BC. Lydia (Lud) is named as an ally of Tyre and Egypt in Ezekiel. From 133 BC it was part of the Roman province of Asia.
Ezekiel 38:2; Obadiah 20; Ezekiel 27:10; 30:5

LYSTRA
A remote town in the Roman province of Galatia (not far from Konya in modern Turkey). Paul and Barnabas went on to Lystra after rough treatment at Iconium, on the first missionary journey. Paul healed a cripple at Lystra, and the people believed

him to be Hermes (messenger of the Greek gods) and
Barnabas to be Zeus himself. But Jews from Iconium stirred up trouble, and Paul was stoned and
left for dead. Some of the people became Christians,
and Paul returned to visit them on his second journey. Lystra (or possibly Derbe) was Timothy's home
town.
Acts 14:6–20; 16:1–5

MAACAH

A small Aramaean state to the south-east of Mt Hermon. It is mentioned in David's campaigns and one of his warriors came from here.
Joshua 12:5; 2 Samuel 10; 23:34

MACEDONIA

A region of Greece stretching north and west from Thessalonica. The Roman province of Macedonia included Philippi and Beroea as well as Thessalonica.

Paul crossed the Aegean Sea from Troas after seeing a vision of a Macedonian man asking him to come over and help them. It was the first stage in bringing the Good News of Jesus to Europe. Three of Paul's letters (Philippians, 1 and 2 Thessalonians) are addressed to Macedonian Christians. They gave generously to his relief fund for Christians in Judea. And several of them became his regular helpers.
Acts 16:8–17:15; 20:1–6; 2 Corinthians 8:1–5; 9:1–5, etc.

MACHPELAH

When Sarah died at Hebron, Abraham still owned no land. So he bought a plot of land with the cave of Machpelah from Ephron the Hittite. Abraham himself was later buried here, and afterwards Isaac and Rebekah, and then Jacob.

Much later, Herod the Great built a shrine round the place believed to contain the cave and the tombs, and this can still be seen.
Genesis 23; 25:9; 49:30; 50:13

MAGOG
See *Gog*.

MAHANAIM
A place in Gilead, east of the River Jordan and near the River Jabbok. Jacob saw God's angels at Mahanaim, before the reunion with his brother Esau. For a short time it was the capital of Saul's son Ishbosheth (Ishbaal). It was King David's headquarters during Absalom's rebellion. One of Solomon's district officers was based at Mahanaim.
Genesis 32:2; 2 Samuel 2:8–10; 17:24–29; 1 Kings 4:14

MAKE-UP
From earliest times women have used beauty aids. In ancient Palestine, Egypt and Mesopotamia women put dark eyeshadow around their eyes. At first this was to protect their eyes against the strong sunshine. But it soon became a matter of fashion. Minerals were ground up in oil or gum with a small pestle and mortar. The women used their fingers, spatulas made of wood or bronze, or fine brushes to put on their eyeshadow. And they had polished metal mirrors in which to study the effect! Lead sulphide (*galena*) was used early on, and copper carbonate (*kohl*) gave a greenish tinge. By Roman times, antimony was more often used. Egyptian

A Greek perfume bottle and jug made of multi-coloured glass.

women used lipstick and powderpuffs. Their toe nails and finger nails were painted red with dye from the crushed leaves of the henna plant. Red iron oxide seems to have been used in Egypt as rouge.

Oil, rubbed into the body to soothe the skin, was almost as essential in a hot, dry climate. The only time it was not used was during times of mourning. But the oil, like the eye-paint, soon became part of the fashion scene and was perfumed. A heavy scent helped disguise body odour where there was not much water for washing! "Good oil" was made from flowers, seeds and fruit, soaked in oil and water. This was then sometimes treated so that the essence could be extracted and strained out. Other perfumes came from gums or resins and were used either in powdered form, dissolved in oil, or mixed to make ointments. Most of these were imported into Israel and were a luxury. Because of their cost, they were kept in very expensive bottles and containers.

MALACHI

The last of the Old Testament prophets (about mid-fifth century BC). The temple had been rebuilt after the return from exile but the people were not serving God wholeheartedly. "Turn back," said Malachi. "Stop cheating God of his dues. Don't test his patience any longer." Malachi's name means "my messenger". As God's messenger he spoke of the coming Messiah and the great day of God's justice and judgement.

MALTA
The modern name of an island in the central Mediterranean Sea, between Sicily and the north coast of Africa. Its ancient name was Melita, and Paul's ship was wrecked here during his voyage as a prisoner to Rome. All the people on board reached land safely and were received kindly by the natives. They spent the winter on Malta before sailing for Italy.
Acts 28:1–10

MAMRE
A place near Hebron. Abraham, and later Isaac, often camped by the oak-trees at Mamre. It was here that Abraham heard that Lot had been captured. At Mamre God promised him a son, and he pleaded with God to spare Sodom.
Genesis 13:18; 14:13; 18; 23:17; 35:27

MAN AND WOMAN
Men and women are part of nature. They are "animals" — yet different from the animals, because God made them to be "like himself" and to enjoy his friendship. They were the crowning glory of his whole creation on earth.

The story of Adam and Eve in Genesis 2 shows the

importance of men and women in God's creation. Adam is put in the Garden of Eden to look after it and to work in it. Work itself is not a necessary evil: it is part of God's original intention. Man was not meant to live alone. God made woman as the ideal partner for Adam, to work alongside him and to share his life. The relationship between man and woman, their sexuality, is part of God's perfect creation.

But when Adam ("man") and Eve ("woman") rebelled against God they lost the open fellowship with God and with one another which they had known. The results of their sin affected every area of their lives. The man's work became burdensome, and the woman's relationship with her husband brought pain as well as pleasure.

The rest of the Bible reflects both the glory and the fallenness of men and women. They are second only to God, crowned with honour. They care for all God has made, sharing his creativity in artistic achievement and caring for the earth's resources. But we see them, too, as spoilers, perverted and degraded, violent and evil.

The New Testament announces the dawn of a new age. Mankind "in Adam" is the same as ever. But men and women are "one in union with Christ Jesus". Both are made new and share in the new creation as equal partners, to live life as God originally intended it.

See also *Fall, Future destiny, Life*.

Genesis 1:26–28; 2; 3; Deuteronomy 5; 8; Psalm 8; Romans 1–3; 5:12–19; 8:18–25; 2 Corinthians 5:17; 6:16–18; Galatians 3:28

MANASSEH

1. Joseph's elder son who was adopted and blessed by Jacob. His descendants formed the tribe of Manasseh.

Genesis 41:51; 48:1ff.

2. King of Judah for fifty-five years (696–642 BC) after his father, King Hezekiah. Manasseh led the nation astray, introducing all kinds of idol worship. He was taken prisoner to Babylon by the Assyrians. When he returned to Jerusalem he turned to God and changed his ways.

2 Kings 21:1ff.; 2 Chronicles 33

3. The land belonging to the tribe of Manasseh. West Manasseh was the hill-country of Samaria as far west as the Mediterranean Sea. East Manasseh was the land east of central Jordan.

Joshua 13:29–31; 17:7–13

MARESHAH

A town in the low hills nearly 20 miles/32 km south-west of Jerusalem. It was fortified by Rehoboam. Later King Asa destroyed a great army from Sudan here. The prophet Micah foretold disaster for Mareshah.

Joshua 15:44; 2 Chronicles 11:8; 14:9–12; 20:37; Micah 1:15

MARK (JOHN)

The writer of the second Gospel. John Mark lived in Jerusalem. His mother, Mary, allowed the first Christians to meet in her house. Mark later went with Paul and Barnabas, his cousin, to Cyprus on Paul's first missionary journey. He left them halfway through and Paul refused to take him when they set out again. Instead Mark went back to Cyprus with Barnabas. Later Paul and Mark were together in Rome, and Paul wrote of him as a loyal friend and helper. Peter describes him as "my son Mark" and, by tradition, it was Peter who gave Mark much of the story of Jesus told in Mark's Gospel.

Mark 14:51; Acts 12:12, 25; 13:13; 15:36ff.; Colossians 4:10; 2 Timothy 4:11; Philemon 24; 1 Peter 5:13

MARK'S GOSPEL

Mark — the second of the four Gospels which tell the life of Jesus — is a gospel of action. It is full of life. Its author concentrates on what Jesus did, and where he went — rather than what he said and taught.

Mark is the shortest Gospel, with only sixteen chapters. It may also be the earliest. It was probably written about AD 65–70. Writers in the first centuries after Christ believed it was written down by John Mark from the account he heard from the apostle Peter. John Mark's name comes often in Acts and the New Testament letters. He shared part of Paul's first missionary tour and was later with Peter. In the Gospel, the writer often takes trouble to explain Jewish customs, so clearly he had non-Jewish readers in mind.

Mark keeps the pace of events moving. After a short introduction which covers John the Baptist and Jesus' baptism and testing, the first nine chapters deal with Jesus' healing and teaching in Galilee. Mark shows how Jesus' followers gradually began to understand him better. But his enemies became more and more hostile. Chapters 11–15 describe Jesus' last week in Jerusalem, and are followed by reports of his resurrection — how he came back to life (chapter 16). The ending, Mark 16:9–20, does not appear in many old texts and may have been added by early Christians, to make a less abrupt end to the book.

Mark shows Jesus as a man of action, a man of authority. He teaches powerfully, has power over evil spirits, and forgives people their sin. He is clearly more than an ordinary man. Yet he makes himself one with us. He came to give his own life to set people free from sin.

MARRIAGE

The story of creation in Genesis 1 and 2 shows the pattern of marriage — one man to one woman for life — as God's original design. But it was not long before a code of rules was needed because standards had fallen.

Rules and customs The law-code of King Hammurabi of Babylon (about 1700 BC) implies that:

A man would not take a second wife unles the first was unable to have children.

The husband was allowed a secondary wife (a concubine), or his wife might give him a slave-girl, to have children by her.

The children of the slave-girl might not be sent away.

It is clear from the story of Abraham that he, too, observed these customs. That is why he was so worried when Sarah insisted on sending away the slave-girl Hagar and her son (Genesis 16:1–6; 21:10–12).

The customs of Jacob's and Esau's time were less strict and allowed more than one wife. This practice grew until, by the time of the Judges and the Kings, a man could have as many wives as he could afford. But having several wives could lead to all kinds of problems. It must have been all too easy to have favourites. Deuteronomy 21:15 seems to recognize this problem when it says that a man must not take away the inheritance of his firstborn son to give to the child of his favourite wife. No doubt at first it made good economic sense to have more than one wife: more children meant more workers. But the time came when it cost more to keep several wives than the family gained by having more children.

By New Testament times the usual practice was once again to have only one wife (although at one time King Herod the Great had nine). In this respect the people had returned to the standard set out by Moses and the prophets.

It was very unusual for a man not to marry — there is no Hebrew word for "bachelor" — and people in Israel married very young. The legal ages for marriage were thirteen and over for a boy, and twelve and over for a girl. It was probably because they were so young that marriages were arranged by parents, normally within the same clan in Old Testament times, and ideally with a first cousin. Marriage to someone from another nation worshipping other gods was forbidden. The law also forbade marriage between close relatives (Leviticus 18:6ff.). Arranged marriages did not always mean that the young people had no say. Shechem (Genesis 34:4) and Samson (Judges 14:2) both asked their parents to arrange a marriage with a particular girl. It was also possible to marry a slave or a war captive.

Marriage was a civil rather than a religious affair. At engagement (betrothal) a contract was made in front of two witnesses. Sometimes the couple gave one another a ring or bracelet. The engagement was as binding as marriage. During the waiting time before the wedding, while the girl was still living at her father's house, the man was excused from going to war (Deuteronomy 20:7).

A sum of money, a bride-price (called the *mohar*) had to be paid to the girl's father. It could sometimes be paid partly in work by the man. The father seems to have been able to use any interest the *mohar* could earn, but he was not allowed to touch the *mohar* itself. It was returned to the daughter on the death of her parents, or if her husband died. Jacob's father-in-law, Laban, seems to have broken with custom and spent his daughter's bride-price (Genesis 31:15).

The girl's father, in return, gave her, or her husband, a "dowry" (wedding gift). This could be servants (as in the case of Rebekah and Leah), or land or property.

The wedding This took place when the bride-groom had the new home ready. With his friends, he went to his bride's house in the evening. She was waiting, veiled and in her wedding dress. She wore jewellery which the bridegroom had given her. Sometimes he gave her a head-band of coins. (It may have been one of these coins which was lost in the "lost coin" story — told by Jesus — Luke 15:8.) In a simple ceremony, the veil was taken from the bride's face and laid on the bridegroom's shoulder. The bridegroom, his "best man" (called a "companion") and his friends (called the sons of the bridechamber) then took the bride back to his own or his parents' home for a wedding feast to which all their friends were invited. The friends waited at the roadside in their best clothes and went in torchlight procession to the new home, sometimes with music and dancing.

The law of Moses allowed a man to divorce his wife. But he had to write out divorce papers which gave the woman her freedom before he sent her away. In New Testament times the Jewish teachers often argued about the reasons for divorce. Some allowed divorce for anything which displeased the husband — even poor cooking! Others believed there must be a serious moral lapse, such as adultery. But, typically, there was a different standard for women. A wife could never divorce her husband, though under certain circumstances she could force him to divorce her.

When questioned about divorce, Jesus firmly reinstated the principle of God's original design for marriage. Paul, too, underlined the same point that in marriage two people become "one flesh".
Genesis 1:26–31; 2:7, 18–25; Deuteronomy 24:1–4 and Matthew 19:3–12; Proverbs 5:15–20; 12:4; 18:22; 19:13–14; 21:9, 19; 25:24; 31:10–31; 1 Corinthians 7; Ephesians 5:22–33; 1 Peter 3:1–7
Passages reflecting wedding customs:
Genesis 24; 29; Judges 14; Matthew 22:2–14; 25: 1–12; Luke 14:7–14; John 3:1–10; Revelation 21:2

MARTHA

The sister of Mary and Lazarus. She lived at the village of Bethany, close to Jerusalem. Jesus often visited their home. When Lazarus was ill the sisters sent for Jesus. Their brother died before Jesus came. Martha went to meet Jesus and said, "If you had been here, my brother would not have died." Jesus replied, "I am the resurrection and I am life . . . Do you believe this?" "Lord, I do," Martha answered. And to her great joy, Jesus restored her brother to life.
Luke 10:38–42; John 11:20ff.

MARY

1. Jesus' mother. While she was engaged to Joseph, a carpenter, an angel told her she was to be the mother of Jesus, the Messiah and Son of God. Before Jesus was born, Mary visited her cousin Elizabeth. There Mary spoke the wonderful song of praise to God known as the *Magnificat*. Mary and Joseph went from Nazareth to Bethlehem to register for a Roman census. There Jesus was born. When the shepherds came, with their story of angels singing, "Mary remembered all these things and thought deeply about them." When Jesus was presented at the temple, a few days later, Simeon spoke to Mary about the future: "Sorrow, like a sharp sword, will break your own heart." While Jesus was still a baby, Mary and Joseph took him to Egypt because King Herod wanted to kill this rival. After Herod's death they returned to Nazareth.

When Jesus was twelve his parents took him to the temple for the Passover Festival. They were terribly worried when he stayed behind, alone, to talk with the teachers. Mary was with Jesus when he worked his first miracle at the wedding feast in Cana. At his crucifixion she stood by the cross, and Jesus asked one of his disciples (see *John*) to look after her. Mary was with the disciples when they met together to pray after Jesus' ascension.

Matthew 1:18–25; 2:11; 13:55; Luke 1–2; John 2:1ff.; 19:25–27; Acts 1:14

2. Sister of Martha. She lived in Bethany with her sister and brother Lazarus and loved to listen to Jesus. Just before Jesus' death she anointed him with precious oil and wiped his feet with her hair. (See also *Martha, Lazarus*.)

Luke 10:38–42; John 11; 12:3ff.

3. Mary Magdalene became a disciple of Jesus after he had healed her. She was the first person to see Jesus after the resurrection and ran to tell the apostles.

Mark 16:9; Luke 8:2; 24:10; John 20:1ff.

4. Mary, mother of James and Joseph. She was present at the crucifixion and was one of the group of women who found Jesus' tomb empty on the resurrection morning. This Mary is probably the same person as "the other Mary" and Mary, wife of Clopas.

Matthew 27:56, 61; 28:1; John 19:25

5. Mary, the mother of John Mark. The first Christians met in her house in Jerusalem.

Acts 12:12

MATTHEW
One of the twelve apostles, and traditionally writer

of the first Gospel. Matthew, also called Levi, was a tax collector before Jesus said to him, "Follow me." Matthew 9:9; 10:3; Luke 5:27–32

MATTHEW'S GOSPEL

There are four "Gospels", telling the story of the life and teaching of Jesus. Each has its own special purpose. The Gospel of Matthew was written, in the first place, particularly for the Jews. It tells the good news that Jesus is the promised Saviour — the Messiah, or Christ, whom the Jews had been expecting for so long. With Jesus, all the promises God had made to his people in the Old Testament came true.

The Gospel does not give the name of its author. From very early on Matthew has been accepted as its writer. He was the tax collector who became one of Jesus' twelve close friends. If he did not write it all, he was almost certainly the author of a collection of Jesus' sayings included in the book. Matthew's Gospel was written some time between AD 50 and 100. Much of it is very similar to the story in Mark's Gospel. But there are ten parables and a number of incidents which come only in Matthew.

Matthew opens with the family tree and birth of Jesus (chapters 1–2). After describing John the Baptist's work, it records Jesus' baptism and his time of testing in the desert (chapters 3–4).

A large part of Matthew is taken up with Jesus' preaching, teaching and healing in Galilee. Matthew shows Jesus as a great teacher, with much to say about God's "kingdom" — his reign in the world (chapters 4; 12–18). This teaching is presented in five main sections:

Chapters 5–7: the Sermon on the Mount. This answers many questions about the kingdom and gives us the basis of Jesus' teaching on moral questions.

Chapter 10: Jesus' instructions to his twelve disciples before sending them out.

Chapter 13: parables about the kingdom.

Chapter 18: Jesus' explanation about what it means to follow him.

Chapters 24–25: Jesus' words about the fall of Jerusalem, the end of this age, and the coming of a new age.

Matthew then describes Jesus' journey from Galilee to Jerusalem (chapters 19–20) and the events of his last week in that city (chapters 21–27). The account of Jesus' death on the cross is followed by the account of how he came back to life — the resurrection (chapter 28).

MATTHIAS
Chosen by the disciples after the death of Judas Iscariot to take the traitor's place as one of the twelve.
Acts 1:21–26

MEALS
In the peasant home, meals were very simple. There was no formal breakfast. If anything was eaten at all, it was as a snack carried and eaten on the way to work. The midday meal was usually bread and olives, and perhaps fruit. The evening meal was a vegetable stew, with a piece of bread used as a spoon

to dip into the common pot. The whole family ate together for this meal, and if any important guests were present, meat might be added to the cooking pot. The family sat on the floor to eat.

In a wealthy home it was different. There was more elaborate food with plenty of meat. In New Testament times guests reclined on couches round three sides of a square table. Instead of one dish, there were many.

A Roman, or Roman-style, dinner party followed this pattern: first came the hors d'oeuvres, and wine mixed with honey. Next, three main courses were served on trays. The guests ate with their fingers, though they used a spoon for things like soup! After this course, at a Roman meal, pieces of food were thrown into the fire as a token "sacrifice" — a kind of "grace". Finally pastries and fruit were served as dessert. This was followed by drinks and entertainment. The "religious" element — the offering to the gods — was one of the reasons why a Jew could never eat with a Gentile. The strict Jewish food-laws was another (see above). But God showed Peter in a vision that the old barriers between Jew and non-Jew must be broken down: Christians, whatever their nationality, belong to one family.

Among the nomadic, tent-dwelling people, a traveller was always welcome to stay — for three days and four hours! — the length of time the hosts believed their food sustained their guests. Flat loaves of bread, and milk, were basic to the meal. For the time of his stay the traveller became one of the clan. Both Old and New Testaments teach the importance of hospitality. As the author of the letter to the

Hebrews writes: "Remember to welcome strangers in your homes" (Hebrews 13:2).

MEASURES
See *Weights and Measures*.

MEDES
In north-west Persia, Assyrian kings met Median tribes from the ninth century BC onwards. They were on fairly good terms for two hundred years. Then the Medes joined with the Scythians, in alliance with Babylon, to bring about the downfall of Assyria (612 BC). The Medes had already been under Scythian pressure for some decades. But this time the Median king, Cyaxares, had built up his own strength, and was able to extend his rule as far as the Lydian frontier in Turkey, and over the Persians to his south.

Astyages, next king of the Medes, was overthrown by his son-in-law, Cyrus the Persian, in 549 BC.

The head of a Median noble, carved on the stairway of Darius' palace at Persepolis, Iran.

Media then became a province of the new Persian Empire. They played their part in the fall of Babylon. Media's capital, Ecbatana (modern Hamadan) became the Persian capital. Median officers held high positions in the Persian court, and Median words were adopted into Persian. Median influence was so strong in the Persian Empire that we find the joint phrase "Medes and Persians" being used. And the Greeks called their great Persian war "the war with the Medes".

One tribe of Medes, the Magi, had a special religious position (like that of the Levites in Israel). Jeremiah 25:25; 51:11, 28; Daniel 5:28

MEDIATOR

A "go-between" who brings together (reconciles) two people who are estranged from each other.

When Adam first disobeyed God his sin broke the friendship between them. The Old Testament therefore recognizes the need for a mediator between man and God. The Old Testament prophets spoke in God's name and made God real to their hearers. The priest who offered sacrifices to God represented the people before God. Moses combined both roles as Israel's mediator.

But, important as Moses was, he could never be the perfect mediator between God and the people, because he shared the sinful nature of every human being. Only Jesus, who was both man, but sinless, and the Son of God could be the perfect mediator who arranges a new covenant. This is the main theme of the letter to the Hebrews.

See also *Reconciliation*.

Exodus 32:30–32; 33:11; Leviticus 16; Numbers 12:6–8; Deuteronomy 5:4–5; Galatians 3:19–20; 1 Timothy 2:5; Hebrews 7:24–25; 8:6; 9:15; 12:24

MEDICINE

Even where symptoms are described in the Bible, it is not always possible to be sure what diseases were involved. Some form of leprosy was fairly common. Shortage of food in drought, combined with the heat and poor water supply, often led to dysentery, cholera, typhoid and beriberi ("dropsy"). The dust-filled air made blindness very common. Then there were the deaf and the crippled. The number of deaths among children was clearly quite high.

Mental illness was not uncommon. But the Bible often does not make any distinction between this and being possessed by evil spirits. There may also have been a popular belief that "fits" could be caused by the moon. (In Matthew 4:24, "epileptic" translates a word which literally means "moonstruck".)

2 Samuel 12:15; 2 Kings 4:20; 1 Kings 17:17; 2 Kings 5:1–14; 1 Samuel 19:9; Daniel 4:33

Attitudes to disease The attitude to illness in Israel was always quite distinct from that of Israel's neighbours. The Mesopotamians and the Egyptians in early times regarded illness as invariably caused by the malice of evil spirits. Treatment was therefore in the hands of exorcist-priests and involved incantations and magic, alongside other methods. Israel also regarded health as a religious matter, but this was because the people firmly believed that God was all-powerful. From him came both good and evil. Health was a divine blessing. Disease was a sign that the spiritual relationship between a person and God had broken down. Magic was therefore officially forbidden, although no doubt the ordinary people practised it to some extent. The discovery of many small images, probably used as charms, seems to indicate this.

This attitude to illness, however, also had its drawbacks. God was the only true healer. He had given his people a set of rules. If they obeyed, they would enjoy good health. If they disobeyed, they would not. Occasionally God would use his prophets as healers. But this was exceptional and there was no recognized place for doctors, no reason to explore the physical causes of disease, and little place for medical skills.

The Babylonian king, Hammurabi, had drawn up a code of laws in about 1750 BC. It fixed doctors' fees, and set out penalties for surgeons who were careless in performing operations. The Egyptians were also doing surgery, studying anatomy by dissecting dead bodies, and writing medical and surgical notes on papyrus. But this was unthinkable in Israel. The first reference to doctors in the Bible is critical: "Asa was crippled by a severe foot disease; but even then he did not turn to the Lord for help, but to doctors." The Book of Job, however, challenges the view that disease is always the direct result of a person's sin.

By the second century BC the prestige of doctors had increased. In Ecclesiasticus it is said that although God is the healer, he has given gifts of healing to men and has provided medicines for the cure of illness. Jesus resisted the view that it is specific sin which always causes illness. He saw disease as evidence of the power of evil in the world as a whole. In healing diseases he was attacking the kingdom of Satan, but this implied no criticism of the work of doctors. General attitudes, however, were hard to change, as certain recorded Jewish sayings show. "Physician, heal yourself." "Live not in a city whose chief is a medical man, for he will attend to public business and neglect his patients." "Even the best among doctors is deserving of Gehenna" (hell). Leviticus 26:14–16; Deuteronomy 7:12–15; 2 Chronicles 16:12; John 9:3; Luke 13:16; Mark 2:17; Luke 4:23

Treatment of disease It is interesting to notice how Israel's laws compensated for their general ignorance about hygiene. To obey these laws was part of their religious duty, but obedience obviously contributed to keeping them healthy as well.

First there must be one day of complete rest each week for physical and spiritual refreshment.

Then there were certain foods which must not be eaten. This included pork which, in a subtropical climate, carries a high risk of food poisoning. And water must be free from contamination.

All males must be circumcised — an operation believed to prevent venereal disease.

A man must not marry members of his own family.

Careful attention must be paid to cleanliness, in daily personal habits and in sexual relationships.

This is the earliest evidence we have of preventive medicine. The priests were expected to enforce these laws and to take special action in the case of "leprosy" (though this may not have been the leprosy which we know today).

The prophets occasionally concerned themselves with health. Elisha neutralized poisonous herbs, purified the water of Jericho, and helped to cure Naaman and the Shunammite woman's son. In 2 Kings 20:1–7 Isaiah advises Hezekiah to apply a poultice of figs to a boil — the only real "prescription" in the Old Testament.

Various oils and perfumes were used in personal hygiene — myrtle, saffron, myrrh and spikenard. Olive oil and "balm of Gilead" (a spicy resin) were swallowed or put on wounds and sores. Isaiah's description of Judah throws light on the treatment of wounds: "You are covered with bruises and sores and open wounds. Your wounds have not been cleaned or bandaged. No ointment has been put on them." Certain herbs may have been used as painkillers, for example the "wine mixed with a drug called myrrh" offered to Jesus on the cross. Many effective herbs must have been known, but there must also have been a good deal of superstition. It was widely believed, for example, that mandrake roots would help women to conceive children.

Broken arms and legs were bound up tightly and crutches may have been used. But there is no evidence of radical surgery being done in Old Testament times in Israel, except for the discovery of three skulls in eighth-century Lachish, with holes bored in them. This kind of operation was widespread to relieve pressure (or release demons).

There were, of course, Israelite midwives from the very earliest times. Even before the exodus they may have formed a kind of guild, with their own code of ethics and recognized leaders (two are named in Exodus 1:15). Mothers sometimes died in childbirth, but often the midwife was very skilled. Tamar successfully gave birth to twins who seem to have been locked in a difficult position (Genesis 38:27–30). Ezekiel, speaking about Jerusalem, throws light on what was normally done after a birth: "When you were born, no one cut your umbilical cord or rubbed you with salt or wrapped you in a cloth." Midwifery was perhaps the only honourable public duty in which a woman could be employed.

Exodus 20:8; Leviticus 11:13–23; 2 Kings 4:41; 2:19–22; 5; 4:18–37; Jeremiah 8:22; Luke 10:34; Isaiah 1:6; Mark 15:23; Genesis 30:14; Ezekiel 30:21; 16:4

New Testament times   In Greece, medicine and surgery had become a highly developed skill, though still mixed with a certain amount of magic. It was the Greek, Hippocrates, who laid down the principles

Hippocrates, the Greek doctor who laid down principles for the practice of medicine. He lived from about 460 to 377 BC.

that the life and welfare of the patient should be the doctor's first consideration; that male doctors should not take advantage of women patients, or procure abortions; and that they should not reveal confidential information. At one time state doctors were employed, paid a salary and gave free medical attention.

The Romans later adopted some of these practices. Surgical instruments and prescription labels have been found in excavations of Roman cities, and there was a school of medicine at Alexandria in Egypt. Paul's companion, Luke, was a doctor. The language he uses in Luke and Acts sometimes includes technical Greek medical expressions.

In Palestine itself the rabbis required that every town should have a physician and preferably a surgeon, too (the woman with the haemorrhage who came to Jesus had been to many doctors). There was always a doctor among the temple officials. His work was to look after the priests, who worked barefoot and were naturally liable to catch certain diseases.

Dentistry was practised even among the ancient Egyptians (some of the mummies have gold-filled teeth!), and the Greek historian, Herodotus, tells us that in 500 BC the Phoenicians were making false teeth. There is no evidence of such a practice in Israel.

Colossians 4:14; Luke 5:12; 13:11; 14:2; Acts 12:23; Mark 5:26

MEGIDDO

An important Old Testament city on the edge of the plain of Jezreel, guarding the main pass through the

Carmel hills. About 20 miles/32 km from modern Haifa. So many battles took place here that the New Testament (Revelations 16:16) uses the name symbolically for the site of the great last battle: "Armageddon", "the hill of Megiddo".

Joshua defeated the Canaanite king of Megiddo when the Israelites conquered Canaan. It was given to the tribe of Manasseh. They made the Canaanites who lived at Megiddo work for them, but did not drive them out. King Solomon chose Megiddo, with Hazor and Gezer, to be one of his main fortified cities, with stabling for large numbers of horses and chariots. King Ahaziah of Judah died at Megiddo after being wounded by Jehu's men. So too did King Josiah, attempting to stop the advance of Pharaoh Neco of Egypt.

Archaeologists have discovered twenty main levels of settlement on a mound now 70ft/21m high and covering, at the top, an area of more than 10 acres. The earliest settlement goes back to before 3000 BC. Excavation has uncovered, among other things, a Canaanite "high place"; the city's water supply system; a fortified gateway built to the same pattern as others at Gezer and Hazor; a hoard of carved ivory

This remarkable seal, discovered at Megiddo, is carved with a roaring lion and inscribed "Shema, the servant of Jeroboam".

objects; and a series of stables (probably from King Ahab's time).
Joshua 12:21; Judges 1:27–28; 5:19; 1 Kings 9:15; 2 Kings 9:27; 23:29

MELCHIZEDEK
A king and priest of God Most High at Salem (Jerusalem) who met and blessed Abraham after a battle. In the New Testament letter to the Hebrews Jesus is called a high priest "for ever, in the line of succession to Melchizedek". Like Melchizedek, Jesus is both king and priest — king of God's kingdom and a priest because he offered the sacrifice of his own life.
Genesis 14:18–20; Psalm 110:4; Hebrews 5:6–10

MEMPHIS
The ancient capital of Egypt, on the River Nile not far south of modern Cairo. The pyramids at Giza are also near to Memphis. The city remained important for many centuries, up to the time of Alexander the Great. Several of the Old Testament prophets refer to Memphis when they condemn Israel's trust in Egypt.
Isaiah 19:13; Jeremiah 2:16; 46:14; Ezekiel 30:13

MENAHEM
One of the last kings of Israel (752–742 BC). When King Shallum had reigned for only one month Menahem killed him and made himself king instead. Menahem was a cruel and wicked king who worshipped idols. During his reign Tiglath-pileser III (Pul) of Assyria invaded Israel. Menahem paid the Assy-

rians a large sum of money to continue as king.
2 Kings 15:14–22

MEPHIBOSHETH
The son of Jonathan, David's great friend, and
grandson of King Saul. When David was king he
gave Mephibosheth a place at the palace and servants
to wait on him.
2 Samuel 4:4; 9; 16:1ff.; 19:24–30; 21:7

MERAB
A daughter of King Saul. Saul promised David he
could marry her, but gave her to another man instead.
1 Samuel 14:49; 18:17ff.

MERARI
One of Levi's sons. His descendants, the Merarites,
formed one of the three groups of Levites.
Exodus 6:16ff.; Numbers 3

MERCY
The Hebrew word often translated "mercy" occurs
nearly 250 times in the Old Testament. It refers to
God's loving patience with the people of Israel, his
kindness and readiness to forgive. God had made his
covenant-agreement with them, and although they
often broke their side of the agreement, he did not
disown them. He is faithful and has "mercy" on
them. Some English versions translate the word
"loving kindness".

In the New Testament, "mercy" is a loving pity
for those in need. God is "the merciful Father, the

God from whom all help comes". It is because of his mercy that we are saved. Jesus himself was often moved with pity to respond to the needs of those around him. Christians are expected to show to other people the same mercy which they have experienced from God himself.

Exodus 34:6–7; Deuteronomy 7:9; Nehemiah 9:7, 31; Psalms 23:6; 25:6; 40:11; 51:1; 103:4, 8; Daniel 9:9; Jonah 4:2; Micah 6:8; Matthew 5:7; Luke 6:36; 18:13; Romans 9:15; 12:1; 2 Corinthians 1:3; Ephesians 2:4

MERODACH-BALADAN

A king of Babylon (in Babylonian, Marduk-apla-iddina II) who sent messengers to King Hezekiah in Jerusalem. Merodach-Baladan hoped to make Hezekiah join with Babylon against Assyria.

Isaiah 39

King Merodach-Baladan (on the left) granting land to an official; from a Babylonian boundary stone.

MESHACH
See *Abednego*.

MESOPOTAMIA
The land between the Tigris and Euphrates rivers. Harran and Paddanaram, where some of Abraham's family settled, are in Mesopotamia. It was the home of Balaam, the prophet who was sent to curse the Israelites, and the country ruled by Cushanrishathaim at the time of the Judges.

People from Mesopotamia were in Jerusalem on the Day of Pentecost and heard Peter and the apostles speak to them in their own languages.
Genesis 24:10; Deuteronomy 23:4 and Numbers 22; Judges 3:8, 10; Acts 2:9

MESSIAH
"Messiah" and "Christ" both mean the "anointed one" — Messiah is the Hebrew word and Christ is the Greek equivalent.

Throughout the troublesome history of the nation of Israel the hope gradually grew that God would one day send a great Messiah-king to establish his universal and everlasting kingdom. By the time of Jesus many Jews were longing for that day to come. So when they heard of his teaching and miracles they asked, "Is he the Messiah?"

The New Testament shows plainly that the first Christians identified Jesus as the Messiah. At his baptism, "God poured out on (anointed) Jesus of Nazareth the Holy Spirit and power." Afterwards he applied to himself the prophecy of Isaiah that "the time has come when the Lord will save his people".

But Jesus normally avoided directly calling himself the Messiah because the people understood it in political terms. The Gospels tell of only one occasion on which Jesus claimed to be the Messiah — to a poor, sinful woman at a well. When Peter told Jesus, "You are the Messiah", he was asked to keep it quiet. Jesus wanted genuine disciples; he was no "rabble-rouser", out to make a name for himself.

However, when the Jewish authorities began to put the pressure on Jesus, the key question asked by the high priest at his trial was, "Are you the Messiah, the Son of the Blessed God?" "I am", answered Jesus, and the high priest, enraged by this "blasphemy" (insult to God) secured a unanimous verdict of guilty. Jesus was sentenced to death.

The verdict of the New Testament is that the Jewish court made a mistake. Jesus was the Messiah — and God proved this by raising him to life again. As Peter declared on the Day of Pentecost, "All people of Israel, then, are to know for sure that this Jesus, whom you crucified is the one that God has made Lord and Messiah!" See also *Jesus Christ*.
Deuteronomy 18:15–22; Psalms 2; 45:6–7; 72; 110; Isaiah 9:2–7; 11; 42:1–9; 49:1–6; 52:13–53:12; 61:1–3; Jeremiah 23:5–6; 33:14–16; Ezekiel 34:22–25; Daniel 7; Zechariah 9:9–10; Matthew 1:18, 22–23; 16:16, 20; 26:68; Mark 8:27–30; 14:61–64; Luke 2:11, 26; John 4:25–26; 7:26–27, 31, 41–42; 9:22; Acts 2:36; 3:20–21; 4:26–28; 10:38; 18:28; 26:22–23

METHUSELAH
Remembered as the oldest man who ever lived. He

died, in the year of the flood, 969 years old.
Genesis 5:22–27

MICAH
The prophet Micah lived about the same time as
Isaiah, Amos and Hosea, in the eighth century BC.
He brought a message for both Israel and Judah.
Like Amos, Micah denounced the rulers, priests and
prophets. He attacked them for exploiting the poor
and helpless, for business frauds and sham religion.
God's judgement would fall upon Samaria and Jeru-
salem.

But Micah also brought a message of hope. He
promised that God would give worldwide peace; that
a great king would come from the family of King
David, bringing peace with him. In one verse Micah
sums up much of the message of the prophets: "what
God requires of us is this; to do what is just, to show
constant love, and live in humble fellowship with
our God" (6:8).

MICAIAH
A prophet who lived in the reign of King Ahab.
When Ahab planned to fight a battle against the
Syrians he asked many prophets if he was going to
win. Four hundred prophesied success, and only
Micaiah foretold defeat. Ahab was angry at this
answer and threw Micaiah into prison, but his prediction came true.
1 Kings 22

MICHAEL
An archangel described in Daniel as the guardian of
the Jewish people.

Daniel 10:21; 12:1; Jude 9; Revelation 12:7

MICHAL

King Saul's younger daughter and David's wife. She helped David to escape from Saul and saved his life, but Saul gave her to another man.
1 Samuel 14:49; 18:20ff.; 25:44; 2 Samuel 3:13–16; 6:16ff.

MICHMASH

A place about 7 miles/11km north-east of Jerusalem, at a village still called Mukhmas. It was separated from Geba by a deep valley. But an important route, "the passage of Michmash", crossed an easy part of the valley. The Philistines invaded Israel and camped in force at Michmash, threatening King Saul's capital at Gibeah. Jonathan and his armour-bearer surprised the Philistine garrison by climbing across from Geba at a steep place down the valley, and in the panic which followed Saul defeated the Philistines. Michmash was on the route by which the Assyrians approached Jerusalem from the north. It was reoccupied after the exile.
1 Samuel 13–14; Isaiah 10:28; Ezra 2:27; Nehemiah 7:31; 11:31

MIDIAN

The Midianites lived south of Edom along the Red Sea coast, engaging in trade and riding in on camels to raid the settled lands. Moses met them in the Sinai Desert and married a Midianite wife. The Midianites were descendants of Abraham through his second wife, Keturah.

Genesis 37:28; Judges 6–8; Exodus 2:16ff.; 3:1; Genesis 25:1–6

MILETUS

A sea-port on the west coast of present-day Turkey. Paul stayed at Miletus on his way to Jerusalem at the end of his third missionary journey. To save time, the elders from the church at Ephesus came to meet him there and heard his farewell message. At another time Paul, writing to Timothy, says that he had left his helper Trophimus at Miletus because he was ill.

Acts 20:15–38; 2 Timothy 4:20

MINING AND METALWORK

In Deuteronomy 8:9 Moses promises the Israelites that the land of Canaan will be rich. "Its rocks have iron in them, and from its hills you can mine copper." In fact these are the only two metals native to the region of Israel. Gold, silver, tin and lead had to be imported.

Gold and silver   Gold was probably the first metal known to man, because it is found in a pure state and needs no complicated process to cast it. When the Israelites left Egypt, the Egyptians had been using gold for many centuries. They took ornaments of gold and silver with them out of Egypt. And they knew how to work these metals.

To make solid objects the metal was melted and poured into moulds. Exodus 32:4 describes Aaron taking ear-rings, melting them and pouring the gold into a mould to make a gold bull. Gold could also be beaten into sheets, to cover objects, or beaten into a particular shape. The different Hebrew words for gold in the Old Testament, usually translated "pure gold", "fine gold", and "choice gold", may indicate differences in colour and quality, but the exact meanings are unknown.

A gold adze, dagger and sheath from about 2600 BC, found in the Royal Graves at Ur.

When the Israelites entered the land of Canaan, gold and silver formed part of the spoils of war. Craftsmen probably made ornaments and jewellery for those who could afford them and, in times of religious decline, they adopted the practices of the surrounding nations and made idols of silver or overlaid with gold. (This custom was strongly criticized by the prophets.) Israelite craftsmen cannot have been very experienced. When Solomon needed intricate gold and silver work for the temple and other buildings, he employed experts from Phoenicia. He imported gold from "Ophir" and is said to have made silver "as common in Jerusalem as stone".

The process of refining gold and silver — melting it to separate off the impurities — is often used in the Bible as a picture of the purifying effects of suffering.
Exodus 11:2; 32:4; 25:11, 31; Joshua 6:19; 22:8; Judges 17:1–4; Isaiah 2:20; 40:19; Hosea 8:4; 2 Chronicles 2:7; 1 Kings 10:1–27; Zechariah 13:9; Malachi 3:2–3; 1 Peter 1:7

Copper Copper was the most plentiful metal in early Israel. It was extracted from ore by heating (smelting) and, although the metal was rather spongy, it could be hardened and shaped by cold hammering. At some time before 2000 BC it had been discovered that if up to four per cent of tin was added, the copper was stronger and harder. Its melting-point was also lower, and it could be poured into a mould and cast into shape. The result is bronze. However, the Hebrew words for copper and bronze are the same, so it is not clear when the Israelites began to make bronze. It would certainly have been needed for the finely shaped work of Solomon's temple — the great bronze basin ("sea"), resting on twelve bronze bull-calves, and the bronze pillars whose tops were decorated with lilies and pomegranates.

Copper ore is to be found in the Sinai peninsula and in the Arabah, the desert area between the Dead Sea and the Gulf of Aqaba. Archaeology has shown that this area was being mined while the Israelites were in Egypt, and even much earlier. There is a site at Timnah, fifteen miles north of Elath, where the underground shafts penetrate for hundreds of yards in all directions and at several levels. The deeper workings are hundreds of feet below the surface, and ventilated through air channels.

Job 28 describes the work of mining for silver and, although they did not mine silver in Israel, the picture applies equally to mining for copper and iron. "They search the depths of the earth and dig for rocks in the darkness. Men dig the shafts of mines. There they work in loneliness, clinging to ropes in the pits."

Some have suggested that the Israelites learned the art of smelting and working copper from the Kenites (or Midianites), the desert tribe into which Moses married. Another suggestion is that there were travelling tinkers or smiths attached to communities from an early period. An Egyptian tomb-painting shows a group of Asiatics with what seem to be goat-skin bellows.

A furnace from the Judges period has been found at Bethshemesh. Here copper was smelted on a small scale, and the heat was intensified, probably through pottery blowpipes or bellows.

Other furnaces dating from the time of Solomon have been found in Israel, some for treating copper, others for iron. The smiths would receive the metal, melt it in a clay pot over the fire and then shape the articles, sometimes using stone moulds. Their main products were for army and home use: arrow-heads, lances and spear-tips, swords, daggers, axes, plough-points, adzes, chisels, needles, safety pins, tweezers, bracelets, bowls and pails.

It is not clear how much mining and smelting activity went on in Solomon's time. At one time archaeologists thought that there had been a minor "industrial revolution". They had discovered a number of mining sites and small smelting furnaces in the Arabah. The furnaces were of different shapes — some round, some square and some with two compartments. There were also traces of encampments, where the workers, probably slaves, lived. Brick buildings discovered at a site at the head of the Gulf of Aqaba were identified with the town the Bible calls Ezion-geber. They were thought to belong to a giant smelting-plant to which copper was sent to be prepared for export, after the initial smelting on the site.

But these proposals are now seriously doubted. More recent excavations have shown that the most impressive mining works were used only at a much earlier period, even before the conquest of Canaan — while the brick buildings may have been a large fortified inn on an important trade-route.

Iron The use of iron spread very slowly in Israel. It needed to be heated as it was being worked, and so was difficult to produce. When the Israelites entered Canaan, the Canaanites already had chariots with iron fittings and other equipment. This put the Israelites at a disadvantage.

When the Philistines defeated the Israelites in the days of Samuel and Saul, they would not let them have blacksmiths of their own in case they made strong swords and spears. If the Israelites wanted their copper tools sharpened or repaired they had to go to the Philistines, who charged crippling prices. David, however, had great stores of iron. He "supplied a large amount of iron for making nails and clamps". And, from this time on, iron objects became more plentiful. Iron ore was also discovered and mined in the Arabah.

Joshua 17:16; 1 Samuel 13:19–22; 1 Chronicles 22:3

The New Testament period In New Testament times there was a smiths' bazaar in Jerusalem. But workers in bronze and iron were not allowed to work on certain religious feast days because of the noise they made. The extravagances of King Herod's court meant an increased trade in luxury goods.

In the temple that Herod built in Jerusalem the double gate, thresholds and lintel were overlaid with gold and silver. The walls inside were covered with gold plating. There were gold and silver lamps and bowls and there were even spikes of gold on the roof to keep the birds away! A thousand priests had to be trained to do much of this work, because no one else was allowed to enter the sacred temple area.

MIRACLES

One of the striking things about Jesus' life and work is the fact that he did miracles. Even his enemies agreed on this. The miracles described in the Gospels range from curing physical illnesses and casting out devils to calming a storm and bringing the dead back to life.

The miracles are sometimes described as "mighty works". They are done through the power of God.

The most important display of God's power, the greatest miracle, is the resurrection of Jesus.

Jesus' miracles are also called "wonders". They often amazed those who saw them. But Jesus did not want to be seen as a mere wonder-worker. This was why he refused to jump from the highest point of the temple, as the devil suggested in his temptations. Jesus did not want people to follow him just to see his miracles. So he often told the people he cured to tell no one about it.

John's Gospel makes it plain that Jesus' miracles were above all "signs". They were signs that he was the Messiah, signs that the new age, the kingdom, had really come. When John the Baptist wanted to know if Jesus really was the Messiah he was told of the miracles Jesus did and left to draw his own conclusions. By doing miracles Jesus was showing people the kingdom of God. He was giving examples of the fact that in the new age sin and death and sickness would be no more.

Jesus gave his disciples power to do miracles. They continued to heal in the power of Jesus after Pentecost, and miracles remained part of the experience of the early church. One of the "gifts of the Spirit" mentioned by Paul is the working of miracles, another the gift of healing. But the one who heals is always God himself, never the Christian, or the church.

Mark 10:27; Romans 1:4; Matthew 4:5–7; 11:2–6, 20–21; Luke 9:1; Acts 3:6; Galatians 3:5; 1 Corinthians 12:9–10

Jesus' healings: Matthew 8:2–3, 5–13, 14–15, 28–34; 9:2–7, 20–22, 27–31, 32–33; 12:10–13, 22;

15:21–28; 17:14–18; 20:29–34; Mark 1:23–26; 7:31–37; 8:22–26; Luke 13:11–13; 14:1–4; 17:11–19; 22:50–51; John 4:46–54; 5:1–9; 9

Jesus' command over the forces of nature: Matthew 8:23–27; 14:25, 15–21; 15:32–38; 17:24–27; 21:18–22; Mark 11:20–26; Luke 5:1–11; John 2:1–11; 21:1–11

Jesus brings the dead to life: Matthew 9:18–19, 23–25; Luke 7:11–15; John 11:1–44

Some Old Testament miracles: Exodus 14; Joshua 2; 1 Kings 17:17–24; 2 Kings 2; 4–5; Daniel 6 and many other passages

MIRIAM

Sister of Moses and Aaron. She watched over her baby brother Moses in the reed basket until he was found by the daughter of Pharaoh. After the Israelites had crossed the Red Sea, Miriam led the woman, singing and dancing for joy. Later she quarrelled with Moses, because she was jealous of him as leader. For a short time, as punishment, she suffered a terrible skin disease. But Moses asked God to heal her. Miriam died at Kadesh before the Israelites reached Canaan.

Exodus 2:4, 7–8; 15:20–21; Numbers 12; 20:1

MITYLENE

The most important city and port on the Greek island of Lesbos, off the west coast of Asia Minor (Turkey). Paul stopped there overnight on his last voyage to Jerusalem.

Acts 20:14

MIZPAH/MIZPEH

The name (meaning "watchtower") of a number of different places. When Jacob and Laban made a peace agreement they called the place Mizpah. A Mizpah in Gilead (perhaps the same as Ramoth-gilead) features in the story of Jephthah, at the time of the Judges.

The most important Mizpah is a town a few miles north of Jerusalem. The Israelites met together here at the time of Samuel and the Judges. The town was on Samuel's circuit as a Judge. And at Mizpah he presented Saul to the people as their king. Later, King Asa of Judah fortified the town. After Jerusalem fell to the Babylonians the governor, Gedaliah, lived at Mizpah.
Genesis 31:44–49; Judges 10:17; 11; 20:1; 1 Samuel 7:5–16; 10:17; 1 Kings 15:22; 2 Kings 25:23

MOAB

The Moabites lived south of the River Arnon, a river which flows into the east side of the Dead Sea. These people, related to Israel and Ammon — through Lot, Genesis 19:37 — would not let Israel pass through their land when they wanted to reach Canaan. And they constantly harassed the Israelites for much of the Old Testament period. Moab is listed among the countries attacked by Ramesses II of Egypt (about 1283 BC). The city of Dibon was taken. Here, much later, King Mesha recorded his triumph over Israel on a famous stone (the Moabite Stone). The inscription shows that his language was similar to Hebrew. His belief that his god (Chemosh) acted in history was also very much like Israel's belief.

Numbers 21; Judges 11:17; 3:12–30; 1 Samuel 14:47; 2 Samuel 8:2, 12; 2 Kings 13:20; 24:2; 1:1; 3:4–27

MONEY

Money as we know it was first used in Bible lands in the eighth century BC, in Lydia (part of modern Turkey). Early coins were made of electrum (an alloy of silver and gold) and the weight of the metal was guaranteed by the stamp on the coin. From this time on the Jewish people rarely had their independence. They were exiled to Babylon, then subject to Persia, Greece and Rome — so not many Jewish coins were minted.

In the Greek period, coins were issued from Acco, on the coast of Israel. Roman coins were used throughout the Empire. The only Jewish coins minted were the small bronze coins first allowed by the Seleucid kings (the Syrian Empire which followed the death of Alexander the Great). The Jewish leaders (Hasmoneans) in Jerusalem coined these to their own designs. At the time of the rebellion against the Romans in AD 66 the Jews minted their first coins in silver. There were so many different coins about, that it was necessary for the buyer and the seller to know their equivalent values.

Old Testament gold and silver coins
Shekel (approx. 11.4 gm)
Mina (approx. 500 gm) = 50 shekels
Talent (30 kg) = 60 minas
New Testament coins   There were three different

currencies used in Palestine in New Testament times. There was the official, imperial money (Roman standard); provincial money minted at Antioch and Tyre (Greek standard); and local Jewish money which may have been minted at Caesarea. Money for the temple (including the half-shekel tax) had to be paid in the Tyrian coinage (the 2-drachma piece), not Roman. It is not surprising that money-changers flourished! Money was coined in gold, silver, copper and bronze or brass. The commonest silver coins mentioned in the New Testament are the Greek *tetradrachma*, and Roman *denarius*, which was a day's wage for the ordinary working man.

Jewish coins
lepton (bronze)
shekel
Greek coins
drachma (silver)
stater (or tetradrachma) (silver)
mina
Roman coins
quadrans
as (bronze) = 4 quadrans
denarius (silver) = 16 as
aureus (gold)
1 Jewish **shekel** = 1 Greek stater (tetradrachma) = 4 Roman denarii
30 Jewish **shekels** = 1 Greek mina = 100 Roman denarii

MORDECAI

Esther's cousin and guardian. Mordecai was a Jew who lived in Susa, capital of Persia. When he heard about a plot to kill all the Jews he persuaded Esther, then queen of Persia, to plead with King Ahasuerus to spare them. Mordecai afterwards became the king's chief minister.

(See *Esther*.)

Esther

MORESHETH/MORESHETH-GATH

The home town of the prophet Micah, probably near Mareshah in the low country south-west of Jerusalem.

Jeremiah 26:18; Micah 1;1, 14

MORIAH

The mountains to which Abraham was told to go for the sacrifice of his son, Isaac. The writer of 2 Chronicles says that the site of Solomon's temple was "in Jerusalem, on Mount Moriah". (The Samaritans claimed that the place of Abraham's sacrifice was not Jerusalem, but Mt Gerizim.)

Genesis 22:2; 2 Chronicles 3:1

MOSES

The great leader who freed the Israelites from slavery in Egypt and led them through the desert to the borders of Canaan. Moses was born in Egypt, brought up by the daughter of the king, and educated as an Egyptian. When he was grown up, Moses was so angry at the cruel way the Israelites were treated that he killed one of the Egyptian overseers. When Pharaoh heard about it, Moses was forced to escape from Egypt. He lived as a shepherd in the desert and married a daughter of Jethro, the man who gave him a home.

After forty years God appeared to Moses. He saw a desert bush which flamed but did not burn up, and knew God was speaking to him. God told him to go back to Egypt and ask Pharaoh to let his people go. Pharaoh refused, and the Egyptians suffered ten plagues. Then Pharaoh let Moses lead the Israelites out of Egypt. But he quickly changed his mind; the Egyptians pursued the Israelites as far as the Red Sea. The Israelites escaped into the desert but Pharaoh's army was drowned.

After three months the people reached Mt Sinai. Here Moses the leader became Moses the law-giver. God gave him the Ten Commandments and instructions for building the worship tent (tabernacle). Moses led the people on to the oasis at Kadesh. From there, spies were sent into Canaan. Ten came back with frightening tales. The people shouted and rebelled against Moses, forgetting the power of God. Because they rejected God they were condemned to wander in the desert until all those who rebelled had died. Moses gave God's law to the new generation before he handed on the leadership to Joshua. When he had blessed the people Moses climbed Mt Nebo so that he could see Canaan, the land he was not allowed to enter because of his own earlier disobedience. Moses was 120 years old when he died in the land of Moab.

At the transfiguration, when they saw Jesus' glory, the disciples also saw Moses and Elijah, the two great Old Testament leaders, talking with Jesus about his coming death.

Exodus 2–Deuteronomy 34; Luke 9:28ff.

MOUNT OF OLIVES

A 2,700ft/830m hill overlooking Jerusalem and its temple area from the east, across the Kidron Valley. In Jesus' day it was planted with olive trees.

King David passed this way when he fled from Jerusalem at the time of Absalom's rebellion. King Solomon built an altar for idols on the Mount of Olives. Later, during the exile, the prophet Ezekiel saw the dazzling light of God's glory leave Jerusalem and move to the Mount of Olives. The prophet Zechariah foresaw God, on the Day of Judgement, standing on the Mount, which would split in two.

When Jesus rode in triumph into Jerusalem he came from the Mount of Olives. Seeing the city from the Mount, he wept over its fate. When he stayed at Bethany on his visits to Jerusalem he must have walked into the city round the shoulder of the Mount of Olives. The Garden of Gethsemane, where he prayed on the night of his arrest, was on its lower slopes. From the Mount of Olives Jesus was taken up to heaven.

2 Samuel 15:30; 2 Kings 23:13; Ezekiel 11:23; Zechariah 14:4; Luke 19:29, 37, 41–44; 21:37; 22:39; Acts 1:12, etc.

MUSIC

Music and dancing have been part of life in all cultures, as far back in history as we can go.

There were three kinds of instrument in Israel — string, wind and percussion. They played together in unison rather than in harmony. And the music seems to have been strongly rhythmic rather than melodic, although there were set tunes to some of the psalms. Because the description of the instruments is rather vague it is not possible to identify them all. But we *do* know something about the following:

Strings The *kinnor* is normally translated "harp" in the Bible. It may have been a harp or a lyre. It was a small, eight- or ten-stringed instrument with a wooden frame, and could be carried about. We do not know if it was played simply by plucking, or if a plectrum was used. The *kinnor* may be the instrument shown on ancient tomb-paintings at Beni-Hasan in Egypt.

An Egyptian timbrel made from wood and painted skin.

The *nebel*, called a "psaltery", was another stringed instrument in a wooden frame, played by plucking with the fingers. The word *nebel* means a "skin bottle" or jar, which suggests a swollen sound-box like a lute. David was able to play both *kinnor* and *nebel*.

Wind The *halil* (pipe) was the ordinary person's hollow pipe, made of cane, wood or bone. *Halil* means "to bore", and describes the way the instrument was made. A reed was used in the instrument, and the player carried spare reeds about in a bag.

The *geren* (cornet, horn) was made from the horn of an animal and was used as a trumpet. If the horn used was a ram's horn, the instrument was called a *shofar*, also translated trumpet in some versions of the Bible. It was used on religious and public occasions.

The *hazozra* was a metal trumpet, which in Bible times was made of silver. A continuous call on two silver trumpets was the sign to gather at the tabernacle. One was sounded to call the chiefs together.

Percussion The *menaanim* is a percussion instrument and was probably made of discs rattled along metal rods, suspended in a wooden frame.

Meziltaim are copper cymbals. They were used by Levites in the temple to mark the beginning, ending, and pauses in the chapters which were sung.

The *tof* was a percussion instrument with a membrane, and is called a "timbrel" or tambourine in English versions. It was used to accompany singing and dancing. At the time of the exodus Aaron's sister Miriam "took her tambourine, and all the women followed her, playing tambourines and dancing" (Exodus 15:20).

Unfortunately, because the Israelites were not allowed to portray human figures in their art, we do not know exactly how these instruments were played. But pictures of similar instruments from Egypt, Assyria and Babylonia give us a fair idea. Instruments were made from a wide variety of materials — cedar-wood, sandal-wood, leather, gut, ivory, shell, gold and silver.

Music had an important place in the worship at the temple. 1 Chronicles 15:16–24 describes how David organized the temple choir and orchestra "to sing and to play joyful music". In the temple the

Two sistrums and a pair of rattles in plaited cane, from Egypt.

singing was often in parts — one line of a section being sung by one group, and the next sung in response by another. Dancing, too, was often part of the people's joyful expression of worship. When the Covenant Box (the ark) was brought to Jerusalem "David and all the people danced with all their might to honour God" (1 Chronicles 13:8).

MUSTARD
God's kingdom, Jesus said, is like the tiny mustard seed, which grows into a great plant. He was probably talking about the black mustard, whose seeds were grown for oil as well as flavouring. Usually

Flowers and leaves of the mustard plant.

about 4ft (120cm) high, these plants can grow to 15ft (460cm).
Matthew 13:31–32

MYRA

A port in Lycia, in the south-west of modern Turkey, where Paul and his party changed ships on his voyage to Rome. Myra was a regular port for the corn-fleet which carried grain to Rome from Egypt.
Acts 27:5

MYRRH

Pale yellow gum from a shrub which grows in Somalia, Ethiopia and Arabia. Used as a spice and a medicine, and in making the holy oil for the tabernacle and temple, Myrrh was brought to Jesus by the wise men. It was mixed with the drink offered to him on the cross as a pain-killer. And Joseph and Nicodemus later embalmed Jesus' body with myrrh and aloes.
Exodus 30:23–24; Matthew 2:11; Mark 15:23; John 19:39–40

MYRTLE

An evergreen with fragrant leaves and sweet-scented white flowers which were used as perfume.

MYSIA

A land in the north-west of Asia Minor (Turkey), forming part of the Roman province of Asia. Paul came to this district during his second missionary journey, but God prevented him from crossing the border from Asia into Bithynia. He passed through

Mysia, travelling west, and came to Troas before it became clear where he should go next.
Acts 16:7–8

NAAMAN

The Syrian general cured of leprosy by the prophet Elisha.
2 Kings 5

NABATAEA

After the time of Alexander the Great, the Nabataeans, an Arab tribe made their home in Edomite and Midianite territory, building up a strong kingdom by controlling the trade which brought incense from southern Arabia to Damascus and across to Gaza. For a few years they ruled Damascus (2 Corinthians 11:32) but were conquered by Trajan of Rome in AD 106. Their chief city was Petra.

NABOTH

Owner of a vineyard in Jezreel next to King Ahab's palace. Ahab tried to buy the vineyard from Naboth, but he refused to sell. The king sulked at this. Jezebel, his wife, promised Ahab that she would get the vineyard for him. She bribed two informers to say that Naboth had cursed God and the king. Naboth was found guilty and stoned to death. Ahab had the vineyard — but God sent Elijah to tell him that because of this murder his whole family would be wiped out.
1 Kings 21

NADAB
Aaron's eldest son. He became a priest but died when he and Abihu, his brother, dishonoured God.
Exodus 6:23; Leviticus 10

NAHOR
1. The father of Terah and grandfather of Abraham.
Genesis 11:22–25
2. Abraham's brother.
Genesis 11:26–29; 22:20ff.; 24:10ff.

NAHUM
A prophet from Elkosh, probably in Judah. His name means "comforter".

The Book of Nahum is a poem. The prophet Nahum predicts that Nineveh, capital of Israel's enemy, Assyria, will fall. The prophet rejoices in the judgement of God on a cruel and arrogant nation.

Nineveh fell to the Babylonians and Medes in 612 BC, and the book was probably written about that time.

NAIN
A town near Nazareth in Galilee where Jesus restored a widow's son to life.
Luke 7:11

NAOMI
The mother-in-law of Ruth. Naomi and her husband Elimelech came from Bethlehem. They had two sons, Mahlon and Chilion. The family moved to Moab because of a famine. There Mahlon and Chilion married Moabite girls. After her husband and

sons had died, Naomi returned to Bethlehem and Ruth went with her. Naomi arranged for Ruth to marry Boaz. Their son was King David's grandfather. Naomi looked after the child as her own son.
Ruth

NAPHTALI

The fifth son of Jacob; father of the tribe of Naphtali. Also the name of the land belonging to the tribe, in Galilee.
Genesis 30:8; 49:21; Joshua 19:32–39

NATHAN

Best-known of several Nathans is the prophet who lived in King David's reign. David told Nathan he wanted to build a temple for God. "God says, not you, but your son will be the one to build," Nathan answered. After David had taken Bathsheba from her husband and engineered his death, Nathan confronted David with his crime. When David was old, he ordered Nathan and Zadok the priest to anoint Solomon king.
2 Samuel 7; 12; 1 Kings 1; 1 Chronicles 17

NATHANAEL

One of Jesus' twelve apostles. He is mentioned only in John's Gospel but may be the disciple known in the other Gospels as Bartholomew. Nathanael heard about Jesus through Philip.
John 1:45ff.; 21:2

NAZARETH

A town in Galilee, the home of Jesus' parents, Mary

and Joseph. Jesus grew up in Nazareth but made his base in Capernaum when he began his public work. His teaching in the synagogue at Nazareth made the people so angry that they tried to kill him.

Nazareth was close to a number of important trade-routes, and so in contact with the wider world. There are rock-tombs at Nazareth dating from New Testament times, and similar to the Gospels' description of the grave in which Jesus himself was buried.
Luke 1:26; Matthew 2:22–23; Luke 2:39, 51; Mark 1:9; Matthew 4:13; Luke 4:16–30; John 1:45–46, etc.

Houses built in traditional style in the town of Nazareth.

NEAPOLIS
The port for Philippi, in Macedonia (northern Greece). This was the place where Paul first set foot in Europe, in answer to a call for help from Macedonia. He later sailed from here on his last voyage to Jerusalem. The place is modern Kavalla.
Acts 16:11; 20:6

NEBO

A mountain east of the north end of the Dead Sea, in Moab. Before he died, Moses climbed Mt Nebo and saw the whole of the Promised Land spread out before him. Jebel Osha (3640ft/1120m high) has a viewpoint from which it is possible to see as far north as Mt Hermon, as well as the Dead Sea and the Negev. This is probably Mt Nebo.
Deuteronomy 32:48–52; 34:1–5

NEBUCHADNEZZAR/NEBUCHADREZZAR

King of Babylon 605–562 BC. He was the son of Nabopolassar who conquered the Assyrian Empire. Nebuchadnezzar led his father's army against the Egyptians and defeated them at Carchemish in 605 BC. Babylon gained control of the countries which had been subject to Egypt, including Judah. For three years Judah paid tax to Babylon. In 597 BC King Jehoiakim rebelled. Nebuchadnezzar attacked Jerusalem. He took Jehoiachin, who was now king, prisoner to Babylon along with the most important citizens. Nebuchadnezzar made Zedekiah king instead. When Zedekiah rebelled he besieged Jerusalem. The city was destroyed in 586 BC and the leaders of the people taken into exile in Babylon. Daniel was one of an earlier group of Jews taken captive. He was trained at Nebuchadnezzar's court. When he was able to explain the meaning of Nebuchadnezzar's dreams, he was made his chief adviser. Nebuchadnezzar's success made him proud. "Look how great Babylon is. I built it as my capital city to display my power and might." But God humbled him through a strange madness. When his

sanity returned he was a changed man. "Now I, Nebuchadnezzar, praise, honour and glorify the King of heaven," he said.
2 Kings 24–25; 2 Chronicles 36; Jeremiah 21:2–52:30; Ezekiel 26:7ff.; 29:18ff.; 30:10; Daniel 1–4

NEBUZARADAN

The captain of King Nebuchadnezzar's guard. Nebuzaradan was responsible for sending the Judeans into exile in Babylon after Nebuchadnezzar had captured Jerusalem. He burned down the temple and reduced the city to ruins. However, he carried out Nebuchadnezzar's command to treat Jeremiah kindly and let him stay in Judah.
2 Kings 25; Jeremiah 39ff.

NECO

See *Pharaoh*.

NEGEV

A dry scrubland and desert area in the far south of Israel. The Negev merges with the Sinai Desert on the way to Egypt. Abraham and Isaac camped in various places in the Negev. So too did the Israelites before they settled in Canaan.
Genesis 20:1; 24:62; Numbers 13:17; 21:1; Isaiah 30:6

NEHEMIAH

Nehemiah, a Jewish exile, was given permission by the Persian king, Artaxerxes, to lead a group of Israelites back to Jerusalem in 445 BC. The Book of Nehemiah, written as his memoirs, shows him as a born leader, and a man who trusted God completely. For Nehemiah it was almost as natural to pray as it was to breathe.

The book can be divided into three parts.

Chapters 1–7: Nehemiah returns to Jerusalem. He inspires his people to rebuild the walls of the city against fierce opposition. He introduces much-needed religious reforms.

Chapters 8–10: Ezra reads the law of God to the people. They are deeply moved, confess their wrong-doing and turn afresh to God.

Chapters 11–13: Nehemiah's work as governor of Judah, appointed by the Persian emperor.

NEW BIRTH

Long before the time of Jesus, the prophet Jeremiah had seen that men and women need to be completely remade from within if they are to have a renewed relationship with God. In his discussion with the Jewish leader Nicodemus, Jesus made the same point. He said that only a complete "new birth" would allow people to make this fresh start.

This fundamental change occurs when a person becomes a Christian. "When anyone is joined to Christ, he is a new being; the old is gone, the new has come." Baptism is the outward sign of this new life. The new life is given by the Holy Spirit, the eternal life of God's kingdom, shared with others in the family of the church.

See also *Baptism*.

Psalm 51:10; Jeremiah 31:31–34; John 3:1–21; 2 Corinthians 5:17

NEW MOON
See *Feasts and Festivals*.

NEW TESTAMENT TEXT
In the case of the Old Testament we have barely enough evidence for the text. With the New Testament we have almost too much! Scholars are faced with many thousands of different ancient manuscripts of the New Testament. They have to decide which of these are most trustworthy and which have preserved the most accurate version of the original.

The New Testament was originally written down in Greek. Scholars have many thousands of Greek manuscripts to which they can refer. In addition they possess early translations of the New Testament — in Latin, Syriac, Egyptian (Coptic) and other languages. They can also refer to quotations which some early Christian writers and theologians made from the New Testament (though these are sometimes inaccurate).

Many of the Greek manuscripts contain a text of the New Testament which was standardized in the fifth century AD. The first printed edition of the Greek text came in 1516 — in a form prepared by the Dutch scholar Erasmus. Up until then no-one had questioned the accuracy of this text.

During the next two centuries, some Bibles included notes to indicate where certain other manuscripts varied from the standard version of the New Testament. Particularly important examples include the text of Stephanus, used in translating the King James' Version in England (1611), and the edition of Elzevir (1633), which became the standard for New

The opening page of Mark's Gospel from the illuminated manuscript made on the island of Lindisfarne, England, in about AD 700.

Testament translations in Europe (it came to be known as the Received Text, *Textus Receptus*).

But during the eighteenth and nineteenth centuries, scholars began to delve deeper into the history of the New Testament text. They discovered that many older manuscripts of the New Testament differed from the fifth-century standard text. They showed that it was more important to ask how old a manuscript was and how good it was, than how many copies survived. Other scholars found that manuscripts could be grouped together in "families" which share a similar kind of text. Older "families" of texts such as the "Alexandrian" and the "Western" texts are now known to preserve a more accurate version of the original writings than the standard fifth-century text.

How the manuscripts were copied Before the invention of printing in the West, in the fifteenth century, all writing had to be hand-copied for circulation. This was usually done by a group of scribes, each of whom wrote out his copy of the manuscript as the head scribe dictated. If a scribe did not hear clearly, or failed to concentrate, mistakes would occur. Even a single copyist working from an original manuscript sometimes misread the writing, or accidentally introduced his own mistakes.

Very few private individuals could afford to own a handwritten manuscript. They were expensive to make, and Christian churches would usually own manuscripts which all their members could share. At first the New Testament books must have been written on scrolls made of papyrus, leather or parchment. But from about the second century Christians probably began to use the book form which we use today (the *Codex*). This was much easier to handle than an awkward scroll.

A reliable New Testament text Two of the most important groups of manuscripts for our New Testament are the Bodmer Papyri (one of which dates from the late second century) and the Chester Beatty Papyri (probably from the early third century). But these contain only parts of the New Testament. The *Codex Sinaiticus*, which dates from the fourth century, contains the complete New Testament; and the *Codex Vaticanus* has everything up to Hebrews 9:13. Both of these manuscripts were probably made by professional copyists in Alexandria, Egypt.

These two codex manuscripts were the main sources for the Greek text of the New Testament prepared in the nineteenth century by the scholars Westcott and Hort. Most scholars agree that they are more accurate than the standard fifth-century text which so many previous versions had used. The two papyrus collections were discovered after the time of Westcott and Hort. They in turn have been used with others to achieve an even more accurate version of the New Testament text. Since then, still more papyrus evidence has been discovered. No single manuscript is clearly the best. The evidence of each has to be weighed carefully.

Over the last 250 years many careful scholars have worked hard to make sure that we have a New Testament which is as close as possible to what its authors originally wrote. The few small areas of doubt which remain are over minor matters of wording. But none of these questions raises any doubt whatever about the basic meaning of the New Testament.

How the New Testament books were collected Although there is little direct evidence from the earliest years, we have a good idea of how the New Testament took on its present shape. The first gatherings of Christians probably followed the practice of the Jewish synagogues and had regular readings from the Old Testament during their meetings. Since they were worshipping Jesus Christ, it was natural for them to add an account of some part of his life and teaching.

At first this may have been in the form of a first-hand account from someone who had known Jesus during his lifetime. But then, as the churches grew in numbers, and as the eye-witnesses began to die, it became necessary to write these stories down. This was the way the four Gospels (Matthew, Mark, Luke and John) came into being, and they obviously had an important place in the worship and life of the early churches.

Then the apostles and other leaders had written a number of letters to various churches and individuals. Since these often gave general guidance on Christian life and beliefs, their usefulness for the whole church was soon recognized. Acts was accepted because it continued the story from Luke's Gospel. It preserved the only full account of the beginnings of Christianity.

We know that by the year AD 200 the church was officially using the four Gospels — and no others, although fictitious tales about Jesus and writings by other Christian leaders who came after the apostles were in circulation. But the mainstream church clearly accepted only the Gospels of Matthew, Mark, Luke and John as their authority for the life and teaching of Jesus. By this time, too, Paul's letters were generally accepted as of equal importance with the Gospels.

It was only later that the remaining books of the New Testament became generally accepted. Revelation, for example, was certainly read in the second century. But not until the third century was it circulating widely. Hebrews was read towards the end of the first century, but took longer to become accepted in the Western churches. It was not generally acknowledged by the church in the West until the fourth century, partly because of doubts as to whether Paul wrote it.

It took longer, too, for 2 Peter, 2 and 3 John, James and Jude to be accepted by the church as basic Scripture. Perhaps this was because of questions about the content of these books. The New Testament books were mainly used at first for public reading. If they were unsuitable for this purpose, their usefulness must have seemed limited.

It is clear that no church council arbitrarily decided that certain books composed the New Testament. Rather, over a period of time, the church discovered that certain writings had a clear and general authority, and were helpful and necessary for their growth. At the Council of Laodicea (AD 363) and the Council of Carthage (AD 397) the bishops agreed on a list of books identical to our New Testament, except that at Laodicea Revelation was left out.

Above all, the churches were concerned to make sure that the documents they included in the "New Testament" truly represented the witness and experience of the apostles — the men who lived closest to Jesus.

NEW YEAR
See *Feasts and Festivals*.

NICODEMUS
A Pharisee and a member of the supreme Jewish council (the Sanhedrin). He came to talk to Jesus secretly, at night. "No one can see the Kingdom of God," Jesus said, "unless he is born again." Nicodemus did not understand what he meant then, but later he spoke up for Jesus when the Pharisees wanted to arrest him. After Jesus' crucifixion Nicodemus brought spices to embalm his body.
John 3:1–20; 7:50ff.; 19:39–42

NILE

The great river of Egypt on which the country's whole economy depended. The Nile flows from Lake Victoria in the heart of Africa, about 3,500 miles/5,632km to the Mediterranean Sea. The fertile valley of the Nile (never more than about 12 miles/19km wide in Upper Egypt) is flanked on either side by desert. Every year the river flooded its banks in spring, leaving behind a layer of fertile mud. Crops would grow wherever the water reached. Too high a flood meant destruction; too low a flood, starvation. The river was also a useful means of transporting goods from one part of the country to another. About 12 miles/19km north of modern Cairo the Nile divides into a western and an eastern branch. Between them is the flat marshy land known as the Delta.

The Nile features in the dreams of Joseph's pharaoh. The pharaoh at the time of Moses' birth ordered his people to drown all Hebrew boy babies in the Nile. Moses himself was hidden in a basket in the reeds at the river's edge. The Nile also features in the sequence of plagues sent by God when the pharaoh refused to free the Israelites. It is often mentioned by the prophets.
Genesis 41:1–36; Exodus 1:22; 2:3–10; 7:17–25; 8:1–15, etc.; Isaiah 18:2, etc.

NINEVEH

An important city in Assyria, notably in King Sennacherib's reign. The Bible says that Nineveh was founded by Nimrod the hunter. The site certainly has a very long history, going back to about 4500

BC. From about 2300 BC the city had a temple to the goddess Ishtar.

Nineveh grew in importance from about 1250 BC, as Assyria's power increased. Several Assyrian kings had palaces there. Sennacherib undertook a great deal of rebuilding and other work.

Reliefs carved on the walls of his new palace show his victories, including the siege of Lachish in Judah. At Nineveh, too, archaeologists discovered a clay prism (the Taylor Prism) which describes how King Hezekiah was "shut up like a bird" in Jerusalem.

King Ashurbanipal and his queen feasting in their garden at Nineveh; from a seventh-century BC Assyrian relief.

Ashurbanipal, the next king but one, added to Nineveh's greatness. Whole libraries of inscribed tablets, including the *Epic of Gilgamesh* (containing a flood story) and the creation epic (*Enumaelish*), have been discovered at his palace and in the temple of Nabu. Nineveh fell to the Babylonians in 612 BC.

In the Bible, Jonah was sent to save Nineveh; Nahum prophesied against it. See also *Assyria*. Genesis 10:11; 2 Kings 19:36; Jonah 1:2; 3; Nahum 1:1; Luke 11:30

NOAH

Noah was a good man at a time of great evil and violence. It was so bad, God could no longer tolerate it and sent a terrible flood. Only Noah and his family were saved. Noah followed the instructions God gave him and built a large boat about 430 feet/133 metres long. People saw what he was doing but refused to listen to his warning. When the rains came, Noah, his wife, his three sons and their wives, boarded the ark, with pairs of every kind of living creature. The ark floated until the flood went down. It came to rest on a mountain. After the flood God made a promise to Noah for all time: never again would he send a flood to destroy all living things. The rainbow was the sign of that promise. Noah lived to a great age and his sons became the ancestors of many nations.

Genesis 6–9; 1 Peter 3:20

NUMBERS

The book of Numbers tells the story of the Israelites during almost forty years of wandering in the Sinai Desert. It begins two years after their escape from Egypt and ends just before they entered Canaan, the land that God had promised to give them.

The name Numbers comes from the two "numberings" (censuses) of the Israelites at Mt Sinai and on the plains of Moab, across the River Jordan from Jericho. Between the two censuses they settled for a time at the oasis of Kadesh Barnea, and then travelled to an area east of the River Jordan.

The Book of Numbers is one long, sad story of Israel's complaints and discontent. The Israelites were often afraid or disheartened when faced with difficulties. They rebelled against God and their leader Moses. Although they disobeyed him, God continued to care for his people. But only two men who escaped from Egypt, Caleb and Joshua survived to enter the Promised Land.

OAK

There are many kinds of oaks in Israel, some of them evergreen. They are strong trees growing for many years. The wood was used for oars and for carving statues. Absalom was caught in an oak when he fled from King David.

2 Samuel 18:9–10; 1 Kings 13:14; Isaiah 2:13

OBADIAH

1. The book of the prophet Obadiah is the shortest book in the Old Testament. It was written after the fall of Jerusalem in 587 BC.

The Edomites, Judah's old enemies from the mountains south-east of the Dead Sea, took the opportunity to invade Judah.

Obadiah attacked the pride of the Edomites. He prophesied their fall. In the fifth century BC the Arabs defeated them; in the third century BC the Nabataeans overran them. They finally disappeared from history.

In contrast, Obadiah prophesied the return of Israel to her homeland.

2. A steward in charge of King Ahab's household. When Queen Jezebel gave orders for all God's prophets to be killed, Obadiah hid 100 of them in caves and fed them until the danger was over. He

risked his life again when Elijah asked him to arrange a meeting with Ahab.
1 Kings 18

OG

King of Bashan, a land east of the River Jordan. The Israelites, led by Moses, defeated Og and captured his sixty fortified cities. The land of Bashan was given to half the tribe of Manasseh.
Numbers 21:32ff.; Deuteronomy 3; Joshua 22:7

OLD TESTAMENT TEXT

The Old Testament is made up of the first thirty-nine books of the Christian Bible. These books are the holy writings — or scriptures — of the Jewish people, and their religion, Judaism. They were first written down in Hebrew and Aramaic, the ancient languages of the Jews. Many of these writings are so old that little is now known of their origins. The Jewish scribes used to make new copies of the Hebrew sacred writings from time to time. But documents did not last long in the climate of the Bible lands, and so we rarely find very old copies of the writings.

Until 1947 the oldest known Hebrew manuscripts of the Old Testament dated from the ninth and tenth centuries AD. They were copies of the first five books of the Bible — the Pentateuch. Then in 1947 came the remarkable discovery of the Dead Sea Scrolls. These were early manuscripts from the library of a Jewish religious group who flourished at Qumran, near the Dead Sea, about the time of Jesus. These manuscripts are about a thousand years older than the ninth-century AD documents. Amongst the Dead Sea Scrolls are copies of all the Old Testament books except Esther.

These early manuscripts from Qumran are very important because they have essentially the same text as the ninth-century manuscripts. The text of the Old Testament had changed very little for a thousand years. The careful copyists had made few errors or alterations. Of course there are a few places where different words and expressions are used. And sometimes it is no longer possible to discover exactly that the Hebrew words meant. But we can be confident that the Old Testament as we now have it is substantially the same as its authors wrote many centuries ago.

The text of the Old Testament has also come down to us in other early translations. Some of these, too, confirm the accuracy of the Hebrew text of the Old Testament that we use today.

One of the most important translations is the Greek version of the Old Testament, the *Septuagint*. Greek-speaking Jews and many Christians used the *Septuagint* in the first Christian centuries. Another early document, *The Letter of Aristeas*, suggests that the *Septuagint* was compiled for Jews living in Egypt during the reign of Pharaoh Ptolemy Philadelphus (285–246 BC).

Greek was the main language of the Roman Empire, and several other Greek versions of the Old Testament were in use during the first Christian centuries. Sometimes the Greek translation helps to make clear obscure parts of the Hebrew text, but often it is not precise. The other translations can help occasionally in this way. For examples, study the notes in any modern translation. Later, as Christianity spread to people who spoke other languages, the Old Testament was translated into Latin (the Vulgate), Syriac (the Peshitta) and Egyptian (Coptic).

It is not possible to know for certain how the Old Testament came together in the collection of books we now know. But we do know which books made up the Old Testament in the period just before the birth of Jesus, and we can know which books Jesus and his apostles would have regarded as their "Bible".

The Jews have a strong tradition that the scribe Ezra (whose story is told in the Book of Ezra) arranged and collected the books of the Old Testament. But collections of the first five books ("the books of Moses", or the Pentateuch) and of some of the sermons of the prophets were in existence much earlier, as were the psalms and proverbs.

The Jews arranged their sacred books into three groupings: the Law, the Prophets and the Writings. "The Law" consisted of the first five books of the Old Testament (Genesis–Deuteronomy). Although Genesis contains no "law" as such, it was included because all five were thought to have been written by Moses. "The Prophets" contained not only the messages of men like Amos, Jeremiah, Isaiah, and many others, but also the books of history — Joshua, Judges, 1 and 2 Samuel, and 1 and 2 Kings. These books were included in this section because they are concerned not only with the facts but also with the meaning of history as God sees it. The Writings included the books of Wisdom (wise sayings) — Proverbs, Ecclesiastes, Job — some books of history that were written later, such as Ezra, Nehemiah and Chronicles, and one book of prophecy, Daniel.

It is clear that by the time of Jesus the Hebrew Scriptures usually consisted of the thirty-nine books we know today as the Old Testament. Most of the books of our Old Testament are quoted somewhere in the New Testament. This makes it likely that Jesus and his followers were familiar with the Old Testament as we know it.

As well as the thirty-nine books of the Old Testament, the Jews had other sacred writings. In the Greek version, these were given the same respect as the other Old Testament books. But these additional books, known as the *Apocrypha*, were not given the same recognition as the other Old Testament books in the Hebrew version.

OLIVE

One of the main tree-crops of ancient Israel. The berries were harvested in about November, by shak-

Olive tree.

ing or beating the branches with poles. Some olives were eaten pickled, but most were taken in baskets to the presses, where the valuable oil was crushed out. Olive oil was used for cooking, as fuel for lamps, and as a soothing lotion for the skin. In ancient Israel it was also used to anoint kings and priests. It was the way a person was set apart for special work. The trees themselves can live to an age of several hundred years. The wood can also be carved and polished for fine work, as in Solomon's temple.

Deuteronomy 24:20; Judges 9:8; 1 Kings 17:12–16; 1 Samuel 10:1; 1 Kings 6:23

OLIVES, MOUNT OF
See *Mount of Olives*.

OMRI
Commander of the army of King Elah of Israel. His fellow officers made him king when they heard that Zimri had murdered Elah. Omri was a strong and vigorous king. He reigned twelve years (885–874 BC). He chose Samaria as his new capital — well-sited at the top of a steep hill and easily defended. Omri lost some of his cities to Syria but conquered Moab. As a result Moab paid a heavy tax to Israel each year. Omri worshipped idols, and his son, Ahab, followed his example.

1 Kings 16:15–28; 20:34

ON
An ancient city in Egypt, famous for its worship of the sun-god Ré. Joseph married the daughter of the

priest of On, and they had two sons, Ephraim and Manasseh. On is mentioned later in the prophets, once by its Greek name "Heliopolis" (city of the sun).
Genesis 41:45, 50; 46:20; Ezekiel 30:17; compare Isaiah 19:18; Jeremiah 43:13

ONESIMUS
A slave who belonged to Philemon, a Christian friend of Paul living at Colossae. Paul met Onesimus, probably in Rome, after he had run away from his master. While he was with Paul, Onesimus became a Christian. Paul wrote the letter to Philemon asking him to forgive Onesimus and accept him as a brother-Christian. Onesimus travelled back with Tychicus who was taking Paul's letter to the Colossians.
Colossians 4:9; Philemon

ONESIPHORUS
A Christian who helped Paul when he was at Ephesus. He later encouraged Paul by visiting him when he was in prison at Rome.
2 Timothy 1:16ff.; 4:19

OPHIR
A country famous for its gold. It may have been in South Arabia, or East Africa (Somalia), or even India.
1 Kings 9:28, etc.

ORNAN
See *Araunah*.

ORPAH
A Moabite girl who married one of Naomi's sons.
Ruth 1

OTHNIEL
The first of the Judges in Israel. Othniel stopped the
Israelites worshipping idols. As a result God gave
him victory over Cushan-Rishathaim, king of Meso-
potamia.
Joshua 15:16–17; Judges 3:7–11

OWL
Owls are night-time hunters, flying on almost silent
wings to swoop down on the small creatures they eat.
The Eagle Owl (the largest), Tawny Owl, Barn Owl
and Scops Owl (the smallest) are all known in Israel.
In the Bible the owl is pictured as the inhabitant of
ruined and desolate places.
Leviticus 11:16; Isaiah 34:15

An Eagle Owl.

PADDAN-ARAM
The area around Harran in north Mesopotamia. Abraham sent his servant to Paddan-aram to choose a wife for Isaac from the branch of the family which had settled there. Jacob later fled from Esau to his uncle Laban, who was living at Paddan-aram.
Genesis 25:20; 28:2

PALM (DATE)
A tall tree with a straight trunk topped by a tuft of huge 6ft (2m) leaves, amongst which the clusters of dates grow to provide valuable food. The palm became a national symbol of Israel, standing for victory. The people waved palm leaves when Jesus rode in triumph into Jerusalem. The shape of the palm was often copied for decoration in stone carving.
John 12:13

PAMPHYLIA
A region on the south-west coast of modern Turkey. The town of Perga, visited by Paul, was in Pamphylia. Jews from this region were in Jerusalem and heard Peter and the apostles on the Day of Pentecost.
Acts 2:10; 13:13

PAPHOS
A town in the south-west of Cyprus. Paul visited

Paphos on his first missionary journey. Here he met the magician Elymas; and the governor of the island, Sergius Paulus, believed God's message.
Acts 13:4–13

PAPYRUS

A sedge which grew in the marsh areas of the Nile Delta (and still grows in northern Israel), from which the paper of the ancient world was made. Its mop-like flower-heads are 10ft (3m) high or more. The three-cornered stems were cut into thin strips.

Papyrus.

Two layers, one at right-angles to the other, were laid out on a hard wooden surface and hammered together. These sheets of paper were then pasted end to end to form a roll. Much of the Bible would have been written on papyrus. It was also used to make boats and baskets (like the one in which Moses' mother put her baby son), ropes and sandals.

PARABLE

A way of teaching spiritual truths by using a picture

or short story. Much of Jesus' teaching was given in parables. See *Jesus' teaching*.

PARAN
A desert area near Kadesh-barnea, where Hagar's son Ishmael grew up. The Israelites passed through it after the exodus. From here they sent spies into Canaan.
Genesis 21:20; Numbers 10:12; 12:16; 13:1–16, etc.

PARENTS
See *Family Life*.

PARTRIDGE
The name probably includes three kinds of partridge: the Rock Partridge, the Desert Partridge and the Black Partridge. All are game birds whose flesh and eggs can make a good meal. The Rock Partridge hides itself so well that it is more often heard than seen.
1 Samuel 26:20

A Rock Partridge.

PASSOVER
See *Feasts and Festivals*.

PATMOS
An island off the west coast of modern Turkey. The

place where John had the visions written down in the book of Revelation.
Revelation 1:9

PAUL (SAUL)

The great apostle and missionary whose letters form a large part of the New Testament. Paul was a Jew, and a Roman citizen. He was born in Tarsus and educated by the Rabbi Gamaliel in Jerusalem. He was a Pharisee opposed to the Christians and present at the stoning of Stephen. Paul was on his way to Damascus to arrest the Christians when he saw a dazzling light and heard Jesus say to him, "Why do you persecute me?" Blinded by the light, he was led to Damascus. Ananias was sent by God to visit him and restore his sight, and Paul was baptized. At once Paul started preaching about Jesus in Damascus. When the Jews plotted to kill him, he went to Jerusalem. The Christians there were afraid of Paul but Barnabas introduced him to the apostles. After a plot to kill him, Paul returned to Tarsus.

Some years later, Barnabas fetched him to help the church at Antioch in Syria. The two men were later sent to Cyprus and then to Asia Minor (Turkey) to take God's message to many peoples. After the Cyprus visit he was known as Paul, which is the Greek form of the Hebrew name Saul. Paul returned and reported back to the church in Antioch. He also helped the Jewish Christians in Jerusalem to accept the fact that Jesus Christ was the Saviour of all nations, not just the Jews.

On his second journey Paul took Silas as his helper. They visited the converts in Galatia. At

Lystra, Timothy joined them as another helper. From Troas they sailed to Greece where Luke, the writer of the Gospel and Acts also joined them. A Christian church was started in Philippi, but Paul and Silas were beaten and thrown into prison. After their release, they travelled through Greece. Paul preached in Athens and then stayed in Corinth for eighteen months. Then he returned to Jerusalem with gifts for the poor from Christians in Greece and Asia Minor. For a while Paul stayed in Syria. Then he set out again for Ephesus. For almost three years he preached to Jews and Greeks there. After visiting Corinth again, Paul returned through Greece and Asia Minor to Jerusalem. He was arrested and sent to Caesarea to be tried by Felix. For two years he was kept in prison, waiting for his case to be heard. By the time he was tried, Festus had replaced Felix as the Roman governor. Paul appealed to Caesar and was sent for trial in Rome. On the way Paul's ship was wrecked just off Malta, but no one drowned. When they reached Rome, Paul was kept under house arrest for more than two years. He was probably set free after his trial and may have preached in Spain. After a second arrest, Paul was executed in Rome by Nero, about AD 67. He had taken Christianity to Europe, left the priceless legacy of his writings to the church for all time, and kept his faith to the end.

Acts 7:58ff.; 9–28; the letters of Paul: Romans to Philemon

PEACE

The Hebrew word for "peace" has a very broad

meaning. It really means "wholeness" and describes fullness of life in every aspect. It can refer to bodily health, or a long life which ends in a natural death. It is also used to describe safety, and harmony for the individual and for the community. Peace is the most precious of all gifts, and it comes from God himself. "The Lord is peace." On the other hand, "There is no (peace), says the Lord, for the sinners."

Peace becomes the hallmark of the future age when God will establish his kingdom. God's Messiah, who was to bring in this new age, is called the "Prince of Peace". So the New Testament declares that Jesus, "has brought us peace". He "came and preached the Good News of peace to all" — a peace bought by his death on the cross. His gift to every Christian is peace with God; and peace with our fellow men. It is also a deep peace of heart and mind unaffected by circumstances. "Peace," he told his disciples on his last evening with them, "is what I leave with you; it is my own peace that I give you. I do not give it as the world does. Do not be worried and upset; do not be afraid."

See also *Reconciliation*.

Genesis 15:15; Psalms 4:8; 85:8–10; Judges 6:24; Isaiah 48:22; 2:2–4; 9:6; Romans 5:1; Ephesians 2:14–18; John 14:27; 2 Thessalonians 3:16

PEKAH

A captain in King Pekahiah's army who seized the throne of Israel (740–732 BC). He was an evil king who worshipped idols. Pekah made an alliance with King Rezin of Syria and both countries invaded Judah. King Ahaz of Judah appealed to Tiglath-

pileser III of Assyria for help. As a result the Assyrians invaded Israel and captured several cities. Shortly after this Pekah was murdered by Hoshea.
2 Kings 15:25–16:5; 2 Chronicles 28:5–6

PEKAHIAH
King of Israel after Menahem, his father, 742–740 BC. Pekahiah allowed the Israelites to continue worshipping idols. He was assassinated in the second year of his reign by Pekah, a captain in his army.
2 Kings 15:22–26

PENTECOST
See *Feasts and Festivals*.

PENUEL/PENIEL
A place near the River Jabbok, east of the Jordan, where Jacob wrestled with the angel.
Genesis 32:22–32

PERGA
A town just inland from Antalya (Attalia) on the south coast of modern Turkey. Paul visited Perga on arrival from Cyprus on the first missionary journey, and again when he returned to the coast.
Acts 13:13; 14:25

PERGAMUM
The administrative capital of the Roman province of Asia (west Turkey). The first temple to be dedicated to Rome and the Emperor Augustus was built at Pergamum in 29 BC. Pergamum was also the centre of the pagan cults of Zeus, Athena, and Dionysus.

There was a centre of healing connected with the temple of Asclepius (a fourth great pagan cult).

Pergamum was one of the seven churches to which the letters in the Book of Revelation are addressed. The phrase "where Satan has his throne" may refer to emperor worship.
Revelation 1:11; 2:12–16

PERSIA

The Persians were nomadic Indo-Europeans who entered Iran not long before 1000 BC. By the seventh century they had settled east of the Persian Gulf in an area still called Farsistan. They were ruled by the family of Achaemenes. The first we know of in history is Cyrus I, about 640 BC. Cyrus's grandson, Cyrus II (the Great), overthrew the Medes (550 BC), then defeated Lydia (547 BC) and Babylon (539 BC). He established Persian rule over most of the Old Testament world. Cyrus's son, Cambyses, added Egypt to the empire (525 BC), and his successor, Darius, parts of the Black Sea coast.

Cyrus's empire allowed subject peoples to follow their own customs and religion, as long as they remained loyal. Governors were often local princes. But the highest government jobs were kept in the hands of noble Persian and Median families. Persia outstripped Babylon in land and wealth. This can be seen in the magnificent buildings of Persepolis and Pasargadae and the quantities of gold plate and jewellery found in Persia (descriptions in the Book of Esther agree with this). Craftsmen from every province were employed on the great king's buildings.

Although the Persian language was written for

A bearded sphinx which decorates the palace staircase at Persepolis, Persia (Iran).

display in a cuneiform script, Aramaic and Elamite were used for most of the administration.

Persians were nature worshippers at first but, probably in the reign of Darius I (522–486 BC), adopted the teachings of Zoroaster. He taught that there was one god, Ahuramazda, the Good — seen in purifying fire and water — and a dark power of evil, Angramainyu (Ahriman). Revolts and intrigues weakened Persia, so that the empire fell to the Greek, Alexander the Great, in 331 BC.

PETER

Leader of the apostles and of the early church. Like his father and brother Andrew, Simon Peter was a fisherman. When Jesus called him to be a disciple he changed Peter's name from Simon to Peter, which means "rock". Later, Jesus asked his disciples who people thought he was. Peter answered, "You are the Christ, the Son of the Living God." Jesus replied, "You are Peter and on this rock I will build my church." Peter was one of Jesus' closest disciples. He was with Jesus at his transfiguration and in the Garden of Gethsemane just before his death. After Jesus' arrest Peter was afraid and said three times that he did not know him. But at once he was bitterly sorry. Knowing this, Jesus appeared specially to Peter after his resurrection. At Lake Galilee he told Peter to care for the Christian "flock" as a shepherd.

On the Day of Pentecost Peter preached boldly about Jesus to the crowds in Jerusalem. About three thousand people became Christians that day. At first Peter preached only to the Jews. But at Joppa God gave him a special dream to show him he must share the Good News with non-Jews, too. King Herod arrested Peter and put him in prison, but the Christians prayed and God set him free. Peter wrote two of the New Testament letters, probably while he was in Rome. Mark probably got some of the story of Jesus for his Gospel from Peter. Peter is said to have died in Rome during the persecution begun by the Emperor Nero — crucified, like Jesus, but upside down.

Matthew 4:18–19; 10:2; 14:28–33; 16:13–23; 17:1–9; 26:30ff.; Mark 1:16–18, 29–31; 5:37; John 1:40–42; 18:10–11; 20:2–10; 21; Acts 1–15; Galatians 1–2; 1 and 2 Peter

PETER'S LETTERS

1 Peter A letter addressed to scattered groups of Christians in the five Roman provinces which covered much of what is now western and northern Turkey. It was probably written by Peter in Rome at the time when the Emperor Nero was persecuting the Christians (AD 64). Peter's purpose was to encourage and strengthen Christians who were facing suffering.

Peter reminds his readers of the Good News about Jesus Christ. God the Father has given us "new life by raising Jesus Christ from death. This fills us with a living hope". He urges them to regard their suffering as a "test" of their faith. The letter is full of comfort and encouragement to lead lives worthy of people who belong to Jesus Christ. No matter what trouble comes, God is in control: "he cares for you" (5:7).

2 Peter   A letter addressed to a wide circle of early Christians "from Simon Peter". It was written at a time when Christians were confused by false teaching — particularly about how they should behave, and about the return of Jesus Christ.

The writer emphasizes true knowledge — the first-hand account of Jesus which those who saw and heard him have passed on (chapter 1). False teachers who disrupt the church will be punished (chapter 2). The return of Jesus is certain. It could happen any day, and Christians must be ready (chapter 3).

PETRA
See *Sela*.

PHARAOH
Title of the kings of Egypt. Several "pharaohs" are mentioned in the Old Testament including:
1. The pharaoh visited by Abraham.
Genesis 12:10ff.
2. The pharaoh who made Joseph his prime minister.

Colossal statues of Pharaoh Ramesses II at the entrance to the rock-cut temple of Abu-Simbel, Egypt.

Genesis 40ff.
3. The pharaoh who was forced to let Moses lead the Israelites out of Egypt, probably Ramesses II, who built great store cities.
Exodus 5ff.
4. The pharaoh who sheltered Hadad after David defeated the Edomites.
1 Kings 11
5. The pharaoh who gave Solomon his daughter in marriage.
1 Kings 9:16
6. Shishak. He encouraged Jeroboam to lead the ten tribes in revolt against King Solomon's unpopular son, Rehoboam. Later he raided Jerusalem and took away the temple treasure.

1 Kings 11:40; 14:25–26
7. So, who was asked by King Hoshea of Israel to form an alliance against Assyria.
2 Kings 17:4
8. Tirhakah led his army against Assyria during the reign of King Hezekiah. The Assyrian army had to abandon its attack on Jerusalem to meet the Egyptian forces.
2 Kings 19:9; Isaiah 37:9
9. Neco, 610–595 BC. He killed King Josiah of Judah at the Battle of Megiddo. For four years Neco made Judah pay tribute to him, but then he was defeated by Nebuchadnezzar of Babylon at the battle of Carchemish (605 BC). After that Judah was in Babylon's power. Neco spent his later years defeating Egypt and trying to strengthen his country.
2 Kings 23:29ff.; 24:7; 2 Chronicles 35:20–36:4
10. Hophra, 587–570 BC. He supported King Zedekiah's rebellion against Nebuchadnezzar of Babylon.
Jeremiah 37:5; 44:30; Ezekiel 17:15ff.; 29:2

PHARISEES

The name may mean the "separated ones". The Pharisees were a strict, religious sect, probably beginning in the second century BC. They were mostly ordinary Jews — not priests — who kept closely to the Jewish Law. They often extended the way the laws applied, so that they became very hard to keep. The forbidding of work on the sabbath is an extreme example. Pharisees counted as "work": walking more than ⅗ miles (about 1 km) from one's town; carrying any kind of load; lighting a fire in the home. Strict rulings like this often led to people being so concerned to keep the law in every detail that they lost sight of the "spirit" behind it. But the motive was good. Pharisees believed that their rules "built a fence around the Law". By keeping these other rules people would be in less danger of disobeying the actual Law of God.

Although the Pharisees were the largest Jewish sect in the time of Jesus, there were only about 6,000 of them. Many Pharisees were very godly men. But they tended to despise those who did not, or could not, keep their burdensome laws, and referred to them as "sinners". Jesus frequently argued with the Pharisees. He condemned their self-righteousness and legalism. And he identified himself with the common people whom the Pharisees, as religious leaders, had written off. Nicodemus, who became a secret follower of Jesus, was a Pharisee. So too was Paul.
Matthew 12:1–42; 22:34–23:36; Mark 7:1–23; Luke 18:9–14; John 18:3; Acts 23:6–10

PHARPAR
See *Abana*.

PHILADELPHIA
A town in the Roman province of Asia (modern Alashehir, in western Turkey). Philadelphia was one of the seven churches of Asia to which the letters in the book of Revelation are addressed.
Revelation 1:11; 3:7–13

PHILEMON
A private letter from Paul to Philemon, a Christian convert and friend at Colossae (western Turkey).

Philemon owned a slave named Onesimus, who had run away. Onesimus eventually met Paul in prison and became a Christian. Paul wrote urging Philemon to forgive and welcome back his slave as a Christian brother. The letter was probably sent back to Colossae along with Onesimus, and the letter to the Colossian church.

PHILIP

1. One of the twelve apostles. He came from the lakeside town of Bethsaida in Galilee, the home town of Peter and Andrew. Philip went straight to Nathanael, told him he had found the Messiah, and introduced him to Jesus. Faced with a crowd of five thousand hungry people, Jesus tested Philip's faith. "Where can we buy enough bread to feed all these people?" he asked. Philip was wondering where the money would come from. But Jesus fed them all from five small loaves and two fish. At the last supper, when Jesus said, "No one goes to the Father except by me," Philip asked Jesus to show them his father. "Whoever has seen me," Jesus answered, "has seen the Father."
Matthew 10:3; John 1:43–46; 6:5–7; 12:21–22; 14:8–9; Acts 1:13

2. Son of Herod the Great. His wife, Herodias, left him to marry his half-brother, Herod Antipas. John the Baptist was beheaded because he condemned this marriage.
Mark 6:17

3. Another son of Herod the Great, brother of Antipas and Archelaus. He became ruler of Ituraea.
Luke 3:1

4. Philip the evangelist. One of seven men chosen to help the apostles in the work of the church at Jerusalem. He fled to Samaria when the Christians in Jerusalem were being persecuted by Paul. There he preached and healed many people. An angel sent Philip to meet the Ethiopian chancellor, travelling from Jerusalem to Gaza. This man became a Christian and was baptized. Philip then went and preached in every town along the coast from Ashdod to Caesarea. Philip's four daughters were also involved in making God's message known. About twenty years later Paul stayed at Philip's home in Caesarea. Acts 6:1–6; 8; 21:8–9

PHILIPPI

A town 8 miles/12km inland from Neapolis on the coast of Macedonia (northern Greece). It was named after Philip of Macedon. Philippi was annexed by

Prisoners taken captive by Ramesses III. They are, from left to right, Libyan, Syrian, Hittite, Philistine and Syrian.

the Romans in 168 BC. It was the site of a famous battle between Antony and Octavian (Augustus) against Brutus and Cassius in 42 BC. Some years later, Octavian made Philippi a Roman colony, which gave its people the same rights and privileges as any town on Italian soil.

Paul visited Philippi on his second missionary journey, after seeing a vision of a Macedonian man appealing to him for help. The first Christian church in Europe was established at Philippi. Paul and Silas were illegally imprisoned here but later released with an apology when they made it known that they were Roman citizens. The letter to the Philippians was written to the church at Philippi.
Acts 16:6–40; 20:6; Philippians 1:1, etc.; 1 Thessalonians 2:2

PHILIPPIANS
Paul founded the church at Philippi — the first in Europe — in about AD 50. He wrote this letter from prison, possibly in Rome about AD 61–63. Or it may have been from Ephesus, in about AD 54.

Paul explains his situation to the Christians at Philippi, and thanks them for gifts they had sent him. He encourages them in the faith. He urges them to forget pride, and follow the example of Jesus, "who was humble, and walked the path of obedience." He sets out the joy and peace which belong to those who trust Christ.

Although Paul was worried by false teachers in the church at Philippi, his affection for the Christians there shines through.

Despite the dark background of prison, his letter

is full of the joy, confidence and hope of the Christian life.

PHILISTINES

The Philistines lived in five cities to the south-west of the land of Israel: Ashdod, Ashkelon, Ekron, Gath, and Gaza. They controlled the coast road from Egypt. It was perhaps to avoid them that God did not take his people into the Promised Land "by the road that goes up the coast to Philistia, although it was the shortest way" (Exodus 13:17).

War with the Israelites   In the days of the Judges, and of Samuel, Saul, and David, the Philistines were a constant threat to the Israelites. Both peoples wanted control of the same land. Their military pressure was one factor in Israel's demand for a king. ("We want . . . our own king . . . to lead us out to war" — 1 Samuel 8:20.)

Only after fierce struggles were their attacks finally ended by David, who drove them "back from Geba all the way to Gezer" (2 Samuel 5:25). Yet the Philistines remained independent, and caused occasional disturbances in later times. They extended their rule northwards along the coast, and inland, whenever they could. Although they were never in control of much of the country for long, it was the Philistines who gave their name — as Palestine — to the whole of the land west of the Jordan.

Rulers   Each Philistine city was ruled by a "lord". This title (*seren*) is a non-Semitic word, probably belonging to the Indo-European speech of the Aegean area. A word for helmet (*koba'*) found in stories about the Philistines (for example, Goliath in 1

Samuel 17:5) and the names Goliath and Achish may belong to the same family of languages. This evidence from two words and two names can be linked with information from Egypt. There, in the thirteenth and twelfth centuries BC, pharaohs recorded how they beat off invasions by the "people of the sea". One of these peoples was the Philistines. After defeating them, the Egyptians used some as soldiers to garrison provincial and frontier forts, and allowed others to settle along the coast of Canaan, an Egyptian province.

"Sea Peoples" While the Sea Peoples' warriors reached Egypt by ship, and fought the Egyptians on water, their families and household goods trekked down the coast of Syria and Canaan, according to an Egyptian text. These details, and some items in Egyptian pictures of Sea Peoples, point to them as intruders into the Near East. Amos 9:7 states that they came from Crete (Caphtor). Deuteronomy 2:23 says that this was where the men of Gaza came from. "Philistine" pottery found in Israel is evidence of this link. The pottery belongs to the Mycenean type made in Greece, Crete, and Cyprus. It is found in levels of occupation dating from 1200–1100 BC, especially at sites on the coast. Nothing else has been found that can be called "Philistine" as distinct from Canaanite or Israelite.

Religion and culture The Old Testament gives Philistine gods Semitic names: Dagon, with temples at Gaza and Ashdod; Baalzebub, worshipped at Ekron; and Ashtoreth (Astarte). We know too little about their cities as yet to be sure whether they had their own designs for houses or temples. Metal-working, especially in iron, was a Philistine skill. Goliath's armour was impressive, and the Israelites had to pay their neighbours to sharpen their iron tools.

Early Philistines   Long before Israel entered the Promised Land, their ancestors met Philistines in southern Canaan. Many scholars consider that these stories were composed much later, after the Philistines had settled there in the thirteenth century BC. Or the name Philistine may have been used by a later editor to replace an out-of-date name in the story (as St Petersburg would be replaced by Leningrad). There are some objects from the Philistine area which show that there were connections with the Greek region as early as 1900 BC. But apart from the documents of the Old Testament, no others have yet been found which specifically mention the people of the district at that time.
Genesis 21:32, 34; 26; Judges 16:21ff.; 1 Samuel 5; 13:19–22; 17; 31:9, 10; 1 Kings 1:2

PHINEHAS
1. The son of Eleazar and grandson of Aaron. When the Israelites were mixing with Midianite women and worshipping their god, Phinehas executed two of the worst offenders. His action stopped an epidemic which had already killed 24,000 people. His faithfulness to God was rewarded with the promise that he and his descendants would always be priests.
Exodus 6:25; Numbers 25; 31:6; Joshua 22:13ff.; Judges 20:28
2. One of Eli's two sons. (See *Hophni and Phinehas*.)
1 Samuel 2:12ff.; 4

PHOENICIANS

The Israelites never occupied all of the land God originally promised to them. The Canaanites whose homeland it had been for centuries remained in some areas, particularly on the coast to the north-west — modern Lebanon. One of their towns was the ancient city of Byblos, possibly the place where the alphabet was invented. At any rate the Greeks, who borrowed the alphabet, also borrowed the name of the city as their word for book (*biblos*).

Trade   Byblos had a flourishing merchant shipping trade from at least the eighteenth century BC. But it is two nearby ports that are most often mentioned in the Bible. The power of Tyre and Sidon increased and overtook Byblos after 1000 BC. It was about this time that David and Solomon formed trade alliances with King Hiram of Tyre. He supplied fine wood, and gold, and skilled craftsmen for building the temple and palaces at Jerusalem, in return for twenty towns in Galilee (1 Kings 9:10ff.). Hiram and

Phoenician boats with horse-headed prows and high sterns transporting logs; from an eighth-century BC Assyrian relief.

Solomon also combined in operating a fleet on the Red Sea. The ships brought back gold and jewels.

The chief exports of Tyre and Sidon were cedar-wood from the mountains of Lebanon and purple dye from cuttle-fish. But the people built their empire on trade. They were middlemen, dealing in linen from Egypt, silver, iron and tin from Spain, ivory and ebony from the coastlands (Ezekiel 27 gives a very full description). They spread their colonies across the Mediterranean, to North Africa, Italy, and Spain, where they were known as the Phoenicians. Their language was a form of Canaanite, similar to Hebrew, but their literature is known only at second-hand. Their religion, too, continued Canaanite ideas. (see *Canaanite Religion*). It was brought into Israel by the marriage of King Ahab to Jezebel, daughter of the king of Sidon. Ahab built a temple to Baal at his capital and Jezebel and the prophets of Baal threatened Elijah's life (1 Kings 18).

PHRYGIA

A land in the centre of Asia Minor (modern Turkey), the home of an Indo-European group. In Assyrian records and the Old Testament it is called Meshech. According to Ezekiel it was a warlike nation, trading in copper and slaves. Several of the rulers were named Midas (though this may be a title, like "pharaoh") and were buried in richly furnished tombs around Gordium, the capital, which has recently been excavated. After the middle of the seventh century BC, Phrygia came under Lydian rule (an event reflected in Ezekiel 38 and 39). In 116 BC it

became part of Roman Asia. From 25 BC the eastern part was counted as being in Galatia.
Ezekiel 32:26; 38:2, 3; 39:1; 27:13; 38; 39

PILATE

Roman governor in Judea AD 26–37. He was cruel and unpopular with the Jews. When Jesus was brought to him to be tried Pilate knew that Jesus was innocent. But he was afraid there would be a riot, and the Emperor would remove him as governor. So he condemned Jesus to death.
Matthew 27; Mark 15; Luke 3:1; 13:1; 23; John 18–19

PISGAH

One of the peaks of Mt Nebo.

PISIDIA

A mountainous inland area inland from the south coast of modern Turkey. Paul passed through this remote and dangerous region on his first missionary journey, on his way from Perga to Antioch.
Acts 13:14; 14:24

PITHOM

One of Pharaoh's two store-cities, built by Israelite slave labour. It lay east of the Nile Delta in Egypt. See also *Raamses*.
Exodus 11:1

POMEGRANATE

Scarlet flowers contrast with deep-green leaves on this large shrub. The yellowy-brown edible fruits are

the size of an orange. Inside the hard rind is a juicy pulp, full of seeds. The shape was copied in embroidery round the edge of the high priest's robe, and carved on the pillars in Solomon's temple.
Exodus 28:33; 1 Kings 7:20

PONTUS

The ancient name of the Black Sea, and so of the land along its south coast. This became a Roman province, stretching along most of the northern coast of Asia Minor (Turkey). This was one of the lands to which Peter sent his first letter. The Christian message may have reached Pontus very early, as Jews from there were in Jerusalem on the Day of Pentecost.
Acts 2:9; 18:2; 1 Peter 1:1

POPLAR

Jacob peeled poplar shoots when he tricked Laban. The white poplar has fast-growing shoots and gives a dense shade. The "willows" of Babylon, where the exiles mourned, were probably a kind of poplar.
Genesis 30:37; Psalm 137:2

POTIPHAR

Egyptian official who bought Joseph as a slave. (See *Joseph*).
Genesis 37:36; 39

POTTERY

By comparison with the products of her neighbours, Israel's pottery seems poor and not very artistic. There is an immense difference between the painted pottery of the Canaanites and Philistines and the limited designs of the Israelites when they eventually occupied the land. But this is because the Israelites were making their pots with a view to usefulness rather than decoration. The forms were good and they were carefully produced.

At the time of King David, craftsmanship improved. There were new shapes and there was some form of decoration. This progress went on and, during the time of the kings, the making of pottery developed into a minor industry with small "factories", mass production, some standard shapes, and trade marks. Many more pots were made, but the standard was high.

In New Testament times it seems that a good deal of fine pottery was imported.

The potters It is possible, especially during the time of the later kings, that several potters worked together, with their apprentices (often their own sons). There is evidence that potters kept the temple worshippers supplied with pots fit to use for cooking a sacrificial meal in the temple courts.

There also seems to have been a royal guild of potters "in the service of the king" (1 Chronicles 4:23). They probably produced large jars for storing produce from the king's private estates. Jars have been found (holding about 10 gallons/45 litres) with a stamp on the handles: "Belonging to the king". Underneath is the name of one of four cities: Hebron, Ziph, Socoh, or Memshath. These may have been the sites of royal vineyards, or centres where the people brought their taxes in the form of produce.

Pottery

Israelite pottery.

The potter's workshop The whole process of producing pottery was probably carried out on one site. There had to be a handy water supply (a stream or cistern), wheels for shaping the clay, and kilns for firing it. The yard of the potter's house or workshop would be used for preparing the clay and no doubt also became the place where broken pottery or rejects from the kiln (potsherds) would pile up.

Jeremiah 19:2 speaks of the "Potsherd Gate" near the Valley of Hinnom. Presumably there was a potter's house there. In Nehemiah 3:11 and 12:38 we read of the "Tower of the Ovens" or "Tower of the Furnaces" and these expressions may refer to pottery kilns in Jerusalem.

Preparing the clay Pottery was made from the local red clay. The potter did not alter the quality of the clay, except by mixing it occasionally with ground limestone, which was readily available. This enabled the finished pot to withstand heat (useful in the case of cooking-pots), but it meant that the potter had to fire the clay at a lower temperature, otherwise the limestone would decompose.

The raw clay was exposed to the sun, rain and

frost to break it up and remove impurities. Then water was added and it was trampled into mud (see Isaiah 41:25). This needed skill. The water had to be measured and poured on evenly, and the air removed.

Working the clay When the clay had been prepared, three methods of working it were open to the potter.

1. The clay could be pressed down in a mould. Canaanite plaques were made this way, and so also were most of the lamps of New Testament times. Job 38:14 refers to the imprint of a seal on clay.

2. The clay could be modelled free-hand. In Israel the only things made in this way seem to have been toys, ovens and a few pots.

3. Or the clay could be shaped on a wheel — and this was the usual method of working.

The earliest type of potter's wheel known was a circular disc, rotating on a vertical shaft. But about the time of the exodus a different type came into use. This had a second, larger disc, mounted below the first. This speeded the turning and may have been kept moving by the potter's assistants. Potters' wheels were probably used everywhere, but the Bible only mentions one once (when Jeremiah visits the potter's house — Jeremiah 18:3), and wheels are rarely found. Perhaps they were usually made of wood or clay and so have not survived. Stone wheels have been found at Megiddo, Lachish and Hazor. There is no evidence of a foot-operated wheel before 200 BC, although it was widely used in New Testament times.

When the pot had been shaped, it was allowed to

harden. Then it could go back on the wheel and be turned into more delicate forms. At the time of the later kings production was speeded up in various ways. Sometimes a very large lump of clay was put on the wheel and pots were shaped from the top of it, each one being "pinched off" as it was completed. Sometimes unskilled workers shaped the clay roughly on the wheel. They used cheap clay and made thick pots, which were then turned into the desired shape and thickness by skilled potters.

Firing The firing of the clay objects in a kiln was the ultimate test of a potter's art. Different clays needed different treatment. But the methods of firing are not known. A number of kilns have been found. Some of them have a U shape, but it is not easy to tell whether they were used for pottery or for copper.

Decoration The Israelites did not glaze their pottery but they had three main ways of decorating it.
1. They could use a "slip". Fine clay with a rich iron content was thinned with water and then brushed over the parts which the potter wished to decorate.
2. Sometimes they painted a line of red or black around the shoulder or middle of the jar or jug.
3. They could "burnish" pots either by hand or on the wheel. To do this, a tool of stone, bone or wood would be rubbed against the clay after drying but before firing. These areas would then shine after firing.

The "slip" and "burnish" were sometimes combined.

Some of the perfume jugs which have been found

are.black. It is not clear how these were made. They may have been dipped in milk or olive oil before firing and then lightly polished.

Glazing was used by the Greeks and Romans.

Articles made by the potter Pottery articles can be divided into two basic designs.

The bowl This could range from a large banquet bowl with four handles, to a small cup (which rarely had handles). Bowls were used for mixing wines, serving food, holding coal, cooking, and so on. The household oven was really an inverted bowl with the bottom missing. The clay would simply be moulded into shape. It hardened when used as an oven. Broken bits of pot were plastered round the outside to moderate the heat.

Lamps were thrown in the same way as a bowl, and the rims were pinched in while the clay was still soft. Their style changed considerably during the history of Israel, but the basic design was the same. The gradual changes, at different stages, enable the experts to use them as an indication of date.

The jar or pitcher There were jars for wine, for water and for oil. Jars were also used for storing documents. And small juglets were specially produced for perfume.

Other objects made of pottery included water bottles for a journey; articles for industry (crucibles, clay moulds, spindle whorls, loom-weights); toys (dolls, horses, camels), and clay objects connected with the Canaanite religion.

If pots were broken, they were sometimes mended with rivets or wires. Sometimes notes or letters were written on pieces of broken pottery. For example, we know of a series of letters (the "Lachish Letters") written on pieces of pottery (ostraca), from the commander of a smaller garrison to his superior at Lachish during King Nebuchadnezzar's final attack on Judah.

PRAISE

The joy God's people have in him is expressed in "praise". They praise him as their Creator and as their Redeemer (Saviour).

One of the Old Testament words for praise comes from a Hebrew word which means "to make a noise". It appears in our word "hallelujah". Israelite worship included joyful shouting and singing and the sound of many musical instruments. We see this again and again in the psalms (the hymns sung in the temple).

This same note of praise characterizes the Christian church. Christians rejoice above all in the great act of salvation brought about through the life, death and resurrection of Jesus. Angels sang when Jesus was born. Praise is a constant part of Christian prayer — rejoicing, asking God with a thankful heart. Heaven itself continually rings with praise.

See also *Creeds and hymns*.
Psalms 136; 135; 150; 34:3; 35:18 and many other passages; Luke 2:13–14; Philippians 4:4–8; Revelation 4:6–11

PRAYER

Men and women were made to live in fellowship with God. In this "sharing", prayer was the normal relationship through which God fulfilled his purposes. It is because of the coming of sin and evil that this relationship is often broken now, and so prayer can seem unnatural or unreal.

But those who trust in God share their life with him in prayer. We pour out our hearts before him. We are open to God in confessing our sin. We ask things of God, confident that God answers prayer. And our prayers always include thanksgiving to God.

The faithful Israelite prayed three times each day. Samuel was so sure of his duty to pray that he considered it a sin if he failed to pray for those in his care. There is no particular pattern laid down for Christians to follow but Paul expects prayer to have a central place in the life of the Christian and the church. It will have a natural place in the restored relationship of God and his people.

Prayer is a Christian family activity. Jesus' model prayer begins "Our Father . . ." It is the work of the Holy Spirit to help Christians to pray, tuning their minds more and more to the mind of God. "The Spirit himself pleads with God for us in groans that words cannot express," wrote Paul to the Romans.

As well as the private prayers of individuals, the New Testament often mentions groups of Christians praying together. From the very beginning Christians shared in "the fellowship meals and . . . the prayers". They prayed for courage when the Jewish Council banned Peter and John from preaching. They prayed for Peter when he was imprisoned. They prayed for the success of the missionary work of Barnabas and Paul. These prayers were spontaneous, but they are full of the spirit and language of the Old Testament.

Some of the actual words of early Christian prayer are still known.

Marana tha (1 Corinthians 16:22). These are two Aramaic words, meaning "Our Lord, come!" They were addressed to Jesus, calling him by the same name, "Lord", that Jews had reserved for God alone. *Marana tha* comes again in the last prayer of the Bible: "So be it. Come. Lord Jesus!"

The word **abba** (Mark 14:36) was used by Jesus himself in addressing God. It is an Aramaic word meaning "dear father" or "dad". A child would use it to speak to his own father. Jews would have thought it an irreverent way to speak to God. They used the word *abinu*, "our father", instead. But Jesus' relationship with God was so close that he could use this family word, and encourage his disciples to do the same. The word comes twice in Paul's letters: "when we cry out to God, 'Abba, my Father!', God's Spirit . . . declare(s) that we are God's children." And: "To show that you are his sons, God sent the Spirit of his Son into our hearts, the Spirit who cries out, 'Father, my Father'."

Amen This is a Hebrew word used in the temple and synagogue services at the end of prayers. It means, "It is sure", or even, "There is no doubt about that." So, in the worship in heaven described in Revelation 5, when the cry goes up, "The lamb who was killed is worthy to receive power, wealth, wisdom and strength" the prayer is concluded with a great "Amen". "Amen" ends a prayer in Romans 15:33, a blessing on God in Romans 9:5, an expression of praise in Galatians 1:5, and a blessing upon fellow Christians in Galations 6:18.

Psalm 62:8; 1 John 1:9; Mark 11:24; Philippians 4:6; 1 Samuel 12:23; Colossians 4:2; James 1:5–6; Acts 12:12; Romans 8:26

Jesus' teaching on prayer:
Matthew 6:5–15; 7:7–11; 26:41; Mark 12:38–40; 13:33; 14:38; Luke 11:1–13; 18:1–14

Prayers of Jesus:
Matthew 6:9–13; 11:25–26; 26:36–44; Mark 14:32–39; Luke 10:21; 11:2–4; 22:46; 23:34, 46; John 11:41–42; 12:27–28; 17

Some other great Bible prayers:
Exodus 15; 32; 33; Deuteronomy 32–33; Joshua 17; 10; Judges 5; 6; 1 Samuel 1; 2; 2 Samuel 7; 22; 1 Kings 3; 8; 18; 19; 2 Kings 19; Ezra 9; Nehemiah 1; 9; Job 42; Psalms; Daniel 2; 9; Jonah 2; Habakkuk 3; Luke 1:46–55, 68–79; 2:29–35; Acts 4:24–30, and many prayers in the New Testament letters

PRIESTS AND LEVITES

The Levites were originally just one of the twelve tribes of Israel, descended from Levi, one of the sons of Jacob. But they were given a special position among God's people, because they defended his honour at the time when the rest of the people worshipped the golden calf. So they were dedicated to serve God. They became his own tribe in a special way.

They were set apart from the other tribes for religious duties. As they did not own any land, they had to be supported by the other tribes. To do this

A model of Levites offering sacrifices in front of the tabernacle.

the people gave a "tithe" (a tenth) of all their harvests and livestock to God. In Israel forty-eight towns were set aside for the use of the Levites.

Levi had three sons (Kohath, Gershon, and Merari) and their descendants formed the three clans of Levites. During the time in the desert the Kohathites were responsible for carrying the tabernacle furniture; the Gershonites carried its curtains and coverings; and the Merarites carried and set up the tabernacle itself.

One family, belonging to the Kohathite clan, was set apart for special service. This was the family of Aaron, the brother of Moses. He and his descendants were appointed priests. Only priests could offer sacrifices. The other Levite families did the more menial jobs, and were virtually servants of the priests. So the priests were the most "holy" group within Israel. That does not mean, of course, that they were the most godly; many were not (for example, Eli's sons, who are described in 1 Samuel 2:22–

25). "Holy" is used in the special sense of "belonging to God". These men were the professional officials of the tabernacle and temple. Because of their special position they were subject to strict rules. A man of this family became a priest at the age of thirty.

The man in charge of the priests was the chief or "high priest". He had one privilege allowed to no one else. He could enter the "holy of holies" once a year, on the Day of Atonement.

Levites: Exodus 32:25–29; Numbers 3:12–13; 18:21–24; 35:2–8

Priests: Exodus 28–29; Leviticus 8–10; 16; 21–22

The duties of the priests and Levites are mostly connected with the tabernacle and temple sacrifices and worship. But they also had a number of other duties. A group of men from each of the three Levite clans formed the temple choirs, and they may have composed several of the psalms (for example, Psalms 85 and 87).

The priests and Levites also had to give answers in God's name to questions that could not otherwise be decided (for example, whether it was the right time to go out to battle). For this purpose they used the sacred stones called Urim and Thummim, which were kept in a pouch worn on the high priest's chest. If the priest pulled out the Urim stone, the answer was "no", but if it was the Thummim stone, the answer was "yes".

More important, they were also responsible for teaching the people the Law of God. When Moses blessed the tribes of Israel he said that the Levites will first "teach your children to obey your Law";

and, secondly "offer sacrifices on your altar". The Book of Nehemiah describes one occasion when Ezra and the Levites held a reading of the Law to all the people. The prophet Malachi sums up their role: "It is the duty of the priests to teach the true knowledge of God. People should go to them to learn my will, because they are the messengers of the Lord Almighty." Sadly, the prophets often had to call the priests and Levites to task for failing in these duties. 1 Chronicles 6:31–48; Leviticus 13; Deuteronomy 33:8–11; Nehemiah 8:1–12; Malachi 2:7; Jeremiah 23:11–32; Ezekiel 34

PRISCILLA
See *Aquila*.

PROPHETS
The great prophets whose messages we have in the Old Testament appeared on the scene at times of crisis in the nation's history. They were God's men for the moment and their messages were generally concerned with particular times and places. They remain valid and helpful because the same kind of situations have recurred again and again in history.
The early prophets The prophets first emerged as a group in the time of Samuel, who is often described as "the last of the Judges and first of the prophets in Israel". The Philistines were a great threat to Israel at the time. These early prophets, with their enthusiasm for Israel's God, strengthened the Israelites' determination to be free and independent. When the young Saul met them he was overcome by their sense of God's dynamic energy. He

joined in excited prophesying as God's power took control of him.

Samuel himself does not seem to have been caught up in the ecstasies of these prophetic groups. He played an important role as a judge of the people. He also reproved them for worshipping foreign gods, and prayed to God on their behalf for forgiveness. (These were also important aspects of the work of later prophets.) Samuel obviously also had other, supernatural gifts. When Saul was out looking for his father's lost asses Samuel could tell him they were found — and also predict what would happen to him on his way. But these are comparatively trivial matters. Samuel is best remembered for the fact that he, like many of the prophets, was the one through whom God's choice of a king was made known. He anointed Saul, and later David, as God's chosen rulers.

While David was still king, the prophet Nathan was similarly involved in king-making. But it was not until the middle of the ninth century BC that prophecy came to the fore with work of Elijah and Elisha.

A crisis in the northern kingdom of Israel formed the backcloth to the work of these prophets. Foreign gods had been imported into the worship of Israel by Jezebel, wife of King Ahab. She had brought from her home city of Tyre 850 prophets of Baal and Asherah, a Canaanite god and goddess. Elijah realized that he must challenge this false religion and uphold faith in Israel's God.

So Elijah challenged the Canaanite prophets to a contest on Mt Carmel where God proved by fire that

"The Lord is God; the Lord alone is God!" Elisha continued Elijah's mission. He performed miracles of healing and later in his life had Jehu anointed king of Israel. He gathered a number of disciples — "sons of the prophets" — who preserved the memory of his deeds.

1 Samuel 7:3–17; 9–10; 2 Samuel 7; 1 Kings 1:11–40; 17–19; 2 Kings 1–9

Later prophets None of the "older" prophets have left us any books of their prophecies, though we do know a little of what they said and did. But in the "classical" period of prophecy, from the eighth to the fifth centuries BC, many of the prophets' messages were written down and compiled into the Old Testament books we now have: Isaiah, Jeremiah, Ezekiel, and the Book of the Twelve Prophets (the "minor" prophets — Hosea to Malachi), plus the Book of Daniel.

The crisis behind this new period of prophecy was the changing political scene that led first to the exile of Israel (the northern kingdom) after its capital, Samaria, was captured in 721 BC, and then to the exile of Judah (the southern kingdom) after Jerusalem had been destroyed in 586 BC.

The message of these prophets centres on the exile. Some looked ahead to it. Others reflected on its meaning. And the later prophets encouraged the nation to rebuild itself out of the disaster.

Before the exile The prophets warned that judgement was inevitable. Amos and Hosea did so in the northern kingdom in the eighth century; Jeremiah in the southern kingdom in the late seventh century. They called on the people to repent. It was not yet too late for God to change his mind. But the prophets were forced to realize that the people were in no mood to repent. They had been given many chances, but they refused to take them. At this point Amos speaks for all the prophets. This is God's message: "Get ready to face my judgement!"

What had Israel done to make God so angry? Different prophets exposed different aspects of Israel's sin. Amos attacks social injustice; Hosea Israel's unfaithfulness to God; Micah the sins of Israel's rulers; Jeremiah the false gods and the unchecked corruption in Judah. For these sins, the righteous God must punish his people, even though it pained him to the heart to do so.
Amos 9:1–4; Hosea 11:5–7; Jeremiah 25:8–11; Amos 5:14–15; 14:6–12

The exile and after Once Judah as well as Israel had gone into exile, some, at least, began to realize that they had deserved this punishment. From this time on, the prophets were able to stir up hope. Ezekiel foresaw a day when the nation, lifeless as a heap of dead bones, would begin to live again as the Spirit of God breathed new life into the people. He looked forward to the rebuilding of the temple and a new settlement of the land. The prophecies of Isaiah 40–55 also brought a message of assurance to the people. God was about to bring the exiles back from Babylonia to Jerusalem.

Then, after the first exiles had returned, and the excitement of the beginning of temple rebuilding had worn off, a new generation of prophets was needed to meet the crisis of disillusionment and despair. If Haggai and Zechariah had not encouraged the people to work on the temple, it would never have been completed. The return from exile would have been a failure if the worship of God had not been properly restored.

Ezekiel 37; 40–48; Isaiah 40:1, 9–10

The role of the prophets The prophets are best understood as messengers. Their speeches (or "oracles") often begin with the words "God says" or "God spoke". This is the way a messenger in the ancient world would begin a message he was bringing by word of mouth. The prophets were called by God to hear his plans and his messages. Then they were sent by him to bring this message to Israel and the nations. Sometimes they saw visions; sometimes they preached sermons; sometimes they used parable or poetry or drama to speak to the people. They tell us little about how they actually received their messages. But they were completely convinced that what they said came from God.

The prophets were usually against the mainstream of opinion. When all seemed well, they attacked the evils of their society and predicted its doom. When their people were pessimistic, they prophesied hope. They brought these disturbing, challenging words from God because God's call had broken into their own lives and changed them drastically.

The prophets were also teachers calling Israel back to obey God's laws. They were not preaching a new religion, but applying the word of God to their own day.

The Old Testament owes a great deal to the prophets. Not just the books of the prophets, but many of the history-books, especially those from

Joshua to 2 Kings, were written either by prophets or by men who had learned much from the prophets' teaching. They wrote history as God sees it.

Jeremiah 23:18, 21–22; Amos 7:1–2; Zechariah 1:7–21; Jeremiah 7; 18; 19; Isaiah 1; Ezekiel 5:17; 1 Kings 18:19; Amos 7:14–16; Isaiah 6; Jeremiah 1

False prophets   All through Israel's history there were false prophets who claimed that their messages came from God, when in fact they did not. A prophet might begin his preaching with "God says", but that was no guarantee at all that it really was a word from God. It needed spiritual insight to decide, in a particular case, what actually came from God. The Law in Deuteronomy recognized the problem and gave two helpful rules. If a prophet predicted something and it did not happen, he was a false prophet. And if his message led people away from God and his laws, it was false.

1 Kings 22; Jeremiah 28; Micah 3:5–7; Jeremiah 23:13–32; Deuteronomy 13; 18:21–22

The message of the prophets   Jeremiah saw that the exile meant the end of God's covenant with Israel: "Both Israel and Judah have broken the covenant that I made with their ancestors."

Yet the prophets believed that God would not desert Israel even though they no longer had any claim upon God. That is why even those prophets who pictured a dreadful future for the people could still look beyond the tragedy to a time of hope. In Amos it is promised that the family of David will be restored to the throne; in Hosea that God will heal Israel's faithlessness; in Jeremiah that God will re-make the covenant.

So the prophets' message looked to the past, recalling Israel to obedience; to the present, dealing with the crisis of faith in which the people found themselves; and to the future, because they believed that God had committed himself to Israel. The commitment might mean the destruction of Israel for a time but it would end in rebuilding. The time when Israel would be destroyed and rebuilt was sometimes called the "Day of the Lord". The hope of a Messiah who would bring about a restoration has its roots in the Old Testament, but it became important only in the last centuries before Christ. For the prophets, it was God who would step in to restore Israel.

Jeremiah 11:10; Amos 9:11–12; Hosea 14:4; Jeremiah 31:31–34; Amos 9:9; Zechariah 13:8–9; Isaiah 2:12–17; Zephaniah

Prophecy in the New Testament With the outpouring of God's Holy Spirit on all believers, everyone, men and women, can proclaim God's message. But there is still a gift of "prophecy" mentioned in the New Testament. This is one of God's special gifts given to various members of the church in order to build it up.

The prophecies of the Book of Revelation, like those in the Old Testament Book of Daniel belong to a type of literature called "apocalyptic". This contains a special kind of imagery and symbolism which can be understood only if it is applied first to the time in which these books were written.

Acts 2:17; 1 Corinthians 11:5; 14:24, 29; 1 Corinthians 12:10, 29

PROVERBS

Proverbs is a book of wise sayings and proverbs intended to guide a young man in a good and godly life. Much of it is blunt day-to-day advice, set down in forms which were popular at the time of writing, not just in Israel but also in neighbouring countries.

Much of the book probably dates from the time of the first kings of Israel, although the final editing was much later. King Solomon — famous for his wisdom — is named in the title of the book, but it is not clear what part he played in the collection.

The book sets out what is right and wrong. Its basis is the principle that "to have knowledge you must first have reverence for the Lord". It then applies this wisdom to every area of life: marriage, home, justice, decision making, attitudes; everything a person does, says or thinks.

The short sayings in the book reveal the views of Israelite teachers about how people should behave in various situations. Proverbs underlines the need for such qualities as humility, patience, concern for the poor, hard work, loyalty to friends and respect within the family.

The book begins with a section in praise of wisdom (chapters 1–9). The rest of the book contains six collections of sayings (10:1–31:9) and a poem on the ideal wife (31:10–31).

PSALMS

The Book of Psalms is a collection of hymns, prayers and poems. They were composed over a long period by different writers. They were read, sung and chanted by the people of Israel in their worship. It is difficult to give an accurate date to particular psalms, but they were collected from the time of David — or earlier — through to the time after the exile.

The Psalms include poems of contrasting types. There are prayers for help, for God to rescue and protect; songs of praise and worship to God; calls for forgiveness; outpoured thanks for God's goodness. There are also requests that God will punish enemies. Some psalms are concerned with the feelings of individuals; others deal with national needs. A frequent theme is the greatness of God in creation, and his loving care for the nation of Israel.

The Psalms express every type of human emotion and experience. This has helped make them favourite reading all down the ages. Above all they express a deep faith in the living God.

The Psalms often use picture language, like poetry from many other countries. A characteristic feature of the poetry of the Bible is the way in which the thought expressed in one line is echoed in the following line ("parellelism"). There are many examples of this in the Psalms.

The Book of Psalms is made up of five separate sections: Psalms 1–41; Psalms 42–72; Psalms 73–89; Psalms 90–106; Psalms 107–150.

PTOLEMAIS

The Greek name of an ancient city on the coast of northern Israel; Old Testament Acco. Paul sailed here from Tyre on his last visit to Jerusalem, and spent a day with the Christians here. The city is now

again known by its early name Akko (Acre), but has lost much of its importance since the growth of modern Haifa near-by.
Judges 1:31; Acts 21:7

PUL

See *Tiglath-pileser*.

PURIM

See *Feasts and Festivals*.

PUT

An African country, probably part of Libya (as in some modern Bible versions).
Genesis 10:6; Jeremiah 46:9; Ezekiel 27:10, etc.

PUTEOLI

The port near Naples in Italy where Paul landed on his way to Rome as a prisoner. The town is now called Pozzuoli.
Acts 28:13

QUAIL

Quails provided the Israelites with meat as they journeyed from Egypt at the time of the exodus. Twice a year vast numbers of quails fly across this region, migrating north in summer, south in winter. Exhausted by the long flight, they fly low above the ground and are easily caught.
Exodus 16:13; Numbers 11:31–35

Quails.

QUIRINIUS (CYRENIUS)

Roman governor of Syria at the time of the census which brought Mary and Joseph to Bethlehem.
Luke 2:2

RAAMSES/RAMESES

Egyptian city near the coast on the east side of the Nile Delta. Pharaoh Ramesses II had a palace here. Earlier this was the Hyksos pharaohs' northern capital, Avaris. Exodus records that the Israelites built the cities of Pithom and Raamses as supply centres for the king. It was from Raamses that they set out on their escape from Egypt.
Exodus 1:11

RABBAH

The capital city of the Ammonites (see *Ammon*), sometimes also called Rabbath-Ammon. The Israelites defeated Og, king of Bashan, whose "iron bed" (or coffin) was preserved in Rabbah. This territory east of the Jordan was given to the tribe of Gad. But it was still occupied by the Ammonites until David's general Joab captured Rabbah. When David fled from his rebellious son Absalom he received help from Rabbah. After Solomon's death Ammon seems to have become independent again, and to have been once more a cruel enemy. The prophets denounce the wickedness of Rabbah and prophesy its destruction.

The city later took the Greek name Philadelphia, and became one of the ten cities of the Decapolis (see *Decapolis*). The name of the ancient people, the

Ammonites, is preserved in the modern name, Amman. It is now the capital of Jordan.
Deuteronomy 3:11; Joshua 13:25; 2 Samuel 11:1; 12:26–31; 17:27; 1 Chronicles 20:1–3; Jeremiah 49:2; Ezekiel 21:20; 25:5; Amos :14

RABSARIS, RABSHAKEH, TARTAN
Titles given to Assyrian officials sent by King Sennacherib to bully King Hezekiah and his subjects into surrendering when Jerusalem was besieged.
2 Kings 18–19; Isaiah 36–37

RACHEL
Beautiful daughter of Laban. Jacob worked seven years without pay for Laban because of his love for Rachel: then a further seven, after Laban tricked him into marrying Leah first. For many years Rachel was childless: then Joseph was born. When Jacob left for home, Rachel secretly stole her father's household gods. In Canaan Rachel died giving birth to a second son, Benjamin.
Genesis 29–30; 35:18–20

RAHAB
A prostitute who lived in a house on the wall of Jericho. She hid Joshua's two spies because she believed God would give Canaan to the Israelites. In return the spies promised to save Rahab and her family when they captured Jericho. Rahab's name is given as the mother of Boaz in Matthew's list of Jesus' ancestors.
Joshua 2; 6; Matthew 1:5; James 2:25

RAMAH

A Hebrew name meaning "height", and used of several towns on hills. Two of these are important in the Old Testament story.

One was at er-Râm, 5 miles/8 km north of Jerusalem. Near here the prophetess Deborah lived. This Ramah was later close to the border between Judah and Israel. It was captured and fortified by Baasha, king of Israel, and recaptured by Asa of Judah. Isaiah pictures the Assyrians approaching Jerusalem by way of Ramah. Later, when Jerusalem actually fell to the Babylonians, Jeremiah was set free at Ramah. The place was resettled after the exile in Babylon. Rachel's tomb was said to have been near Ramah, and Jeremiah spoke of her weeping for her children. Matthew refers to this prophecy about Ramah in his account of what happened after Jesus' birth.
Judges 4:5; 19:13; 1 Kings 15:17, 22; 2 Chronicles 16:1, 6; Jeremiah 31:15; 40:1; Isaiah 10:29; Ezra 2:26; Nehemiah 11:33; Matthew 2:18

The second Ramah was about 12 miles/19km further north-west. It was probably the birth-place and home of the prophet Samuel, and may have been the same as New Testament Arimathea. It was also called Ramathaim-Zophim.
1 Samuel 1:1; 2:11, etc.

RAMOTH-GILEAD

A city of refuge east of the Jordan which changed hands several times in the wars between Israel and Syria. It may be the same as Mizpah in Gilead, and so the home of Jephthah at the time of the Judges.

One of Solomon's twelve district governors was stationed at Ramoth. King Ahab of Israel was killed in battle here. And Jehu was anointed king.
Joshua 20:8; Judges 11; 1 Kings 4:13; 22; 2 Kings 9:1–10

RAVEN

The name probably includes crows and rooks as well as ravens. All are large, black, flesh-eating birds. After the flood, Noah sent out a raven to see if the land was dry. Ravens are also said to have fed Elijah in a time of famine.
Genesis 8:7; 1 Kings 17:4

Raven.

REBEKAH

The wife of Isaac and mother of Esau and Jacob. Rebekah grew up in Harran, the city where Abraham lived on his way to Canaan. Her father was Abraham's nephew. When Abraham decided it was time for Isaac to marry he sent Eliezer, his chief steward, back to Harran to find a suitable wife. The first person who came to the well where he was resting his camels was Rebekah. With her family's blessing Rebekah set off for Canaan. Isaac loved her on sight. For twenty years Isaac and Rebekah prayed for a son. Then twin boys — Esau and Jacob — were born. Home-loving Jacob was Rebekah's favourite;

Isaac preferred Esau. When Isaac was old and nearly blind Rebekah helped Jacob to trick his father into giving him the blessing which belonged to Esau, the elder twin. To save him from Isaac's anger, Rebekah sent Jacob to her brother Laban in Harran.
Genesis 24; 25:19–26:16; 27

RECONCILIATION

To "reconcile" two people is to bring them together when they have been enemies. The story of man in the Bible begins with the break in relationships between him and God. It is followed immediately by man's hostility to his fellow man (Cain murders Abel). It is only when the relationship with God is restored that relations between people can be truly healed. This is the effect of the "reconciliation" which God offers to all.

So it is not surprising that people are often described in the Bible as enemies of God. They are opposed to all that God is and all that he stands for. Mankind is cut off because of sin. It is impossible to reconcile ourselves to God. But, as Paul explained, "God was making all mankind his friends through Christ."

This was done in the life, death and resurrection of Jesus himself. It is possible now for people to be friends, in fact children of God, rather than enemies. Sin, the reason for the original estrangement, has been dealt with by Jesus. Yet we are not automatically reconciled to God. It is a gift he offers and which we must accept. But it is a gift that is available for all, and so Christians are expected to explain the "way of reconciliation" to others.

Reconciliation not only brings peace with God but also peace between one man, or woman, and another. Those who once were enemies find themselves members of the same family when they are reconciled to God. The things that divided them are unimportant compared to the relationship with God which now unites them. This is the solution the New Testament offers to the most bitter racial conflict of Bible times — the split between Jews and non-Jews.

See also *Atonement, Cross, Peace.*

Genesis 3; Romans 5:10–11; 11:15; 2 Corinthians 5:18–20; Ephesians 2:11–18; Colossians 1:19–22

RED SEA

The meaning of the Hebrew word translated Red Sea is "sea of reeds". In the story of the exodus it refers to the area of lakes and marshes between the head of the Gulf of Suez and the Mediterranean Sea (the Suez Canal area). It is also used for the Gulf of Suez, the Gulf of Aqaba (the northern arms of the Red Sea proper) as some modern Bible versions make plain.

Exodus 13, etc.; Numbers 33:10; Deuteronomy 1:40

REDEMPTION

To "redeem" something is to buy it back. Jesus said that he came to "give his life to redeem many people".

The picture is that of a slave being "ransomed". Man is said to be a "slave to sin". Even if we want to give up sinning we cannot do so. But by his life, death and resurrection Jesus paid the price that would set us free.

Christians are therefore "the redeemed", just as the Israelites who had been brought out of slavery in Egypt were "the redeemed" in the Old Testament. They now belong to God. Paul urges his readers to consider the price that was paid for their redemption and give themselves wholeheartedly in the service of God. A redeemed person is also a free person, so Paul urges his readers not to fall back into the old ways but to allow God to rid them of the marks left by their former slavery to sin. But even the Christian will not experience full freedom immediately. That must wait until the end of the age, when Jesus returns and his people will know the perfect freedom of living in the presence of God himself.

See *Cross, Freedom, Sons of God.*
Mark 10:45; John 8:34; 1 Peter 1:18–19; Exodus 13:11–16; 1 Corinthians 6:20; Romans 6:12–14; 8:19–23

REGENERATION
See *New birth.*

REHOBOAM
Son of King Solomon. Rehoboam became king after his father's death but was so unwise a leader that the people rebelled. As the prophet Ahijah had predicted, the ten northern tribes made Jeroboam their king. Only Judah and Benjamin stayed loyal to Rehoboam. From this time on, the northern kingdom was known as Israel, and the southern kingdom Judah. Rehoboam was defeated by Egypt and for

much of his reign was at war with Jeroboam.
1 Kings 11:43–14:31; 2 Chronicles 9:31–12:16

RELIGION OF ISRAEL

Abraham The starting-point of Israel's religion is
the day when God spoke to Abraham, telling him to
leave his land and his family home and go to a new
country. On that day God promised to make Abraham the founder of a great nation. Abraham took
God at his word. "He put his trust in the Lord, and
because of this the Lord was pleased with him and
accepted him."

So the very first and most basic belief of the
Jewish and Christian religions is the certainty that
God is a real person, and that human beings —
individually or as a group — can know him. Abraham, we are told, did as God said. He moved to
Canaan, and in various places where he set up camp
he built an altar and worshipped God.

Abraham's faith in God was at times shaky. But he
knew that God had committed himself to him and to
his family, that was to grow into the nation of Israel.
Genesis 15:6

Jacob The history of Israel as a nation begins with
Abraham's grandson Jacob (renamed Israel) and his
twelve sons, from whom the twelve tribes were
descended. "I am the Lord, the God of Abraham
and Isaac," God said to Jacob. "I will give to you
and to your descendants this land . . . I will be with
you and protect you wherever you go, and I will
bring you back to this land. I will not leave you until
I have done all that I have promised to you." Famine
came. Jacob and his sons followed Joseph into

Egypt. Their decendants remained there for centuries. But God's promise still held. This family and nation were his people. When the Egyptians made slaves of them and they cried out for help, God heard.

Moses One day, in the desert, God spoke to Moses. "I am sending you to the king of Egypt," he said, "so that you can lead my people out of his country." Moses needed to know how he could describe God to the people, and so God explained more about the kind of God he was. He revealed his own personal name, Yahweh ("the Lord"), and also his mysterious name "I am", or "I will be who I will be". That name showed two things. God was unchanging: he was completely reliable. But also he was always alive, active, creative. It was the knowledge of this God that Moses brought to his people.

But God did not just give information about himself. He proved by what he did that he was that kind of God.

A model of the seven-branched candlestick first made for the tabernacle. This candlestick came to symbolize religious freedom.

When he rescued the Israelites from Egypt to keep the promises he had made to their ancestors, he showed his reliability. But also, when he led them through the unknown wilderness, he met their need for food and water and cared for them in spite of their rebellions. Here was the living God in action.

The Exodus and Mt Sinai In Moses' time, God made himself known as a God who acts and speaks. At the exodus from Egypt he proved that he was the defender of oppressed people and the enemy of the unjust. That in itself was a revelation of his character. At Mt Sinai he revealed himself still further. He told Moses that he was "a God who is full of compassion and pity, who is not easily angered and who shows great love and faithfulness". He also revealed his will for his people in the commandments. The Israelites could see from them what he required of them and what his own character was like. The law was to become the pattern of their life — moral, social, religious. The feasts and festivals and sacrifices were to be a constant reminder of their relationship to God. (See separate entries.)

The time of David and Solomon In this age, Israel became an independent state for the first time. The Israelites were impressed by the pomp and splendour of kingship, but they recognized that the dignity of their earthly kings was only a shadow of the greatness of the Lord, the King of kings. A new sense of the grandeur of God can be seen in the temple and its worship and in the psalms sung in the temple, hailing God as a "mighty God, a mighty king over all the gods". Along with the solemnity of the temple worship went a strong sense of joy: "The

Lord is king! Earth, be glad! Rejoice, you islands of the seas!" Gladness and reverence went hand in hand, as many of the psalms show.

In the age of David and Solomon God also made a new promise: he would make David's kingdom a lasting one; his dynasty would never end. This kept Israel loyal to the kings of David's family line even when they did not deserve it. And it developed in the end into the hope that God would send a new David, a son of David who would rule justly. So in that promise to David lay the seeds of an expectation of a Messiah.

Psalm 95:3; 97:1; 2 Samuel 7

The prophets The greatest contribution the prophets made to Israel's faith was not a new revelation from God, but a new challenge to be faithful to what God had already made known of himself, and to return to God in repentance. The prophets never tired of hammering home the fact that true religion is not just a matter of ritual, or even of belief, but also of behaviour. They mercilessly attacked the religion of their day, not because it did not follow the patterns laid down in the law-books like Leviticus, but because it was not matched by right behaviour. The prophets spoke to the conscience of Israel. They gave warning of the approaching disaster of the exile. And when God's punishment had come upon Israel, they offered hope and God's promise for a new future.

Amos 5:21–24

The exile The exile was not a gap in the history of Israel, an unhappy experience best forgotten as quickly as possible. Though it was a time of misery for many thousands of Jews, it was one of the most creative periods in Israel's history. For in it the people of Israel found again both themselves and their God. In the exile they came to recognize, in a way they had never needed to before, how much the two things were connected. Israel had no reason for existing apart from the treasure it possessed in knowing God. Unless they saw themselves as the people of God, Israel was no different from any other nation on earth. It could be wiped off the map as easily as many nations have been in the course of history. Many Israelites saw the exile only as a disaster. But those who saw in it God's discipline of his people could also see the exile as a time of purification.

The Jews who returned to the land, "whose heart God had moved, got ready to go up and rebuild the Lord's Temple in Jerusalem". They realized that they would only survive by keeping themselves separate from other nations and by insisting on obedience to the letter of God's Law. This was the only realistic attitude; and although, eventually, it led some of them into legalism, it produced a piety that is very praiseworthy.
Ezra 1:5

After the exile The Jews who returned to Israel had no king, but the high priest became their natural leader, assisted by a new class of "scribes" who were able to explain the Bible's laws. The lesson had been learnt so well that after the exile the prophets never had to rebuke the Jews for worshipping foreign gods, though they did protest at their laziness in rebuilding the temple and their reluctance to pay their tithes.

The Jewish community of returned exiles was a small one, probably less than 75,000 people. It was very aware of being different from the surrounding nations. Three things which stressed this "difference" were specially emphasized at this time: strict observance of the sabbath, of the rite of circumcision, and of the Jewish food laws.

The focus of religious life was to be not so much the temple but the synagogue, the local place of meeting and teaching, that had been developed in the years of exile.

Haggai 1; Malachi 3:7–11; Nehemiah 13:15–27; Isaiah 56:6–7; Genesis 17; Leviticus 11
(see also Daniel 1)

Between the Testaments Hopes for the future were very much alive in the time of Christ. Several centuries before, the prophets had predicted the end of Israel as a nation-state, and those prophecies had been fulfilled by the exile. Some of their prophecies seemed, though, to reach beyond the near future into a distant future when God would, as Haggai put it, "shake heaven and earth" and a totally new age would dawn.

From the second century BC on, a new type of writing called apocalyptic (meaning "revelation") was produced. The writers of these apocalyptic books were sure that the end of the world was close. God was about to step in, destroy the foreign rulers, whether Greeks or Romans, and begin a new era in history. One apocalyptic group was the community of the Dead Sea Scrolls (see *Essenes*).

The Messiah Many of the hopes for the new age

centred on the Messiah. In the Old Testament the Hebrew word "Messiah" meant simply "someone who has been anointed" and could be applied to kings, priests, or prophets. Some prophets, such as Isaiah, spoke of a future king descended from David who would "reign in righteousness" and upon whom God's Spirit would rest.

In the century and a half before the coming of Christ, many people began to look forward eagerly for such a ruler. The men of the Dead Sea sect looked for two "Messiahs", one would be a priest, the other a king. The collection of hymns from the first century BC called the *Psalms of Solomon* was one of the first writings to use the phrase "the Lord Christ (that is, Messiah)" (or, "the Lord's Christ") for this coming ruler (compare Luke 2:11).

Most often the Messiah was expected to be a warrior who would rid the Jews of hated foreign rulers. It is not surprising that Jesus, whose kingdom "does not belong to this world" was reluctant to let himself be called "Messiah". It created the wrong impression. But the disciples, who in the end understood what kind of a king he was, often used this title for him: "Jesus the Christ".

Isaiah 9:1–7; 11:1–9; John 18:36; Mark 8:29–30; Luke 22:67

Resurrection Another hope had also developed: for personal resurrection. In Old Testament times the Israelites generally believed that after death good and bad people alike entered the land of *Sheol*. This was a kind of underworld existence which was only a shadow of real life, and from which no one could return. Occasionally the prophets expressed hope for the resurrection of the nation — as in Ezekiel's vision of skeletons which became men again. But the nearest the Old Testament comes to a hope of resurrection of individuals is in Daniel 12:2, "many of those who have already died will live again".

But by the time of Jesus, most Jews (except the *Sadducees*) probably believed in a resurrection for everyone. The righteous would "rise again into life eternal" (*Psalms of Solomon* 3:16) in the "garden of life" (1 *Enoch* 61:12), or "Abraham's bosom". The wicked would be thrown into Gehenna, the underworld equivalent of the Valley of Hinnom, the rubbish dump of Jerusalem, where fires always burnt.
Job 7:9–10; Ezekiel 37; Daniel 12:2; Luke 16:22
Belief in angels and demons Israelites had always pictured God as a king surrounded by his courtiers, the angels. God's decisions were made in his councilroom, and the prophets thought of themselves as listening in. Not much attention was paid to "bad" angels. But when they are mentioned, they are clearly under God's control.

In the time between the Old and New Testaments there was great debate about the names and duties of the angels and demons.

The evil angels were sometimes identified with the "sons of God" or "supernatural beings" mentioned in Genesis 6:1–4. They and their assistants, the demons or unclean spirits, were held responsible for evil in the world. In the Old Testament Satan was "the tester", trying to find grounds to accuse man before God. But now he was regarded as a demon prince opposed to God. He was also called Belial and Beelzebub.

Job 1–2; Jeremiah 23:18, 21–22; 1 Samuel 16:14; Daniel 10:13; 8:16; Matthew 12:24; 1 Peter 5:8

Other developments   As well as these changes in belief, there were two other important developments in the last centuries before Christ. It was a time when the Law was studied, and extended, as never before (see *Pharisees*). And during this time various religious and political groups sprang up. We meet some of them — Pharisees, Sadducees, scribes — in the New Testament. But even those not named had an effect on the Jewish religious "climate" of New Testament times.

See also *Feasts and Festivals*, *Law*, *Priests and Levites*, *Sacrifices*, *Synagogue*, *Tabernacle*, *Temple*, *Worship*.

REPENTANCE

"Repent sincerely and return to me", God said through Joel, "with fasting and weeping and mourning. Let your broken heart show your sorrow; tearing your clothes is not enough."

Jesus called for the same inward change of heart. Repentance means more than saying sorry, or even being sorry, for sin. It involves a decision to leave it behind. Jesus' parable of the Pharisee and the tax collector shows the importance he placed on an inward change of heart.

Jesus' message links repentance and faith. "Turn away from your sins and believe the Good News." Repentance is not something which comes naturally to people. It is the gift of God. But when men and women meet Jesus for themselves, they repent. There is no other way into the kingdom of God. God "commands all (people) everywhere to turn away from their evil ways".

See also *Forgiveness*.

Joel 2:12–13; Luke 18:9–14; Mark 1:15; Acts 11:18; Luke 19:1–10 (and other examples); Acts 17:30

RESURRECTION

The claim that Jesus rose from the dead is the key fact of the Christian faith. "If Christ has not been raised, then your faith is a delusion and you are still lost in your sins," wrote Paul. There was no doubt, however, in the apostles' minds that Jesus had risen from the dead, as he had said he would. They had seen him on various occasions, and this to them was evidence enough. Paul lists the people who had seen Jesus alive. The disciples were transformed overnight, from being a weak and cowardly bunch into being a fearless group of people who preached and performed miracles in the power of their risen Lord. The grave was empty, and the Jewish authorities could not produce a body to disprove the claim that Jesus was alive.

Paul teaches that Jesus' followers will share in his resurrection. When a person becomes a Christian he already experiences the life of the risen Jesus working in his own life. And in the future, Christians can look forward with confident expectation to their own resurrection at the end of the age. Believers must face physical death, like everyone else, but they are assured of a future with Christ in a new spiritual existence. Christianity does not look for the immortality of a soul (a Greek idea), but the resurrection of the complete person in a new and more wonderful body.

See also *Heaven*.

Matthew 28; Mark 16; Luke 24; John 20; 1 Corinthians 15; Acts 1:3; 4:10; Romans 1:4; 6:4–13

REUBEN
Eldest son of Jacob and Leah. He tried to save Joseph's life when his brothers plotted to kill him. Years later he offered his own two sons as hostages to guarantee Benjamin's safety. Reuben was founder of the tribe named after him.

Genesis 29:32; 37:21–22; 42; 49:3

Also land belonging to the tribe of Reuben, east of the Dead Sea.

Joshua 13:15–23

REUEL
Another name for Jethro.

REVELATION
Human beings can never know God unless God chooses to "reveal" himself. In his purity and majesty, he "lives in the light that no one can approach". We can know something of God's character through the world he has created (even *this* is revelation) and our own experience of it. But otherwise we can know nothing unless he shows it to us. Moses' encounter with God in the burning bush is a clear example of God revealing to a person what he could never have found out for himself.

In the history of Israel God most often revealed

himself through what he did, particularly in delivering his people from slavery in Egypt. But time and again they failed to see God at work in their history. So God sent prophets through whom he spoke directly to his people to explain to them what he was doing.

"In the past God spoke to our ancestors many times and in many ways through the prophets, but in these last days he has spoken to us through his Son," wrote the author of the New Testament letter to the Hebrews. Jesus Christ himself is the final and complete revelation of God. He is God shown to us in a form we can understand, living as a person on earth.

The Bible itself is "revelation". It is the written record of what God did and said in history and through Christ — of his message to his people, from the call of Abraham to the time of the New Testament apostles. Its books were written by people under the guidance of God himself.
Ecclesiastes 5:2; Isaiah 58:8–9; 1 Timothy 6:16; Exodus 3; 6:7; Isaiah 1:3; Amos 3:7; Hebrews 1:1–2; John 1:14; 2 Peter 1:21; 2 Timothy 3:16; John 14:26; 16:13

REVELATION, BOOK OF

Revelation was written to Christians who were being persecuted for their faith. Its author is named as John, and it may have been written about AD 90–95, when the Emperor Domitian was persecuting Christians and John was an exile on the island of Patmos (off the west coast of modern Turkey).

The writer wanted to encourage his readers in their time of suffering. He wrote down a series of visions or "revelations" in vivid picture-language (a special style of writing known as "apocalyptic" and found in the Old Testament Book of Daniel). Christian readers would understand their meaning, but not outsiders.

The great message of the book is that God is in control. Jesus is the master of history. At the end of time God will totally defeat all his enemies, through Christ. His faithful people will be rewarded in a new heaven and a new earth.

Chapters 1–3: the book opens with a vision of Christ, and a series of letters with special messages for the seven churches of Asia Minor.

In chapter 4 the scene changes to heaven and a great vision of God.

John begins to see the things that "must happen after this" (4:1). He sees a scroll with seven seals which the Lamb breaks open; a vision of seven angels with seven trumpets; a woman, the dragon and the two beasts; the seven bowls of God's anger; the destruction of "Babylon"; the wedding-feast of the Lamb; and the final defeat of the Devil, followed by the great judgement (chapters 4–20).

The book closes with a dazzling picture of the new heaven, the new earth, the new Jerusalem (chapters 21–22), where God is with his people, and sin, death and suffering are gone for ever.

REZIN

The last king of Syria. Rezin made an alliance with King Pekah of Israel. When Rezin and Pekah attacked Judah, King Ahaz appealed to the Assyrian King Tiglath-pileser III for help. Tiglath-pileser

captured Damascus, the capital of Syria, and killed Rezin.
2 Kings 15:37–16:9; Isaiah 7:1ff.

RHEGIUM

A port on the toe of Italy, on the Strait of Messina opposite Sicily; the modern city of Reggio di Calabria. Paul's ship called here on his voyage to Rome.
Acts 28:13

RIBLAH

A town in Syria on the River Orontes. King Jehoahaz of Judah was taken prisoner at Riblah by Pharaoh Neco of Egypt. Later, King Nebuchadnezzar of Babylon had his headquarters here. And King Zedekiah, the last king of Judah, was taken to him at Riblah for sentence following rebellion.
2 Kings 23:33; 25:6–7

ROADS

There were few paved roads until the Romans began to build a system of fine roads, connecting the provinces of the Empire to Rome, but not with each other. This is why "all roads led to Rome".

Before the Romans, conquest, rather than trade, was the usual incentive for road-building. The Romans built roads to keep their Empire together, to make it possible to move troops, goods and send Imperial despatches long distances at speed. A courier on the Roman roads could cover about 75 miles/120 km a day.

Roman roads were superbly constructed, and many sections remain intact, even today. They were paved with flat stones or with specially-cut blocks of stone on top of two or three layers of foundation material. The road-builders overcame every obstacle. They built bridges over rivers, causeways through marshes, and tunnelled through rock. Altogether the Romans built more than 50,000 miles/ 80,000 km of roads.

Even so, the roads only went where the Romans wanted them to go. There were still many journeys that had to be made on the old "roads", unsurfaced and worn by travellers over the centuries.

In towns the streets were not very clean, so the Romans provided pedestrians with raised pavements and stepping-stones to allow them to avoid the dirt and mud.

ROCK HYRAX

(In the Authorized Version, "coney", Revised Standard Version, "badger".) A small, shy animal about the size of a rabbit, with neat ears and no tail. The hyrax lives in colonies in rocky places.
Proverbs 30:26

ROMANS

Paul wrote his letter to Christians in Rome in about AD 57, after his three major missionary journeys. He had not yet been to Rome, but intended to go there. He was writing to prepare the Christian group, some of whom he knew (see chapter 16), for his visit.

The letter sets out at length Paul's understanding of the Christian message. It was written after his letters to the Thessalonians, Galatians and Corinthians. It might be called Paul's manifesto. It gives us his fullest and most clearly reasoned statement of basic Christian beliefs.

Paul opens the letter by greeting the Christians in Rome. He explains the basis of his letter: "the gospel reveals how God puts people right with himself: it is through faith from beginning to end" (1:17).

Paul then shows how all people need God's remedy for sin, both Jews and non-Jews. We can be put right with God through faith in Jesus Christ (chapters 3–4).

Paul describes the free pardon and new life God gives us through Christ. He explains the relevance of God's laws and the work of God's Spirit in the life of every Christian (chapters 5–8).

In chapters 9–11 Paul tries to see what place Israel now has in the plan of God. He believes that the Jews will not always reject Jesus.

Paul continues (chapters 12–15) with some plain words about how Christians should behave. He talks about Christians and the government. He talks about our duties to one another, and how to live in a non-Christian world. He also deals with some tricky questions of conscience.

The letter ends, characteristically, with personal messages to friends and praise to God (chapter 16).

ROME

The beginnings of the city of Rome are lost in legend. The story was that it had been named after its founder, Romulus, whose ancestors had escaped from the Greek destruction of Troy. The date was said to be 753 BC. That was the year from which the later Romans counted the beginning of their history.

Early history   For centuries Rome was a small and struggling city-state. But it was well placed at a crossing of the River Tiber in the centre of Italy. At first it had kings, and some of them probably belonged to a mysterious and almost forgotten nation, the Etruscans. These kings were at last driven out, and Rome became a "Republic", headed by two "consuls" elected for a year and a council called the "Senate". After times of strife, poverty and war, Rome slowly won ground, and by 275 BC controlled all Italy.

Rome grew partly by war, but also by a policy of alliances in which Roman citizenship and other rights were freely granted to allies. Right from the start the Romans were good organizers. They built fine roads and unified the whole of Italy. They were very different in character from the Greeks. They were not very original. But they were practical men, loyal to the state, hard-working and disciplined.

Wars   It was not long before Rome faced a new

The forum, the political and business centre of ancient Rome.

enemy, Carthage. Carthage was on the coast of modern Tunisia, and controlled the sea-routes and trade of the western Mediterranean. The struggle was to last for over a century. The Carthaginians had a leader of genius, Hannibal. He is best remembered for his bold crossing of the Alps with elephants. He invaded Italy and defeated Rome on her own soil, but he got no support and finally had to retreat. The Romans destroyed Carthage in 146 BC.

By this time Rome had also been drawn into the affairs of the East, where Hannibal had joined Rome's enemies. The Romans defeated Antiochus III of Syria and gave his lands in Asia Minor to their ally Eumenes II of Pergamum. They destroyed Corinth in 146, and began direct rule over Greece. In 133 the last king of Pergamum left his lands to the Romans. Out of them they made the province of "Asia".

World power So Rome became a world power. But there were great changes. The Greeks had a remarkable influence on their conquerors. Romans studied Greek language and thought and copied Greek styles of art and writing. But there were also other changes, for the worse. Asia, in particular, was very rich, and Roman officials began to use their new position to enrich themselves by robbing their subjects. The Senate in Rome was not able to control them. And this was only part of a larger problem. It was not possible to govern a world empire in the same way as a small city. Large armies and regular organization were needed. Ambitious men began to struggle for power. As a result, there were several civil wars in the first century BC.

In 63 BC the Roman general, Pompey, occupied Jerusalem. From that time Rome had a controlling influence on Palestine. Later, Pompey became the Republican champion, against the ambitious Julius Caesar. But Caesar defeated him and took the title "dictator", a position which gave him special emergency powers. Caesar was a brilliantly able and vigorous ruler. But he was murdered in 44 by the Republicans Brutus and Cassius. Caesar's friend Antony and his heir Octavian defeated the Republicans in 42 at Philippi in Macedonia, a city well known in the New Testament. Then the two victors quarrelled. Octavian defeated Antony and his ally Cleopatra, queen of Egypt.

The Empire and the emperors   People were weary of so many years of war. Octavian gave them peace. In 27 BC he received the title "Augustus". He claimed to have brought back the Republic and was careful to disguise his real power. He kept control of the army and became, in fact, the first ruler of what we call the "Empire", though he never used the word. He united the whole Mediterranean world under one peaceful government. It became possible to travel safely by land or sea to every part. There was great thankfulness everywhere for Augustus. He died in AD 14.

Jesus was born in the time of Augustus (Luke 2:1). His teaching, death and resurrection took place in the reign of the next emperor, Tiberius (AD 14–37). Paul travelled during the reigns of Claudius (AD 41–54) and Nero (AD 54–68), the "Caesar" to whom he appealed at his trial (Acts 25:11).

The Romans and the Jews   Palestine was occupied

by the Romans in the time of Jesus. They tried at first to rule there through kings of the Herod family. When this failed in Judea, they sent a Roman governor called a "procurator". Although the first emperors were usually careful to respect the feelings of their subjects, they found it difficult to cope with the religion and nationalism of the Jews. Pontius Pilate (AD 26–36) and his successors angered them by their harsh misrule, and in AD 66 there was a desperate rebellion against Rome. When Nero died, rival generals fought for power in Rome. Vespasian, commander of the Syrian frontier army, finally won and became emperor (AD 69–79). It was his son Titus who ended the Jewish rebellion. He destroyed Jerusalem and its temple in AD 70.

Rome had often favoured and protected the Jews in the past. Paul was both a Jew and a Roman citizen. He naturally looked to Rome for justice and protection. Rome had provided the peace and freedom to travel and spread the gospel. When Paul was treated unjustly he used his right as a Roman to appeal to the Emperor. He may not then have known what an evil man Nero was becoming.

Life in Rome Rome was now the centre of the world, a city of well over a million people. We have vivid pictures of its life: the tall buildings and narrow, congested streets where people lived in fear of fire, and the constant noise of carts kept them awake all night. The emperors and nobles lived in great luxury, but also in fear. There were free men and slaves of many races thronging the streets. The emperors tried to keep the peace by organizing corn from Egypt and bloodthirsty public shows where men or beasts fought to the death. When a great fire broke out in Rome in AD 64, Nero blamed the Christians, and tortured many of them to death.

The good and the bad For all its achievements there was clearly a bad side to Roman civilization. We can understand how Rome was hated in the occupied country of Palestine. Governors like Pilate, Felix and Festus had no interest in the matters of faith which Jews and Christians debated. Yet Jesus commended a Roman's faith (Luke 7:1ff.) and Peter found another Roman officer, Cornelius, to be a man who sincerely sought God (Acts 10:11).

After the fall of Jerusalem Christians faced new problems. The Emperor Domitian (81–96) insisted on being worshipped as a god. A faithful Christian could not obey. Rome became an enemy. The Book of Revelation was written when Christians needed strength to meet Roman persecution. Rome on its seven hills (Revelation 17:9) was pictured as a luxury loving prostitute, like ancient Babylon.

See also *Greek and Roman Religion*.

"ROSE"

The word often translated "rose" in the Bible is not the rose as we know it: but probably the narcissus in Isaiah 35:1, and a mountain tulip in the Song of Solomon 2:1.

Two plants may be called "rose" in the Bible: a mountain tulip and narcissus.

RUTH

The peaceful story of Ruth contrasts with the violent times of the Book of Judges, in which it is set.

Ruth, a Moabite woman, married an Israelite. When he died, Ruth showed unexpected loyalty to her Israelite mother-in-law, and trust in the God of Israel. Finally she found a new husband among the relatives of her dead husband. By this marriage she became the great-grandmother of King David, and an ancestor of Jesus himself.

Although religion generally was weak in these times, the Book of Ruth shows the faith of an ordinary person — a foreigner who turned to the God of Israel.

SABBATH
See *Feasts and Festivals*.

SACRIFICES
The practice of animal sacrifice goes back to very early times. Genesis 4 tells how Abel killed one of his lambs and gave the best parts as an offering to God. Noah made a sacrifice of animals and birds after his escape from the flood. The agreement between God and Abraham was sealed with a sacrifice.

The details of the sacrifices are described in the Book of Leviticus. There we learn certain basic facts about their meaning.

1. Sacrifice is always made to God himself. So only the best is good enough. Sacrifice was also a way of setting apart for God something belonging to a man.

2. Sacrifice is a way of approach given by God. He gave the rules for sacrifice. It is not simply man's own attempt to earn favour with God, it is God's way for men to make their peace with him. All the same, a person must freely wish to make use of the ritual which God has laid down.

3. Sacrifices are for everyone. In most religions, rituals like these are the secret of the priests. The fact that they alone know how to approach the god helps them to keep their special position in the

community. But in Israel, the laws of sacrifice (that is, the Book of Leviticus) are part of the Scriptures that belong to everyone. And in fact in Israel most sacrifices were actually carried out by the worshipper, and not by the priest.

4. There are limits to the effectiveness of sacrifice. In most cases, the sacrifices could only compensate for accidental or "unwitting" sins. For deliberate disobedience sacrifice could only express repentance. If a sinner is to be pardoned, he must seek pardon directly from God. The New Testament also makes it clear that the blood of bulls and goats could not take away sin.

5. Sacrifice is a substitution. Sometimes, the death of the sacrificed animal was seen as taking the place of the person who brought the sacrifice. Sin that deserved death could not be atoned for by sacrifice, but a person who had repented of his sin and had been forgiven by God, would often bring a sacrifice as a sign of his sorrow for sin. In the New Testament, the death of Jesus is understood as a sacrifice which *did* take the place of the sinner.

Genesis 4; 8:20; 15; Leviticus 1–7; 16–17; 4:2; 13, 22, 27; Psalm 51:16–17; Hebrews 10:4; 9:11–12; 10:12

There were several types of sacrifice:

Burnt-offering The whole animal, except for the skin, which went to the priests, was sacrificed to God. The worshipper placed his hands on the animal to show that it was a sacrifice for his own shortcomings. The animal had to be in perfect condition (only the best is good enough for God). The blood of the animal was sprinkled on the altar as a further sign that the life of the animal given in death had been dedicated to God.

Leviticus 1

Grain-offering This was an offering of flour, baked cakes, or raw grain, together with oil and frankincense. It was a good-will offering to God. Part of it — a "memorial portion" — was burnt on the altar. So it was a way of asking God to "remember" the worshipper for good. It was also a contribution to the upkeep of the priests. Again, it was a sacrifice of the best the worshipper could give.

Leviticus 2

Peace (fellowship)-offering The ritual was similar to that for the burnt-offering, except that here only the fat — which the Israelites considered the best portion — was burnt on the altar, and the meat was shared by the worshipper and his family. Since God also shared in the sacrifice, it was thought of as a friendship meal with God too.

Leviticus 3

Sin-offerings These sacrifices were offered when a person had sinned against someone else or against God. This sin "defiled" (contaminated) the holy place of tabernacle or temple, and so it needed to be cleansed. The blood of the sacrifice was sprinkled as a sign that the defilement had been removed through the death that had taken place. Some of the sacrifice was taken as food for the priest. When the worshipper saw the priest eat the meat without being harmed he knew that God had accepted his act of repentance.

Leviticus 4; 5; 7

The ritual of sacrifice on the Day of Atonement

(Leviticus 16) is somewhat different. Here, as well as other sacrifices, two goats were used. One was killed as in the usual sin-offering, but the other was sent into the wilderness as a symbol that the sins were being removed. (See *Atonement*.)

SADDUCEES
This group was smaller than the Pharisees, but more influential. Most Sadducees were members of the families of priests. They supported the Hasmonean high-priest kings and later the Roman rulers. We have little reliable information about the Sadducees, since most of it comes from their opponents. But we do know that they did not accept the Pharisees' extensions of the Law (the oral law, as distinct from the Old Testament written law). That is why they could not believe in resurrection, for it is not clearly taught in the Old Testament Law (Genesis to Deuteronomy).
Matthew 16:1–12; Mark 12:18–27; Acts 4:1–2; 5:17–19; 23:6–10

SAINT
See *Holiness*.

SALAMIS
A commercial centre on the east coast of Cyprus. A number of Jews lived here, and when Paul visited the town he preached in synagogues.
Acts 13:5

SALEM
See *Jerusalem*.

SALOME

One of the women who looked after Jesus and his disciples while they were in Galilee. Salome was present at the crucifixion. On the resurrection morning she was one of the women who took spices to the tomb to embalm the body. Many believe that Salome was the wife of Zebedee and mother of James and John.
(Matthew 27:56) Mark 15:40; 16:1

SALT SEA

The Old Testament name for the Dead Sea, given because the water contains very heavy deposits of salt.
See *Arabah*.

SALVATION

God's act of rescue. People are helpless to escape from the situation in which sin has ensnared them. Only God can bring deliverance.

There is a past, present and future tense in the use of "salvation" in the New Testament. God sent Jesus into the world to "save his people from their sins". Sin was dealt with by Jesus in his death and resurrection. By faith in him we can now be "saved". This free gift is offered to all, no matter what their religious, racial or social background. "Everyone who calls out to the Lord for help will be saved." Christians are already "saved", because they already have forgiveness and new life. But they will not experience the full meaning of salvation until the end of the age and the return of Jesus Christ. In the meantime they are "being saved".

In the Old Testament, salvation is more than just spiritual deliverance. The major act of salvation was when God freed the Israelites from actual slavery to the Egyptians. The New Testament also teaches that God's salvation affects far more than a person's "spiritual" life. It concerns the whole person. Nearly a third of the references to salvation in the New Testament are concerned with being set free from specific ills such as imprisonment, disease and demon possession. When a person becomes a Christian, Christ's salvation affects the whole of life, physical as well as spiritual. But no part of him will be completely whole until he is finally "saved" at the return of Christ.

See also *Atonement, Freedom, Redemption.*
Matthew 1:21; Ephesians 2:8–9; Romans 10:13; 13:11; 1 Corinthians 1:18; Philippians 2:12; Matthew 9:21–22; Luke 8:36 (where "saved" is translated "cured")

SAMARIA
Capital of the northern kingdom of Israel. The city was on the main north/south trade-route through Israel and was built on top of a hill so that it could easily be defended. The work of building the city was started about 875 BC by King Omri. It was continued by his son Ahab, who added a new palace. So much carved ivory was used to decorate the palace that it became known as the "ivory house". Over 500 pieces of ivory, some covered with gold leaf, have been discovered by archaeologists in the ruins of the palace.

From the start, the people of Samaria followed

One of the beautiful ivory carvings which once adorned King Ahab's palace at Samaria.

pagan religions. Several Old Testament prophets condemned their idol-worship and warned that the city would be destroyed.

The Syrians attacked and besieged Samaria many times, but it was the Assyrians who finally captured the city in 722/1 BC. The people were exiled to Syria, Assyria and Babylonia. They were replaced by colonists from different parts of the Assyrian Empire. When Samaria fell, the kingdom of Israel ceased to exist. The whole area, not just the city, became known as Samaria.

By New Testament times the city of Samaria had been rebuilt by Herod the Great and renamed Sebaste (Greek for Augustus). A few half-caste Jews still remained in Samaria and claimed to worship God there, but these "Samaritans" were despised and hated by the Jews in Judea. Jesus showed his concern for them by travelling through their land and staying with them. After Jesus' death and resurrection Philip went to Samaria to preach the gospel, and his work was followed up by Peter and John.

A small group of Samaritans still live in Nablus and Jaffa and worship on Mt Gerizim.

1 Kings 16:24, 32; Isaiah 8:4; Amos 3:8; 2 Kings 6:8–7:17; Luke 17:11; John 4:1–43; Acts 8:5–25

SAMSON

A Judge in Israel famous for his great strength. Before Samson was born, an angel told his mother he was to be specially dedicated to God as a Nazirite and destined to save Israel from the Philistines. As a sign of this his hair was never to be cut. When Samson grew up he harassed the Philistines single-handed, although he never fully freed his people. His weakness for women was his undoing. In the end he told a Philistine girl, Delilah, the secret of his strength. Samson was captured. His hair was cut. He was blinded and put in prison. As his hair grew long again his strength began to return. At a festival Samson was taken to a Philistine temple to amuse the crowd. He grasped the two pillars which supported the temple, prayed and heaved with all his might. The building crashed to the ground, and Samson died with the Philistine leaders and people. Judges 13–16

SAMUEL

The son of Elkanah and Hannah who grew up to be the last great Judge in Israel and one of the first prophets. When Samuel was born, Hannah's heartfelt prayer for a son was answered. In return she kept her promise to God and took Samuel to the shrine at Shiloh to be trained by Eli, the priest. One night Samuel received a message from God that Eli's family would be punished because of his son's wickedness. When Eli died, Samuel faced a difficult situation. Israel had been defeated by the Philistines and the people felt God no longer cared about them. Samuel told them to destroy their idols and obey God. Samuel ruled Israel all his life and under his leadership there was peace. When Samuel was old he made his sons judges and handed his work over to them. But the people were not happy and asked for a king. At first Samuel was against this, but he was guided by God to anoint Saul. After Saul had disobeyed God, Samuel anointed David as the next king. Everyone in Israel mourned when Samuel died.

1 Samuel 1–4; 7–16; 19:18ff.; 25:1

BOOKS OF SAMUEL

The two books of Samuel give a history of Israel from the last of the Judges to the final years of King David. They are named after Samuel, the last great Judge, not because he wrote them, but because he towers over the early chapters. They were originally one book in the Hebrew Bible.

Samuel anointed Israel's first two kings, Saul and David, as God's chosen rulers. The books cover roughly the period 1075–975 BC. The author/historian several times refers to the separate kingdom of Judah. This means that the books must have been compiled in their final edition after 900 BC. But they contain much material that is contemporary with the events they describe — especially the story of intrigue at the court of David in 2 Samuel 9–20, which many scholars believe to be the work of professional court secretaries who actually witnessed what they wrote about.

The books of Samuel are mostly concerned with the story of God's dealings with the nation of Israel.

1 Samuel tells how Israel changed from rule by the Judges to rule by kings.

Chapters 1–8: Samuel's years as Judge of Israel.

Chapters 9–15: the story of Saul, first king of Israel.

Chapters 16–30: the relationship between David and Saul. The book ends (chapter 31) with the death of Saul and his sons. Although the people now had a king, both he and they were seen as living under the rule and judgement of God.

2 Samuel tells the history of David's reign as king, first of Judah in the south (chapters 1–4) and then of the entire nation, including what later became the kingdom of Israel in the north. We read how King David enlarged his kingdom and became a powerful ruler. He was a man of deep faith in God, and very popular. But he was sometimes ruthless in his efforts to gain his own ends — for example in his determination to have Bathsheba, wife of one of his generals, for himself. The book contains David's famous lament over the death of his close friend, Saul's son, Jonathan.

SANBALLAT
A Samaritan governor who tried to stop Nehemiah rebuilding the walls of Jerusalem.
Nehemiah 2:10, 19; 4; 6; 13:28

SAPPHIRA
See *Ananias*.

SARAH

Abraham's wife; the mother of Isaac. Abraham married Sarah while he still lived in Ur. Because she was beautiful Abraham twice passed her off as his sister instead of his wife, to protect his own life. When it seemed she would never have any children to inherit the blessing God had promised, Sarah gave her maid Hagar to Abraham, and Ishmael was born. Abraham and Sarah were both old when an angel told Abraham that Sarah would have a son. At first she laughed at the idea, but in due course Isaac was born. He was Abraham's heir. Sarah sent Hagar and her son Ishmael away after Isaac's birth. When Sarah died Abraham bought a cave near Hebron as her burial-place.
Genesis 11–12; 16–18:15; 20–21

SARDIS

A city in the Roman province of Asia (in modern Turkey) situated at the point where two main trade-routes met. In Roman times there were thriving dyeing and woollen industries here. One of the seven letters to churches in Asia, in the Book of Revelation, was addressed to the Christians at Sardis. The church had become apathetic. They relied on the past instead of concentrating on the present — an attitude typical of the city as a whole. It had been the capital of the kingdom of Lydia and at one time ruled by Croesus. His wealth was legendary; gold was easily obtained from a river which flowed close to the city. The first gold and silver coins were minted at Sardis.
Revelation 1:11; 3:1–6

SATAN

Satan is the Hebrew name and Devil the Greek name for the being who personifies all that is evil and opposed to God. Both names mean "accuser", showing that Satan is the one who tries to tempt people to do wrong so that he can accuse them before God.

The battle between good and evil is not an equally balanced contest. God is all-powerful and eternal; Satan often appears to be in control, but his work is limited by God. He destroys and undermines by tricks and cunning, rather than power. But within the world he holds such power that he can be called its ruler.

Jesus came "to destroy what the Devil had done", and through his victory over evil in his death and resurrection Satan has been defeated. Although he is still active within the world his defeat will be total at the end of the age.

We can see clearly how Satan set himself against God's work in the life of Jesus. Jesus was tempted by the Devil in the desert. Peter was used as a tool of Satan and had to be rebuked by Jesus. The betrayal by Judas Iscariot was another part of Satan's work. Jesus had many clashes with evil spirits under Satan's control, but his many exorcisms showed that his power was far greater than that of Satan and the forces of evil.

2 Corinthians 11:14; Ephesians 6:11; John 14:30; 1 John 3:8; John 12:31; 1 Peter 5:8; Revelation 20:10; Matthew 4:1–11; 16:23; Luke 22:3; Matthew 12:22–28

SAUL

First king of Israel. Saul was the son of Kish, a man from the tribe of Benjamin. The Israelites asked their leader, the prophet Samuel, for a king, like other nations. God was their real king but he allowed Samuel to do as they asked. Samuel was guided by God to anoint Saul, the tallest and most handsome man in Israel. Saul was acclaimed as king after he had proved himself in battle.

To begin with he was humble, but he soon became proud and deliberately disobeyed God. Samuel was sent to tell Saul that God had chosen another man to be king. Saul began to suffer from fits of madness. David was known for his skill on the harp and was sent for to soothe the king with his music.

At first Saul treated David kindly, but soon grew jealous of his popularity and tried to kill him. David was forced to escape to the mountains. Saul's power as a leader failed and he was unable to overcome the Philistines. When the Philistine army was preparing to attack Israel again, Saul turned to a medium for help. In the battle which followed, Saul and Jonathan his son were both killed.
1 Samuel 8–31; 2 Samuel 1ff.

SCRIBES

The scribes were the experts in the Law and are also called lawyers or teachers (rabbis). They interpreted the Law and applied it to everyday life. Jesus had not been to one of the schools for rabbis, but his own disciples called him "teacher" (rabbi). So too did many of the professional rabbis. They were greatly impressed by his understanding of the Law. Later,

Paul came to Jerusalem as a student of Rabbi Gamaliel.
Mark 7:28–29; Luke 2:41–47; Acts 4:5–7, 18–21; 6:12–14; 22:3

SCYTHIANS
The horse-riding Scythians ("Ashkenaz") came from central Asia in the seventh century BC. Some groups of Scythians burst into the Near East. They destroyed Urartu, and joined with the Medes, in alliance with Babylon, to overthrow Assyria. In due course they provided men for the Persian army. One Scythian troop marched through Syria to raid Egypt, reaching Ashkelon about 630 BC.
Jeremiah 51:17

Bronze models of Scythian archers on their horses: from about 500 BC.

SECOND COMING OF JESUS
In his first coming to this world Jesus came quietly, lived the life of the humble servant of God and died

on the cross. But during his life he promised that he would return at the end of the world, this time with power and glory for all to see. Many people ignored Jesus when he first came, but when he returns no one will be able to ignore him, and for many it will be a time of grief because it will be the day of judgement. For those who believe, both dead and living, it will be the moment of their final salvation, when Jesus will take them to be with him for ever in a totally re-created world order.

There is no way of finding out when the great day will be. Jesus said that before he comes, the gospel will be preached to all nations. Before he comes, sin will increase and worship be offered to one who falsely claims to be God. But no one can calculate when he will come, for it will be "at an hour when you are not expecting him". The Christian must always be ready, so that he is not caught out and ashamed when Jesus returns.

Matthew 24; 26:64; Mark 13:26; John 14; Acts 1:11; 3:19–21; Philippians 3:20; Colossians 3:4; 1 Thessalonians 1:10; 4:13–5:11; 2 Thessalonians 1:5–2:12; 2 Peter 3:8–13; Revelation 19–22

SEIR
Another name for **Edom**.

SELA
Capital of Edom. The name means "rock" or "cliff" and was given to this fortress-city because it was built on a rocky plateau high up in the mountains of Edom. About 300 BC the Nabataeans took Sela and carved the city of Petra (the Greek word for rock)

out of the rocky valley at the foot of the original settlement.
2 Kings 14:7; Isaiah 16:1; 42:11

SELEUCIA (SELEUCIA PIERIA)

The port of Antioch in Syria. It was built by, and named after, the first Seleucid king. Paul and Barnabas set sail from here for Cyprus on their first missionary journey.
Acts 13:4

SENIR

Another name for Mt Hermon. It is also used to describe a nearby peak and the whole range of mountains.

SENNACHERIB

King of Assyria, 705–681 BC. He strengthened the Assyrian Empire, sending armies to put down rebel

A relief of Sennacherib praying to the god Assur.

subject nations. After Hezekiah refused to pay tax, Sennacherib attacked Jerusalem. Although he had captured several cities in Judah, Isaiah encouraged Hezekiah not to surrender. Jerusalem was saved. The Egyptian army threatened from the south and death struck the Assyrian army. Sennacherib returned to Nineveh, where he was murdered by two of his sons.
2 Kings 18–19; 2 Chronicles 32; Isaiah 36–37

SEPHARVAIM
A town as yet unidentified, captured by the Assyrians. People from here were brought to Samaria after the Jews had been sent into exile.
2 Kings 17:24, 31; 18:34

SERGIUS PAULUS
Roman governor of Cyprus. He was interested in religion and came under the influence of a magician named Elymas. (See *Elymas*.)
Acts 13:7ff.

SETH
Third son of Adam and Eve, born after Cain had murdered Abel.
Genesis 4:25ff.

SHADRACH
See *Abednego*.

SHALLUM
1. The son of Jabesh; he murdered King Zechariah and made himself king of Israel, 752 BC. Shallum

reigned for only one month. He was assassinated by Menahem.
2 Kings 15:10–15
2. A son of King Josiah, usually known as Jehoahaz. (See *Jehoahaz*.)
1 Chronicles 3:15; Jeremiah 22:11

SHALMANESER
Name of several kings of Assyria. Shalmaneser V (727–722 BC) defeated King Hoshea of Israel and made him pay tax to Assyria every year. When Hoshea rebelled, Shalmaneser besieged Samaria, capital of Israel. After three years Samaria fell and the Israelites were exiled to Assyria.
2 Kings 17

SHAMGAR
One of the Judges in Israel. Shamgar fought off the Philistines.
Judges 3:31; 5:6

SHAPHAN
Best-known of several men of this name is one of King Josiah's important officials. He helped supervise the temple repairs and reported to Josiah the finding of a scroll of God's laws.
2 Kings 22; 2 Chronicles 34

SHARON
The coastal plain of Israel. It extends from Joppa to Caesarea — about 50 miles/80 km and is about 10 miles/16 km wide. Today the plain is one of the richest agricultural areas in Israel. In Bible times few

people lived here. The land was used as pasture for sheep, but much of it was left in its natural state of thick scrub. The writer of the Song of Solomon (Songs) refers to the "rose of Sharon", one of the many beautiful wild flowers which grew on the plain.

1 Chronicles 27:29; Song of Solomon (Songs) 2:1

SHEBA

A country in south-west Arabia, now the Yemen. Sheba became a wealthy land by trading spices, gold and jewels with the Mediterranean world. In the tenth century BC a queen of Sheba travelled over 1,000 miles/1,600 km by camel caravan to visit King Solomon and test his wisdom. She possibly also wished to arrange a trade agreement. The remains of a great dam and a temple to the moon-god Ilumquh have been discovered at Marib, once the capital of Sheba.

Psalm 72:15; Isaiah 60:6; 1 Kings 10:1–10, 13

SHEBNA(H)

One of King Hezekiah's most important officials, sent to negotiate with King Sennacherib's spokesmen.

2 Kings 18–19; Isaiah 22:15–25; 36–37

SHECHEM

1. The son of King Hamor, a Hivite king. Shechem raped Dinah, Jacob's daughter.
Genesis 34

2. An ancient Canaanite town which became an important religious and political centre for the

Israelites; in the hill-country of Ephraim, near Mt Gerizim.

Abraham stopped at Shechem on his journey from Harran to Canaan. While he was here God told him, "This is the country that I am going to give to your descendants." Jacob also visited Shechem and set up camp outside the town.

When the Israelites had conquered Canaan Joshua gathered all the tribes together at Shechem. Here they renewed their promise to worship the God who had rescued them from Egypt, and to have nothing to do with foreign gods. But in the time of the Judges Canaanite worship was practised in Shechem. The inhabitants of the town gave Gideon's son Abimelech money from the temple of Baal-berith so that he could pay to have his seventy brothers killed. Abimelech made himself king of Shechem but the people soon turned against him. In revenge he destroyed the town.

After the death of King Solomon ten of the Israelite tribes rejected Solomon's son Rehoboam at Shechem. Jeroboam, the first king of the new northern kingdom, started to rebuild Shechem, and for a short time made it his capital.

Shechem survived the fall of Israel. It became the Samaritans' most important city and they built a temple here. A few Samaritans still live in Nablus, the modern town north-west of the site of Shechem. Genesis 12:6–7; 33:18–35:4; 37:12–18; Joshua 24; Judges 9; 1 Kings 12

SHEEP AND GOATS
From very early times, before there was settled

farming, nomads depended on their flocks of sheep and goats for milk, cheese, meat and clothes. Goat-skins were the standard water-bottle. Black goat-hair was woven into strong cloth for tents. Wool from the sheep was spun and woven into warm cloaks and tunics. Both sheep and goats were killed in the tabernacle and temple sacrifices. They were well suited to rough hill pasture. Shepherds often looked after mixed flocks of sheep and goats, protecting them from wild animals and leading them to fresh grazing and watering-places.
Genesis 27:9; 4:2; Exodus 26:7; Leviticus 1:10; Matthew 25:32; John 10:1–12

Much of Israel's wealth depended on sheep and goats.

SHEM
Noah's eldest son. He survived the flood and became the ancestor of several "Semitic" nations, the group of people to which the Hebrews belonged.
Genesis 6–10

SHESHBAZZAR
Sheshbazzar led the Jewish exiles back to Jerusalem when King Cyrus of Persia allowed them to return to rebuild the temple. Cyrus handed over to him the

treasures Nebuchadnezzar had taken from the temple in Jerusalem before he destroyed it. Sheshbazzar laid the foundations of the new temple.
Ezra 1:8ff.; 5:14ff.

SHILOH
The town where the worship tent (tabernacle) was set up after the conquest of Canaan. Shiloh became the centre of Israel's worship, and the tent was replaced by a more permanent building. Each year a special festival was held here. Hannah and Elkanah travelled to Shiloh to worship God. On one of these visits Hannah, praying for a son, promised that she would give him back to serve God. When Samuel was born Hannah kept her promise. She brought him back to Shiloh and he grew up in the temple, under the care of Eli the priest.

Archaeological evidence shows that Shiloh was destroyed about 1050 BC, probably by the Philistines. Jeremiah the prophet warned that the temple in Jerusalem would be destroyed just as the place of worship at Shiloh had been. But it seems that some people lived on the site of Shiloh, at least until the time of the exile.
Joshua 18:1; Judges 21:19; 1 Samuel 1–4; Jeremiah 7:12; 41:5

SHINAR
Another name for Babylonia. See *Babylon*.

SHIPS
In Bible times travel by sea was even more difficult than land travel. The Mediterranean was safe for

sailing only in the summer. Between November and March, ships set sail only in an emergency.

The great seafaring nations of the Old Testament period were the Egyptians and the Phoenicians. They built warships and trading vessels, powered by sails and oars. Israel's only successful attempt to develop a navy came during the golden age of Solomon's reign, at a time when the Phoenicians ruled the waves of the Mediterranean Sea.

Israel's border had been extended south to the Red Sea, and Solomon's alliance with Hiram, king of Tyre in Phoenicia, provided him with expert help in constructing a merchant fleet based on the town of Ezion-geber, at the head of the Gulf of Aqaba. Ezion-geber became an important trading-post. From here Solomon's ships carried copper and iron to "Ophir" (probably southern Arabia, at the other end of the Red Sea) and returned with luxury goods. The round trip — about 1,250 miles/2,000 km each way — took three years.

A century later, in about 850 BC, King Jehoshaphat attempted to revive the trade but his fleet was wrecked by a violent storm, and Israel's brief seafaring history was over.

In the New Testament the Gospel writers record several occasions when Jesus crossed the Sea of Galilee by boat. These journeys were probably made in the fishing boats used on this inland lake, 7½ miles/12km wide. The wind funnelling through the surrounding hills can whip the lake into sudden violent storms.

Paul's missionary travels included sea journeys as well as long treks overland. The account of his

A Roman merchant ship built to carry large cargoes of grain.

voyage to Rome given in the Book of Acts reads like a ship's log, with details about weather conditions, seamanship, and even a passenger list. It is one of the most vivid descriptions of a voyage in the whole of ancient literature.

Rome controlled the Mediterranean Sea at the time of Jesus. Corn grown in Egypt and exported from Alexandria on the Nile Delta was vital to the economic stability of the Empire. State-run grain-ships, some as much as 200 ft/60 metres long, carried the corn to Italy. During the summer the winds took the ships straight across the sea from Egypt to Italy, but out of season the safer course was by shorter stages, or round the coast. Paul sailed in a corn-ship taking the safer route in late September or early October. When the ship was wrecked, the rest of the cargo and even the ship's tackle were thrown overboard before the valuable grain. It was another ship from Alexandria that took Paul on from Malta to Italy after the shipwreck.

Puteoli, on the Bay of Naples, was the main port of Rome until New Testament times when the harbour at Ostia, nearer to Rome, was improved and eventually became the principal port for the capital city of the Empire.

1 Kings 9:26–28; 10:11–12, 22; 22:48; Mark 4:35–39; Acts 27–28:15

SHITTIM

A place on the plains of Moab, across the Jordan from Jericho, also known as Abel-shittim, "field of acacias". The Israelites camped here just before they crossed the River Jordan into Canaan. They were probably at Shittim when the king of Moab tried to persuade Balaam to curse them. Preparations were made here for the conquest of Canaan. A census was taken of men able to fight; Joshua was chosen as Moses' successor; and two men were sent to spy out Jericho.
Numbers 25:1; 22–24; 26; 27:12–23; Joshua 2; 3:1; Joel 3:18

SHUNEM

A place in the Valley of Jezreel, in northern Israel, modern Sôlem. The Philistines camped here before the battle on Mt Gilboa when Saul and Jonathan were killed. Elisha was the guest of a woman of Shunem, and he restored her child to life. The girl Abishag, who served David in his old age, was also a Shunnamite. The young woman called a "Shulammite" in the Song of Solomon (Songs) may have come from the same place.
Joshua 19:18; 1 Samuel 28:4; 1 Kings 1–2; 2 Kings 4:8–37; Song of Solomon (Songs) 6:13

SHUR

A desert area in the north-west part of the Sinai peninsula. Traders followed the "Way of Shur" across the desert towards Egypt. Hagar fled this way after Sarah had treated her unkindly. When the Israelites had crossed the Sea of Reeds after escaping from Egypt they had to travel through this desert, and complained bitterly about the lack of water. Genesis 16; Exodus 15:22–25

SIDON

A Phoenician (Canaanite) port on the coast of modern Lebanon. Many skilled craftsmen worked in Sidon. Carved ivory, gold and silver jewellery and beautiful glassware were among its exports. Each Phoenician city was virtually self-governing.

When the Israelites conquered Canaan they failed to take Sidon. In the time of the Judges the people of Sidon attacked and harassed the Israelites. The cultures began to merge and the Israelites were accused of worshipping the gods of Sidon — Baal and Ashtoreth. Jezebel, who promoted Baal worship in Israel, was the daughter of a king of Sidon. Because Sidon was opposed to Israel and the worship of God,

The harbour at present-day Sidon.

the Old Testament prophets predicted the town's downfall. Sidon was captured, in turn, by Assyrians, the Babylonians and the Persians. Later it came under Greek and Roman control.

In the time of Jesus most of the inhabitants of Sidon were Greek. Many travelled to Galilee to hear him preach. Jesus also visited Sidon and the neighbouring city of Tyre. He compared Chorazin and Bethsaida, two towns in Galilee, with Tyre and Sidon, saying how much more readily the non-Jewish cities would have responded to him. Paul stopped at Sidon on his journey to Rome and stayed with friends in the city.

Judges 1:31; 10:12, 6; 1 Kings 16:31; Isaiah 23:1–12; Ezekiel 28:20–24; Luke 6:17; Mark 7:24–31; Matthew 11:20–22; Acts 27:3, etc.

SILAS

A leader of the church at Jerusalem who travelled with Paul on his second missionary journey, in place of Barnabas. At Philippi (in northern Greece) both Paul and Silas were beaten and thrown into prison. After an earthquake shattered the prison they talked to the jailor about Jesus and he became a Christian. Silas stayed in the nearby town of Beroea while Paul went south to Athens, but joined him again in Corinth. He is almost certainly the Christian called Silvanus in some of the New Testament letters. Silvanus helped Peter write his first letter and may well also have helped Paul with his letter-writing. Paul sends greetings from Silvanus in his two letters to the Thessalonians.

Acts 15:22–17:15; 18:5; 2 Corinthians 1:19;

1 Thessalonians 1:1; 2 Thessalonians 1:1; Peter 5:12

SILOAM

A pool, originally underground, which was one of Jerusalem's main sources of water. The water in the pool came through a tunnel from the Gihon Spring outside Jerusalem. When the Assyrians threatened to besiege Jerusalem Hezekiah knew that in order to survive the city must have its own water supply, and gave orders for work on the tunnel. It is 1,750ft/538m long, cut through solid rock.

When Jesus healed a man who had been blind all his life he first put clay on his eyes and then told him to wash in the Pool of Siloam. The tower of Siloam which collapsed, killing eighteen people, probably stood on the slope of Mt Zion, above the pool.
2 Kings 20:20; John 9:1–12; Luke 13:4

SIMEON

1. Second son of Jacob and Leah. When Simeon and his brothers went to Egypt to buy corn, he was left behind as a hostage to make sure they brought Benjamin with them next time. Simeon was the ancestor of one of the twelve tribes of Israel.
Genesis 29:33; 34:25ff.; 42:24ff.; 49:5
2. An old man who had been told by God that he would not die until he had seen the Messiah. In the temple he took the baby Jesus in his arms and praised God. His prayer is known as the *Nunc Dimittis*.
Luke 2:22–35
3. A teacher at the church in Antioch. He was probably an African and may well be the Simon of

Cyrene who carried Jesus' cross.
Acts 13:1–2
4. The land given to the tribe of Simeon in the Negev, the southernmost part of Israel. It seems that the area was considered an extension of Judah's territory.
Joshua 19:1–9; compare Joshua 15:20–32

SIMON

1. Simon Peter. (See *Peter*.)
2. One of the twelve apostles. He had been a member of the Zealots, an extreme Jewish nationalist group pledged to drive out the Romans.
Matthew 10:4; Acts 1:13
3. A brother of Jesus.
Matthew 13:55
4. A leper who invited Jesus to his house in Bethany. While Jesus was there, a woman anointed his head with expensive perfume.
Matthew 26:6; Mark 14:3
5. A Pharisee who invited Jesus to his house. At dinner a woman wept at the feet of Jesus, dried them with her hair and poured perfume on them.
Luke 7:40ff.
6. Simon of Cyrene, who was ordered to carry Jesus' cross.
Matthew 27:32
7. Simon Magus, a magician at Samaria who tried to buy the apostles' God-given power.
Acts 8:14–24
8. A tanner with whom Peter stayed in Joppa.
Acts 9:43ff.

SIN

The Bible uses many words to describe sin. It is rebellion against God, as the story of Adam and Eve shows. Men and women are therefore enemies of God. Sin is also often described as "missing the mark" or falling below the standard required by God. A person can be held guilty for *failing* to do what God requires, as much as for deliberately disobeying God's commands. But the essence of all sin is that it is an offence against God. Because of this, men and women are cut off from God and face his anger and judgement. Because of sin, suffering and death came into the world.

The Bible does not concern itself with the thorny problem of where evil comes from. It accepts it as a fact. Satan is its source, but men and women are not allowed to blame Satan for their own downfall, although Adam and Eve tried hard to do so. They are responsible and held guilty for their own sin. In Jesus Christ God has dealt with the problem of sin, and there will come a day when sin and evil are no more.

See also *Death, Fall, Forgiveness, Hell, Judgement, Suffering*.
Genesis 3; Psalm 51; Isaiah 1:18–20; 59; Romans 1:18–2:11; 3:9–26; 5–8; Revelation 20–21

SINAI

A mountain in the Sinai peninsula and the area of desert around it. Three months after leaving Egypt the Israelites reached the mountain and set up camp. Here, at Mt Sinai, God gave Moses the Ten Commandments and other laws. The exact identification

of Mt Sinai is not known. It was probably one of two peaks — Gebel Musa or Ras es-Safsafeh — in the south of the peninsula.
Exodus 19–32

SISERA

Captain of the army of Jabin, king of Hazor. He had under his command 900 iron chariots and for twenty years made life unbearable for the Israelites. Sisera was defeated by Deborah and Barak. He escaped on foot, but was killed by Jael when he hid in her tent.
Judges 4–5

SLAVES

Some projects — for example, the building and mining works of the Old Testament kings, and the building works of Herod the Great and his successors — needed enormous numbers of workmen. In Old Testament times slavery was accepted in Israel, but it was not widespread. Men and their families became slaves to better-off households when they were unable to meet their debts. Prisoners-of-war were also made slaves. The Old Testament laws about slaves are remarkably liberal for their time, although people may not always have lived up to these ideals. The Israelites were never allowed to forget that they, too, had once been slaves in Egypt. So they were to free their slaves after six years' service.

King David, however, forced prisoners-of-war to work on his projects. And Solomon organized a system of forced labour using Israelites as well. They were expected to work for the king one month in three. These men, with the slaves, built the roads, fortresses and temples that made Solomon famous. They looked after the king's farms and worked in his factories and mines. Long before, the prophet Samuel had warned the people that having a king would mean compulsory armed service and forced labour. State slavery, if not conscription, probably continued all through the time of the kings of Judah.

In New Testament times there were both Jewish and non-Jewish slaves in Palestine. But they were not forced to do heavy work. For the most part they were servants in the houses of the wealthy and of the court. There do not seem to have been many of them. Workmen for the building projects were more usually hired by the day (as in Jesus' parable of the workers in the vineyard — Matthew 20:1–16). When the temple begun by Herod the Great was completed — AD 62–64 — more than 18,000 men were thrown out of work.

Paul and Peter gave advice to Christian slaves in their letters to various church groups. These men

A Roman slave badge which reads "Seize me if I should try to escape and send me back to my master".

and women lived in the wider Roman Empire, and probably had a much harsher life than that in Palestine.

Deuteronomy 15:12–18; 2 Samuel 12:31; 1 Kings 5:13–18; 1 Samuel 8:11–18; Ephesians 6:5–9; Colossians 3:22–25; 1 Timothy 6:1–2; Philemon; 1 Peter 2:18–25

SMYRNA

A port serving one of the main trade-routes across Asia. It is now the city of Izmir in modern Turkey. In New Testament times it was a beautiful city with many splendid public buildings. One of them was the temple built in honour of the Emperor Tiberius, where emperor-worship was practised. One of the letters to the seven churches in the Book of Revelation is addressed to the Christians at Smyrna.
Revelation 1:11; 2:8–11

SODOM

The town where Lot settled and which became notorious for its immorality. Sodom was suddenly destroyed, along with Gomorrah. Lot was warned of the impending disaster and escaped. Sodom probably now lies submerged at the southern end of the Dead Sea.
Genesis 13:8–13; 14; 19

SOLOMON

The son of King David and Bathsheba. Israel's most famous king. David had fought many wars to create a strong kingdom; Solomon inherited peace. He protected his country by keeping up a strong army and building fortresses. He also made marriage-alliances with the kings of surrounding countries. Israel became a rich country under Solomon's rule. He traded copper and horses for precious cargoes of gold and jewels. Solomon's God-given wisdom made him famous. The Queen of Sheba (south-west Arabia) visited him to test his wisdom.

Solomon built the first temple for God in Jerusalem. The building materials and skilled workmen were provided by Hiram, king of Tyre, in exchange for wheat and oil. It was a magnificent building and stood for 400 years until Nebuchadnezzar destroyed it in 586 BC. He also built palaces for himself and Pharaoh's daughter, one of his wives. Solomon's reign was spoilt by his ill-treatment of his subjects and by his many marriages. He made his subjects angry by demanding free labour and high taxes from them to carry out his building programmes. In the end, Solomon's foreign wives made him turn away from the true God to worship their own gods. When Solomon died, the ten northern tribes rebelled against Rehoboam, his son, and made the rebel leader, Jeroboam, their king.
2 Samuel 12:24; 1 Kings 1–11; 1 Chronicles 22:5–23:1; 28–2 Chronicles 9

SONG OF SONGS
The Song of Songs is a collection of love poems between a man and woman. It is sometimes called the Song of Solomon because it is probably credited to Solomon in the Hebrew text.

The poems are set in the countryside in springtime. They are full of the passion and joy of human love. They express frankly the delights of physical attraction.

Both Jews and Christians have seen the love expressed in the Song as a picture — of God's love for Israel, or of Jesus' love for the church. There is no backing for this either in the book itself, or anywhere else in the Bible.

SOSTHENES

1. Appointed chief official of the synagogue at Corinth when Crispus, the previous ruler, became a Christian. Sosthenes was beaten up after a group of Jews had failed to persuade Gallio, the Roman governor of Achaia, to condemn Paul. If he was later converted, this Sosthenes may be the same as 2 below.
Acts 18:17

2. A Christian known to members of the church at Corinth. The first letter to the Corinthians was sent from Paul and Sosthenes.
1 Corinthians 1:1

SOUL

The Bible sees human beings as a unity. It does not speak of an immortal "soul" locked up in a decaying, sinful body. This was a Greek idea, though it has been held by many Christians through the centuries.

When we read the word "soul" in the Old Testament it means the whole of a person's being. When the psalmist says, "Praise the Lord, my soul", he is calling on himself to respond as a whole person to God.

The New Testament uses the word "soul" in a similar way, meaning "people". It is the word used to show that people are more than physical flesh and bone; they have a mind and will and personality. For instance, Jesus said, "Do not be afraid of those who kill the body but cannot kill the soul; rather be afraid of God, who can destroy both body and soul in hell."

See also *Body, Flesh*.
Psalm 103:1; Matthew 10:28, and so on

SPARROW

The word is often used to mean any small bird suitable for eating, but in some places refers specifically to the Hedge Sparrow. Larks and finches as well as sparrows have often been trapped or shot to be cooked and eaten. Jesus used the sparrow to emphasize how much God loves his creatures. If he cares, even for the smallest birds, how much more will he care for people.
Matthew 10:29–31; Luke 12:6–7

SPIKENARD (NARD)

A sweet-smelling ointment was made from this plant which grows in India. It was imported to Israel in

The fragrant spikenard plant.

sealed alabaster jars to preserve the perfume. This was the costly gift that Mary lavished on Jesus. Song of Solomon 4:13; Mark 14:3; John 12:3

SPINNING
See *Clothes-making*.

SPIRITUAL GIFTS
When Christ left this earth to go back to his Father, he gave "gifts" to his followers. These gifts are given by the Holy Spirit to individuals within every local Christian church so that they can continue Christ's work. They show the supernatural nature of the church. As a community of God's people, its work is not limited to its members' natural abilities. The Spirit of God gives those gifts which are needed to build up the church. He gives as he thinks fit.

In Ephesians 4 Paul lists some of the gifts which marked people out as having a special work as leaders of the church — apostles, prophets, evangelists, pastors and teachers. In 1 Corinthians 12 Paul takes other examples, this time emphasizing those which would be found among the members — wisdom, knowledge, faith, healing, miracles, speaking and explaining God's message, speaking in strange tongues and explaining what is said. At the end of the chapter he adds to the list those who have the power to help or direct others. Romans 12 lists some other gifts: service, encouragement, sharing with others and acts of kindness. None of these lists claims to be complete.

Paul believed that in every local church each member should be free to use his God-given gift of

ministry. Gifts of the Spirit are not given for private enjoyment but for the good of all, and for this reason Paul deals at some length with the question of speaking in tongues. Paul himself spoke in tongues and was keen for others to have the same gift, but he insisted that there must be someone to interpret. Otherwise no one would understand it, and no one would be helped.
Romans 12; 1 Corinthians 12 and 14; Ephesians 4

SPORT
See *Games and Sport*.

STEPHANAS
Stephanas and his family were the first people to become Christians in Achaia (southern Greece). They were amongst the few Christians whom Paul baptized personally at Corinth.
1 Corinthians 1:16; 16:15ff.

STEPHEN
A Greek-speaking Jew who was the first Christian to die for his faith. Stephen was one of seven men chosen by the apostles to arrange care for poor widows in the church at Jerusalem. He had great faith in God. As well as looking after practical matters Stephen preached and worked miracles. He was arrested and brought before the supreme Jewish council (the Sanhedrin). At the end of a brave speech he accused the Jews of killing God's Son. He was stoned to death, but as he died asked God to forgive his murderers. Paul who was at that time still perse-

cuting the Christians, saw Stephen die.
Acts 6 and 7

STORK

Both White and Black Storks pass through Israel
every year, flying north from their wintering-places
in Arabia and Africa. The larger and more numerous
White Stork is seen most often. Storks live mostly on
small animal life — snakes, fish, mice, worms and
insects.
Jeremiah 8:7

SUCCOTH

1. An Egyptian town. The Israelites made their first
camp here on their journey out of the country.
Exodus 12:37; 13:20; Numbers 33:5–6
2. A town in the Jordan Valley which became part
of the territory of Gad. Jacob stayed for a while in
Succoth after he and his brother Esau agreed to go
their separate ways. In the time of the Judges the
people of Succoth refused to provide Gideon and his
army with food while he was fighting the Midianites.
When Gideon was victorious he returned and
punished the town officials.
Joshua 13:24, 27; Genesis 33:12–17; Judges 8:4–16

SUFFERING

Suffering is seen in the Bible as a *misfortune*. It
entered the world because of sin; it is a result of the
continuing activity of Satan. Jesus came into the
world to free men and women from suffering and
death. In his life on earth he showed his love and

care by healing many people. And in the new heaven and earth there will be no suffering.

Suffering is also a *problem* in the Bible. As God has total control, suffering must ultimately come from him. Yet how can a God of love allow the innocent to suffer? It is easy to see that sin brings suffering, and not just to the individual but to his whole family. And it is possible to accept that God allows suffering in order to discipline his children. But the Book of Job is an honest attempt to discuss the problem of the suffering of innocent people. Job discards all the theories that are offered him, and in the end accepts his suffering. He does not find a rational explanation, but he sees in God a certainty which can overcome all his doubts and fears.

In the life and work of Jesus we are shown suffering as a way of life. He lives out the life of the suffering servant outlined in Isaiah 53. He is innocent. He is not suffering for his own sin, but he is suffering because of the hatred of sinful people, and in order to save them from their sin. The Bible does not give us a rational answer to the problem of suffering, but it does give us a practical answer. God took responsibility for it in the death of his son. Genesis 3:15–19; 2 Corinthians 12:7; Romans 8:21; Revelation 21:4; Amos 3:6; Psalm 39:11; Hebrews 12:3–11; Job; Isaiah 53

SUSA

Capital of the Elamite Empire until King Ashurbanipal of Assyria destroyed the city in 645 BC and exiled its inhabitants to Samaria. Under the Medes and Persians it once again became an important city.

A winged bull from the palace of Darius I at Susa, built in the sixth century BC.

Darius I built a splendid palace here. The ruins, in modern Iran, can still be seen.

The story of Esther, the Jewish girl who became queen of Persia, took place at the royal court in Susa. It was here, too, that Nehemiah acted as royal cupbearer. The city was later captured by Alexander the Great.

Ezra 4:9–10; Esther 1:2, etc.; Nehemiah 1:1

SYCHAR

A Samaritan town close to Jacob's well, where Jesus met and talked to a Samaritan woman who had come to draw water. Many people from Sychar believed Jesus was the Messiah when they heard what the woman said about him. The exact site is unknown.

John 4:1–42

SYENE

A place on the southern border of Egypt; modern

Aswan. Isaiah pictures dispersed Jews returning to Jerusalem from as far away as Syene. Papyrus deeds found here record activities of Jewish settlers about 450 BC (the Elephantine Papyri).
Isaiah 49:12; Ezekiel 29:10; 30:6

SYNAGOGUE
Synagogues probably first began during the exile, when there was no temple and the people were far away from Jerusalem. By the time of Jesus, most Jews outside Jerusalem normally met together on the sabbath at the local synagogue. The service at the synagogue was mainly for readings from the Bible (usually a passage from the Law and one from the Prophets) and prayers.

The service began with the *Shema*: "Hear, O Israel, the Lord our God is one Lord; and you shall love the Lord your God with all your heart, and with all your soul, and with all your might." The Bible passages were read in Hebrew. But since most Jews in Palestine at the time of Christ spoke Aramaic, an interpreter gave a verse-by-verse translation and explanation (a *targum*). Sometimes there was also a sermon.

A reconstruction of a synagogue based on plans of the third-century AD synagogue at Capernaum.

Every synagogue had a chest ("ark") in which the scrolls of the Law were kept. The leaders sat in front of the ark, facing the people. Men and women sat separately.

Jesus went regularly to the synagogue, and read and taught there. Paul, on his missionary journeys, went first to the synagogue in each town, and spoke there.

The synagogue served as the local school and as the centre for local government as well as worship. Deuteronomy 6:4–5; Luke 4:16–30; 6:6; Acts 13; 14–18; 14:1, and other references in Acts

SYRACUSE
An ancient city in Sicily, where Paul spent three days on the last stage of his voyage to Rome after shipwreck on Malta.
Acts 28:12

SYRIA
In the Old Testament, Syria is the land occupied by the Aramaeans to the north and north-east of Israel. The capital of Syria was Damascus.
See *Aramaeans*.

T

TABERNACLE

The tabernacle was a large tent made by the Israelites to a design given to Moses at Mt Sinai. It was the place where they worshipped God on their journey from Egypt to Canaan. Each time they camped (see Numbers 1:50–2:31), the Levites set up the tabernacle. It stood at the centre of the camp, with the Levites' tents around it on all four sides. Behind them were the tents of the twelve tribes of Israel, three tribes on each side. The tabernacle was the centre of Israel's religious life. It was a sign that God was always with them. Even though they had been kept out of the Promised Land for forty years because of their disobedience, still God was willing to protect and go with them. So the tabernacle is often called the "tent of meeting" (between God and man) and "the dwelling place" (of God).

The tabernacle and its furniture The tent was supported by a frame of acacia wood. It was about 45ft/14m long, 13½ft/4m wide, and 15ft/5m high. Four types of coverings were draped over this frame. First came linen curtains, decorated with blue, purple and scarlet tapestry which could be seen inside. Next came a set of curtains made of goats' hair. These were a little longer than the linen ones, and one of them formed the door of the tent.

On top of these curtains went a weatherproof covering, made of rams' skins, dyed red.

Finally, there was another waterproof covering made from the skin of some other animal (translated "badger", "porpoise" or simply "fine leather").

Inside, the tent was divided into two rooms. The smaller one, furthest from the door, was called the "holy of holies" or "the most holy place". Only the high priest, once a year, was allowed to enter the "holy of holies". A linen curtain separated this from the larger room, which was called "the holy place". The entrance to it was covered by another embroidered linen curtain.
Exodus 25–27; 30:1–10, 17–21

The Covenant Box/Ark of the Covenant This was a rectangular box (about 4x2½x2½ft/115x70x70cm). Like the framework of the tabernacle, it was made of acacia wood, a very durable timber which grows in the Sinai Desert. The wood of the box was overlaid with gold. The box was carried by poles pushed through rings at the four lower corners. It contained the two tablets of the Ten Commandments, a golden pot of manna, and Aaron's rod that blossomed overnight. The lid was of solid gold and at both ends were the figures of two creatures (cherubim) with wings spread out as a sign of God's protection.

The Covenant Box stood in the "holy of holies". It was thought of as the place where God was invisibly enthroned because he said, "I will meet you there, and from above the lid between the two winged creatures I will give you all my laws for the people of Israel." It was sometimes carried into battle, as a symbol of God's protection. The fact that on one occasion it was captured by the Philistines showed it had no power of its own.

Exodus 25:10–22; Deuteronomy 10:1–5; Hebrews 9:4–5; Joshua 6:6, 8; 1 Samuel 4:3

The incense altar   In the holy place, in front of the curtain which screened the holy of holies, stood a small altar on which incense was burnt each morning and evening. It was made out of acacia wood, overlaid with gold. It had a horn at each corner, and rings were attached to two of the sides to make it easy to carry.
Exodus 30:1–10

The golden lampstand   The seven-branched lampstand was hammered out of one piece of gold, weighing 66lbs/30kg or more and decorated with flowers and buds like almond blossom. It was the only source of light in the tabernacle.
Exodus 25:31–39

Table of showbread/Bread of Presence   Each sabbath, twelve new loaves, one for each tribe, were placed as an offering on the gold-overlaid table that stood in the holy place.
Exodus 25:23–30

Courtyard   The tabernacle itself stood in the western part of a courtyard about 150x75ft/50x25m. The courtyard itself was enclosed by a screen of linen curtains. There was an entrance on one side, with a curtain of embroidered linen drawn across it.
Exodus 27:9–19

Laver   The laver was a huge bronze basin on a bronze base. It was used by the priests for washing their hands and feet each time they were about to enter the tabernacle or offer a sacrifice.
Exodus 30:17–21

Altar of burnt offering   Here sacrifices of lambs,

bulls, and goats, and other animals were made. (See *Priests, Levites and Sacrifices*.) This altar, like several objects in the tabernacle, was made of wood overlaid with bronze. It was about 7½ft/2.5m square and 4½ft/1.5m high. Halfway up the altar was a ledge on which it seems the priests stood to make their sacrifices. The altar may have been filled with earth, or empty and used like an incinerator.
Exodus 27:1–8

TABERNACLES
See *Feasts and Festivals*.

A reconstruction of the tabernacle based on the description given in the Bible.

TABITHA
See *Dorcas*.

TABOR
An 1800ft/550m steep-sided mountain rising from the Plain of Jezreel. The place where Barak gathered his army at the time of the Judges.
Judges 4; Psalm 89:12; Hosea 5:1

TAHPANHES
An Egyptian town in the east part of the Nile Delta.

The prophet Jeremiah was taken to Tahpanhes after the fall of Jerusalem and probably died there.
Jeremiah 43:5–10; Ezekiel 30:18

TAMAR

1. The daughter-in-law of Judah and mother of his twin sons.
Genesis 38
2. David's daughter, raped by Amnon, her half-brother.
2 Samuel 13

TARSHISH

The distant place for which Jonah set sail when he disobeyed God's command to go to Nineveh. A source of silver, tin, iron and lead. It may be Tartessus in Spain. (Some modern Bible versions translate it as Spain.)
Jonah 1:3; Isaiah 23:6; Jeremiah 10:9; Ezekiel 27:12

TARSUS

A town on the Cilician plain 10 miles/16km inland from the south coast of modern Turkey. An important university city in New Testament times, housing 500,000 people. Tarsus was a meeting-place of East and West, of Greek and Oriental. Paul was born at Tarsus and proud of it. He returned there not long after becoming a Christian. But Barnabas brought him to Antioch to help teach the new Christians.
Acts 9:11; 21:39; 22:3; 9:30; 11:25–26

TARTAN

See *Rabsaris*.

TEKOA

A town in the Judean hills about 6 miles/10km south of Bethlehem. A wise woman from Tekoa pleaded with King David to allow his son Absalom to come back to Jerusalem. Tekoa was also the home of the prophet Amos.
2 Samuel 14:2, etc.; Amos 1:1

TEMAN

Part of Edom. The people of Teman were famous for their wisdom. It was the home area of Job's friend Eliphaz.
Jeremiah 49:7; Job 2:11

TEMPLE

Solomon's temple When the Israelites conquered Canaan the tabernacle was no longer carried about with them. For a long time it remained at Shiloh. The Covenant Box was taken into battle and captured by the Philistines. But it brought them trouble and they sent it back.

Eventually King David brought it to Jerusalem. He had bought a piece of land just north of the city, and planned to build a permanent temple there for God. But although he longed to do this he was unable to do so. As he explained to his people, it was because "I am a soldier and have shed too much blood". So he had to be content with getting materials together. Solomon, his son, became the builder of the first temple in Jerusalem.

This temple was not large by today's standards, but it must have been the largest building the Israelites had constructed up to this time. It measured about 30x87ft/9x27m, and was 43ft/13.5m high. No other temple quite like it in plan has been found, though a Canaanite one recently excavated at Hazor, and a ninth-century BC shrine found in Syria have the same basic three-room design. The temple was very similar in layout to the pattern of the tabernacle.

The priests entered the temple through a large porch. Then came the main room, the "holy place". In it stood the incense altar, the table for showbread, and five pairs of lampstands.

The inner room, as in the tabernacle, was the "holy of holies" (the most sacred part of all). It was probably approached by steps from the holy place. It contained two cherubim made of olive-wood and covered with gold. They were the symbols of God's protection of the most important object in the holy of holies: the Covenant Box (ark; see *Tabernacle*).

The walls of each room were panelled with cedar, carved with flowers, palm-trees and cherubim, and overlaid with gold. No stonework could be seen from inside the building. The holy place was dimly lit by high windows and by the lampstands. But the holy of holies — the place of God's presence — had no windows and so was completely dark.

Incense was burnt in the temple itself, but the sacrifices took place in the courtyard outside. Only priests and Levites were allowed inside the temple building.

A full account of how the temple was built and furnished is given in 1 Kings 5–7. All the skill and resource King Solomon could muster went into the construction and decoration of the temple. It was

God's temple. Even the stones were prepared at the quarry "so that there was no noise made by hammers, axes or any other iron tools as the temple was being built".

When it was finished, Solomon held a great dedication service. The cloud of God's presence filled the temple and King Solomon himself led the worship:

"You, Lord, have placed the sun in the sky,
yet you have chosen to live in clouds and darkness.
Now I have built a majestic temple for you,
a place for you to live in for ever."

From this time on the centre of worship was the temple at Jerusalem, though the ten tribes who later broke away to form the northern kingdom of Israel set up their own temples in other places.

King Solomon's temple was finally destroyed by King Nebuchadnezzar of Babylon when he captured the city of Jerusalem in 587 BC. Its remaining bronze and gold and silver furnishings were taken to Babylon.

2 Samuel 6; 7; 24:18–25; 1 Chronicles 28:2–3; 1 Kings 5–8; 12; 2 Kings 16:5–9; 24:10–13; 25:8–17

Zerubbabel's temple (the second temple) When Cyrus allowed the Jews to return from Babylon to Jerusalem in 538 BC, he commanded them to rebuild the temple. He also gave them back all the gold and silver objects which Nebuchadnezzar had taken from Solomon's temple. They began work straight away, but soon became discouraged. Only after the prophets Haggai and Zechariah had spurred them on was the temple completed in 515 BC.

Although it stood for 500 years we know very little about this temple. It almost certainly followed the plan of Solomon's temple, but was not nearly so splendid.

When the Syrian ruler Antiochus IV banned sacrifices in the temple in 168 BC and defiled it by offering a pagan sacrifice, a revolt broke out (the Maccabean revolt). Three years later the temple was re-dedicated — the event still remembered at the Jewish festival of *Hanukkah*. (See *Feasts and festivals*.) It was destroyed by the Roman general Pompey in 63 BC.
2 Chronicles 36:22–23; Ezra 1; 3–6

Herod's temple In 19 BC King Herod the Great began work on a new temple at Jerusalem. He wanted to win favour with his subjects and to impress the Roman world with his splendid building. The main building was finished by about 9 BC, but work continued for many years afterwards. Built on the same plan as Solomon's temple, this temple was

Herod's temple, surrounded by the Court of the Gentiles. The Fort of Antonia, in the north-west corner, was garrisoned by Roman soldiers.

by far the grandest. It was twice as high as Solomon's temple, and covered with so much gold that it was a dazzling sight in the bright sun.

The most impressive feature was the great temple "platform", still in existence today, where pilgrims gathered and sacrifices were offered. The walls of this platform extended beyond the summit of the hill to enclose an area of 35 acres. At its southern end, it stood 100–150ft/30–45m above ground level. One of the southern corners of the platform is probably the "pinnacle" from which the devil tempted Jesus to throw himself down.

A covered cloister (where Peter and John taught the people) ran right round the outer courtyards. The main entrance was from the south, and led to the Court of the Gentiles. Anyone could enter this part of the temple. But notices in Greek and Latin forbade non-Jews to enter the inner court of the temple. The result of breaking this rule was likely to be death. Acts 21, describing Paul's arrest, gives an idea of the intense feelings aroused by the suggestion that a non-Jew had "defiled the holy place". The next court was the Court of the Women. This was as far as women were allowed to go into the temple itself. Men could go further, into the Court of Israel, and they could even enter the Priests' Court for a procession round the altar at the Festival of Tabernacles.

The temple was destroyed by the Romans at the time of the Jewish rebellion in AD 70, and its treasures taken back to Rome.
Matthew 4:5–6; Mark 13:1; Acts 3:11
Jewish worship in the temple In New Testament

times the temple was still at the heart of Israel's religious life. Crowds of pilgrims went there for the great annual festivals. It was also a centre for religious teaching. And, as in Old Testament times, the priests serving in the temple carried out the rites and sacrifices of the law.

Each day began with the recitation of Bible passages and prayers. The chief rituals were the morning and evening sacrifices. Then the priests would address the worshippers with the words of the ancient blessing:

"May the Lord bless you and take care of you;
May the Lord be kind and gracious to you;
May the Lord look on you with favour and give you peace."

Hymns were sung by the temple choirs of Levites, but sometimes the people joined in, especially in the torchlight procession at the Festival of Tabernacles.

The Gospel of Luke describes Jesus' first visit as a boy to the temple, for the Passover Festival. John's Gospel records that when he grew up, Jesus often went to Jerusalem for the festivals, and much of the teaching in that Gospel was given in Jerusalem, in the temple courtyards. After Jesus' ascension his followers met and taught there, too.
Luke 2:41–49; John 2:13–25; 5:7–8; 10:22–38; 12:12 and following; Acts 2:46; 3; Mark 14:58

TEMPTATION
God allows his people to be tempted, or tested. Such testing reveals the worth of their love for him. And every test that is overcome strengthens and leads them forward. The word "temptation" is more com-

monly used to refer to the activity of Satan in trying to lead men into sin, as in the temptation of Jesus. The other classic example of temptation is in the story of Adam and Eve. The serpent gradually leads the woman into doubt and confusion about the will of God; she then sees the fruit, recognizes what it is worth, desires it, realizes what it could do for her, and finally takes it.

Christians are told to be on their guard against temptation. They also have God's promise that he will not allow the testing to become too great to bear. He will provide the power to endure it.

See also *Satan, Sin.*
Genesis 3; Exodus 20:20; Deuteronomy 8:1–6; Matthew 4; 6:13; 1 Corinthians 10:12–13; Ephesians 6:10–18; Hebrews 2:18; James 1:12–16; 1 Peter 1:6–9; 4:12–16

TEN COMMANDMENTS
See *Law.*

TENT
See *Tabernacle.*

TERAH
Father of Abraham. He set off from Ur with Abraham, intending to go to Canaan. Instead he settled at Harran and died there.
Genesis 11:27–32

TEREBINTH
A spreading tree, less than 25ft (7m) high, common in warm, dry hilly places in and around Israel.

THEBES
The ancient capital city of upper Egypt, on the River Nile, about 330 miles/531km south of modern Cairo. Two great temples of the god Amun (Karnak and Luxor) mark the site. From about 1500–1000 BC, when Amun was the official god of the Egyptian Empire, wealth and treasures poured into Thebes. But despite the city's remoteness it fell to the Assyrian King Ashurbanipal in 663 BC. The prophets Jeremiah and Ezekiel pronounced judgement on Thebes (No-Amon) and other Egyptian cities.
Nahum 3:8–10; Jeremiah 46:25; Ezekiel 30:14–19

THEOPHILUS
The person to whom Luke addressed his Gospel and the Acts of the Apostles. He knew something about Christianity but Luke wanted him to have a much fuller explanation. The name "Theophilus" means "friend of God".
Luke 1:3; Acts 1:1

THESSALONIANS
1 Thessalonians Thessalonica, a free city, was capital of the Roman province of Macedonia (in northern Greece). Paul started a church there during his second missionary journey. When he reached Corinth, Paul heard from his fellow-worker, Timothy, that the Jews at Thessalonica were still making trouble because the non-Jews were so interested in Paul's message.

Paul wrote 1 Thessalonians in response. It is one of his earliest surviving letters, and dates from about AD 50, only twenty years after Jesus' death.

In the letter Paul encourages and reassures the Christians at Thessalonica. He thanks God for the good news from them and recalls his visit (chapters 1–3). He urges them to lead lives that will please God (4:1–12). And he answers some problems about Jesus' expected return (4:13–5:11). When will he come again? What will happen to Christians who die before he returns? He ends with practical instructions, a prayer and greetings (5:12–28).

2 Thessalonians Despite Paul's letter (see 1 Thessalonians, above) the Christians at Thessalonica remained puzzled about Jesus' return. Some thought the day of his return had already come. In this second letter, written a few months after the first, Paul warns that before Jesus comes again, there will be a time of great wickedness (chapter 2). He finishes his letter by urging the Christians to keep the faith, and keep at their work (chapter 3).

THESSALONICA
The chief city of Macedonia (northern Greece), on the Egnatian Way, the main Roman road to the East. Thessalonica (now Thessaloniki) is still a major city. Paul visited Thessalonica on his second missionary journey. But the anger of the Jews forced him to move on to Beroea. His two letters to the Thessalonian Christians were written soon after he left.
Acts 17:1–15; 20:4; 27:2; Philippians 4:16; 1 Thessalonians 1:1; 2 Thessalonians 1:1, etc.; 2 Timothy 4:10

THEUDAS
Leader of a band of 400 rebels. When he was killed,

his men scattered and the movement died out. Gamaliel quoted this example when the apostles were on trial. The movement Jesus had started would similarly come to nothing, unless God was behind it.
Acts 5:34ff.

THISTLES, THORNS AND TARES
Thistles and thorns abound in dry lands like Israel — over 120 kinds, some growing to over 6ft/2m. Some, such as the milk-thistle, have beautiful flowers, but can quickly suffocate young plants at the edges of fields (as in Jesus' story of the sower and the soils). Thorns were plaited into a mock-crown for Jesus at his trial. The "tares" in the story of the wheat and the weeds are darnel, which looks exactly like wheat in its early stages.
Genesis 3:18; Matthew 13:7; Mark 15:15, 17–18; Matthew 13:24–30

A thistle (on the left), the weed called darnel or "tares", and thorns.

THOMAS
One of the twelve apostles. His name means "twin".

Jesus decided to go to Judea when he heard that Lazarus was ill. Thomas knew that the Jewish leaders there might again try to kill Jesus, but was willing to go and die with him. Thomas's question at the last supper led Jesus to declare, "I am the way, the truth and the life." Thomas was not with the disciples when Jesus appeared to them on the first Easter day. He said he would not believe Jesus was alive again unless he saw and touched the scars. A week later, Thomas saw Jesus for himself. "My Lord and my God," he said. There is a later tradition that Thomas went as a missionary to India.
John 11:16; 14:5–7; 20:24ff.; 21:1–14; Acts 1:12–14

THYATIRA

A town in the Roman province of Asia (now Akhisar in west Turkey). Thyatira was a manufacturing centre for dyeing, clothes-making, pottery and brasswork. Lydia, the business woman from Thyatira who became a Christian when she met Paul at Philippi, was a "dealer in purple cloth". One of the seven letters in the Book of Revelation was addressed to the church at Thyatira.
Acts 16:14–15; Revelation 1:11; 2:18–29

TIBERIAS

A spa town on the west shore of Lake Galilee. It was founded by King Herod Antipas and named after the Roman Emperor Tiberius. It was a non-Jewish town, and there is no record that Jesus ever went there. Tiberias is still a sizeable town today, unlike

all the other lakeside places mentioned in the Gospels.
John 6:23

TIBERIUS
Emperor of Rome in Jesus' lifetime. He ruled AD 14–37. In the Gospels he is simply referred to as "Caesar".
Luke 3:1

TIGLATH-PILESER
Tiglath-pileser III (Pul) was king of Assyria, 745–727 BC. He increased Assyrian power by going to war against smaller nations. Israel was one of the countries he invaded. King Menahem paid Tiglath-pileser a large sum of money so that he could remain king of Israel. After King Pekah of Israel and King Rezin of Syria had attacked Jerusalem, Tiglath-pileser responded to King Ahaz's appeal for help by capturing Damascus and several cities in northern Israel. Ahaz became subject to Tiglath-pileser.
2 Kings 15:29; 16:7ff.; 2 Chronicles 28:16ff.

Tiglath-pileser III standing in his state chariot, shielded from the sun by a parasol.

TIGRIS
The second great river of Mesopotamia. The Tigris

rises in the mountains of eastern Turkey and flows for more than 1,400 miles/2250km, joining the River Euphrates 40 miles/64km from its mouth on the Persian Gulf. The Tigris floods in spring and autumn. The great Assyrian cities of Nineveh, Calah and Assur were all built on the banks of the Tigris. The Bible mentions it as one of the four rivers of Eden.
Genesis 2:14; Daniel 10:4

TIME

Time was not rushed in the Jewish home. Before the Greeks and Romans used candle clocks and water clocks, the usual way of measuring time in small units was by the movement of a shadow (although the Egyptians were using hour glasses much earlier than this). Three different systems seem to have been used in Bible times.

Early in the Old Testament period, when Canaan was under Egypt's influence, the day started at sunrise. There was a twelve-month calendar of thirty days with five extra days at the end of the year. The days of the month were marked by putting a peg into a bone plate which had three rows of ten holes.

Later, perhaps under Babylonian influence, the calendar seems to have changed. The day began at moonrise (1800 hrs) and a whole day became "an evening and a morning". The evening was divided into three four-hour watches.

The Romans changed this into four three-hour watches. A new month also began with the moon. The first sign of the new moon was signalled by lighting bonfires on the hills. Months were then only

28/29 days long, so there had to be an extra month at the end of some years to keep the calendar right with the sun. The priests decided when to add this month.

TIMNATH-SERAH, TIMNATH-HERES
The town which Joshua received as his own. He was later buried here. The place was in the hill-country of Ephraim, north-west of Jerusalem.
Joshua 19:50; 24:30; Judges 2:9

TIMOTHY
A Christian from Lystra who was a friend and helper of Paul. His mother was a Jewish Christian; his father Greek. Paul chose Timothy to help him while he was on his second missionary journey. After Paul had left Thessalonica Timothy went back to encourage the persecuted Christians there. Later Paul sent him from Ephesus to Corinth to teach the Corinthian Christians. Timothy became leader of the church at Ephesus. He often lacked confidence and needed Paul's encouragement. But he was always loyal and faithful. The two letters which Paul wrote to the younger man are full of wise advice on the leadership of the church.
Acts 16:1–3; 17:13–15; 1 Corinthians 4:17; 1 Thessalonians 1:1; 3:1–6; 1 and 2 Timothy

TIMOTHY, LETTERS TO
1 Timothy Timothy was a young Christian, son of a Greek father and a Jewish mother. He came from Lystra in the Roman province of Galatia (central

Turkey). He travelled with Paul and helped him on his later missionary journeys. He was a rather shy man, and not strong physically. He needed encouragement and support.

When Paul wrote to him, Timothy was looking after the church in Ephesus. The letter offers much advice and help in church affairs. It warns against false teaching in the church, particularly about a mixture of Jewish and Gnostic ideas about salvation and the nature of the physical world. Timothy is given instructions about how the church should be organized and led (chapters 1–3), and the letter closes with more personal advice to Timothy about his service to the church (chapters 4–6).

Because it is difficult to fit this letter, along with 2 Timothy and Titus, into what we know of Paul's life, and also because it is so different in character from the other letters of Paul, many scholars believe that it came not from Paul himself but from one of his followers. He may have written all three of these letters after Paul was dead, but using material that Paul himself had left behind.

2 Timothy Much of this letter is taken up with Paul's personal advice to Timothy. He urges Timothy to stay faithful to the Good News of Jesus Christ. He encourages him to stand fast as a teacher and evangelist, despite opposition and persecution. Paul warns against pointless arguments, and encourages Timothy with the example of his own faith, which is still strong after a lifetime of suffering. "I have run the full distance," Paul writes, "and I have kept the faith. And now there is . . . the prize" (4:7–8).

TIRHAKAH
See *Pharaoh*.

TIRZAH
A town in northern Israel, noted for its beauty. It was one of the places captured by Joshua. Later it was the home of Jeroboam I, and the first capital of the northern kingdom of Israel. King Omri later moved the centre of government to his new city of Samaria. The site of Tirzah is Tell el-Far'ah about 7 miles/11km north-east of Shechem (Nablus).
Joshua 12:24; 1 Kings 14–16; 2 Kings 15:14, 16; Song of Solomon (Songs) 6:4

TISHBE
The place from which Elijah, "the Tishbite", presumably came. It was in Gilead, east of the Jordan, but the actual site is unknown.
1 Kings 17:1, etc.

TITHING
Each year a "tithe" (a tenth of one's produce) was given to God for the upkeep of the priests. A second tax was used for a sacrificial meal, in which the worshipper and his family shared at one of the festivals. A third tax was used to help the poor.
Leviticus 27:30–33; Numbers 18:21; Deuteronomy 14:22–29; Matthew 23:23

TITUS
A non-Jewish (Gentile) Christian who was a friend and helper of Paul. Titus was with Paul on one of his

visits to Jerusalem and probably travelled with him quite often. For some time Titus worked with the Christians at Corinth. He smoothed over the bad feeling between the Corinthian church and Paul. When Titus rejoined Paul and told him how much better things were, Paul wrote the second letter to the Corinthians. Titus went back to Corinth with this letter and helped organize a collection there for needy Christians in Judea. He was working in Crete when Paul sent his letter to Titus.

The church there had problems similar to those Timothy faced in Ephesus: problems of false teaching and pointless arguments.

The letter reminds Titus that Christian leaders should be of good character (chapter 1). It explains his duties to the different age-groups in the church (chapter 2) and closes with general warnings and advice about behaviour and attitudes among Christians.
1 Corinthians 16:10; 2 Corinthians 2:13; 7:13ff.; 8; 12:18; Galatians 2; 2 Timothy 4:10; Titus

TOB

A region south of Damascus. At the time of the Judges Jephthah lived there as an outlaw. The people of Tob helped the Ammonites against David.
Judges 11:3; 2 Samuel 10:6

TOBIAH

An Ammonite who tried to force Nehemiah to stop rebuilding the walls of Jerusalem.
Nehemiah 2:10ff.; 4; 6; 13

TOPHETH

The place in the Valley of Hinnom where children were sacrificed. The shrine was destroyed by King Josiah.

2 Kings 23:10; Jeremiah 7:31; 19:6, 11–14

TOWNS

The difference between a town or city and a village in Bible times was not its size but its defences. Villages were unwalled settlements. Towns had walls around them. They were built on top of a hill (or a mound formed by the ruins of earlier towns) for defence. They also needed a good water supply close by. At Megiddo a tunnel was dug from the city to its spring, to bring water inside in case of siege. Towns were usually built in fertile parts of the country, where crops were good and people needed to get together to protect themselves against invaders. They were also often sited at a cross-roads or junction of trade routes.

A reconstruction of the town of Lachish, surrounded by double walls built by Rehoboam in the tenth century BC. The large building in the centre is the Israelite palace.

Towns

Towns in early Israel Towns were very small —
often only about 6–10 acres — the size of a modern
city square (640 acres make a square mile). There
would be about 150–250 houses inside the walls,
with 1,000 people living there. From a distance the
towns in Canaan looked rather like castles. When the
tent-dwelling Israelites first entered the country
their spies reported seeing "cities with walls that
reached the sky" (Deuteronomy 1:28). These fortresses first began when nomadic clans decided to
settle permanently. The clan chief became a "king"
over his own territory. There was no central government, and the kings of different towns often squab-
bled and fought.

To begin with the Israelites simply patched up the
houses and buildings in the cities they captured from
the Canaanites. They had to learn building skills
from their neighbours. In times of peace there was a
large "overspill" from the towns, and people
camped outside the walls, grazing their cattle and
working the land.

Life in the towns was very cramped. Houses were
poorly built and joined on house to house. Where
the ground sloped, houses were built one above the
other. There were no real streets — just spaces
between houses — narrow alleys leading to nowhere
in particular. There was no paving. Drains were
open channels. Mud and rubbish — garbage, broken
pots, old mud-bricks — piled up outside, so that the
level of the alleys was often higher than the ground-
floor of the houses. Rain turned the whole mess into
a swamp. In winter, people were cooped up in the
damp and filth. The summer sun helped, though the

smells remained. But by then most of the people had moved away, to live and work in the fields. In peacetime they were country-dwellers for two-thirds of the year, townsmen for one-third.

The fortified gateway was the main open space in each town. In daytime the gates were noisy and crowded, bustling with life — merchants arriving; people buying and selling; elders meeting in council; others settling disputes and hearing cases. Beggars, pedlars, workmen, scribes, visitors, traders and shoppers — with their asses, camels and even cattle — all gathered at the city gate.

In the bigger towns there was more space for the shopkeepers. Sometimes each trade had its own area, but there were no specially-built shops. Each tradesman set out his goods on a stall at the side of the street. At night they were packed away. The city gates were closed and barred.

Important buildings Most towns had one or two larger buildings, as well as houses. From King Solomon's time, when government became more centralized, the town grew more important as an administrative centre for the district. At his capital, Jerusalem, Solomon had his "cabinet" — including a head of administration, secretary of state, keeper of the palace, chancellor of the exchequer and minister of forced labour. He organized twelve tax districts from which he collected food. This involved putting up buildings in which the food could be stored, and providing lodgings for his royal servants and officials in the main towns of each district.

Some of the most important buildings in Israel were connected with religion. There were important religious centres not only at Jerusalem, but also at Dan and Bethel. Most towns had their own small shrine with an altar, very like the Canaanite shrines (the "high places") which were supposed to have been destroyed.

Solomon introduced slave and forced labour to carry out a great building plan. At Jerusalem he built the temple, palaces for himself and his queen, and other large halls (one probably to store arms; one as a court of justice). They were impressive stone buildings with cedar beams and panelling. The temple was beautiful, with olive-wood doors decorated with carved figures, all covered in gold. The Israelites, taught by skilled craftsmen from Tyre, had come a long way since their nomadic life in the desert (though even then they were able to produce beautiful work, as the making of the tabernacle shows).

Solomon also rebuilt and fortified a number of cities, to strengthen his country's defences. The three most important were Gezer, Megiddo and Hazor. The double walls and massive gateways in all three were built to the same plan. There were also warehouses, and stables for horses and chariots.

When the Jews were in exile in Babylon they could no longer go to the temple at Jerusalem. Instead they met together on the sabbath (Saturday) to listen to the law and hear it explained. When they returned, they built local meeting-houses for this purpose. These were the first "synagogues" (the Greek word *synagein* means "to meet together").

New Testament times With the coming of the Greeks and Romans, towns were planned more carefully. The great cities of New Testament times were very different from the fortress towns of early Israel. Antioch in Syria (the city which was Paul's base) had wide streets, some paved with marble, baths, theatres, temples and market-places. It even had lights at night. Many towns now had tall buildings, several storeys high, set in narrow streets.

King Herod the Great rebuilt Samaria (renamed Sebaste) and Caesarea in the Roman style, with a main street through the centre of the city, lined with shops, baths and theatres, and crossed at right angles by smaller streets. Houses were built in blocks of four. The Romans built aqueducts to bring piped water into the cities. They built public baths and introduced more efficient drainage works to take away waste water and sewage. Life in the cities, for the rich at least, was now much pleasanter than in earlier times. The poor, and those in more remote places, were less affected by these changes.

In Jesus' day, the most dazzling sight in Jerusalem was the great temple being built by the Herods out of white marble, with parts of the walls covered in gold. The temple drew pilgrims from all over the Mediterranean world, especially for the great religious festivals. There may have been as many as a quarter of a million people living in the city. Its streets were crowded with people buying and selling. The shops and stalls sold everything, from necessities like sandals and cloth, meat, fruit and vegetables, to the luxury goods offered by goldsmiths, jewellers, silk, linen and perfume merchants. There were seven different markets, and two market days each week. Jerusalem had its restaurants and wine shops for ordinary people as well as its grander buildings — the palaces, Roman amphitheatre, and the fortress of Antonia.

TRACHONITIS

A district linked with Ituraea (see *Ituraea*). Together they made up the territory ruled by Herod Philip at the time when John the Baptist began his preaching. Trachonitis was a rocky volcanic area, the haunt of outlaws, east of Galilee and south of Damascus. Luke 3:1

TRADE AND COMMERCE

Sale of land One of the earliest business deals recorded in the Bible is Abraham's purchase of a field and cave from Ephron the Hittite. From the time when the Israelites settled in Canaan the buying and selling of land was disapproved of. Men held their land in trust from God. They were not the owners. Each family had received a plot of land as its own inheritance. It should therefore remain as part of that family's property.

So there were laws of "redemption", which provided that, if a man became so poor he had to sell land, a member of his own family must buy it. There were also the laws concerning the "Jubilee" years, which laid down that every fiftieth year, all land must be returned to its original owner. How far, and at what times in history, these laws actually operated is not known. The system certainly did not operate successfully under the kings. King Ahab of Israel engineered the death of his subject, Naboth, in order to take his property. And rich men bought up the land of those who were unable to pay their debts.

There were ancient customs connected with acquiring land. In the Book of Ruth the seller takes off his shoe and hands it to the buyer. This may have symbolized taking possession by placing one's foot on the land. When Jeremiah bought a field there was a deed of contract and a copy was stored in a clay jar (the Old Testament equivalent of a safe deposit). Genesis 23; Leviticus 25:8–34; 1 Kings 21:1–16; Isaiah 5:8; Ruth 4:7–8; Psalm 60:8; Jeremiah 32:6–15

Local trade Israelite farmers were poor. They generally only produced enough for their family's needs, and there were few things they needed that they could not make themselves — apart from pottery, and metal tools and weapons. Travel and transport were difficult. The ass carried most of their loads, as a pack animal, and carts were small. So, for a long time, local trade was probably very simple. But market-places gradually developed around the gates of towns and cities. Farm produce, sheep and goats were sold there. Potters and smiths made and sold their goods, and visiting foreign merchants set up their stalls.

International trade Three factors led to Israel's involvement in international trade, especially at the time of the kings.

The first was the growth of "industries" which needed important raw materials. Metal-working and clothes-making were the most important of these.

The second was Israel's conquest of new territories which were on the international trade routes.

Thirdly, the kings themselves had an interest in creating wealth and buying luxury goods.

Trade and commerce

The fact that traders were popularly called "Canaanites" probably reflects the fact that for a long time the Israelites were confined to the hills and so were not involved in foreign trade. The prophet Isaiah talks of Tyre "whose merchant princes were the most honoured men on earth" (23:8). But Hosea declares: "The people of Israel are as dishonest as the Canaanites; they love to cheat their customers with false scales" (12:8).

Trade routes by land Israel stood at the junction between Asia Minor (Turkey and Syria), Egypt and Arabia. The Israelites made good use of this fact, although it was nomadic desert tribesmen who actually carried the goods by camel caravan.

From Asia Minor they travelled over the Taurus mountains, west of the Syrian desert, through Aleppo, Hamath, and Damascus to Israel.

From Mesopotamia they went north of the Syrian desert via Harran and Aleppo, then south into Israel.

From Arabia their route was by the Red Sea shore and at Aqaba, either north to Damascus, via Moab and Gilead, north-west to Jerusalem, or west to the port of Gaza.

Trade routes by sea Right up to Roman times sea transport was controlled by the Phoenicians. They travelled to the west Mediterranean, perhaps as far as Britain, and operated a coastal route from Lebanon to Egypt, calling at such places as Ugarit, Byblos, Sidon, Tyre, Acco, Caesarea, Jaffa and ports serving the Philistine plain. As time went on, wharves and warehouses were built and extended. There was also a route down the Red Sea and the east coast of Africa, but trade with this area fluctuated.

Royal projects   Some of the kings of Israel formed alliances with neighbouring lands, especially Tyre. This may have been done deliberately to help foster trade, as well as to ensure peace. Tyre at this time became the largest sea power in the Mediterranean, with colonies and ports all around the coast.

Solomon also seems to have acted as a middleman between various countries. It seems he imported horses from Cilicia and chariots from Egypt, and then exported them both to Syria.

When the Queen of Sheba visited Solomon, she may have been part of a trade delegation from South Arabia (where incense was produced). And when Solomon fortified Tadmor (Palmyra), it may have been to make it easier for traders to cross over the Syrian desert.

Solomon enlisted the help of the Phoenicians to build ships at Ezion-geber, at the head of the Gulf of Aqaba. They manned them and sailed to "Ophir" (probably on the north-east coast of Arica). Later Jehoshaphat, king of Judah, had a joint venture with the kings of Israel and Tyre to renew this trade, but the ships were wrecked in a storm.

It seems to have been a practice for kings to try to secure the right to open markets in foreign cities to sell their own produce. King Ahab of Israel had this right in Damascus.

Under some of the kings the nation grew prosperous, and wealth poured into the country. But the prophets viewed this situation with strong disapproval. Prosperity bred pride, corruption, debt and slavery. There was more for the rich, but less and less for the poor. What was worse, imports included not only material goods but also foreign religions. Ezekiel 27; 1 Kings 5; 9:11; 10:28–29; 2 Chronicles 9:28; 1 Kings 10:1–13; 2 Chronicles 20:35–37; 1 Kings 22:48–49; 20:34

New Testament times The "Roman peace", especially when Pompey had cleared the seas of pirates, provided ample opportunities for trade. In Palestine the profession of merchant was held in great respect, and even the priests engaged in commerce. The range of exports and imports increased.

Trade routes by land had come under the control of the Nabataeans, whose capital was at Petra (in modern Jordan). Camel caravans were often long and there was always danger from robbers. This seems to be particularly true around the area of Jerusalem, although King Herod took measures to suppress it.

Jewish records show that, in spite of Jerusalem's remote highland position, no fewer than 118 different kinds of foreign luxury goods were being sold there. There were seven different markets. Those who brought goods to market paid heavy taxes, and prices were high. There was a busy trade in goods required for worship at the temple, especially animals for sacrifice. Jesus objected to the fact that this trade went on in the temple court, the only place where non-Jews could worship. The temple was probably the most important factor in Jerusalem's commerce. Every Jew had to make payments to the temple treasury, and this no doubt helped Jerusalem to pay for imports.

The Jewish rabbis had strict rules for business deals, and there were market inspectors to see that

they were carried out. Scales and weights had to be cleaned regularly. Buyers had the right to complain. And no interest was to be charged to fellow-Jews. Personal belongings could be handed over as security against a loan. But essentials such as cloaks, ploughs and millstones were not to be sold in the event of non-payment. These rules clearly have their roots in the Old Testament law, but they were especially emphasized at the time of Jesus.
Luke 10:30–37; Leviticus 19:35–36; Deuteronomy 25:13–16

Payment In the earliest times trade was by bartering. In Genesis 33:19 and Joshua 24:32 the word used for "money" means literally "cattle", which originally no doubt fixed the price of the goods. Gold and silver were soon introduced, but coins were not used until the seventh century BC and after. A shekel was not a coin, but a weight of gold or silver. So trading involved carrying about large amounts of metal, and merchants were needed to weigh and test the ingots. There is no evidence of any banking systems in Israel before the exile, though these did exist in Mesopotamia.

By New Testament times there were local currencies and a regular system for banking. Trade between countries with different currencies called for the services of money-changers.

TRANSFIGURATION

The transfiguration of Jesus came at a turning-point in his life. Peter had just recognized Jesus as the Messiah, and Jesus went on to teach his disciples about his coming death and resurrection. Then he went up a mountain (traditionally thought to be Mt Hermon) with Peter, James and John. There they saw Jesus transformed by a heavenly glory, and Elijah and Moses talking with him. The experience ended with a voice from heaven, similar to that at the time of Jesus' baptism, which said, "This is my Son, whom I have chosen — listen to him."

Moses and Elijah represented the two major parts of the Old Testament, the Law and the Prophets. By their presence they showed that all was fulfilled in Jesus. Peter wanted tents to be put up, to make the experience last. But that was not the point. The transfiguration confirmed the rightness of the way Jesus had chosen. It pointed to the glory that would one day be his. But before that time he had to die on the cross. This was the topic of conversation with Moses and Elijah — Jesus' "exodus". But the disciples did not understand this until after the resurrection.
Matthew 17:1–8; Mark 9:2–8; Luke 8:28–36

TRAVEL AND TRANSPORT

The Bible describes many journeys: Abraham moving home from Ur to Canaan; Jacob going down into Egypt; the Israelites journeying through the desert; the Queen of Sheba visiting King Solomon. These are just a few of the journeys recorded in the Old Testament. In the New Testament the travels of Paul and other Christian leaders are recorded in some detail in the Book of Acts, and Jesus himself must have covered very considerable distances during his public ministry.

Pedestrians In Bible times most journeys were

made on foot. Not everybody could afford to keep a pack-animal and, even if a family owned an ass, on a family journey someone would have to walk.

This terra-cotta model of a covered wagon was made in about 2500 BC.

Animals   Although the nomads of the desert kept camels, the main beast of burden throughout Bible times was the ass. The ass was domesticated long before either the horse or the camel, and was always the most popular means of general transport.

Abraham possessed camels, though he probably acquired them after he left Harran. When Jacob settled in Canaan, he seems to have had no further use for them, for they are not mentioned among his property when he went down to Egypt. His son Joseph sent him provisions for the journey on asses. With the development of international trade, particularly the Arabian spice trade, camels were used more and more in Israel from about 1000 BC.

Horses were usually kept for war. They were expensive to feed compared with camels and asses and could not carry as much. But by New Testament times they were often used for civilian purposes, when chariots for transport developed from the basic war-chariot.

"Caravan" convoys Traders travelled together as a "caravan" — a convoy of asses and camels — for company, safety and as a protection against thieves. Joseph was sold to one such group of travelling merchants.

The caravan routes crossed Israel in all directions. With the Mediterranean Sea to the west and the Syrian desert to the east, all traffic between Mesopotamia and Arabia, Egypt and the rest of Africa had to pass through a narrow corridor about 75 miles/120 km wide.

Great cities grew up at strategic points on these routes. One of these was Palmyra ("Tadmor in the wilderness"), a desert city fortified by King Solomon.

Vehicles In Old Testament times the use of wheeled transport was limited. Horse-drawn chariots were used by armies and by noblemen — chariots may even have been an indication of rank. (Joseph, for instance, was given a royal chariot to ride in; his family travelled to Egypt in wagons or carts; and the goods were carried by asses.) But without properly made up roads, the condition of the ground restricted the use of chariots. The Egyptian chariots pursuing Moses and the Israelites stuck in the mud of the sea bed and, many centuries later, King Ahab had to race back to Jezreel before the rain came.

Carts drawn by asses or cattle were used on farms. On two occasions it seems that the sacred Covenant Box (ark) was carried in an ordinary farm cart. And the prophet Amos describes the people of Israel groaning "like a cart loaded with corn".

By New Testament times the Romans had built first-class roads, and chariots of various types were used — from the light chariots raced in the games, to more substantial carriages with room to seat at least two people.

Most streets in towns were very narrow, and those who could afford it travelled in litters. These litters were couches with a framework so that curtains could conceal the traveller. They rested on poles which were carried by men or sometimes by horses. Genesis 41:43; 45:19; Exodus 14:23–25; 1 Kings 18:44–45; 1 Samuel 6:7–8; 2 Samuel 6:3; Amos 2:13; Acts 8:29–31

Inland waterways Apart from the Nile, the Tigris and the Euphrates, not many rivers in Bible lands were navigable. Barges (with sails) were used on the Nile, bringing corn to the seaport, but there was no other important river traffic. Although canals were often planned by Roman emperors (Nero, for example, wanted to join the Adriatic and the Aegean Seas by a Corinth canal), few were actually constructed. See also *Roads, Ships.*

TRINITY

This word is not used in the Bible. It is the name given to the statements about God in the creeds drawn up in the early centuries of the church to explain what is meant by saying that God is Father, Son and Holy Spirit. This is the teaching of Jesus and the New Testament as a whole. From earliest times it was stated at every Christian baptism.

The Jewish teaching was that there is only one God. Nothing and no one must compromise that belief. Yet the New Testament writers clearly show God as the Father who created and sustained everything in his love and power, as the Son who came into this world, and as the Spirit who worked in their own lives.

After the end of the New Testament period the church found it necessary to work out carefully-worded statements about three persons in one God, in order to uphold the truth of the New Testament against false beliefs.

See also *God, Holy Spirit, Jesus Christ.*
Matthew 28:19; John 5:19–29; 8:23–29, 58; 14–17; Acts 2:32–33; 2 Corinthians 13:14 and so on; Exodus 20:2–6; Deuteronomy 6:4; Isaiah 45:5

TROAS
A port about 10 miles/16km from Troy, in what is now north-west Turkey. Paul used the port a number of times on his travels. It was at Troas that he had his vision of a Macedonian man calling for help, and he sailed from there on his first mission to Europe. On a later visit to Troas he restored Eutychus to life after he had fallen from an upstairs window while Paul was preaching.
Acts 16:8–12; 20:5–12; 2 Corinthians 2:12; 2 Timothy 4:13

TROPHIMUS
A Christian from Ephesus who travelled with Paul to Europe and Jeusalem.
Acts 20:4; 21:29; 2 Timothy 4:20

TYCHICUS

A friend and helper of Paul, probably from Ephesus. It is almost certain he travelled with Paul to Jerusalem because he had been chosen by the churches of Asia Minor (Turkey) to take the money they had collected for needy Christians in Judea. Tychicus was with Paul while he was in prison. Paul trusted him and sent him to Colossae and later to Ephesus with the letters he had written. During his last imprisonment in Rome, Paul sent Tychicus to Ephesus to help the Christians there.
Acts 20:4; Ephesians 6:21–22; Colossians 4:7–9; 2 Timothy 4:12; Titus 3:12

TYRE

An important port and city-state on the coast of Lebanon. Tyre had two harbours, one on the mainland, the other on an off-shore island. In about 1200 BC the Philistines plundered Sidon, the other important Phoenician port 20 miles/32km or so to the north. From that time on Tyre became the leading city.

Tyre's "golden age" was the time of David and Solomon. King Hiram of Tyre supplied wood and skilled men to build the temple at Jerusalem. Trade flourished. Tyre's own specialities were glassware and fine-quality purple dye made from local sea-snails.

King Ahab of Israel married the daughter of the king of Tyre. The city is often mentioned in the Psalms and by the prophets, who condemned Tyre's pride and luxury. In the ninth century BC Tyre came under pressure from the Assyrians. The city paid heavy tribute in return for a measure of freedom. In the same year as the fall of Samaria, Sargon II of Assyria captured Tyre. When Assyria lost power Tyre became free and prosperous again. For thirteen years (587–574 BC), King Nebuchadnezzar of Babylon besieged the city. In 332 BC Alexander the Great managed to take the island port by building a causeway from the mainland.

In New Testament times Jesus himself visited the area around Tyre and Sidon and spoke to the people. See also *Phoenicia*.
2 Samuel 5:11; 1 Kings 5; 9:10–14; 16:31; Psalm 45:12; Isaiah 23; Ezekiel 26; Matthew 15:21; Luke 6:17; Acts 21:3

UR

A famous city on the River Euphrates in south Babylonia (modern Iraq); the home of Abraham's family before they moved north to Harran. The site of Ur had been occupied for several thousand years before it was finally abandoned about 300 BC. Excavations have uncovered thousands of inscribed clay tablets describing the city's history and life. The Royal Graves (about 2600 BC) contained many treasures, examples of beautiful craftsmanship: gold weapons, an inlaid mosaic gaming-board, the famous mosaic standard showing scenes of peace and war, and many other things. Ruins of a great stepped temple tower (ziggurat) still remain.
Genesis 11:28–31, etc.

Drawing of a partial reconstruction of the great ziggurat at Ur, built about 2100 BC as a temple to the moon-god Nannar.

URARTIANS

The Urartians lived in the east of Turkey, around Lake Van. They may have been related to the Hurrians and Armenians. The mountains in the land were named after the kingdom. The highest of all is now called Mount Ararat. It was on one of the mountains of the Ararat range that Noah's ark came to rest. About 750–650 BC strong Urartians kings tried to dominate northern Syria and check the Assyrians. They gave sanctuary to the sons who murdered King Sennacherib. Their temples and palaces show distinctive designs and decoration. But they used the cuneiform script to write their language. The Urartians worshipped a god called Haldi, and called themselves the children of Haldi. Genesis 8:4; 2 Kings 19:37

URIAH

1. A Hittite soldier in King David's army, and husband of Bathsheba. Because David was in love with Bathsheba, he had Uriah sent to the front line, to get him killed.
2 Samuel 11
2. A priest in Jerusalem. He obeyed King Ahaz's instructions and redesigned the temple to a pattern approved by the Assyrians.
2 Kings 16:10ff.
3. A prophet at the time of Jeremiah; killed by King Jehoiakim because he spoke out against the people of Judah.
Jeremiah 26:20ff.

UZ

The home country of Job, probably in the region of Edom.
Job 1:1

UZZAH

One of the men who helped King David take the Covenant Box (the ark) from Kiriath-jearim to Jerusalem. He drove the cart on which it was placed. When the oxen stumbled, Uzzah put out his hand to steady the ark and died.
2 Samuel 6:3–7

UZZIAH

See *Azariah*.

V

VASHTI
The queen King Ahasuerus divorced when she refused to obey him.
Esther 1

VILLAGES
The "village" of Old Testament times was simply an unwalled farming settlement. Villages grew up near a stream or spring that would provide water all the year round. As soon as animals were domesticated and people began to grow crops for food, they tended to settle in one place rather than move about. People were farming at Jericho, using picks, axes and digging sticks, as long ago as 6000 BC. At this stage there were only villages and no towns.

The possibility of towns (large settlements) came with the invention of the bronze ploughshare (some time after 4000 BC), when food production increased. Towns (fortified villages) were needed because of the struggle between the settled people and the nomadic people who wanted the same water supplies. Towns were therefore built up as larger, protected centres of civilization (see *Towns*). In peacetime, people lived out in the villages, but when invasion threatened they gathered to the safety of the town. During the summer months, too, the population left the towns for the villages, to work in the fields.

Ownership of land   Abraham and his family lived a partly nomadic, partly settled life. They moved about with their flocks but they also cultivated crops. In Mesopotamia, where Abraham had come from, there had been a "feudal" system of allocating land. The king provided gifts of land ("fiefs") in return for a promise of personal service, and the land was passed on from father to son. When the Israelites entered Canaan the idea stayed in a new form. God was their king, and he gave them their land. Each family received their land by lot (Joshua 15), just as the fiefs had been given by lot in Mesopotamia.

Because it was God's land, he told them how to make proper use of it and how the produce was to be shared. One plot of land was given to each family, and it seems to have become the family burial-ground as well as the place to grow food. Each person's land was the gift of God (Isaiah 34:17), not to be casually bought and sold. (This was why Naboth would not sell his plot to King Ahab — 1 Kings 21:1–16.) If a family fell on hard times, it was the duty of their nearest relative to buy the land and keep it in the family. As far as we know, the family property went to the eldest son, so it was very important to have a son to carry on the family name and property. Every fiftieth year was a year of Jubilee, when any land which had been mortgaged to pay off a debt, was to be returned to the family. This helped keep everyone on the same level and avoided a sharp division between rich landowners and poor labourers. It also emphasized the importance of the family holding.

The land immediately around the village was

therefore private property. The land further outside the villages was looked upon as common land. It was divided into plots, which were distributed by lot to families each year. Under the kings, beginning with David and Solomon, the old equality began to break down. A new wealthy class of rulers and officials grew up. They oppressed the poor and bought up land. Big estates took the place of small family farms. The people who had lost their land had to hire themselves out as farm labourers. The poor were very poor, and suffered great hardship. The prophets spoke out against all this (Isaiah 5:8; Micah 2:2).

The change in the ownership of land led to a change in housing. In the tenth century BC, all the houses in a town or village were the same size, but by the eighth century BC, some houses were bigger and better and were grouped in a particular part of the town.

Daily work   In early Old Testament times almost everyone in the village was a farmer, growing what was needed for food (see *Farming*). They kept sheep, goats and cattle. These provided food for the family — and also manure for the ground.

The seasons set the pattern of work for the year. The wet season, from October to April, was used for ploughing, sowing (by hand from an open basket), harrowing and weeding. Then the harvesting began — first flax, then barley (April/May), then wheat. Work on the vines began in the spring, when the plants had to be pruned. As they grew, trailing branches had to be propped up clear of the ground. Grapes were ready for picking from July to October.

Most people also had fig and olive trees. The main crop of figs came in August/September. The olive harvest was last, in October/November, when the grape gathering was over.

Every day the women baked bread. First came the back-breaking effort of grinding the grain into a coarse flour. This was mixed with salt and water to make dough. Usually some of the fermented dough from the day before was mixed in and the bread left to rise before baking. Another vital job each day was to fetch water from the local spring or well. Only a few houses had their own well or water-storage cistern underground. The women carried the heavy water-pots home on their head or shoulder. There was always plenty to do, from dawn to dark. There might be milk to make into cheese and yoghurt. There was also wool to be spun and woven. The work in the fields was not all left to the men. Everyone helped with the harvest and with crushing the grapes and olives in the presses. The working day ended at sunset, when the whole family gathered together for the main meal of the day.

Progress and problems   Country life changed very little down the centuries. The plough and other implements improved. But even in New Testament times they were still primitive, the plough cutting one furrow at a time. As time went by there was more specialization on large estates. There were skilled professionals to prune the vines, to drive the teams of oxen and to plough. "Unskilled" workers weeded the fields, spread manure, and did countless other tasks.

The main problems also remained the same. Water

was the first concern in a hot country with no rainfall at all for three or four months in the summer. The village well had to provide drinking water for the family and their animals, and water for the land. Sometimes an endless chain of leather buckets was used to bring the water to the surface and run it along irrigation ditches to the roots of the crops.

Locusts were another problem. Without warning they could arrive in swarms to eat every bit of living greenery. Wild animals — wolves, jackals, lions — could kill the livestock, too.

A third problem, completely disrupting village life, was a human one. Time and again invading armies attacked or passed through the country, taking prisoners or conscripting young men. If they came at the end of the wet season, the new growing crops were destroyed. If they came at harvest, the crops were taken away as booty or used to feed the army. Either way the villagers were likely to starve.

VINE
A trailing shrub producing grapes, one of the most important of all fruit-crops. Moses' spies brought back huge clusters of grapes as a sign of the richness of the Promised Land. Vines were planted in rows in carefully prepared vineyards on the sunny hill slopes. Each spring the vines were pruned, and as the grapes ripened the owner kept a sharp lookout for intruders — animal or human — from a special watch-tower. At harvest time the grapes were picked and taken to be trodden out at the wine-press. Some were also made into raisin-cakes. The fermenting wine was stored in new skins or pottery jars to

mature. The vine was a national emblem in Israel, a symbol of peace and prosperity. Jesus used it in five of his parables, and described himself as the true vine on which the branches (his followers) depend. Numbers 13:20, 24; Matthew 9:17; 20:1–6; 21:28–32, 33; Luke 13:6–9; John 15:1

WAR

War is a dominant theme in the Old Testament, despite the fact that God's law protected life and stood firm against murder. The reason is that God himself was vitally involved with a single nation, Israel. They lived in troubled times. "The Lord is a warrior," sang Moses, after the escape from Egypt. Then, when the people of Israel set out to enter Canaan God told them that the battle was his: "The Lord your God is going with you, and he will give you victory." The former inhabitants of the land must all be destroyed ("devoted" to God). It was a "holy war". But its ultimate goal was peace and well-being. Israel should trust and obey God, otherwise their enemies would win. This is the message of the Book of Judges.

The prophets often continued this theme. When the kings went to war for political reasons and put their trust in horses, chariots and cavalry, defeat was often seen as God's way of punishing his people for their lack of faith.

But after the exile, when the people came back to their homeland, things changed. The Jews had experienced many defeats and so the idea grew that war was more the work of Satan than of God. They hoped that God would send his own warrior-king to fight a final battle and bring victory and peace to his people, either in this world or in the next. This was the Jewish hope, centred on the coming Messiah.

Jesus himself rejected this view of the Messiah. He came to bring God's peace. There would be division between those who believed and those who did not, but men were not to be regarded as enemies. Only in the visions in the Book of Revelation is Jesus seen as a warrior. But Christians are pictured as soldiers engaged in a spiritual war against evil. Victory in this war is certain, for Jesus by his death and resurrection defeated Satan. Physical, historical wars are among the signs that the end of the age is near. Exodus 15:3; Deuteronomy 20:4; Isaiah 31:1; 5:25–30 and many other passages; Revelation 19:11; Ephesians 6:10–17; John 12:31

The army From the early days of Israel's history every man was called to be a soldier. He could be summoned by a tribal leader, as Abraham led men out to rescue Lot from his captors. Each of the tribes was responsible for occupying the land assigned to them. They sometimes helped one another in the task, as they rallied under one leader to resist the Canaanites and Philistines, and to defeat the desert tribes who were constantly raiding Israel. Any tribe which did not respond to a call for help was treated with scorn.

There was no standing army until Saul became king. He appointed 3,000 men as a permanent army, under his direct command but with Abner in charge. King David was a military genius. Joab, his commander-in-chief, captured Jerusalem and taught the Israelites new methods of warfare. David was the first king to have a personal bodyguard of great warriors. These men had been with him when he was an outlaw and had proved their loyalty to him.

The Bible speaks of "fifties" and "hundreds", with their commanders, but very little is known of the detailed organization of the army. For a long time the army was composed almost entirely of foot-soldiers, some equipped as archers or slingers, others for hand-to-hand combat. The cavalry and chariots used by the Egyptians, Philistines and Canaanites, were introduced in Israel under Solomon but the Israelites fought mainly in the hills where these methods were impractical. "The gods of Israel," say the officials of King Benhadad of Syria, "are mountain gods." The later kings of Judah still sent to Egypt for chariots and horsemen. King Ahab of Israel, however, kept a huge force of chariots, and his stables have been discovered at Megiddo.

Assyrian soldiers sack the city of Hamaan.

After the exile there was no Jewish army except for one short period, when non-Jewish as well as Jewish soldiers were employed and paid a wage. Herod the Great had his own forces. They, too, included foreign mercenaries, and were under Roman command.

Genesis 14; Judges 1; 5:15–17; 1 Samuel 23:1–5; 25; 13:1–2; 17:55; 2 Samuel 23:8–39; 1 Kings 10:26; 20:23–25; 2 Kings 18:24

War in the Old Testament There were three kinds of weapons used in fighting. In hand-to-hand fighting, clubs, axes, short and long swords were used. There were darts, spears and javelins for throwing. And there were many missiles, from stones and boulders to bows and arrows.

The soldier wore armour to protect himself and carried a shield for defence. The Israelites seem to have used two types of shield. A small round one was carried by the light armed infantry, and a large rectangular one was used by the men at the front, so that the battle line presented a solid front. The shields were made of a wicker or wooden frame covered with leather, which needed regular oiling. Inside the shield was a handle for holding it. There is little information about the soldiers' armour. Before David's battle with Goliath, King Saul tried to dress him in a helmet and a "coat of mail" (breastplate). But it was so heavy that he could not walk! There may also have been "greaves" to protect the legs, and a lower skirt of mail.

The kings built fortresses to protect their land. Saul fortified his capital, Gibeah. David, in addition to work on Jerusalem, built the fortresses of Libnah, Lachish, Gezer and Beth-horon in the foothills as a defence against the Philistines. Solomon strengthened many cities, especially Gezer, Hazor and Megiddo, guarding the strategic pass through the Carmel hills. When the kingdom was divided, border fortresses were established at Geba and Mizpah.

(See also *Building*.)

1 Samuel 17:4–7, 37–40

Fighting methods   Israel suffered a great deal from raiding bands of desert tribes, especially before the time of the kings. Their attacks were swift and unpredictable. Often they rode in on camels. They plundered the villages, destroyed crops, and took cattle and captives.

Where there was open combat a trumpet gave the signal for attack. And sometimes there was an arranged war-cry, like Gideon's "a sword for the Lord and for Gideon". A line of men carrying rectangular shields and long lances would advance, and the archers let fly a volley of arrows to cover them. When the lines met, fighting was hand to hand. Sometimes the issue was decided by contest between two or more champions. Often the army was divided into two companies, to close in on the side and the rear of the enemy. Under King David the general strategy and tactics of open warfare began to be more skilfully planned.

An attack on a city often took place just before dawn to take the defenders completely by surprise. A favourite ruse was to advance with only half the army and then retreat. When the inhabitants joyfully pursued, the other half of the army would enter the city. In David's time the Israelites began to adopt the practice of laying siege to a city. Usually, though, they were the victims, rather than the initiators of this kind of warfare.

The experts in this were the Assyrians. Spies would be sent to discover a city's weaknesses, and, if a succession of towns had already fallen, a delegation

was sent to try to frighten the town into submission. All lines of communication were cut off, and they took control of all the water supplies in the neighbourhood. It was to prevent this that King Hezekiah of Judah diverted water into the city by digging a tunnel. The enemy then prepared for a long stay, while conditions in the city grew gradually more horrible. To hasten defeat the Assyrians would construct causeways up to the walls, and wooden machines on wheels. These served as platforms from which arrows could be shot at the defenders, and as battering-rams to weaken the walls. Sometimes they would try to tunnel under the wall. Finally an all-out attack was made. The archers kept up heavy fire, while the rest of the army, protected by shields, scaled the walls with ladders. The defenders meantimes hurled down burning arrows, boiling oil and stones in an attempt to keep them off.
Judges 6:1–6, 11; 2 Chronicles 13:12; Judges 7:20; 20:29–36; 2 Samuel 12:27; 2 Kings 18–19; 6:24–7:20

The aftermath of battle   When a city was taken, it was the usual practice to kill, mutilate or enslave all male inhabitants. Women and children were taken captive. The walls were broken down and buildings burnt, and the soldiers were usually free to take whatever plunder they could find, though the more valuable items were claimed by the king. If a city submitted, hostages were taken and a heavy tribute demanded.

The Roman army   In New Testament times the Mediterranean world was at peace under Roman government. No book of the New Testament is written against a background of war, though occasionally the Roman army is present. From time to time Jews rebelled and these rebellions were fiercely crushed by the Romans. The province of Syria, of which Palestine formed a part, being on the border of the Empire, was a potential source of danger. It was therefore under the direct command of the emperor, with detachments of soldiers permanently stationed there.

Roman soldiers often behaved as if the Jews were their servants. But some, especially the officers, won respect from the people. A company of Roman soldiers, detailed to keep the peace in Jerusalem at the time of the Passover Festival, took part in the arrest of Jesus and enjoyed some rough horse-play at the prisoner's expense. In general, however, the Romans had a reputation for justice. Roman soldiers prevented Paul being lynched in Jerusalem, and brought him safely under armed escort to their headquarters at Caesarea, when there were threats against his life.

The emperor had a personal bodyguard, the Praetorian guard, stationed in Rome and some other provincial centres (including Ephesus). When Paul was in prison the "whole palace guard" knew that he was there because he was "a servant of Christ".
Luke 13:1; Matthew 5:41; Luke 7:1–10; Acts 10; John 18:3; Mark 15:16–20; Acts 21:30–36; 23:16–24; Ephesians 6:14–17; Philippians 1:13

WATER
Israel has the desert at its door and the rain comes only in winter. It is a land where it has always been

important to save and store water. The Jordan is the only river of any size, and that empties uselessly (from the point of view of conserving water) into the Dead Sea — where water evaporates from the surface at a rate of 60in/1,500mm a year. The Jordan flows all the year round, fed by snow from Mt Hermon. But this is exceptional. Most streams flow in sudden spates, followed by months when their beds are dry. So, from earliest times, the towns and villages of Israel have relied on wells and springs for their water supply. The right of access to a well was a valuable privilege. If the wells in an area were blocked up, the inhabitants were left to die of thirst. As cities grew bigger, the problem of keeping them supplied with water became acute. Jerusalem, high in the porous limestone hills, needed a whole system of waterworks. King Hezekiah "built a reservoir and dug a tunnel to bring water into the city" to safeguard the supply of water if the city was besieged (2 Kings 20:20).

The Romans built aqueducts and irrigation canals to cope with the problem. But after they left, the works fell into disrepair. Only in the twentieth century have they been restored or replaced. However, the modern state of Israel was not content to watch its main water resource — the Jordan — run untapped into the Dead Sea. A project has been developed in recent years for diverting Galilee water to other uses. Part of the problem is, of course, that both the Sea of Galilee and the Jordan are far below sea level and, if their waters are to be used anywhere outside the rift valley, it is necessary to pump water up over the "spine" of Israel. This has now been done, and the water is taken south down the coastal plain in a series of canals and tunnels. These go as far as the Tekuma reservoir, near Gaza. They have made town supply schemes and irrigation possible as far south as the fringe of the desert.

WEAVING
See *Clothes-making*.

WEDDINGS
See *Marriage*.

WEIGHTS AND MEASURES
There were standard weights and measurements of length, dry and liquid capacity, but there was little *exact* measurement. Standard length measurements based on the relative sizes of the human arm and hand arose out of general use. Measurement of distances in Old Testament times were based on a day's journey or even a bowshot.

Foodstuffs were measured by volume rather than by weight. The terms used are often the names of the containers which held the food. A *homer* was an "assload" (perhaps 200 litres) and was the largest measure for cereals. The *ephah* was a container, closed with a lid, holding about one tenth of a *homer*. The *bath* is the same as the *ephah*, but is used for liquids. The *omer* (meaning "sheaf") was the amount of manna gathered each day. Other measurements were also in use in the market. A *letek* is half a homer. A *hin* was six times the amount a man needs to drink in a day. The *log* was another small unit for liquids.

Precious materials and metals were measured by

weight. Small things were weighed on a beam balance with scale pans. The weights were kept in a purse. Merchants sometimes used the fact that they had two sets of weights — one when they were buying, the other when they were selling — to cheat their customers. But the law of God insisted on strict honesty. "Do not cheat when you use weights and measures. Use true and honest weights and measures, so that you may live a long time in the land" (Deuteronomy 25:13). "The Lord hates people who use dishonest scales and weights" (Proverbs 20:23). The verb "to weigh" is *shaqal* in Hebrew and the name has been given to the basic unit of weight — the *shekel*.

Measurements of length

Cubit 17.5in/445mm Measured from elbow to finger-tip; the long cubit was a handbreadth longer 20.4in/520mm New Testament cubit 21.6in/550mm 6 cubits = 1 reed

Finger or digit ¾ in/19mm Measured from the forefinger; ¼ handbreadth

Palm 3in/76mm Width of the hand at the base of the finger

Span 9in/230mm The outstretched hand from thumb to little finger: three handbreadths, or half a cubit

Weights

Table of Old Testament weights

1 gerah = approx. 0.5gm
10 gerahs = 1 bekah (approx. 6gm)
2 bekahs = 1 shekel (approx. 11gm)
50 shekels = 1 mina (approx. 500gm)
60 minas = 1 talent (approx. 30kg)

The heavy royal shekel weighed 13gm.
The heavy, double standard talent weighed 60kg.
New Testament weights
The litra (pound) = approx. 327gm
The talent = 20 to 40kg
Old Testament liquid measures
Kab = 1.2 litres
Hin = 3.66 litres
Bath = 22 litres (10 baths = 1 homer = a "donkey load")
Old Testament dry measures
Log = 0.3 litre
Kab = 1.2 litres
Omer = 2.2 litres
Seah = 7.3 litres
Ephah = 22 litres
10 ephahs = 1 homer = 220 litres

WILLOW
The willows of Israel are shrubs or small trees, often found in thickets beside streams. See also *Poplar*.

WOLF
Fierce and dangerous hunters which usually feed on smaller animals, but will also attack and kill deer, sheep and even cattle. The Bible speaks of cruel and evil leaders as "wolves" and Jesus described his followers as "sheep among wolves".
Matthew 7:15; Luke 10:3

WORD
The "word of God" is a phrase the Bible often uses when it speaks of God revealing himself to men. Just

as we can only know one another well through speech, so God made himself known by his words as well as his acts.

The "word of the Lord" is God's spoken word. The phrase often occurs in the books of the prophets. This word was not always heard; sometimes it was seen. Jesus, the final and full revelation of God, is also described as the Word. This time God's word could be seen, touched and heard. It is this word or message that the Christian church must make known.

The word of God — his whole "revelation" of himself — "endures for ever". It is powerful and does all that God plans for it to do. And no one is to add anything to it or take anything away from it.

See also *Revelation*.

Jeremiah 1:4; Ezekiel 1:3–28; John 1:1–14; 1 John 1:1–3; 2 Timothy 4:2; Isaiah 40:8; Revelation 22:18–19

WORLD

The Greek word *kosmos*, "world", normally means "the physical created world". It is used in this way in the New Testament to describe the world God made.

It is also used to speak of the "state of the world". "The world" is in rebellion against God. So Satan can be called the prince or ruler of "this world", and the whole world is said to lie in his power. "World" (represented sometimes by another Greek word, *aion*, meaning "age" or "spirit of the age") describes all that is in opposition to God.

The "world" hated Christ and shows similar hatred to his followers. And yet God loved the world. Christians do not belong to the world but they live in it. They must not share the world's attitudes or conform to its self-centred materialist standards. But they must live with those who are in rebellion, because God loves them and Jesus died for them.
John 1:10; 14:30; 1 John 5:19; John 15:18–19; John 17:16–17; Romans 12:2; John 3:16–21

WORMWOOD AND GALL
Wormwood is the bitter-tasting absinthe, used in the Bible as a symbol of sorrow and bitterness. Gall may be the juice of the opium poppy.

WORSHIP
"I am the Lord your God," says the first Commandment. "Worship no god but me." To worship is to give God the honour due to him. In the psalms God's people worship him for who he is; for what he has done in creation; for what he has done in redemption, rescuing and freeing his people; and for all his good gifts and blessings to individuals.

In the New Testament when Christians met together, they expressed their gladness by "praising God". Filled with the Spirit they were to speak to "one another with the words of psalms, hymns, and sacred songs," to "sing hymns and psalms to the Lord" with praise in their hearts. Everyone could take part. "When you meet for worship one person has a hymn, another a teaching, another a revelation from God, another a message in strange tongues, and still another the explanation of what is said."

"God is Spirit, and only by the power of his Spirit can people worship him as he really is," said Jesus. Worship must be real. It must come from the heart. In the Old Testament God spoke sternly against the kind of worship which is only an outward show. True worship is a genuine response to God which shows itself in a life lived to please him. Worship centres on God. His message fills it with content and meaning. As Paul wrote: "Christ's message in all its richness must live in your hearts. Teach and instruct each other with all wisdom. Sing psalms, hymns, and sacred songs; sing to God with thanksgiving in your hearts."

The earliest Christians were Jewish, so it is not at all surprising that they drew very much on their Jewish background for their forms of worship. Acts 2:46 tells us: "Day after day they met as a group in the Temple, and they had their meals together in their homes, eating with glad and humble hearts." They continued to worship at the Jewish temple, and added a special Christian meal.

But Christians came to see that the temple sacrifices were no longer necessary, since Jesus' death had been the final, once-for-all sacrifice for sin. So Christians tended to break away from temple worship, especially when there began to be conflict between Jews and Christians. But for several decades many Jewish Christians continued to attend the synagogues. Paul usually began his preaching in any town in the synagogue, and continued worshipping there until he was forced out.

Two aspects of Jewish worship especially influenced Christian worship. The Passover ritual is reflected in the Lord's Supper. And the synagogue service, with its Bible reading, prayer and sermon, formed a model for early Christian services.

Worship is not simply a human activity on earth. In heaven, God's whole creation — humans and angels — praise and worship him.

See also *Creeds and Hymns, Lord's Supper, Praise, Prayer, Priests and Levites, Sacrifices, Synagogue, Temple*.
Exodus 20:1–3; Psalms 29; 136:4–9, 10–36; 116; Acts 2:43–47; Ephesians 5:18–19; 1 Corinthians 14:26–40; John 4:21–24; Micah 6:6–8; Colossians 3:16; Revelation 4; 5; 7; 15

WRITING
Archaeologists working in the Near East have discovered many written documents. These give names of places, kings and other people. They tell of invasions and wars, of famine and inflation. They may describe social customs and behaviour, or disclose them incidentally. Some may be hymns and prayers, reflecting religious beliefs; or they may be spells, relating to magic. There may also be stories of gods and heroes of the past. In fact, once writing had been invented, any aspect of life could be recorded.
Cuneiform Writing was invented in Babylonia between 3500 and 3000 BC (see *Babylonians*). The first language to be written down seems to have been Sumerian. This language used picture symbols to represent words. The Semitic Akkadian language (a name used for Assyrian and Babylonian) quickly followed. That was different from Sumerian, and the

Sumerian word-signs were more often used as syllable-signs to reproduce Akkadian.

Other Semitic languages in the west (Syria and Palestine) were written in cuneiform. So too were the Indo-European dialects spoken in the area of modern Turkey (generally called Hittite), and another different language, Elamite, which was spoken in Persia. Cuneiform writing continued to be used in Babylonia until as late as the first century AD.

Egyptian The idea of writing was carried from Babylonia to Egypt soon after it was invented. Egyptian clerks made up their own system of picture word-signs, which we call hieroglyphs. Some of these were very often written for their sounds only (syllables), as in Babylonia. But they were not used without the word-signs to the extent that they were in cuneiform, and so the system was less easily adapted for other languages.

The Egyptian script kept its picture form for inscriptions on buildings and other monuments until the fifth century AD, when people stopped using hieroglyphs. For ordinary records, letters, accounts and books, a simpler handwriting, called hieratic, was developed. A sort of shorthand, now called demotic, grew out of that after 1000 BC.

Books and everyday documents in Egypt were written on paper made from the papyrus reed. Long thin strips of its pith were laid side by side, with another layer of strips pressed onto them at right angles, to produce a page of writing material. It was rather rougher than modern paper, but just as strong and flexible. Papyrus documents buried in tombs or ruined buildings in the dry sands of Egypt have survived until the present day. But papyrus cost money, and unimportant matters — such as short notes or school exercises — were written on flakes of stone or pieces of broken pottery (called *ostraca*). People usually wrote with reed brushes using black ink made from soot.

Wherever Egypt ruled or traded, the Egyptian writing system followed. Examples of Egyptian writing are found in Palestine and Syria, and far south into the Sudan.

The earliest picture writing: on a stone from Sumer, about 3500 BC.

Other systems   Between 2000 and 1000 BC other scripts were used in different parts of the Near East. In Turkey the Hittites had their own form of hieroglyphs. About seventy signs stood for simple syllables (*ta*, *ki*, etc.), with a hundred or more word-signs. A similar system was used in Crete, where three related forms have been discovered. The last of these, known as Linear B, had about eighty-five syllable-signs and some word-signs. These were scratched on clay tablets to record government affairs in an early Greek dialect. Another branch of that group of written languages was used in Cyprus, and a few examples have been found in Syria.

All these methods of writing were difficult to learn, so that only a few people, the professional scribes, could read and write. Most people who wanted to send a letter, to write a will, or to keep accounts, had to call on a trained man. The scribes' services were also needed to read a letter or a legal deed, or to check accounts. Naturally, some scribes rose to high positions in the royal courts, while others sat at street corners waiting for customers.

The alphabet The scribes' monopoly was broken when the alphabet became widely known. Archaeology has enabled us to recover quite a lot of examples of the alphabet in its early stages. But there are many aspects of its development which are not yet known. It seems that a scribe in Canaan realized that it was possible to write a language without the many signs which the Egyptians and Babylonians had. He studied his language and drew one sign for each consonant. He apparently chose the signs on the scheme "door stands for d". But they were used only for sounds, never as word-signs. There were no separate signs for vowels, and this creates problems in reading Hebrew and Arabic writing even now.

Examples of the early alphabet have been found in Israel. These are very short, probably men's names, written on pottery, stone and metal. Canaanites working in the Egyptian turquoise mines in south-western Sinai scratched prayers on rocks and stones. They used the letters of the alphabet, and have left us the best specimens we have of the alphabet at an early stage (about 1500 BC).

How it developed over the next five hundred years can be seen from more scattered examples. (Unfortunately for us the scribes usually wrote on papyrus, which rots when buried in damp soil.) During that time the letters took standard shapes. Scribes trained in Babylonian traditions at Ugarit in Syria saw the advantages of an alphabet over the other scripts. There they composed an alphabet of thirty letters in cuneiform and wrote their own language with it.

By 1000 BC the alphabet was firmly established. In Syria and Canaan the newly settled Aramaeans, Israelites, Moabites and Edomites adopted it. Soon afterwards the Greeks learned it from the Phoenicians. They made some adjustments to suit their own language, especially the use of distinguishing signs for vowels.

The Aramaean tribes of Syria spread into Assyria and Babylonia, and many were carried off captive by Assyrian kings. They took with them their form of the alphabet. Jewish exiles adopted it and popularized it in Jerusalem in preference to the older Phoenician-Hebrew form. Arab tribesmen (the Nabataeans) borrowed it too, and the modern Arabic script is descended from the letters they developed.

The alphabet brought reading and writing within the reach of everyone. The scribes did not go out of business, nor did everyone become literate, but far more people learned their letters in areas where the alphabet was used. This is made clear by the fact that in seventh-century BC Judah many people had seals with their names on them but no distinctive designs. These would have had no value if their owners and others could not read them.

The scribes in Assyria and Babylonia, and in Egypt, usually worked with great care. There were several checks to make sure that books were copied accurately. The number of lines was counted and compared with the original; and damage to the original was noted; and sometimes a second scribe checked the whole copy. The Israelite scribes no doubt followed the same conventions when they copied the books of the Old Testament.

ZACCHAEUS

A tax collector who lived in Jericho. Because he was a little man, Zacchaeus climbed a tree in order to see Jesus when he came. Jesus looked up and asked if he could visit his house. Zacchaeus was a changed man as a result of his meeting with Jesus.
Luke 19; 1–10

ZADOK

In King David's reign Zadok and Abiathar were the most important priests. At the end of David's reign Abiathar supported Adonijah's claim to the throne. Zadok crowned Solomon as the new king and was rewarded by being made high priest.
2 Samuel 15:24ff.; 17:15; 19:11; 1 Kings 1:7, 32ff.; 2:35

ZAREPHAT/SAREPTA

A small town that belonged to Sidon, later to Tyre. The prophet Elijah stayed with a widow there during a time of drought. Later he restored the widow's son to life.
1 Kings 17:8–24; Luke 4:26

ZEALOTS

This group of nationalists kept alive the spirit of

Judas Maccabaeus — the guerrilla leader who had succeeded in regaining the temple from the Syrians in the second century BC. They refused to pay taxes to the Romans and held themselves ready for the war that would bring in God's kingdom. They engineered several revolts. One of these was ended only by the Roman destruction of Jerusalem in AD 70. At least one of Jesus' disciples, Simon (not Simon Peter), had been a Zealot.
Luke 6:15

ZEBEDEE

A fisherman; the father of James and John, the apostles.
Matthew 4:21–22

ZEBOIIM

One of a group of five early cities, of which the most famous are Sodom and Gomorrah. See *Admah, Sodom, Gomorrah*.

Zeboiim was also the name of a valley near Michmash, in the desert north-east of Jerusalem, the site of a Philistine raid in the days of Saul.
Genesis 14:2, 8; Deuteronomy 29:23; 1 Samuel 13:18

ZEBULUN

A son of Jacob and Leah. Father of one of the twelve tribes of Israel.

Also the land belonging to the tribe of Zebulun, in Galilee.
Genesis 30:19–20; 49:13; Joshua 19:10–16

ZECHARIAH

1. Zechariah, king of Israel, who reigned for only six months and was murdered by Shallum (752 BC).
2 Kings 14:29; 15:8–12

2. A prophet and priest born during the Jewish exile in Babylon. His first message was given in 520 BC and is recorded in the Book of Zechariah. By that time the Jews who had returned from exile in Babylon had lost heart and given up rebuilding the temple. Zechariah encouraged them to carry on with this work and promised a bright future.
Ezra 5:1–2; Nehemiah 12:16; Zechariah

3. A priest: the husband of Elizabeth and father of John the Baptist. He was on duty in the temple at Jerusalem when an angel told him he would have a son who would prepare people for the Messiah. Zechariah and Elizabeth were both old. Because he did not believe the angel, Zechariah remained dumb until John was born.
Luke 1

BOOK OF ZECHARIAH

The prophet Zechariah came from a family of priests. Like Haggai, he was involved in getting the temple rebuilt. The temple was finally completed in 516 BC.

Chapters 1–8 of his book are prophecies delivered between 520 and 518 BC. They come in the form of visions and deal with restoring Jerusalem, rebuilding the temple, purifying God's people, and the promise of a coming Messiah.

Chapters 9–14 are a distinct collection of spoken messages, possibly by a different author. They tell of the expected Messiah and the last judgement.

ZEDEKIAH

1. Last king of Judah, 597–586 BC. He was placed on the throne by King Nebuchadnezzar as his subject. When Zedekiah rebelled, Nebuchadnezzar besieged Jerusalem. After several months the Babylonians captured and destroyed the city. Zedekiah was blinded and taken prisoner to the city of Babylon.
2 Kings 24–25; 2 Chronicles 36:10ff.; Jeremiah 21, 32, 34; 37–39
2. A false prophet who lived in the reign of King Ahab.
1 Kings 22; 2 Chronicles 18

ZEPHANIAH

A prophet who lived in Judah in the reign of King Josiah; probably great-great-grandson of King Hezekiah. Zephaniah's message is recorded in the Old Testament book named after him. He warned people in Judah of God's coming judgement if they continued to worship idols and disobey his laws. He also warned of destruction coming to Israel's neighbours. Injustice would be punished. But for those who returned to God, there would be a bright future.
Zephaniah

ZERUBBABEL

Grandson of King Jehoiachin and a leader of the exiles who returned from Babylon to Judah in 537 BC. He became governor of Judea and worked alongside Joshua, the high priest. Under their leadership the foundations of the temple were laid. The

work ground to a halt until the prophets Haggai and Zechariah encouraged them to spur the people on and finish the task.
Ezra 2:2; 3–5; Haggai; Zechariah 4

ZIKLAG
A town in the south of Judah taken by the Philistine city of Gath. King Achish of Gath gave it to David when he was an outlaw from King Saul. David recovered the captives after Amalekites had raided the town.
Joshua 15:31; 1 Samuel 27:6; 30

ZILPAH
Leah's servant and one of Jacob's wives. She was mother of Gad and Asher, two of his twelve sons.
Genesis 29:24; 30:9–13

ZIMRI
Commander in the Israelite army. Zimri killed King Elah and reigned as king of Israel for seven days (885 BC). He was overthrown by Omri.
1 Kings 16

ZIN
An area of desert near Kadesh-barnea where the Israelites camped after the exodus.
Numbers 13:21; 20:1; 27:14, etc.

ZION
The fortified hill which David captured from the Jebusites to make it his capital, Jerusalem. The

name is often used in the Psalms and by the prophets.

ZIPH

A town belonging to the tribe of Judah, in the hills south-east of Hebron. David hid from Saul in the desert near Ziph, and Jonathan came to encourage him here. But the men of Ziph betrayed him to Saul, and he moved to Maon and Engedi. Later, Ziph was one of the places fortified by King Rehoboam. The site is still called Tell Zif.
Joshua 15:55; 1 Samuel 23:14–29; 2 Chronicles 11:9

ZIPPORAH

Wife of Moses and daughter of Jethro, the man who gave Moses a home when he escaped from Egypt. She was the mother of Moses' two sons.
Exodus 2:16–22; 4:24–26; 18:2–4

ZOAN/TANIS

An ancient Egyptian town in the north-east of the Nile Delta. From about 1100 to 660 BC Zoan was used as the capital of Egypt.
Numbers 13:22; Isaiah 19:11, etc.

ZOAR

One of five cities probably at the southern end of the Dead Sea. Lot fled to Zoar at the time when Sodom was destroyed.
Genesis 13:10; 14:2, 8; 19:18–30

ZOBAH
An Aramaean kingdom defeated by David; it was between Damascus and Hamath.
2 Samuel 8:3; 10:6; 1 Kings 11:23

ZOPHAR
One of Job's three friends who talked to him in his suffering.
Job 2:11

ISRAEL IN OLD TESTAMENT TIMES

Tyre

Abel-beth-maacah

Dan

Kedesh

MAACAH

Hazor

Merom

BASHAN

River Kishon

GALILEE

Lake Galilee

Ashtaroth

Golan

Gath-hepher

Edrei

△ Mt Carmel

Mt Tabor △

Shunem Endor

Lo-debar

Ramoth-gilead

Dor

Megiddo Jezreel

△ *Mt Gilboa*

GILEAD

Taanach

Sharon

Ibleam Beth-shan

Dothan

Brook of Cherith

Abel-meholah

Jabesh-gilead

Samaria

River Jabbok

Mahanaim

Shechem Tirzah

△ *Mt Ebal*

Plain of Sharon

Mt △ Gerizim

Succoth Peniel

ISRAEL

AMMON

Aphek

Timnath-serah Shiloh

Adam

Joppa

Jazer

Beth-horon Bethel

Ai

Rabbah

Mizpah Michmash

Gibeon

Gilgal

Acacia

Gezer Gibeah Geba

Jericho

Bezer

Sorek

Heshbon

Ekron Aijalon Anathoth

Eshtaol Kiriath-jearim Jerusalem

△ *Mt Nebo*

Ashdod Zorah Bethlehem

Timnah Makkedah *Judean wilderness*

Ashkelon Libnah Azekah Adullam Tekoa

Ataroth

Gath

Keilah Beth-zur

Kiriathaim Dibon

PHILISTIA Lachish Mareshah Hebron

Dead Sea

Aroer

Gaza Eglon Ziph Engedi

River Arnon

Gerar Ziklag Maon

MOAB

JUDAH Arad

Ar

Beersheba

Hormah

Kir-hareseth

Negev Desert

| 0 | 10 | 20 | 30 | 40 Km |
| 0 | 5 | 10 | 15 | 20 | 25 Km |

ISRAEL IN NEW TESTAMENT TIMES

Tyre

△ Mt Hermon

Caesarea Philippi

PHOENICIA

ITURAEA

GALILEE

TRACHONITIS

3

Ptolemais

Chorazin

Capernaum ● Bethsaida

Gennesaret

Magdala

Lake Galilee

Sepphoris

2

Tiberias

Cana

Nazareth

△ *Mt Tabor*

Gadara

Nain

DECAPOLIS

Caesarea

Scythopolis

Aenon (near Salim)

Gerasa

Sebaste (Samaria)

Sychar

△ *Mt Gerizim*

Antipatris

Joppa

Arimathea

River Jordan

PEREA

SAMARIA

2

Lydda

1

Jericho

Azotus

Jerusalem

Bethany beyond Jordan

Bethphage ● Bethany

Bethlehem ●

Judean wilderness

JUDEA

Dead Sea

Machaerus

Gaza

Masada

NABATAEA

IDUMAEA

1 Judea: Roman province
2 Galilee and Perea kingdom of Herod Antipas
3 Tetrarchy of Philip

0   10   20   30   40 Km

0   5   10   15   20   25 Km